Imagining Judeo-Christian America

Imagining
Judeo-Christian
America

Religion, Secularism, and the Redefinition of Democracy

K. HEALAN GASTON

The University of Chicago Press
Chicago and London

The University of Chicago Press, Chicago 60637
The University of Chicago Press, Ltd., London
© 2019 by The University of Chicago
Published 2019
Printed in the United States of America

28 27 26 25 24 23 22 21 20 19   1 2 3 4 5

ISBN-13: 978-0-226-66371-5 (cloth)
ISBN-13: 978-0-226-66385-2 (paper)
ISBN-13: 978-0-226-66399-9 (e-book)
DOI: https://doi.org/10.7208/chicago/9780226663999.001.0001

Library of Congress Cataloging-in-Publication Data

Names: Gaston, K. Healan (Katherine Healan), author.
Title: Imagining Judeo-Christian America : religion, secularism, and the redefinition
    of democracy / K. Healan Gaston.
Description: Chicago ; London : The University of Chicago Press, 2019. | Includes
    bibliographical references and index.
Identifiers: LCCN 2019018465 | ISBN 9780226663715 (cloth : alk. paper) |
    ISBN 9780226663852 (pbk. : alk. paper) | ISBN 9780226663999 (e-book)
Subjects: LCSH: United States—Church history—20th century. | Religious
    pluralism—United States. | Religion and politics—United States—History—20th
    century. | Christianity and politics—United States—History—20th century. |
    Democracy—United States—Religious aspects.
Classification: LCC BR525 .G35 2019 | DDC 277.3/082—dc23
LC record available at https://lccn.loc.gov/2019018465

Contents

Acknowledgments

The place of Judeo-Christian rhetoric in American political culture has fascinated me for almost as long as I can remember. Growing up in Chattanooga, Tennessee, during the Reagan years, I witnessed firsthand the tug-of-war over the nation's religious identity that fueled the emerging culture wars of the 1980s. As a progressive Congregationalist in a sea of conservative Protestants, I noticed a telling terminological divide: my evangelical relatives and friends referred to the United States as a "Christian" nation, but those in my liberal Protestant church tended to call it a "Judeo-Christian" nation. Pilgrim Congregational, unlike its counterparts in New England, was hardly a "power church." Yet despite its modest budget and sanctuary, there was great moral force in its prophetic witness.

This religio-political context sensitized me to the potent equation of democracy with religion that fueled the Cold War—and to the competing definitions of religious authenticity the term "religion" itself often carries. Like conservatives elsewhere, Chattanooga's establishment often portrayed secular and religious liberals as un-Christian and even un-American. My early awareness of these logics—and the social cost of exposing them—stuck with me when I went off to Brown University and broadened my understanding of America's religious history. I soon came to see that such accusations had a long and influential career in the United States. As I did so, Brown's Religious Studies faculty, especially Wendell Dietrich, Susan Harvey, Giles Milhaven, and John P. Reeder, and the eminent historians William G. McLoughlin and John L. Thomas helped me grasp the intertwined character of religious, social, and intellectual changes.

Although I wrote my senior thesis at Brown on an early nineteenth-century mission to the Cherokee, as a doctoral student at the University of California,

Berkeley, I became fascinated by another sustained attempt at conversion: mainstream Americans' mid-twentieth-century "mission" to their own fallen neighbors, which generated innumerable jeremiads lamenting religious decline and calling both skeptics and theological liberals back to the fold. As I began to seek the roots of modern American political culture in the interwar, World War II, and postwar years, I took special inspiration from Elaine Tyler May's riveting study of Cold War family life, *Homeward Bound*. That remarkable book, in tandem with works by Reinhold Niebuhr and Perry Miller, convinced me that there was much more to say about religion and political culture in the pivotal postwar years.

Given my interest in religion's role in American history, it was impossible to pass up the opportunity to study with David A. Hollinger at Berkeley. From our very first meeting, David struck me as someone with a remarkable capacity to never be boring. Ever since, I have marveled at his ability to provoke students, colleagues, and readers alike to think deeply and in new ways about hard questions. Although my interpretations depart from his in important ways, I am deeply indebted to David for his support and encouragement over the years, and for his professional and personal example. As I moved toward my oral exams, I came to appreciate more fully the extent of Berkeley's resources for the study of religious history. The expert guidance of Margaret Anderson, Thomas Brady, Jenny Franchot, Jon Gjerde, and Christopher Ocker hit that point home, as did the opportunity to examine the cultural logic of the Cold War as a summer teaching assistant to Ron Robin. I also found many important conversation partners and friends among my inspiring cohort of fellow graduate students, whom I thank for their intelligence, creativity, passionate engagement, kindness, good humor, and solidarity.

Since then, I have been sustained by a remarkable and ever-growing cadre of colleagues, friends, and family members, who have sharpened my own powers of discernment with their keen intellects and kind hearts. This book would not have materialized without a formative fellowship year at Princeton's Center for the Study of Religion. I am particularly grateful to Robert Wuthnow, Jeffrey Stout, Leigh Schmidt, and Marie Griffith for seeing the promise in my work, and to William Storrar of the Center of Theological Inquiry and Robin Lovin, whom I met at the CTI. I am also indebted to the talented colleagues and close friends I made at Princeton, especially Rebecca Davis, James McCartin, and the incomparable Jason Josephson Storm.

As I consider the twists and turns in this book's path, the moral of Aesop's fable "The Lion and the Mouse" comes to mind: No act of kindness, no matter how small, is ever wasted. I have benefited from the innumerable kindnesses, large and small, of family and friends, colleagues and students, acquaintances and perfect strangers. At Harvard, for example, the Social Studies program provided a crucial incubator for the project, as I taught the inspiring students there, alongside Anya Bernstein Bassett and a merry band of fellow tutors.

Another highly generative context has been the North American Religions Colloquium at Harvard Divinity School. I have learned a great deal from my insightful NARC colleagues: Ann Braude, Catherine Brekus, David Hall, David Hempton, David Holland, Dan McKanan, and so many others. The same is true of the wider HDS community. I especially want to thank Harvey Cox, Diana Eck, William Graham, Janet Gyatso, Paul Hanson, Amy Hollywood, Mark Jordan, Karen King, David Lamberth, Jon Levenson, Kevin Madigan, Diane Moore, Stephanie Paulsell, Ahmed Ragab, Dudley Rose, Michelle Sanchez, Elisabeth Schussler Fiorenza, Charles Stang, Andrew Teeter, Jonathan Walton, Cornel West, and Preston Williams.

This book also bears the imprint of the many scholars who have grown from promising young students into colleagues and friends during my time at Harvard. I owe particular debts of gratitude to Robert Long for detailed suggestions on structure and argument; Lucia Hulsether for extensive research assistance; Angel Calvin for helpful work on citations; and, most importantly, Eric Stephen for expert editing help during the book's final stages. Thanks also to Carleigh Beriont, Katherine Gerbner, Elizabeth Jemison, Hillary Kaell, Cody Musselman, Sejal Patel, Kip Richardson, Sher Afghan Tareen, and Louis West for many thought-provoking conversations over the years.

Beyond Harvard, historians, ethicists, and religion scholars too numerous to name have provided valuable inspiration and support. My heartiest thanks go out to all of them for teaching me through their scholarship and believing in the importance of this book. In addition to the many conversation partners included in the bibliographic essay and footnotes, I am especially indebted to Mark Silk for sharing his knowledge and expanding my field of vision and to Tisa Wenger and Susannah Heschel for their intellectual vitality and friendship. At the University of Chicago Press, I have benefited enormously from the wise counsel of two fine editors, Robert Devens and Tim Mennel; the technical assistance of India Cooper and Joel Score; and the helpful suggestions of two anonymous readers.

Along the way, I have been buoyed by the encouragement and camaraderie of many close friends. From Chattanooga days, David Beebe, Joe and Margha Davis, Don and Liz Klinefelter, and Eric and Peggy Swanson deserve special mention. So, too, does Sarah Carriger, whose love of reading and writing decisively shaped me. From Brown and Berkeley, many thanks to Dee Bielenberg, Erbin Crowell and Kristin Howard, Tim and Jenn David-Lang, Dan Geary and Jennie Sutton, Dave Gilson and Lyssa Rome, Jason Grunebaum,

Molly and Daryl Oshatz, Anne Pycha and Ivan Ascher, and Fred Shoucair. In Cambridge and beyond, Melanie Adrian, Cassie and Norman Fahrney, David Greenberg, Maya Jasanoff, Rebecca Lemov and Palo Coleman, Mary Lewis and Peter Dizikes, Jonna Meyler and Charlie Hogg, Claire Rowberry and Tim McLucas, Vanessa Ruget and Prabal Chakrabarti, and Shane Snowdon have truly sustained me.

Without the support of my loving parents, Joe and Kay Gaston, this book never would have come to fruition. During my childhood, they built a safe haven for intellectual exploration; introduced me to Reinhold Niebuhr's writings on power and justice; and taught me to love learning about the past, including historic preservation and other forms of resource and environmental conservation. Under their guidance, I discovered how much the study of the past teaches us about the present—indeed, that knowing about the past is both an ethical responsibility and a political necessity.

The lessons my parents taught me have been reinforced over the years by countless conversations with the many lovers of history and ideas within my wider family. On my mother's side, I am particularly grateful for the influence of my grandmother and grandfather, Healan Brown Baker and Thomas Burl Baker; my uncle and aunt, Tom Baker and Lynne Rudder Baker; and their close friend Kate Sonderegger. The extended Gaston family has also provided inspiration and encouragement. Likewise, my husband's extended family, especially Mary and Howie Ditkof and John and Lisa Jewett, have supported my scholarly efforts in countless ways. So, too, have my sister and her husband, Josephine and Andrew Larson, and their children Erika, Emma, and Eli. This book would not be what it is—just as I would not be who I am—without the contributions of these beloved family members.

Finally, words are insufficient to express my indebtedness to Andrew Jewett and our dear sons, Joseph and Samuel. Andy's brilliance as a historian, deftness as an editor, and devotion as a partner shine through on every page of this book. Our boys, for their part, inspire me every day to keep researching and writing, in the hope of changing our political narratives and brightening our collective future.

Introduction

Dreaming America, Deciphering Judeo-Christianity

"How do you dream America?" Despite this question's stark simplicity, historians still have much to learn about how various groups of Americans have imagined their national project, particularly at the level of language.[1] This book explores one key conceptual and linguistic resource for dreaming America: the idea that the United States is a "Judeo-Christian" country. The term "Judeo-Christian" entered the political lexicon in the 1930s, when cataclysmic world events led many Americans to reassess the ethical and religious dimensions of their political system. Ever since, it has played decisive, albeit shifting, roles in American public life.[2]

By following Judeo-Christian constructions of democracy and national identity from the interwar years up to the present, this book narrates the challenges associated with defining the religious character of a nation, a citizenry, and a form of government. It examines both those who endorsed Judeo-Christian formulations and those who rejected them, whether actively or passively. One person's dream typically turns out to be another person's nightmare. To the extent that democratic visions take concrete form, they almost always produce winners and losers. This has certainly been true of Judeo-Christian constructions. For that reason, the idea of America as a Judeo-Christian nation has been deeply contested since its inception during the interwar years. There have always been influential dissenters from this iconic political discourse, and powerful countervailing dynamics within it.

The conventional understandings of Judeo-Christian formulations omit such conflicts. In popular culture, a common narrative holds that Americans (and Europeans before them) hewed to a stable, unbroken "Judeo-Christian tradition" until the 1960s, when a band of cultural rebels uprooted two millennia of history—and the deepest convictions of a devout majority. Scholarly interpreters, on the other hand, recognize that the "Judeo-Christian tradi-tion" made its entry into popular discourse during the World War II era. They have argued that Judeo-Christian rhetoric served as a powerful tool of liberal inclusion from the late 1930s until the 1970s, when religious conservatives began to appropriate it for their own purposes. In this view, the concept of a Judeo-Christian tradition integrated Jewish and Catholic Americans into the mainstream by creating a tri-faith, liberal-democratic front against fascism. Most recently, critical theorists have reasoned backward from the conserva-tive, religiously exclusive Judeo-Christian formulations in circulation today by arguing that such rhetoric has always encoded whiteness and blunted chal-lenges by African Americans and other racialized groups. In their view, the term "Judeo-Christian" enforces a racially bounded conception of pluralism and a Western civilizational framework that work together to authorize mar-ginalization and even violence against racialized minorities.

This book challenges all three narratives—each of which ascribes a single, clear meaning to Judeo-Christian discourse—by showing that the discourse's meanings have been fundamentally contested since the 1930s, when the term first captured America's political imagination. That era's numerous assertions of Judeo-Christian harmony did in part describe burgeoning new realities on the ground. But they also represented fervent, even wishful, attempts to create such unity. Thus, invocations of the term "Judeo-Christian" must be read as descriptive and aspirational at one and the same time. This double-sidedness characterizes Judeo-Christian discourse as a whole, helping to explain the is/ought slippage it frequently displays as well as some of the most curi-ous aspects of its subsequent development. For instance, many of the mid-twentieth-century figures most strongly identified as champions of Judeo-Christian democracy—Reinhold Niebuhr and Will Herberg foremost among them—largely avoided using the term "Judeo-Christian" itself. Others used it in surprising ways, and for purposes that have been lost to historians.

In addition to those liberal pluralists who employed "Judeo-Christian" to bring Jewish and Catholic Americans into the democratic fold, there were many critics of "secularism" for whom Judeo-Christian formulations placed nonbelievers, and often theological liberals as well, beyond the democratic pale. Scholars have too often missed the World War II era's sharp conflicts within and between religious groups over the meaning of democracy. The usual story of religious pluralism in America, featuring an inexorably widen-ing circle of tolerance and inclusion, foregrounds those liberal Protestants for whom Judeo-Christian language represented an olive branch to groups previously marginalized by the Protestant establishment. But it ignores the numerous other commentators who used that newly minted rhetoric to attack an increasingly secular American liberalism, calling it too long on tolerance and too short on genuine religious commitment. Overall, this study shows, Judeo-Christian discourse in the mid-twentieth-century United States was neither as liberal and inclusive nor as productive of social harmony as scholars have often assumed. At most, it represented a linguistic détente, not a cultural consensus.[3]

Likewise, the assertion that America became a "tri-faith nation" during and after World War II does not mean that cultural and political power was simply carved up into three equal pieces of a national pie, nor that Jewish and Catholic Americans faced common obstacles and confronted Protestant domination arm in arm. Such accounts drastically overemphasize the similarities between the Jewish and Catholic minorities, not to mention the homogeneity of those groups themselves. In truth, various subsets of the Jewish and Catholic populations encountered highly particular forms of suspicion and marginalization. They also differed markedly in the degrees and kinds of cultural and political power they could mobilize. The dynamics between Protestants, Catholics, Jews, nonbelievers, and groups such as Buddhists and Muslims were highly complex. Although Protestants wielded the greatest influence by far, the decentralization and internal fractures of the various Protestant denominations made it difficult for their adherents to effectively promote the interests of a singular "Protestantism," even when they wanted to do so. The religio-racial implications of Judeo-Christian discourse were apparent in the term's exclusion of Muslims from "Western civilization"—and of racialized cultural and religious minorities from "tri-faith America." But the discourse also created important forms of leverage for those marginalized groups that could mobilize the moral power of the Judeo-Christian framework.[4]

Interpreters can either take sides in such disputes or work to delineate the specific contours of the competing paradigms. This book seeks to account for conflicts and complexities by narrating the history of America's Judeo-Christian discourse from multiple perspectives, rather than adopting the viewpoint of either dominant or marginalized groups. One-sided treatments invariably flatten out the complexity of the past, producing predictable narratives and stock casts of heroes and villains. In many respects, the historical record does confirm the views of critical scholars who seek to expose the disciplining power of tolerance and debunk secularism's pretensions to neutrality. But the alternative responses to religious diversity were also partial and coercive, albeit in different ways. Indeed, every conceivable definition of a nation's religio-political culture will involve more and less subtle and costly acts of inclusion and exclusion. It is too simple to dismiss altogether the genuine reverence for tolerance and inclusion that accompanied many Judeo-Christian formulations in the mid-twentieth-century United States.[5]

Approaching this story from multiple angles invites readers to reengage with American democracy and its rich, if profoundly flawed, political culture. Reading an unfamiliar story about a seemingly well-known past can change our perspective in the present by reconnecting us to forgotten arguments, honing our conceptual and linguistic faculties, enlivening our sympathies, and awakening our own political imaginations. This book aims to make its readers wiser critics and consumers of the visions of religious pluralism and secularism now circulating in the United States and around the world, and perhaps even to inspire new conceptual and linguistic approaches to our contemporary political predicaments. It enjoins readers to grapple with the magnitude of the challenge posed by democracy's tendency to presuppose— and in some ways to enforce—a civic "we." Since no perfect universalism has ever existed, we cannot escape the violence and coercion inherent in the fact that all schemes of inclusion also imply exclusion. In this regard, Judeo-Christian reformulations of liberal democracy in the mid-twentieth-century United States operated like every other conceivable "circle of we" in the religio-political realm. Yet, by taking an explicitly multiperspectival approach to the history of Judeo-Christian discourse, this book seeks to capture the complexity of these boundary-drawing exercises and to better understand their implications, both past and present.[6]

Indeed, the history of Judeo-Christian discourse and the underlying religio-political conflicts holds many lessons for today, when political, cultural, and demographic shifts once again inspire conceptual and linguistic innovation. Struggles over religion and American identity took on a new character—and a new bitterness—in the wake of September 11, 2001. After a decade of relative optimism in the 1990s, many Americans once again sensed a powerful, if shadowy, threat from without and within. For some, "radical Islam" came to play the same role in the collective psyche that communism did during the Cold War. This preoccupation with Islam's political meanings has intersected with the growing visibility of the new groups of immigrants that have come to the United States since the immigration reforms of 1965, including not just Muslims but also Hindus, Buddhists, Sikhs, and many other religious minorities from distant shores. On a conceptual level, meanwhile, an inclusive, multicultural sensibility has steadily spread outward from cosmopolitan universities and cities into the wider political culture. Although many commentators still call the United States "Judeo-Christian," that familiar descriptor has faced unprecedented challenges since 9/11. In an in-

creasingly diverse context, Judeo-Christian descriptions of American democracy and national identity strike some as prophetic and others as decidedly
antiquarian—or even highly dangerous.

Presidential rhetoric reveals great instability in how recent administra-
tions have framed American democracy. The Protestant evangelical George
W. Bush, though a staunch champion of conservative social values, took an
inclusive stance toward Muslims in the wake of 9/11 and eschewed the term
"Judeo-Christian" altogether. His successor, Barack Obama, a more liberal
Protestant with family ties to both Islam and atheism, ultimately defined the
United States as a purely civic enterprise. Yet that enterprise, Obama consistently averred, draws on the moral resources of many faiths, even as it takes its
shape from widely shared ideals rather than theologically specific tenets. Most
recently, Donald Trump, though championing the cause of the Christian right
as an interest group, has abandoned the niceties of Judeo-Christian rhetoric
altogether. Not since the 1930s have there been so many different frameworks
at hand for defining the country's religious character—and so little sense
of which framework might prevail in the future. Delving into the history of
Judeo-Christian language, which emerged from that moment of uncertainty
as the leading descriptor of American culture and institutions, reveals more
clearly the contours of the present moment.

*

A central lesson of this book is that the emergence of the widely shared language of Judeo-Christianity did not put an end to tussles over religion and
politics. Here, a historical example helps to illuminate the surprisingly complex, fractured landscape of public religiosity in the mid-twentieth-century
United States. In both the historical record and the popular imagination,
Dwight D. Eisenhower's presidency figures as the heyday of American "civil
religion," a harmonious period of social unity characterized by frequent assertions of the "Christian," "Judeo-Christian," or simply "religious" character
of American democracy. In these consensus-driven portraits, a shared religio-
political vision dominated American public life in the 1950s before giving way
to the "culture wars" of our own day.

There are important kernels of truth in this account. By the time Eisenhower captured the presidency in 1952, Americans routinely identified a
coherent "Judeo-Christian tradition" as the philosophical and historical
source of their democracy. And Eisenhower was the first American president
to employ Judeo-Christian terminology, on the campaign trail and thereafter.
Yet a closer look reveals the kinds of ambiguities that have always characterized the career of Judeo-Christian discourse in American political life. Eisen-

hower did use Judeo-Christian rhetoric during his campaign and first term, but awkwardly and only sporadically. He seems to have recognized the ability of that religio-political language to alienate many groups of citizens at home, as well as allies abroad. Then, after 1954, Eisenhower largely ditched Judeo-Christian terminology altogether. In 1957, he urged his brother Milton, then president of Johns Hopkins University, to replace "Judeo-Christian" with a more inclusive term that accommodated Muslims and Buddhists.

Eisenhower's shifting rhetoric calls for closer attention to the interactions of religion, power, and language in the mid-twentieth-century United States. The Eisenhower era featured endemic conflicts—social, political, religious, and linguistic—rather than an easy consensus around shared religious values. The complexities of Eisenhower's own religious identity reveal important dimensions of these conflicts. Loosely affiliated with the widely despised Jehovah's Witnesses in his youth, he was not even nominally a member of the Protestant establishment (or of any Protestant body, mainstream or otherwise) until a few weeks after his election to the presidency, when he joined the National Presbyterian Church in Washington.

Meanwhile, the divergent backgrounds and sensibilities of Eisenhower's advisers and speechwriters brought the era's religious tensions and crosscurrents directly into the president's public addresses. Eisenhower took cues from prominent mainline Protestants such as his secretary of state, John Foster Dulles. But his inner circle also included the ambitious young journalist Emmet J. Hughes, who helped pioneer the role of presidential speechwriter. And Hughes, who penned many of Eisenhower's best-known public comments on religion, was a devout Catholic, as well as a lifelong Democrat who preferred European-style Christian social democracy to Eisenhower's moderate Republicanism.[7] Indeed, many of Eisenhower's major statements on religion and politics featured language and concepts that were more common among American Catholic thinkers than among either liberal or conservative Protestants.[8]

Such patterns take us a long way from the usual picture of postwar religious harmony. Today's culture warriors look back—either longingly or dismissively—on the mid-twentieth century as a time when all Americans shared a set of conventional religious, moral, and social principles. The contemporary right seeks to recapture a "Judeo-Christian consensus," based on "traditional family values." The left celebrates the demise of such homogeneity, even as it often identifies Judeo-Christian rhetoric as an important stepping-stone to fuller inclusion. There is no place in such understandings of postwar American public life for a deeply devout president who felt uncomfortable within the Protestant establishment, let alone a Catholic speechwriter who decisively crafted that president's religious rhetoric—perhaps helping to pave the way for America's first Catholic president in 1960. In national memory, Eisenhower stands for the arrival of Christian or Judeo-Christian harmony in American national politics. But as is so often the case, the historical record tells a richer story of complexity and conflict.

To be sure, Eisenhower did serve as a genial "pastor-in-chief." But he did not preside over a country whose citizens conformed to one religious mold, whether Protestant, Christian, or Judeo-Christian. It is tempting to view Eisenhower as simply a spokesman for a hegemonic Protestant establishment, a puppet of conservative Christian business interests, an avatar of Judeo-Christian inclusion, or even the leading mouthpiece of a form of secularism that silently enforced core Protestant ideals.[9] But no portrait of a single, dominant postwar perspective can capture the deep tensions in both Eisenhower's own stance and the surrounding cultural and political landscape. Carefully examining the Judeo-Christian rhetoric mobilized by Eisenhower and an array of other commentators reveals a many-sided history of disputes around religious identity that set many of the terms for today's conflicts. When we look closely at the Judeo-Christian formulations of the mid-twentieth century, deciphering their multiple meanings, the reputed consensus quickly disintegrates into a welter of competing voices espousing fundamentally different and often incompatible visions of America.

In short, what we now call the "culture wars" were already raging in the 1950s, beneath the apparent consensus implied by the ascendance of "Judeo-Christian" as a descriptor of American democracy and national identity. Today, conservatives are far more likely than liberals to call their country "Judeo-Christian." Most cosmopolitans on the left now see "Judeo-Christian" as a hopelessly narrow and naïve label for American religious identity. But while linguistic patterns have shifted, the basic contours of today's conflicts over religion in American public life date back to the 1930s and continued largely unchanged through the supposed consensus period of the 1950s. The common tendency to trace contemporary religious and political divides back to the 1960s and 1970s misplaces by at least two decades the origin point of the religio-political realignments that still shape the political world of today. In the 1940s and 1950s, Americans increasingly found themselves at odds over the relationship between religion and democracy. As the United States assumed its new role as the defender of "Western civilization" abroad, the home front witnessed vigorous disputes over the proper relationship between religious and political commitments, set against the backdrop of an expanding welfare state. Exploring the intricacies of Judeo-Christian discourse from the 1930s to the 1970s reveals that the polarization of American political culture characteristic of today's "culture wars" owes much to interwar and post–World War II debates over religion and politics. Surprisingly little has changed in the terms of the controversy, even though the liberal forces have largely ceded the label "Judeo-Christian" to their conservative opponents since the 1970s.

*

The career of Judeo-Christian terminology in the United States offers a particularly revealing lens through which to view nearly a century's worth of struggles over the cultural dimensions of the American project. From the 1940s to the 1970s, Judeo-Christian rhetoric provided the main linguistic battlefield on which champions of competing cultural visions promoted their divergent views of American identity. Some commentators used "Judeo-Christian" loosely as a shorthand term for religious pluralism in general, identifying unbounded diversity and unfettered freedom of belief as the keynotes of democratic life. Others, however, interpreted the Judeo-Christian idiom more narrowly. They argued that democracy required specific theological and ethical resources that were unique to Protestantism, Catholicism, and Judaism—and deeply threatened by tendencies toward pluralization and secularization in American public life. Since the 1970s, the latter interpretation has increasingly prevailed, as the term "Judeo-Christian" has become associated with conservative "family values" and related conceptions of political legitimacy. Scholars can begin to reconstruct those dynamics by analyzing the full range of meanings ascribed to Judeo-Christian rhetoric as it rose in the 1930s, swelled to a chorus in the 1940s and 1950s, and then became a largely conservative resource in the wake of the 1960s. Tracing Judeo-Christian discourse across the decades reveals constantly shifting patterns of conflict over religion and public life that elude historians' retrospective attempts to impose clear labels and neat interpretive frameworks. Past actors, like their counterparts today, lived in the dizzying complexity of their own presents.

This book adopts a comprehensive approach by taking the entire discourse of Judeo-Christianity as its object of analysis. By applying the scholarly term "discourse," it does not imply that using Judeo-Christian terminology was merely a cynical ploy or a form of rhetorical play. Rather, it tries to take seriously all users of Judeo-Christian language, and to understand the who, what, when, where, why, and how of their particular contributions. Part of this task is noticing not only where Judeo-Christian formulations appeared but also where they did not. As it turns out, subtle patterns of presence and absence characterized the use of Judeo-Christian terminology in its mid-twentieth-century heyday. In fact, many of the best-remembered proponents of Judeo-Christian terminology jettisoned it after short periods of frequent use. This book places such hesitations and misgivings alongside more confident assertions of America's Judeo-Christian character. Many commentators in the tumultuous decades of the mid-twentieth century clearly understood that the adjective "Judeo-Christian" was a double-edged sword that excluded as well as included. Its use often reflected strategic choices on a field of sharp ideological conflict, not watery assertions of harmony or mindless conformity to prevailing norms. Making Judeo-Christian discourse itself the primary unit of analysis highlights much that remains hidden when we focus on specific individuals or institutions.[10] It also shows that the emergence of Judeo-Christian language did not stem solely from the actions of believing Protestants, Catholics, and Jews. Of course, such groups, which together comprised the vast majority of Americans at the time, did figure prominently in crafting conceptions of religious difference during the middle decades of the twentieth century. But a wider cast of characters flanked them, including avowed atheists, agnostics, humanists, and naturalists who were their interlocutors, friends, mentors, colleagues, family members, fellow congregants, and, sometimes, fierce critics. Scholars cannot fully understand American political culture without bringing these figures into their purview, alongside religious minorities outside the Judeo-Christian fold.[11]

The many religious communities standing outside the newly constituted Judeo-Christian mainstream, including Buddhists, Hindus, and others, continued to struggle for recognition as genuine believers—and genuine democrats. Not to be seen as "either a Protestant, a Catholic, or a Jew," observed the Jewish writer Will Herberg in his 1955 classic *Protestant-Catholic-Jew*, "is somehow not to be an American. It may imply being foreign, as in the case when one professes oneself a Buddhist, a Muslim, or anything but a Protestant, Catholic, or Jew, even when one's Americanness is otherwise beyond question. Or it may imply being obscurely 'un-American,' as is the case with those who declare themselves atheists, agnostics, or even 'humanists.'"[12]

Some users of Judeo-Christian terminology silently brought nonbelievers and other minorities into the democratic circle of "we" by grounding democracy in tolerance of all belief systems. But many others did not. Instead, they identified particular forms of Protestantism, Catholicism, and Judaism as the cornerstones of democracy. Such conflicts over religion and democracy began to take shape between the wars, emerged clearly in American public culture by World War II, and became firmly entrenched during the formative years of the Cold War.

As mid-twentieth-century commentators ascribed meanings to America's burgeoning Judeo-Christian discourse, they also fleshed out related categories such as "totalitarianism"—a corporate term, centered on the primacy of the state, that encompassed both fascism and communism—and "secularism." The concept of secularism did particularly important work for many postwar thinkers. For its advocates, secularism did not entail a vigorous campaign against all forms of faith in the name of a militant, crusading atheism. Rather, it signaled a preference for a formally secular public sphere grounded in a minimal requirement of tolerance rather than specific faith claims—a commitment that could be combined with various forms of faith or lack thereof. Secularists, whether religious, agnostic, or atheistic, favored a comparatively neutral public culture in which all belief communities could participate (at least in theory) without prejudice and without substantially modifying their own theological commitments. But for critics, the term "secularism" conflated support for strict church-state separation with militant atheism and moral relativism. This usage denied the authenticity of liberal forms of religion whose adherents endorsed a public culture based on tolerance rather than more substantive religious principles. Indeed, it portrayed secularists of all varieties as the advance guard of totalitarianism, asserting that strict separationism cleared the way for authoritarian rule by dynamiting the religious foundations of interpersonal morality, human rights, and limited government.[13]

In the mid-twentieth century, American struggles over religious diversity focused strongly on the status of nonbelievers and those theological liberals who supported a secular public sphere. The demographic shifts of the 1880s to the 1920s, which brought large numbers of Catholic and Jewish immigrants into the country, have led scholars to assume that the central issue of the interwar and postwar periods was how Protestants, Catholics, and Jews could get along in a "tri-faith" nation. In fact, however, by the 1940s and 1950s the main "diversity problem"—at least, outside evangelical Protestant circles—involved the status of nonbelievers, humanists, and advocates of strict separation, not the relationship between Protestants, Catholics, and Jews. At stake was the relationship between religious diversity and secularism: Did embracing a more religiously heterogeneous model of American identity require accepting unbelief and strict church-state separation? Even as believing Protestants, Catholics, and Jews worked to clarify their own identities in relation to one another, they also struggled with the equally vexing problem of how to think about and deal with the others—above all, the nonreligious others—in their midst. Many different kinds of thinkers sought cross-confessional amity, but they disagreed fundamentally on the issue of secularism. They framed the project of religious inclusion in contrasting ways, and they set very different limits to democratic belonging. Exploring the constructions of secularism that accompanied Judeo-Christian discourse in the mid-twentieth century reveals that the basic assertion that Protestants, Catholics, and Jews should be equal partners in American public culture coexisted with many different views of nonbelievers and strict separationism.

Such dynamics ensured that the European immigrants of the industrialization period came to be defined in religious terms, as Catholics and Jews rather than Italians, Poles, Lithuanians, and members of other ethnic groups. Because the national reckoning with cultural difference reflected a felt need to defend democracy from its totalitarian challengers—and perhaps secularism at home as well—it took shape largely as an engagement with religious pluralism, not ethnic diversity. The threats of fascism and communism shaped how mainstream commentators constructed a new national "we," leading them to emphasize shared beliefs and values that many traced back to Christianity and Judaism. This was not a foregone conclusion, once Southern and Eastern European immigrant groups had attained a certain level of social advancement and political maturity. Rather, it reflected a widespread sense that the fate of democracy, and perhaps the survival of Western civilization itself, hung in the balance as totalitarian regimes spread across the globe. It also took much of its texture from long-standing anxieties about Christian identity and newer fears about the inroads of secular modes of life and thought, as well as the sharpening of church-state separation. Ever since the 1930s, Judeo-Christian terminology has operated in the United States as a religio-political discourse, wherein multiple and competing conceptions of religious authenticity—defined in relation to secularism and nonbelief, and to a lesser extent religions beyond Christianity and Judaism—vie for cultural supremacy.

*

By the 1950s, struggles over religion's role in American public life had given rise to a pair of competing sensibilities I call "Judeo-Christian exceptionalism" and "pluralism." Judeo-Christian formulations tended to fall somewhere between these poles, which reflected competing answers to a timeless political question: What sorts of cultural preconditions does democracy require? Judeo-Christian exceptionalists endorsed a confessionally ecumenical, yet still religiously specific, conception of American democracy and national identity. They grounded democracy in core Christian and Jewish principles, insisting that it required a public culture centered on those principles. In the 1940s and 1950s, Judeo-Christian exceptionalists such as Will Herberg and Emmet Hughes's teacher Carlton J. H. Hayes worked to build a cross-confessional alliance against both believing and nonbelieving defenders of strict church-state separation. They argued that separationists would stamp out religion by installing secularism as the official faith of the nation. Judeo-Christian exceptionalists identified the Judeo-Christian tradition as the essence of both American democracy and Western civilization, and they insisted that a merely civic definition of democracy would eradicate religious pluralism by fostering the total secularization of American culture. In short, Judeo-Christian exceptionalists argued that a democracy could not survive unless its citizens hewed to certain modes of Christian and Jewish faith. They gave intellectual specificity and heft to the increasingly widespread notion that democracy required religion as a foil to "godless communism." Even as they expanded the democratic "we" to include Catholics and Jews alongside Protestants, they tended to create a litmus test of religious authenticity within each of those groups that placed Christian and Jewish advocates of strict church-state separation outside the pale, along with nonbelievers and adherents to faiths other than Christianity and Judaism. Exceptionalists used the term "Judeo-Christian" to distinguish an authentic, religiously grounded democratic faith from an American liberalism that they deemed hopelessly corrupted by naturalism, humanism, and secularism.[14]

By contrast, pluralists grounded democracy in religious diversity and intellectual freedom, not Judeo-Christian religion itself. They endorsed a broadly civic definition of American identity, centered on shared commitments to religious tolerance and freedom of conscience. In the middle decades of the twentieth century, many pluralists used Judeo-Christian language as shorthand for a more inclusive outlook that tacitly encompassed nonbelievers and religious minorities beyond Catholics and Jews. Yet they disagreed sharply with the Judeo-Christian formulations of their exceptionalist counterparts. Pluralists argued that replacing the idea of America as a Protestant or Christian nation with another religiously specific conception of American identity obscured the breadth of the country's existing or eventual religious diversity. As they saw it, Americans needed to throw off all exclusive definitions of national identity, not simply shift the existing definition's boundary. In their view, the proper response to growing religious diversity was a full-blown civic nationalism rooted in tolerance for the deeply held commitments of others. Of course, tolerance, too, has its limits.[15] The pluralists' circle of democratic belonging included individuals of any faith or none, but only if they rejected the idea of using public resources to advance explicitly religious claims. Intolerant of what they deemed intolerance, pluralists tended to equate that trait with particular faith traditions, especially Catholicism and fundamentalist Protestantism. At base, then, it was the legitimacy and desirability of a secular public sphere that divided Judeo-Christian exceptionalists from pluralists. The former welcomed Catholics, Jews, and Protestants as equal participants only to the extent that they opposed secularism as a public philosophy, whereas the latter welcomed adherents of any and all belief systems, so long as they embraced secularism. Although each of these sensibilities transcended the older ideal of a Protestant America, they set very different limits to democratic inclusion.

The spectrum of Judeo-Christian discourse thus took its shape from the powerful religious/secular binary that many interpreters have discerned at the heart of modern European and American thought. The poles of Judeo-Christian exceptionalism and pluralism reflected divergent conceptions of religion, and thus of religious authenticity. Indeed, interpretations of religious diversity—like narratives of secularization—always rest on assumptions about religious authenticity: what proper or normative religion is, who has it, and how it can be cultivated.[16] Disagreements on the nature of religion thus mirrored a contest over the meaning and validity of the secular. Judeo-Christian exceptionalists tended to be staunch antisecularists with a yearning for religious orthodoxy; they saw secularism as the relativistic ideology of the modern state. They attached Judeo-Christian language to the claim that Americans must believe in a particular kind of God in order to be loyal citizens. (In fact, many of those who invoked Judeo-Christian formulations used them interchangeably with frank expressions of Christian parochialism and assumed that Judaism's contributions to civilization lay in the distant past.) For Judeo-Christian pluralists, by contrast, the new discourse marked an inclusive definition of democracy with tolerance of divergent views as its cornerstone. They defined secularism as neutral ground on which all belief communities could meet as equals and contrasted it to the authoritarianism they associated with traditional faith. In other words, Judeo-Christian exceptionalists believed that secularism undermined their religious freedom, while pluralists viewed secularism as the precondition for their religious freedom. The former viewed secularism as religion's rival; the latter defined secularism as democracy's religion.

The competing views of secularism and religion that took shape in the 1940s and 1950s tended to line up with competing analyses of totalitarianism's roots. Like the broader Judeo-Christian discourse, Judeo-Christian exceptionalism and pluralism reflected not only the swelling numbers of Catholic and Jewish Americans in the wake of rapid industrialization and mass immigration but also the emerging threat of totalitarianism in the 1930s. As economic collapse and the ensuing growth of centralized states brought sharp divisions over religion and politics to the fore, many commentators began to identify democracy with Judeo-Christian principles, over and against the Nazi and Soviet regimes—and for some, aspects of Franklin D. Roosevelt's

New Deal as well. In this context, groups of mainstream Protestants came to share the long-standing Catholic charge that Protestants had fostered secularization by giving individuals free rein to create and institutionalize their own belief systems.

To be sure, many Americans thought the rise of fascism and communism reflected a narrow-minded bigotry that was best overcome by encouraging a free marketplace of beliefs. But a growing number regarded totalitarianism as the apotheosis of nonbelief—the political outcome of the West's increasing secularity and moral relativism. In this camp, Judeo-Christian exceptionalists argued that modern states invariably threatened religion because they harbored a powerful impulse to deify themselves. Only states whose citizens and leaders saw them as truly "under God" could withstand this temptation and avoid devolving into totalitarianism. To many exceptionalists, even the emerging American welfare state appeared dangerously secular, and thus implicitly totalitarian.[17] Fascism's disappearance from the global stage in 1945 dramatically altered the political climate in ways that favored this comparatively exclusive, theologically committed stance. New groups of Americans came to see their political culture as the outgrowth—and the epitome—of a "Judeo-Christian tradition," and to view Soviet communism as the inevitable endpoint of secular thinking. As Judeo-Christian exceptionalism became the dominant conception of American religious identity during the early Cold War years, its supporters suggested that the official atheism of the Soviets indicted not only nonbelievers but also those Christians and Jews who supported the strict reading of church-state separation enshrined in a series of postwar Supreme Court cases.

Of course, not all mid-twentieth-century Americans embraced either pluralism or exceptionalism as I have defined those positions. The terms are merely ideal types, marking clusters of commitments that appeared with particular frequency in the complex landscape of postwar thinking about American religious identity. Here, as elsewhere, analytical categories should not be allowed to obscure important nuances and exceptions. In the fraught realm of religion and politics, interpretive generalizations can quickly turn into dangerous stereotypes about groups or individuals. On this score, it bears remembering that descriptors such as "radical," "liberal," "moderate," and "conservative" do not map onto theological positions in the same ways that they map onto politics. Likewise, it is never safe to assume a neat correspondence between political and theological views, or to take for granted that individuals shared the beliefs of their coreligionists or followed the teachings of their religious leaders. More generally, historical actors seldom adhered to strict logic in crafting their positions. By exploring Judeo-Christian discourse in the round, this book incorporates instances wherein commentators employed Judeo-Christian terminology in unpredictable or even inconsistent ways.[18]

Some readers will be tempted to view Judeo-Christian exceptionalism and pluralism as monolithic and opposing positions, but it is better to simply recognize the persistence across time of two constellations of interrelated ideas and sensibilities that tended to push concrete human actors in opposite directions. Even as this book tells the story of a discourse, it is first and foremost a book about people: how their ideas shaped their culture and helped to create the world we have inherited. Yet while abstract categories such as "exceptionalism" and "pluralism" cannot capture the full complexity of history, they remain valuable interpretive tools. They reorient our thinking, shifting our vantage point so that we can more critically assess the assumptions that undergird prevailing narratives and the implications of those assumptions for cultural and political practice.[19]

From the start, many commentators used Judeo-Christian rhetoric not only to combat religious bigotry but also to stave off the less clearly bounded—and often formally secular—conceptions of American democracy and national identity that cosmopolitan and civil-libertarian thinkers had begun to develop between the wars. The rift between Judeo-Christian exceptionalists and pluralists opened up by the early 1940s and widened further in the postwar years, when exceptionalists steadily gained ground in American public culture. Indeed, the postwar period witnessed the solidification of a new political paradigm whose architects identified American democracy as an expression of theological principles and ethical ideals shared by the Judeo-Christian faiths. The wide appeal of that vision, then as now, demonstrates that the Judeo-Christian exceptionalists of the 1940s and 1950s spoke for a broad cross-section of Americans who rejected the cultural policies and underlying theoretical assumptions of mid-twentieth-century liberalism. The postwar generation of exceptionalists helped to lay the conceptual foundations for the conservative, neoconservative, and communitarian movements that have flourished since the 1960s.

Whereas postwar pluralists often challenged exceptionalist formulations of the Judeo-Christian tradition, their successors of the 1960s and 1970s ceded that discourse itself to exceptionalists. Most simply dropped what now struck them as an unnecessarily narrow label for American identity. Yet this shift did not spell the end of Judeo-Christian discourse in American life. With the rise of the religious right, a new generation of conservatives mobilized Judeo-Christian discourse to signal their intent to return America to the public piety and "fighting faith" mentality of the early Cold War years. At their head stood Ronald Reagan, whose heavy reliance on Judeo-Christian terminology assured his theologically conservative followers that his vision of the 1980s reflected their shared memory of the 1950s as a time of universal piety, traditional social norms, and religiously grounded harmony. Intimately familiar with the cultural logic of postwar anticommunism, Reagan filled the term "Judeo-Christian" with meanings that fit his admirers' traditionalist dreams for America. For Reagan and like-minded conservatives, as for many American commentators during and after World War II, the term "religion" encoded a highly exclusive, deeply politicized vision of religious authenticity. It is no accident that Reagan became the most prolific presidential user of Judeo-Christian terminology in American history—and the first sitting president to use the terms "secularism" and "secularist" as pejoratives. Since then, Judeo-Christian rhetoric has continued to flourish among members of the religious right, as they wage the "culture wars" against what many now call "secular humanism."[20] Even today, as the Cold War recedes from memory, the recasting of political culture and political language that it inspired in Americans continues to shape our thought and action. The cultural and political logic of the early Cold War period, which identified the ideological threat to democracy as "godless communism," has deeply imprinted the religious dimensions of American political rhetoric ever since. Between the late 1940s and the early 1960s, the widespread preoccupation with communism inscribed a cluster of related categories—not only "Judeo-Christian" but also "secularism" and others—at the heart of American public discourse, where they have remained firmly in place through the intervening decades. The roots of America's culture wars thus lie in the 1940s and 1950s, and not, as scholars have generally argued, in the 1960s and 1970s.

Scholars have been slow to recognize the continuities between today's cultural conflicts and World War II–era debates over religion's role in the American democratic project. This is true in part because they have typically interpreted mid-twentieth-century paeans to the "Judeo-Christian tradition" as signs of an emerging liberal consensus regarding the value of religious tolerance and the importance of integrating Catholics and Jews into the American cultural mainstream. In the years since Mark Silk published his groundbreaking 1984 article "Notes on the Judeo-Christian Tradition in America," which outlined some of the tensions explored in greater depth here, several other historians have emphasized the liberal, antifascist, and "anti-anti-Semitic" uses of Judeo-Christian discourse. They have generally contended that the new terminology's spread both signaled and facilitated the incorporation of Catholics and Jews into American public life, creating a "tri-faith" nation.

Although there is much truth in this account, the advent of Judeo-Christian discourse was not solely a pluralizing response to nativism and fascism. The new terminology reflected the growing influence of Jews and Catholics and a desire to include those groups in the national self-understanding, but it also indexed sharp contests over the legitimacy of secularism in a democratic context. For many Christians, especially, Judeo-Christian language expressed not only ecumenical, antinativist impulses but also a fervent desire to stanch the spreading cultural influence of naturalistic worldviews. This combination of anti-anti-Semitism and antisecularism was especially common among liberal Catholics and "neo-orthodox" Protestants, who figured prominently among the Judeo-Christian exceptionalists who sought a middle path between Christian nationalism and the pluralists' secular public culture.

Understanding such complexities requires disentangling a series of claims and labels that appeared together in various combinations and that historians routinely conflate. One is the actual term "Judeo-Christian" itself, which was usually employed to posit a single, shared set of Judeo-Christian beliefs or values. A second is the "tri-faith" vision of American identity that took shape during the first half of the twentieth century, describing the United States as a nation of Protestants, Catholics, and Jews cooperating on equal terms. The tri-faith ideal predated the familiar, political form of Judeo-Christian discourse—by a number of decades in some instances—and its advocates did not always attach that ideal to Judeo-Christian language. A third layer of argumentation involved political theories such as Judeo-Christian exceptionalism and pluralism. These claims about the relationship of religion to democracy did not necessarily require the use of Judeo-Christian language. Some Judeo-Christian exceptionalists used alternate terms such as "Hebraic-Christian" or "prophetic," or simply asserted that Judaism and Christianity underpinned democracy without using any term indicating a compound religious heritage. Finally, there was the fourth level: church-state theories. As we will see, many mid-twentieth-century Protestants embraced a Judeo-Christian exceptionalist view of democracy but retained their long-standing belief that religious institutions could anchor a democratic culture without official recognition by the state.

On all of these levels, the meanings and uses of "Judeo-Christian" were contested from the discourse's very inception—an insight of Silk's that no subsequent interpreter has systematically developed.[21] That classic postwar language was more controversial, less widely used, often more exclusive, and employed with greater awareness of the boundaries it drew than either today's disputants or our historical accounts have recognized. To understand our own culture wars, we must turn back to earlier rounds of conflict—above all, those of the supposedly homogeneous, consensus-oriented 1950s. When we survey that terrain through the lens of Judeo-Christian terminology, a new vision of postwar America, riven by deep conflicts, comes into view. Pitched battles over the relationship between religion and democracy raged within the apparent consensus fostered by the widespread use of Judeo-Christian language during World War II and the early Cold War years. By deciphering that Judeo-Christian discourse, we can see America's religiously diverse past, present, and future with fresh eyes.

PART ONE

The Genesis of America's Judeo-Christian Discourse

From Hebraic-Hellenic to Judeo-Christian

THE ROOTS OF A DISCOURSE

At the dawn of the twentieth century, virtually all Protestant Americans regarded their nation as "Christian"—by which they meant Protestant. Although the Catholic and Jewish populations were expanding rapidly, due to the massive influx of Southern and Eastern European immigrants that accompanied industrialization, these stirrings of change in the religious landscape had barely touched the collective self-conception of the Protestant majority. Evidence of growing religious diversity could be seen; cross-confessional skirmishes over Bible reading in the public schools, surprisingly common in the late nineteenth century, produced interfaith initiatives in several cities. At the 1893 World's Fair in Chicago, the World's Parliament of Religions dramatized the range of religious diversity at home and abroad. But these were isolated examples, perceptible to the astute observer but easily ignored by those disinclined to see changes afoot. Within decades, the acceleration of such trends would remake many Americans' sense of their nation's religious identity. But in 1900, the idea that America was a "Judeo-Christian" nation and stood in the vanguard of "Western civilization" would have been unfathomable. Indeed, such claims would have been literally meaningless to all but a handful of Americans. Those key terms had not yet taken on their modern meanings in American public culture.

This all changed dramatically, especially in educated circles, by World War II. In the 1930s, cultural leaders increasingly saw the United States as the torchbearer of "Western civilization" rather than the product of a rebellion against Europe. Among most Protestant Americans, Europe had long been synonymous with hidebound traditionalism and fixed classes. By the 1930s, however, American thinkers increasingly perceived a singular "West," defined by a shared set of ethical and perhaps religious principles. Such intellectual constructions of the West strongly influenced the cultural contours of Judeo-Christian discourse in the United States.

In the late nineteenth and early twentieth centuries, ongoing disputes in Europe over Christianity's historical roles bequeathed to Americans important resources—terms, concepts, dichotomies, taxonomies—for analyzing questions of religious difference and religion's role in society. American scholars then crafted their own accounts of the religious dimensions of Western history. By World War II, some had begun to rework these cultural materials into versions of the "Judeo-Christian tradition" that provided a usable past for a nation with distinctive demographic characteristics and cultural and theological divides. Not simply a liberal response to fascism or increased demographic diversity, the emergence of America's Judeo-Christian discourse also involved the articulation of new standards of theological and political authenticity—standards strongly shaped by the New Deal at home and totalitarianism abroad.

The Nineteenth-Century Dialectic of Hebraism and Hellenism

The term "Judeo-Christian" had been around for decades before it took on its modern meaning in the 1930s and 1940s. Its sporadic original uses reflected pressing problems of identity and belief that also shaped a series of other, related concepts. The nineteenth and early twentieth centuries featured a vigorous discourse on the relationships between religion, nationality, and civilization that would eventually pull the term "Judeo-Christian" into its orbit. This discourse on the cultural character of the West, which Americans joined by the 1870s and 1880s, later gave "Judeo-Christian" its familiar meaning, as thinkers proposed various ways of defining Western civilization and differentiating it from other civilizations.[1]

The leading conceptual resource in the earlier period was a distinction between "Hebraic" and "Hellenic" elements of Western culture that recurred throughout the late nineteenth century. Nineteenth-century European thinkers focused intently on Christianity's Hebraic past. The study of the Hebrew language had played a key role at Protestantism's inception, after centuries in which the medieval church evinced little interest in the ancient Hebrews. The Reformers' concept of *sola scriptura* inspired them to learn to read Scripture in the original Hebrew, in search of its true meanings. In the nineteenth century, as Christianity lost its grip as a taken-for-granted framework of absolute truth, many Protestant scholars and church leaders sought to renew its cultural force by again looking to its earliest iterations as a source of ethical guidance and spiritual energy. The painstaking philological work through which nineteenth-century scholars tracked the historical origins of biblical texts reflected a broader search for a kind of religious fountain of youth that could reinvigorate Europe's Christian spirit. As in the Reformation period, this focus on the early church led once again to the ancient Hebrews.[2]

Nineteenth-century arguments over Hebraism intersected with new ways of thinking about social dynamics. Much of the era's discourse on human differences rejected the individualism and universalism of the Enlightenment period and focused instead on the collective forms of identity—especially nations, religions, and civilizations—that mediated between individuals and humanity as a whole. The nation-building and colonial projects of the nineteenth century imparted a deep sense of portent to scholarly work on such questions. Above all, the existence of Jewish populations in self-professedly Christian nations was a primary concern. Modern nationalism portrayed Europeans as separate and essentially homogeneous peoples, but also as Christian peoples. In this view, each people possessed a unifying spirit that manifested itself in a tightly integrated linguistic and cultural tradition and thus shaped literary productions and folklore, as well as religious beliefs. European nationalism redoubled the pressure on Jews to assimilate culturally, and eventually to convert to their nations' dominant versions of Christianity. Throughout Central Europe especially, where national unity had not yet been achieved and the Jewish presence was strong, Judaism represented a pressing problem for nationalist and Christian leaders alike.[3]

This anxiety about persistent religious differences lurked just below the surface of vigorous scholarly exchanges over the chronology and meaning of early Christian history. Questions about Christianity's relationship with Judaism at the moment of the former's origin stood in for larger concerns about the contemporary relationship between Christianity, Judaism, nationalism, and European civilization. What did it mean that Christianity had grown from a Jewish matrix? When had a distinctively Christian religion emerged out of Judaism? Did that emergence signal a total rejection of Judaism by the early Christians, or could one see significant continuities? And what, precisely, differentiated Judaism from Christianity? The meaning of the Hebrew Bible became a battleground as religious thinkers layered new questions about the historical origins and contemporary meanings of Christianity onto late-Enlightenment debates about faith and reason. Scholars studied ancient languages, developed new theories of history, and proliferated schemes for classifying religions, peoples, races, and civilizations. The Protestants who led the charge hoped to use empirical evidence about primordial Christianity's character to rebuild the social unity of medieval Christendom on the foundation of Protestant voluntarism and moralism. With an eye toward im-

perial ventures and the loosely related missionary enterprise, they also sought
to explain why Christianity could and should spread around the globe.

Two distinct but potentially overlapping ways of understanding the role
of Hebraic ideas in Western civilization took shape in the nineteenth century. One was exemplified in the writings of the German philosopher G. W. F.
Hegel, whose complex taxonomy of religious systems became a key reference
point for arguments about Christianity and Judaism as well as an important
link between the discourses of theology and nationalism. Hegel advanced the
"supersessionist" argument that Judaism had played a necessary role in the
development of Christianity but no longer represented a vital force in the
modern world, having fulfilled its historical destiny in the distant past. Many
Europeans followed Hegel in reducing the meaning of Judaism to its historical contribution to Christianity, ignoring the fact that it survived as a living religion and implicitly endorsing a close link between Christianity and the
modern state. To Hegel, Christianity represented "a spiritualized Judaism," a
Judaism made absolute and universal. By fulfilling Judaism's promise, Christianity had rendered modern forms of Judaism obsolete. As the historical criticism of the Bible emerged in Germany, Tübingen School founder F. C. Baur
embedded Hegel's analysis in the early history of the church by arguing that
Christianity had taken its mature form only when the universalism of Paul
and his followers replaced the legalistic and nationalistic orientation of Peter
and the Jewish Christians.[4]

Meanwhile, the British cultural critic Matthew Arnold argued that Western culture represented a compound of two ancient strands, namely, Hellenism and Hebraism. This distinction, which was susceptible to an extremely
wide range of meanings, appeared time and time again in the cultural disputes of the era. Some theorists of Hellenism and Hebraism held that Western
civilization required the elevation of one component over the other. Arnold,
for example, sought to boost the Hellenic content of British culture in the
face of what he saw as a dominant Hebraism, while other Christian writers decried the emphasis on Hellenistic rationalism. Still others contended
that Western civilization required a delicate balance between Hebraic and
Hellenic elements. Speaking implicitly to questions of national identity and
political organization, these seemingly abstract arguments about the relationship between Hebraism and Hellenism also functioned as practical claims
about the cultural basis and educational forms required to sustain Western
modes of social order.[5]

Scholars have identified Arnold's canonical 1869 work *Culture and Anarchy* as the leading antecedent to the language of Judeo-Christianity. There,
Arnold addressed concerns about culture and democracy similar to those

that animated early-twentieth-century American commentators. With the aristocracy fading, he argued, the middle class was destined to rule and to assimilate the working class. Yet the workers would reject the leadership of the middle class, he feared, if it failed to take over from the dying aristocracy "those public and conspicuous virtues by which the multitude is captivated and led—lofty spirit, commanding character, exquisite culture." Arnold traced prevailing cultural values such as industriousness and acquisitiveness to Hebraism's legalistic emphasis on ensuring proper "conduct and obedience" through the rigid enforcement of "strictures of conscience." The middle class, he argued, could truly fill the aristocracy's shoes only if it instead embraced Hellenism, a capacity "to see things as they really are" that was underwritten by "spontaneity of consciousness." According to Arnold, restoring a greater quotient of Hellenism to the British cultural milieu would satisfy "the need in man for intellect and knowledge, his desire for beauty, his instinct for society, and for pleasurable and graceful forms of society."[6]

At the same time, Arnold found much to admire in the Hebraic quest for justice. And he readily admitted that innovation could go too far, especially in the ethical realm, where a focus on creativity rather than rectitude produced hedonism and anarchy. In morality, among other areas, civilization could not do without the balancing force of Hebraic legalism. Describing Hebraism and Hellenism as "rival forces . . . dividing the empire of the world between them," Arnold argued that Christianity offered a perfect synthesis of the two, providing the needed corrective for any European culture that had become unbalanced. Indeed, one of Arnold's primary claims in *Culture and Anarchy* was that a state church was preferable to religious voluntarism or secularity, because the religious establishment would preserve the cultural basis for middle-class rule. As we will see, many American users of the Judeo-Christian language likewise assumed that Christianity neatly balanced the genius of Hebraism with the resources of Hellenism and thus needed to play a central role in a democratic culture.[7]

The German philologist-turned-philosopher Friedrich Nietzsche's contributions to late-nineteenth-century debates on religion and civilization also foreshadowed the mature discourse of Judeo-Christianity. Arnold had worried about the problem of embracing cultural innovation without undermining existing ethical standards. Nietzsche, by contrast, identified those ethical standards as the major obstacle to human freedom. In setting himself against the entire tenor of Western culture, Nietzsche identified a body of "*jüdisch-christliche*" ethical principles as that culture's foundation. He defined Western civilization as essentially Judeo-Christian in character. Nietzsche's writings, especially *On the Genealogy of Morality* (1887) and *The*

Antichrist (1888), described Western culture as an outgrowth of a Jewish-Christian heritage that he portrayed as a set of basic ethical ideals rather than a comprehensive body of doctrines.[8]

The French thinker Ernest Renan, a lapsed Catholic and a leading student of Semitic languages, illustrated perfectly how the nineteenth-century development of the "higher criticism," which placed Jesus in a secular narrative of history, reflected deep concerns about the relations, past and present, between Judaism and Christianity. As a philologist, an interpreter of the historical Jesus, a student of world religions, and a theorist of nationalism, Renan stood at the intersection of virtually all of the paths of thought that later converged in the concept of a "Judeo-Christian tradition."[9] His *Life of Jesus* (1863) championed the empirical study of Christ's life and the text of the Bible. It also challenged Albrecht Ritschl's claim that the emergence of Christianity had entailed the ascendance of Pauline (i.e., Hellenic) ideas over Jewish ones. Instead, Renan argued, Christianity had synthesized Hellenic and Hebraic strands into a new and uniquely successful whole. The German-Jewish writer Abraham Geiger responded sharply the following year, insisting that Jesus had been Jewish and that whatever value Christianity possessed lay in its Hebraic core of monotheism, which had been swamped by a destructive, Hellenistic paganism as Christianity evolved. But Renan still held out for a Christian Jesus, even though he placed Jesus in a direct line of descent from the Hebrew prophets. In response to challenges by Geiger and others, Renan embarked on his massive, five-volume *History of the People of Israel* (1887–93), which helped establish the conception of a dual Hebraic-Hellenic heritage for Europe. Renan, like Arnold, insisted that Christianity perfectly melded the two strands comprising Western civilization.[10]

At the same time, Renan reinforced the supersessionist claim about Judaism's relation to Christianity. His *History of the People of Israel* described the contribution of Judaism to Western civilization as purely historical: The Hebrew prophets, after midwifing Christianity by injecting a fierce passion for justice into Hellenic thought, had retired to the sideline as their offspring flourished. Renan described Western civilization as a "framework of human culture created by Greece" but infused with "the trace of Israel." The Greeks, he elaborated, had provided "our science, our arts, our literature, our philosophy, our moral code, our political code, our strategy, our diplomacy," and even "our maritime and international law." In only one area had the Greeks fallen short: They lacked the moral fervor that gave Western society its inner fire. As Renan put it, the Greeks "despised the humble and did not feel the need of a just God." Fortunately, he went on, the "ardent genius of a small tribe established in an outlandish corner of Syria" had perfectly filled "this void in the Hellenic intellect." Armed with the needed passion for righteous-ness, Greek culture had gone on to its successful historical career as Western civilization. Meanwhile, "having given birth to Christianity, Judaism still continues to exist, but as a withered trunk beside one fertile branch." Renan concluded, "It is through Christianity that Judaism has really conquered the world. Christianity is the masterpiece of Judaism, its glory and the fulness of its evolution."[11]

The supersessionist view of Judaism as a necessary but bygone element in the formation of Christianity took hold just as an emerging "world religions" framework was teaching Europeans to think of themselves as the inheritors of a civilization shaped by both Jewish and Christian principles. In the 1870s and 1880s, prompted in large part by the so-called discovery of Buddhism, the emerging world religions discourse defined Western civilization in essentially religious terms. Indeed, it helped to crystallize the modern understanding of the term "religion" itself, for which European forms of Christianity served as the model. Buddhism challenged prevailing European views in two important ways. First, the widespread belief that Buddhism was atheistic raised the pros-pect that morality and virtue might be possible without belief in God. Mean-while, Buddhism also seemed to share Christianity's great claim to fame, namely, its universalism. Indeed, Buddhism's comparatively ancient roots raised the startling prospect that Christian universalism might derive in some way from its older counterpart. Suddenly the long history of efforts to convert the "pagan" inhabitants of the East to Christianity appeared in an entirely new light. A few liberals in the West adopted Buddhism themselves, finding it compatible with modern science and concluding from its tolerant outlook and "non-violent methods of evangelization" that it was ethically superior to Christianity. Yet the vast majority of Western Christians simply redoubled their efforts to explain how Christianity outdid the alternatives, which now included Buddhism and other world religions as well as the more intimately familiar Judaism. These belief systems were indeed full-fledged "religions," many Christian interpreters now conceded. But when judged as a religion—a concept modeled closely on European Christianity—each fell far short.[12]

Here, as in so much else, Hegel had paved the way decades earlier. He identified Christianity as the "Revelatory Religion," an ideal faith capable of integrating each of the others and relegating them to the past. The general acceptance of Christianity, in Hegel's view, would signal the full actualiza-tion of the spirit of God. The other religions contained elements of truth, he contended, but each fell short of the Christian ideal in particular, remediable ways, whereas Christianity brought together these partial truths into a single, universally valid synthesis. By the late nineteenth century, many European thinkers had adopted the broad outlines of Hegel's analysis, which made room for Buddhism but preserved the popular image of Christian missionaries as bringing the gift of truth to the world. Like theories about the historical role of Judaism in the West, the world religions framework placed Christianity in a separate category from the other faiths. In terms of improving interfaith relations, it was certainly a step forward to redefine "pagans" as adherents to Judaism, Buddhism, and the other great religions. Yet while these systems now appeared on the same scale of measurement as Christianity, most Western commentators still located them far down that scale. Judaism, though historically a direct predecessor of Christianity, figured in the world religions framework as simply another partial faith, and as one whose role on the world stage had diminished radically since ancient days.[13]

Judeo-Christianity Comes to America

This cluster of preoccupations and arguments profoundly shaped the use of the term "Judeo-Christian" as it evolved in the late nineteenth and early twentieth centuries. Sporadic appearances of "Judeo-Christian" (or, frequently, "Judaeo-Christian" or "Judæo-Christian") occurred as early as 1841, when a writer for the *Weekly Messenger* of the German Reformed Church dubbed "Judeo-Christians" a group of Polish Jews that had converted to Catholicism but secretly remained Jewish, the author believed.[14] The term's familiar meaning did not appear until the last decades of the nineteenth century, however. Instead, it was used either as an adjective to describe an interaction between Jews and Christians, as in the phrase "Judeo-Christian relations," or as a noun to refer to one of three groups: the early adherents of Christianity who had come to it from Judaism instead of Greek or Roman belief systems, modern-day Jewish groups that continued to practice their faith in secret after having been forced to convert to Christianity, or Jewish sects that recognized the divinity of Christ.[15] None of these usages suggested that Protestantism, Catholicism, and Judaism possessed a common body of beliefs, though of course they shared the Hebrew Bible. Instead, the term referred to people rather than ideas, and the hyphen symbolized a discursive engagement or a hybrid identity, not the existence of an intellectual heritage shared by the three faiths. Even in these early days, however, the term "Judeo-Christian" pointed to swirling debates about the teachings and justification of Christianity, as well as concerns among nationalists about the thorny question of how Jews figured into Europe's explicitly Christian nation-building enterprises. The emergence of Judeo-Christian formulations must be read against the anxieties of Christian identity produced by the Enlightenment, science, historicism, and secularization, as well as by civilizing projects at home and abroad.

Over time, in this highly charged discursive context, the familiar, modern meaning of "Judeo-Christian" arose and eventually eclipsed the others. In the new usage, the term referred to a broad stream of thought stretching from antiquity to the present—a spiritual heritage that defined and linked the societies of the ancient Near East, classical Greece and Rome, medieval Europe, and the modern West. Already by the 1880s, some commentators had begun to discern a coherent, if not all-pervasive, body of Judeo-Christian ideas in medieval thought. For instance, one writer spoke in 1882 of "the influence exerted on the Vikings by the Christian schools in England, where Judaeo-Christian and Graeco-Roman elements were united."[16] In the first decades of the twentieth century, Americans increasingly described their own society as part of a larger Western civilization that many came to see as "Judeo-Christian" in its origin and character.

Perhaps unsurprisingly, Jewish commentators were particularly attracted to the term. As early as 1894, Rabbi Frederick Cohn, a popular lecturer and writer, used the new compound formulation to claim for Judaism all of the good done by Christianity since its founding. Anticipating a "cultural gifts" model that would flourish in the early decades of the twentieth century, Cohn explained that "Israel's mission" was to bring "the God idea" to the world. Christianity, he said, was simply "Judaism at work in the pagan world. . . . The Hebrews have given the world the only Bible, with all its manifold blessings. . . . Of the Graeco-Roman, the Teutonic-German, and the Judeo-Christian ideas, it is the latter that has done more for the world than any other agency known to history. The time is coming when the whole world will accept the blessings conferred on it by Judaism."[17] Two years later, the Johns Hopkins linguist Maurice Bloomfield likewise invoked a shared Judeo-Christian heritage, contrasting Hindu beliefs to "Judaeo-Christian conceptions."[18]

Scholars seeking a social-scientific account of religion also began to pick up the new terminology. In 1903, William James, then engaged in his pioneering work on the psychology of religion, cited an account of "the Judæo-Christian ideal" offered in a British volume of the previous year.[19] French contributions to the sociology of religion began to reinforce the Judeo-Christian discourse at roughly the same time. In an article reprinted by the *American Journal of Sociology* in 1903, Maurice Vernes defended the project of "subjecting religions to the scientific method of study" and noted that scientists already knew much about the world's great religions, especially "the Hebrew-Christian religion," or "Judaism-Christianity." Identifying monotheism as the distinctive contribution of the Jewish prophets, Vernes described "Judaism, greatly modified by the Christian element grafted upon it," as "the point of departure for the religious history of civilization." Such contributions added the considerable weight of European authority to the nascent American discourse of Judeo-Christianity.[20]

This terminological evolution also overlapped closely with the articulation of the "humanities" in the American universities. Professionalizing humanists emphasized the role of ideas and values, rather than material or political forces, in shaping social life. Dissatisfied with the usual descriptions of the cultural heritage shared by the United States and Europe—rationality, democracy, and Protestantism were the most frequently cited links—many humanists explored the deep roots of what they came to call Western civilization and to define as an application and development of ideas inherited from the ancient Mediterranean world. In so doing, these American thinkers intervened in long-standing European arguments over the precise meaning and historical role of Greek, Roman, Hebrew, and Christian thoughtways.[21]

American commentators worked against the backdrop of the same forces that preoccupied Europeans, namely, science, nationalism, industrialization, and cultural change. Yet each took a peculiar form in the American case. For example, American nationalism was even more relentlessly universalistic than its European counterparts. European theorists of nationalism had developed their ideas in direct response to Enlightenment universalism, and thus exhibited a deep concern for particularity. Americans, on the other hand, viewed themselves as the vanguard of a unified humanity, although their universalism often coexisted with a belief that other racial and religious groups stood far below them on the scale of civilization. Their intense focus on classicism, for example, gained much of its power from a belief in the universal validity of classical ideals. The Civil War also inspired Northerners to define their cause as that of humanity in general, not of a particular section or an economic faction.[22]

By the late nineteenth century, however, industrialization and immigration seemed to have rendered classical ideals insufficient for the task of attaining cultural unity in the absence of a formal religious establishment. Some American thinkers identified the needed unifying force as science or an empiricist philosophy such as positivism or pragmatism. Others, like many of their European counterparts, thought that recovering premodern (or, in some cases, non-Western) cultural resources could breathe a powerful new energy into modern institutions. Liberal Protestantism, which looked to the Hebraic past for renewal, found fertile soil in the United States. Meanwhile, Matthew Arnold's writings spoke even more influentially to American audiences than to his British contemporaries. Ignoring Arnold's call for a religious establishment, Americans assimilated his claims about the unifying potential of culture to their own, more Emersonian emphasis on self-reliance. Seeking to understand their nation's character and place in the world, they mobilized and combined a diverse array of cultural resources.[23]

By 1871, if not earlier, Americans had also begun to offer their own original contributions to the transatlantic discourse on the religious contours of Western civilization. In that year, the Harvard-educated Unitarian James Freeman Clarke published an extensive volume called *Ten Great Religions.* Clarke exhibited the world religions framework's characteristic combination of respect for non-Christian faiths, which he portrayed as the carriers of partial truths, with forthright insistence on Christianity's unique character as a "Catholic" religion, "universal" and "steadily progressive," and thus "adapted to become the Religion of all Races." Book sections such as "The Hindoos have no History," "Judaism as a Preparation for Christianity," and "Mohammedanism a Relapse" presented the faiths in question as "ethnic" religions, each limited to a single "race" or "national civilization" and thus "partial" and "arrested." Clarke placed Islam and Judaism somewhat above the other ethnic creeds, deeming them "temporary and local forms" of Christianity. He described Catholicism as standing in the same relation to genuine, Protestant Christianity as did an ossified, hierarchical Brahmanism to the living fount of Buddhism. Only Protestantism, wrote Clarke, could truly "fulfil" the various partial faiths, "replacing them by teaching all the truth they have taught, and supplying that which they have omitted," while "keeping abreast with the advancing civilization of the world." It could do so because it was "not a creed or a form, but a spirit." Dynamic rather than static and assimilative rather than exclusive, Protestantism alone could accommodate modern progress without losing sight of the timeless meaning of faith.[24]

Like so many other works of the late nineteenth century, Clarke's book demonstrated the decisive role that characterizations of Christianity's past played in efforts to define the present-day cultural character of Western nations. However, not all American commentators portrayed the non-Christian faiths as stunted and provisional. Many, for example, shared in the newfound fascination with Buddhism. Like their European counterparts, they ascribed many different meanings to Buddhism. Some saw in it an antidote to positivism, while others viewed it as a religion uniquely suited to the science-centered culture of the modern West. The late nineteenth century also brought an intensification of interest in Hebrew studies. The Puritans, like all other post-Reformation Protestants, had been heavily invested in Hebraism. They identified themselves as the new chosen people, the inheritors of the ancient covenant. Although the late 1700s and early 1800s witnessed a turn toward

Greco-Roman models in the new American republic, Hebraism reemerged after the Civil War. Leading the charge was the Baptist minister and Hebrew scholar William Rainey Harper, who taught at Yale before becoming the first president of the University of Chicago in 1891. He launched a series of summer schools in the 1880s, at Chautauqua and elsewhere, to teach Hebrew to Protestant ministers and their parishioners. Harper hoped to infuse American culture with spiritual ideals by spreading the language of the ancient Hebrews across the nation.[25]

Supersessionism persisted among American Hebraists, however. Crawford Howell Toy, a Southern Baptist who taught at Harvard from 1880 to 1903, advanced the cause of Hebraism in *Judaism and Christianity* (1890) and several other books. A theological liberal like Clarke, Toy found much to admire in Judaism. Yet he ultimately described it as the nationalistic progenitor of a universalizing Christianity. Among the world religions, he explained, "only three have grown into universal form—Brahmanism into Buddhism, Judaism into Christianity, and the old Arabian faith into Islam." Although ancient Judaism had contained the germs of a universal faith, argued Toy, it had been overly legalistic and thus extremist. Like many other Protestants of his era, Toy harbored a desire to validate Christianity—not even Buddhism or Islam would comport with modern social conditions, he predicted—as well as an equally strong desire to set limits to its dogmatic claims by whittling it down to its ethical core through comparisons with other major faiths. Even the most vigorous Protestant proponents of Hebraism in the late nineteenth century struggled to see Judaism as a viable faith in the modern world.[26]

Debating Supersessionism

Not until the early 1930s would the Judeo-Christian discourse appear in its fullest form, accompanied by all of its component claims: that Judaism and Christianity shared historical and possibly theological continuities, that this compound heritage defined American or Western society, and that it did so in the face of potent totalitarian challengers. But the various components of that view had begun to circulate more widely in the previous decades, as Americans contributed in ever-growing numbers to the transatlantic conversation about the cultural roots and content of "Western civilization." Claims about America's Judeo-Christian character emerged out of a series of arguments concerning the development of modern cultures and—farther in the background but still palpable—debates about how the American state should treat religious beliefs. Liberal Protestants' identification of Christianity as an expression of the social ideals of the ancient Hebrew prophets, American Jews' attempts to counter supersessionism and present their faith as a creative force in the contemporary world, and scholars' efforts to catalog the past and present components of Western civilization all fed into the crystallization of the Judeo-Christian discourse. Well before the struggle against fascism, then, Americans had begun to engage the points of controversy that would structure the competing formulations of the Judeo-Christian tradition.

Around the turn of the century, the most influential scholarly interpretation of America's cultural identity flowed from the pen of Harvard's Charles Eliot Norton. As the nation's leading academic humanist and cultural critic, the Unitarian Norton played a central role in crafting the concept of "Western civilization." Affected deeply by the waning fortunes of institutional Christianity, Norton sought a functional alternative. He identified a religiously inspired tradition of Western art and literature as the needed source of both cultural progress and cultural stability. Norton denied that Christianity held a monopoly on the recognition of moral laws, but he believed moral enervation would follow if its creative, narrative resources were lost to moderns. Like Arnold, he linked his cultural program to the success of political democracy, insisting that courses in Western civilization could help democratic citizens see their societies in the light of millennia of Western history. Also like Arnold, Norton viewed ancient Greece as the fount of the wisdom required to correct an industrializing nation's cultural one-sidedness.[27]

Such arguments persisted into the interwar years. Introducing a 1925 reprint of Arnold's *Culture and Anarchy*, the Sewanee English professor William S. Knickerbocker argued that the American population had been drawn from "the Puritan and Hebraising middle class" in Britain and thus shared "its narrow conception of man's spiritual range." To his dismay, he found Hebraic tendencies utterly dominant in American culture: "From Maine to Florida, and back again, all America Hebraises." For Knickerbocker, as for Arnold, Hebraism entailed the pinched, colorless moralism that many critics in 1920s America called "Puritanism."[28]

These denigrations of Hebraism faced potent challenges in the early twentieth century, however. Following the lead of figures such as Clarke and Toy, a number of important Protestant and Jewish thinkers highlighted the role of the ancient Hebrews—and perhaps even the contemporary Jews—in defining Western civilization. At the same time, they implicitly challenged Norton's privileging of refined taste over ethical character in the maintenance of democracy. Like Norton, these Protestants and Jews sought to move forward by looking backward, recapturing potent cultural resources from the ancient world. But in order to progress, they argued, modern civilization needed the energy and fire of the Hebrew prophets, not the serene contemplation of the ancient Greeks.

As in Europe, claims about the Hebraic roots of Western culture were closely tied to liberalizing tendencies within Protestantism. Across the West, liberal Protestants followed the Reformers before them in seeking to throw off what they deemed inessential, outdated forms and return to the original source of Christianity in the ancient world. Of course, liberal Protestants hardly abandoned the Reformation as a point of reference. Challenging Catholic claims that the Reformation had heralded the decline of civilization, liberal Protestants still described it as the liberation of true Christianity from its shackles. Yet this retort tended to reinforce the historical primacy of Catholicism and to portray Protestantism as a mere reaction. By looking back further, beyond the medieval heritage to the prophetic Christianity of Jesus, liberal Protestants could claim for themselves the authentic, "Hebraic" spirit of the Christian tradition, dating it to a period before the ascendancy of the "Hellenized" Catholic Church. Liberal Protestants worked diligently to Hebraize the Christian tradition, engaging in a tug-of-war with Hellenizers such as Arnold and Norton.[29]

From the standpoint of interfaith relations, the Hebraizing impulse of early-twentieth-century liberal Protestantism had a number of conflicting effects. Not surprisingly, Protestant Hebraists found allies among liberal Jews, who shared many of their cultural goals. On the other hand, much liberal Protestant thought still partook of the supersessionist dismissal of present-day Judaism that permeated Western Christianity at the time. Many liberal Protestants, like their more theologically conservative counterparts, treated Judaism as a historical relic rather than a living entity. Meanwhile, the impact on Protestant-Catholic relations was more straightforward, if often implicit: The liberal Protestant effort to Hebraize the Christian tradition represented a frontal attack on Catholicism, given the latter's close identification with Hellenic thought.

Hebraizing liberal Protestants engaged with secular traditions of thought as well. Scholars today frequently read the Social Gospel of the late nineteenth and early twentieth centuries, which sought to create God's kingdom on earth, as a simple capitulation to the forces of modernity. However, its proponents actually insisted that modern societies would always require religious ideals to complement their scientific knowledge. The resurgent Hebraizing impulse in Protestantism challenged not only Catholicism but also an Enlightenment-inspired reading of historical progress as a product of reason's liberation from obscurantism. Liberal Protestants were far friendlier to post-Renaissance thought than to the medieval church. But they hoped, through a return to the original fount of Christian energy, to permeate modern societies with Christian teachings and recreate the religiously grounded social unity that they associated with medieval Christendom.

The work of the German theologian Adolf von Harnack, a key reference point for American Social Gospel thinkers, illustrates how liberal Protestants drew on the language of Hebraism to position themselves against both Catholics and naturalists. Harnack, whose students included Karl Barth and Dietrich Bonhoeffer, was a renowned philologist and early church historian as well as a prominent religious leader who combined elements of Lutheranism with a deep concern for social justice. Although Harnack found potent resources in the Catholic thought of Saint Augustine, he disapproved strongly of key Catholic teachings and deemed even Luther's form of Protestantism overly enmeshed in that outmoded framework. Yet Harnack worked closely with Catholics in the ecumenical movement of his day, even as he sharply challenged the Church's rationalistic tendencies in his writings. In the final analysis, Harnack believed that Catholicism was too closely wedded to medieval, Hellenistic forms of thought to serve as the needed source of Christian energy in the modern world. Moreover, he contended that the Reformers had not thrown off all of these Hellenistic patterns. Through painstaking studies of Hellenizing tendencies in the early church, Harnack argued that Catholicism and orthodox Protestantism represented deviations from genuine Christianity, having grown out of a Platonism that had deeply infected the Gospels. His views on the Hebraic background of Christianity found a wide American audience through the 1901 volume *What Is Christianity?*[30]

Walter Rauschenbusch, the foremost American proponent of the Social Gospel after 1900, likewise stressed the continuities between the teachings of Jesus and the social criticism of the Hebrew prophets. Rauschenbusch took inspiration from Harnack's writings and shared with the German a belief that the modern world needed a "prophetic" Protestantism to save it from the Hellenistic errors common to Catholicism, orthodox Protestantism, and naturalism alike. A sharp critic of Catholicism, the Baptist Rauschenbusch also held that Protestantism could not fulfill its proper social function until it became thoroughly Hebraized, abandoning both its assertions of biblical literalism and a moral rigorism that emphasized individual salvation over social justice. He distinguished genuine Christianity from "the dogmas on which the Catholic and Protestant theologies are based." These dogmas, he added, were "neither dominant in the New Testament nor clearly defined in it." Rauschenbusch traced them to the early "Hellenization of Christianity," wherein "alien Greek thought" had "streamed into the religion of Jesus Christ and created a theology which he never taught or intended."[31]

A somewhat different rendering of Hebraism's contributions to early Christianity shaped one of the first American uses of the term "Judeo-Christian" to refer to a single religious framework. In 1902, the Johns Hopkins philosopher Arthur O. Lovejoy, a strong proponent of German thought and scientific methods as well as a fervent seeker after a universal faith, argued in the *American Journal of Theology* that the roots of modern historicism—the views that time is progressive or teleological and reality is dynamic rather than static—could be traced to the "early phases of the conjunction of Judeo-Christian and Hellenic ideas" in the early church. Lovejoy, considered the father of intellectual history in the United States, had become fascinated by the historical development of religion during his studies with Crawford Howell Toy and William James at Harvard in the late 1890s. By 1907, Lovejoy had credited to the ancient Hebrews not only historicism but also what he took to be the other half of the moral vision of Jesus: an "ethical inwardness" that brought moral judgment to bear on desires and feelings as well as actions. Christianity, he declared, had always "been nearest to its true and original type when it has been most faithful to the spirit of Jewish prophetism."[32]

Yet Lovejoy's substitution of "Judeo-Christian" for "Hebraic" still reflected his teacher Toy's supersessionist view of the relationship between Judaism and Christianity. In the 1902 essay, for example, Lovejoy credited Christianity with inaugurating the Western idea of a philosophy of history, which he called "a peculiarly Christian contribution to the Occident's stock of general ideas." Although the Jewish prophets had supplied most of the materials for such a philosophy, he contended, the early Christians had actually put the pieces together. Lovejoy's 1907 essay on ethical inwardness again portrayed Hebraic roots flowering into mature Christian forms, with Christianity realizing the implicit promise of the teachings of the Hebrew prophets.[33]

American Jewish leaders worked to allay this perception that Judaism was no longer a living, creative force in the modern world. Although they joined many liberal Protestants in stressing the cultural contributions of the ancient Hebrew prophets, they rejected the image of Judaism as an empty vessel whose contents had been poured into Christianity. By 1900, a growing number of Jewish commentators attacked the presumption that their faith had long since discharged its service to Western civilization by simply giving birth to Christianity and providing it with a few core ideas. Judaism, they insisted, was a living faith, and indeed a world religion in its own right. The result was a powerful contribution to the conversation on Western civilization that prefigured the mature discourse of Judeo-Christianity by challenging the overt or implicit dismissal of present-day Judaism by the likes of Renan, Harnack, and Lovejoy.

One prominent Jewish critic of supersessionism was the German-born Morris Jastrow, who taught Semitic languages at the University of Pennsylvania. Although he rejected the widespread claim that the ancient Hebrews had invented monotheism, Jastrow emphasized Judaism's ongoing vitality. No mere vestigial accompaniment to Christianity, he wrote, Judaism had, like the other major religions, proceeded through a series of developmental stages. Rather than being restricted to one faith, said Jastrow, the turn to monotheism reflected a stage of cultural development that corresponded to factors such as social complexity and nationalism. Still, Jastrow did think the Jews had contributed something unique. He argued that the other monotheistic nations had united religion and ethics at the institutional level, creating "a combined priestly authority." By contrast, the Jewish prophets had preserved "individual authority in the development of religion" by melding religion and ethics philosophically, not institutionally. According to Jastrow, only Judaism and its Christian offshoot rooted social authority in prophets rather than priests. This produced "a system of ethics entirely derived from religious beliefs," ensuring that "culture" remained "an offshoot of religion." Unitarianism, Reform Judaism, and Ethical Culture, which focused on ethics rather than abstruse doctrines or ritual forms, thus represented the highest phase of religious development, in Jastrow's view. To his mind, the full articulation of religion as a source of cultural authority required essentially ethical faiths, coupled with strong church-state separation.[34]

Other Jewish commentators interpreted the cultural value of their faith differently than did Jastrow. The philosopher Horace M. Kallen, like Lovejoy a student of William James, wrote in a series of essays between 1909 and 1911 that Judaism was "more constant, more adaptable and more progressive than other European religions," because it alone shared a "naturalistic and realistic" character with science. By contrast, wrote Kallen, the other "moralistic religions" were "*supernatural.*" Each divided the world into superior and degraded realms and pursued salvation rather than ethical behavior, endurance rather than righteousness, and abstinence rather than action. Only Judaism, according to Kallen, exhibited the ideal "union of *naturalism* with *moralism.*" To be sure, he said, the gradual "naturalization and socialization" of all Western religious thought in the nineteenth century had brought Protestantism and Catholicism closer to Judaism's "logical and sentimental" orientation. But even though Christians had finally discovered the value of the modern outlook—"essentially so Judaistic," he called it—they had not yet abandoned supernaturalism. For the time being, said Kallen, Judaism stood alone in recognizing the everyday world as the true arena of ethical endeavor.[35]

Kallen offered a further distinction between Judaism and "Hebraism" that made it possible to view Jews who rejected the doctrinal tenets of their religious leaders as full participants in the Jewish moral project. Kallen described Hebraism as a deep philosophical matrix surrounding Judaism, calling it "a flowering of the Jewish spirit . . . a flower whose roots are nationality and whose soil is culture." Judaism proper, according to Kallen, was simply one "special aspect" of Hebraistic culture, namely, the set of "sentiments, theories, doctrines and practices which relate to God." Moreover, views of God changed over time, while the essential elements of Hebraic culture persisted: "in metaphysics the vision of reality in flux; in morals, the conception of the value of the individual; in religion, the conception of Yahweh as a moral arbiter." Contemporary Jewish leaders, Kallen charged, would actually undermine the very source of Hebraism's historical success by forcing it back into the narrow box of Judaism, which was "not Jewish philosophy at all" but rather a form of Hellenism. Kallen discerned self-hating, assimilationist tendencies not among those Jews who embraced an Enlightenment-inspired philosophy but rather among those who embraced what he considered an essentially Christian ideal by reducing the lived genius of their community to abstract philosophical tenets about salvation and the afterlife. In Kallen's portrayal, Jews could infuse a modern, scientific civilization with ethical principles only insofar as they remained essentially secular, ignoring the rabbis' attempts to reduce the rich culture of Hebraism to Judaism, a "mere religion."[36]

Kallen thus reversed the meanings Matthew Arnold had ascribed to Hellenism and Hebraism. He equated Hellenism with an otherworldly orientation and Hebraism with a focus on the things of this world. Kallen also infused Hebraism with the dynamic, pluralistic, and antiutopian tendencies of his teacher William James's philosophical pragmatism, while equating Hellenism with an impulse toward pointless metaphysical reification. Rather than rationality and balance, Hellenism meant for Kallen a concern with "*perfection*," with "seeing things as they *ought to be*." Hebraism, meanwhile, connoted "*righteousness*," but in the sense of "making the best of a bad job," not the fanatical pursuit of moral purism. Most fundamentally, for Kallen, Hellenism and Hebraism represented alternative "modes of adaptation to contrasting environments," Hellenism viewing change as unreal and Hebraism seeing it as the essence of reality. Kallen discerned in the entire body of modern thought a sustained "attempt to subordinate the prophets to Plato, revelation to Aristotle . . . to make the dynamic and functional character of the universe an aspect, a mere appearance of the static and structural." Nevertheless, he contended, the functionalist philosophies of James and Henri Bergson signaled a new era in which Hebraic metaphysics was finally gaining ascendance.[37]

The Jewish critique of supersessionism also fueled the "Menorah movement" launched at Harvard by Kallen and others in 1906. That movement and its *Menorah Journal* came to serve as the center of a lively dialogue on the meaning and significance of Hebraism for America and for Western civilization more broadly. The group originally sought to fill a perceived gap between the nationalistic focus of Harvard's Zionist Club and the philological emphasis of the Semitic studies program by demonstrating the relevance of Jewish thought to modern culture. An early campaign to prod Harvard to teach Hebrew alongside Greek and Latin opened up a much larger discussion about the past and present content of Western civilization that continued in the *Menorah Journal* and reverberated among American Jews elsewhere. The movement's central message was clear: that "the Jews were not destroyed with the destruction of their polity, nor have they ceased to develop their religion and their literature down to the present day." At Harvard, as elsewhere, Jews insisted that their faith still had much to offer in the present day.[38]

Engaging Religious Pluralism

The debate over America's entry into World War I gave a powerful impetus to the discourse on the Judeo-Christian antecedents of the modern West. As would their successors during World War II, advocates of American intervention stressed the cultural ties between the United States and Western Europe, while also seeking to explain why the highly civilized Germans seemed to have spectacularly rejected the Western heritage. In the wake of the war, Oswald Spengler's widely read *The Decline of the West*, which postulated a coherent Western civilization but also predicted its imminent collapse, further inspired American commentators to craft their own interpretations of modern intellectual history—though the vast majority ignored Spengler's assertion of a fundamental discontinuity between the ancient world and the modern West. Once confined to small academic communities, the "Western civilization" idea now moved into other areas of public culture, and the more specific concept of a Judeo-Christian "heritage" or "tradition" stretching across the centuries began to find a place in American popular thought as well. The interfaith movement of the 1920s, whose members aimed to stamp out bigotry and sow amity between Christians and Jews, also served as a crucial vector for Judeo-Christian conceptions of Western civilization, and thus of democracy. In hashing out the contemporary relationship between Judaism and Christianity, interfaith activists made sweeping claims about the essential meanings and historical careers of those faiths.[39]

The conversation on Judaism's modern history expanded further after World War I, in the interfaith movement and elsewhere. The Hebraizing impulse among liberal Protestants and the Jewish challenge to supersessionism fed into that interfaith endeavor. So, too, did the virulent Protestant nativism that spread widely in the wake of World War I. In the face of narrowly Protestant definitions of American national identity, interfaith activists argued that the nation was religiously plural at its core and that its strength lay in the preservation of that pluralism. This growing emphasis on the persistence and even the value of religious difference provided fertile ground for the emergence of Judeo-Christian formulations, although even then, the use of that terminology did not always signal an acknowledgment of Judaism's status as a living faith on par with Christianity.

By the 1920s, in both America and Britain, a number of Protestant writers had joined the campaign against supersessionism. Most of them were associated with the interfaith movement, the American branch of which emerged in part to quell the practice of Protestants proselytizing to Jews. In 1927, for example, *The Legacy of Israel*, a British volume edited by Edwyn R. Bevan and Charles Singer, emphasized that Judaism's contributions to Western civilization were those of "a living community" continuing to the present day. Most Gentiles, wrote the editors, viewed Israel's historical role as a thing of the distant past, like the contributions of ancient Greece and Rome. But in fact, Israel had not simply given over its genius to Christianity and vanished. The editors emphasized that Judaism continued to give to human thought its distinctive "gifts," namely, "its devotion to the law and to the community, and to both of these as the command and special concern of God."[40]

Although supersessionist sentiments remained strong in many Protestant circles, an approach such as Bevan and Singer's, which Diana Selig has termed the "cultural gifts" model of pluralism, became the dominant paradigm among American interfaith activists by the late 1920s. The cultural gifts model portrayed diversity in a positive light by describing American culture as a harmonious synthesis of many different subcultures, each making its own distinctive contribution to the overall whole. Yet those subcultures could be defined in various ways. Were ethnic groups the "instruments" constituting the American "symphony," in Kallen's resonant metaphor? Or were the relevant units the broader streams of religious thought—perhaps Hebraism and Hellenism, or Judaism, Protestantism, and Catholicism—said to comprise Western civilization? For the time being, Jewish leaders could draw on the ambiguous status of Jewishness as both an ethnic and a religious identity to invoke both versions of the cultural gifts model at once. By the late 1930s, however, the concept of a Judeo-Christian tradition would lead many interpreters to view America's demographic diversity through the lens of religious traditions rather than ethnic groups, and often to insist that Jews qualified as Jews—and thus as Americans—only insofar as they embraced their community's brand of theism.[41]

In the universities, the burgeoning subdiscipline of modern European history provided additional scholarly authority and ammunition for those who viewed Judaism as an integral component of Western civilization. The historical accounts of the modern West that appeared in the 1920s and early 1930s suggested that broad philosophical ideas of ancient lineage provided the motive force in human affairs. Like theologians, religious leaders, and interfaith activists, historians debated the applicability and the relative weight of various foundational ideas in modern thought. In the universities, these contests included outspoken naturalists as well as those institutionally committed to Christianity or Judaism. But the various groups tended to share a belief in the unity of Western civilization and its dependence on ideas generated in the ancient Mediterranean region—a belief that paved the way for the discourse of Judeo-Christianity.

The American field of modern European history built on the "New History" pioneered by the likes of James Harvey Robinson in the Progressive Era. In his influential courses at Columbia, Robinson rejected Frederick Jackson Turner's "frontier thesis" and other formulations of American exceptionalism and downplayed the political and military episodes long favored by historians. Instead, he emphasized the power of ideas operating outside the boundaries of the formal political system. Robinson focused especially on the development of rational, scientific thought. His approach meshed nicely with the ideological need of American interventionists in World War I to link their nation's cause to that of Europe. Modern European history rapidly gained curricular ground after the war. Its orientation toward long-term trends in culture also shaped newer fields such as intellectual history and history of science that took shape in the 1930s. By the start of World War II, American undergraduates typically learned a version of Robinson's story about their nation's roots in the culture of the West rather than an earlier nationalist narrative positing stark differences between an "Old World" and a "New World."[42]

Overall, historians and other interwar commentators increasingly portrayed Western civilization as a compound of Judeo-Christian and Greco-Roman cultural elements rather than an expression of Christianity, a single religion with Hebraic and Hellenic strands. "No one," claimed a *New York Times* writer in 1927, would now "deny the common Greco-Roman and Judeo-

Christian origin of Western civilization." This interpretation reflected a growing tendency to identify a broader stream of Judeo-Christian faith, rather
than Christianity in particular, as the source of the ethical and spiritual ideals
that complemented and humanized intellectual, institutional, and aesthetic
forms inherited from Greece and Rome.[43]

Prior to World War I, few of those who stressed the ethical continuities
between Judaism and Christianity went on to assert that the Judeo-Christian
heritage already defined American or Western society, as so many commentators would by World War II. In fact, John Spargo, a Christian Socialist who in
1906 described socialism as an updated version of the "old Hebrew Prophet's
dream of world righteousness," held that Judeo-Christian ideals had yet to
make their mark on the Western world. Spargo, who was strongly influenced
by the Social Gospel ministers Walter Rauschenbusch and George D. Her-
ron, insisted that "Judaism and Protestantism are permeated with the Socialist
spirit," especially in the United States. In his 1915 book *Marxian Socialism and
Religion*, Spargo declared that the "Judaeo-Christian religions" also shared an
"ethical core" with "Islam, Buddhism and Confucianism," namely, "the ideal
of human brotherhood." But this universal religious ideal, he insisted, "cannot be realized within the existing capitalistic system." According to Spargo,
the West had not yet implemented the ethical commitments of its Jewish and
Christian leaders.[44]

Interwar debates about the Jewish Jesus pushed interpreters closer to the
familiar understanding of Judeo-Christianity as the foundation of Western
culture. In the mid-1920s, the Reform rabbi and interfaith activist Stephen
S. Wise, who would soon become one of the earliest Americans to use the
phrase "Judeo-Christian tradition," raised a firestorm of controversy by claiming Jesus for Judaism. Speaking in December 1925, Wise heartily endorsed the
Lithuanian-born scholar Joseph Klausner's claim that Jesus sought to reform
Judaism from within, not to break with it. According to Wise, Klausner had
not proposed "that the Jews should accept Jesus as Christ." But he had urged
them—rightly, thought Wise—to embrace Jesus as "a great ethical personality," even "the embodiment of religious and ethical idealism." Wise traced
"the very foundations of morality" to the "unparalleled code of ethics" proclaimed by Jesus. "Shall we not say that this Jew is soul of our soul," asked
Wise, "and that the soul of his teaching is Jewish and nothing but Jewish? The
teaching of Jesus the Jew is a phase of the spirit which led the Jew Godward."
Like Abraham Geiger before them, Klausner and Wise identified Jesus, and
thus Christianity itself, as a product of the genius of the Hebrew prophets. In
the wake of Wise's 1925 speech, numerous crtics accused him of seeking to
convert Jews to Christianity. In response, he reiterated that one could sepa-

rate Jesus's ethical example from the question of his divinity. Indeed, Wise continued, denying the ethical wisdom of Jesus created an unnecessary and divisive contrast between Judaism and Christianity and wasted a golden opportunity to demonstrate the continuing power of Hebraic ideals in the modern world.[45]

Some liberal Protestants—especially Unitarians—likewise emphasized Jesus's Jewish faith and the centrality of the Hebrew prophets to Western civilization. For example, Wise's close friend John Haynes Holmes, the pastor of New York's Community Church, addressed the relationship between Judaism and Christianity in several sermons of the late 1920s and early 1930s. In 1930, Holmes credited Jews with having "discovered the ethical content of religion." They had not, he said, discovered religion itself, as some erroneously claimed; religion was "a part of the universal experience of mankind." Yet it was true, Holmes continued, that "the Jew had a genius for religion, as the Greeks had a genius for beauty and the Romans for law, and this genius displayed itself in the apprehension, altogether peculiar to this one people, that the substance of religion is ethical idealism as worked out in right relations between men." For Holmes, as for many other liberal Protestants, ancient Judaism lighted the path forward for contemporary Christians. What was "best in Christianity," he wrote—namely, its emphasis on "ethical regeneration," as opposed to fruitless "theological speculation"—was "in its origin Jewish." It was Judaism that had given Christians their emphasis on "moral conscience, moral vision, moral culture and endeavor." Holmes's equation of Jewishness with ethical commitment facilitated a major step beyond supersessionist analyses toward a more inclusive portrait of the West's Judeo-Christian heritage.[46]

Writing in Holmes's "Community Pulpit" series, the Protestant theologian Reinhold Niebuhr, an outspoken advocate of "prophetic faith," brought his characteristic emphasis on irony to the 1920s discourse on Hebraism's role in Western civilization. After crediting the West's political models to the Romans and its "energy and diligence" to the Teutons, Niebuhr turned to what he considered the dominant, spiritual side of the Western heritage. Eschewing the usual image of a fruitful synthesis, he instead portrayed an "eternal conflict" between Hebraism and Hellenism. These poles of Western thought, Niebuhr wrote, represented the "prophet" and the "philosopher," the "conscience" and the "intellect." During the centuries of Hellenism's dominance over the Christian tradition, he explained, "the church lost its ethics in an attempt to construct an adequate metaphysics" and thus "sank from a sublime enthusiasm to a common respectability." Foreshadowing his mature writings, Niebuhr sought a middle path between "fanaticism" and "ennui," the respective dangers of Hebraism and Hellenism. He found that path in the difficult

maintenance of "a never ending tension" between "the Hellenic and the Hebraic forces of life, the forces of reason and the forces of moral idealism, the
forces of reflection and the forces of creation." In sum, Niebuhr concluded,
"the poet and the prophet are as necessary as the scientist and the philosopher[,] and life can reach neither truth nor reality without both the faith of
the Hebrews and the reflection of the Greeks."[47]

Wise, Holmes, and Niebuhr all spoke in the language of the interfaith
movement, whose advocates thought of Americans as members of broad religious traditions—as Protestants, Catholics, and Jews, especially—and worked
to improve relations between these faith communities. For the time being,
however, most discussants of the nation's cultural identity continued to sort
Americans into discrete ethnic groups rather than religious confessions. This
certainly held true for Horace Kallen, who later became one of the nation's
leading Judeo-Christian pluralists but made his name in the 1920s by advancing a somewhat different form of pluralism grounded in an expansive,
egalitarian treatment of ethnic identities. By 1927, if not earlier, Kallen had
begun to intermittently refer to the modern West as "our Judæo-Christian
world." Yet as he honed his vision of a secular public sphere that would allow religious pluralism to flourish, Kallen stressed the centrality of ethnic
communities to social organization, as well as the primacy of moral beliefs
in human action. The model he called "cultural pluralism" gave the leading
social and psychological role to ethnic rather than religious groups. He described ethnic communities as both "the essential reservoirs of individuality"
and the sources of the myriad religious orientations to which Americans bore
allegiance. Neither Kallen nor his nativist enemies had yet made one of the
key moves in the development of the Judeo-Christian discourse, namely, the
division of Americans into Protestants, Catholics, and Jews rather than Poles,
Greeks, Lithuanians, Italians, and so forth. Although it is Kallen who holds
pride of place in today's histories of America's evolving national identity, the
likes of Wise, Holmes, and Niebuhr actually pointed much more directly to
the leading mid-twentieth-century themes in that story. These figures helped
pave the way for the advent of America's Judeo-Christian discourse in the
1930s by defining Americans as Protestants, Catholics, and Jews rather than
prioritizing their ethnic identities.[48]

*

These European and American developments fed into the emergence of the
Judeo-Christian discourse in its modern form. However, the constructions
that began to appear in American public discourse during the early 1930s
were decidedly different in kind from their forebears. As we have seen, Judeo-

Christian terminology was mobilized for several purposes in the nineteenth century—to describe a group of early Christians, to characterize intergroup relations, and especially to chronicle the world's religions. By the early twentieth century, that terminology also came to refer to the animating spirit of Western civilization itself. The shift excised legalism and ritualism from the definition of Hebraism, which now focused more squarely on the prophets' views of ethics, God, and history. But it was the rise of communism and fascism around the globe, coupled with the emergence of polemical discourses of "totalitarianism" and "secularism," that truly ushered in modern Judeo-Christian formulations during the early 1930s. The Judeo-Christian tradition took on its familiar resonances only when it was set against new forms of political culture rather than alternative faiths such as Buddhism or Hinduism.

It should come as no surprise, then, that the first Judeo-Christian formulations of a distinctly modern type were not crafted by liberal Protestant or Jewish opponents of fascism. Rather, the British politician and journalist P. W. Wilson appears to have launched the new discourse in a series of *New York Times* articles in the early 1930s. A member of both the British and the American establishments who came from a religiously hybrid background, Wilson was a liminal figure with a global perspective, uniquely situated to modernize the Judeo-Christian discourse. More than a year before Hitler came to power in Germany, Wilson's December 1931 description of the authoritarian and militantly secular regimes of Lenin and Ataturk as "alternatives to the Judeo-Christian faith" arrayed Judeo-Christian civilization against what came to be called totalitarianism.[49] Hitler's rise certainly made the Judeo-Christian language more attractive to liberal critics of fascism. But Wilson's belief that totalitarianism went hand in hand with secularism because it recognized no religious authority above the state was reflected in many of the Judeo-Christian constructions of American democracy that became commonplace in the nation's political rhetoric by the end of World War II. Like Wilson's articles, these later formulations echoed the profound concerns about the changing religious character of the West that had simmered beneath apparently dry, abstruse arguments since the early nineteenth century. As chapter 2 will show, such formulations were also shaped by more immediate political and cultural conflicts unique to the polyglot context of interwar America.

A Protestant Nation No More

FACING RELIGIOUS DIVERSITY BETWEEN THE WARS

The rise of America's Judeo-Christian discourse reflected the unmooring of the image of the United States as a Protestant nation in the 1920s and 1930s. Although Protestant nativism surged in the early 1920s, many Americans, especially in industrial cities, discarded a narrowly Protestant vision of the nation. But what was the United States, if not Protestant? Was its culture purely civic, or did democracy require religious commitments? If so, which ones? Alternatives to Protestant nativism emerged among culturally influential groups of urban dwellers, but the gnawing question of national identity remained open. This struggle did not simply pit Protestants against Catholics and Jews. It was a complex, multisided battle featuring several different approaches. Some theorists of a post-Protestant America favored a religiously neutral public sphere, while others argued that democracy required substantive religious tenets. By the 1940s, commentators of both varieties would increasingly identify the United States as a Judeo-Christian country.

During the 1920s, such theoretical disagreements over the cultural foundations of democracy remained largely obscured by the shared opposition to Protestant nativism among Catholics, Jews, naturalistic thinkers, and many liberal and moderate Protestants. A fragile antinativist alliance weathered tensions over questions such as Prohibition, censorship, and the Mexican conflict. But it succumbed in the 1930s to the crisis of capitalism, the rise of totalitarianism, and the expansion of the American state. These shifts led Protestants, Catholics, Jews, and naturalists to frame their theoretical positions more clearly, creating new alliances and antagonisms. In interfaith circles and elsewhere, Americans clashed over the relative dangers of fascism and communism, the relationship between secularism and totalitarianism, and the meaning of state expansion, at home and worldwide. As the antinativist alliance fractured amid conflict over democracy's cultural basis, the Judeo-Christian discourse emerged as a shared point of reference for many disputants.

That discourse did not always exhibit the liberal slant that scholars have ascribed to it. As battles over democracy's foundations escalated, many mainstream Protestants and a few prominent Jewish leaders turned sharply against secular allies they had long cultivated. They increasingly feared that in deferring to social science as a source of knowledge and a guide to the application of Christian ideals, they had let in the Trojan horse of secularism. These critics argued that nonbelief, and even strict church-state separation, fueled secularizing tendencies that threatened both religion and democracy. This backlash against secularism would continue into the 1950s and produce widespread support for Judeo-Christian exceptionalism by the early Cold War years. Even in the late 1930s, a growing suspicion of secularism profoundly shaped the emerging Judeo-Christian discourse.

Nativism and Its Critics

Mainstream Protestants dominated American public culture into the early twentieth century. An informal but far-reaching "Protestant establishment" performed many of the cultural tasks of a state-prescribed faith, promoting understandings of self, society, and God that mainstream Protestants deemed foundational to democracy. Most of them invoked a foundational dichotomy between freedom and authority that harked back to the Reformation. Viewing their own faith as the natural result of unfettered thought, these Protestants equated freedom with the autonomous, self-governing citizen and associated authority with tyrants, aristocrats, and the Catholic hierarchy.

By the early twentieth century, however, demographic changes challenged the image of a thoroughly Protestant nation. Industrialization brought millions of Jews and Catholics from Eastern and Southern Europe. Rural Protestants streamed to cities, further disrupting traditional religious patterns. These twin migrations decisively shifted the country's cultural center of gravity from the overwhelmingly Protestant rural areas to the industrial cities, where growing Catholic and Jewish communities belied the image of a Protestant America.

Yet most of the non-Protestants were Catholics, creating a massive Christian supermajority. As Italians, Poles, and other Catholic groups joined earlier groups of Irish and Germans, the Catholic population came to far outnumber the largest Protestant denomination. By 1945, the twenty-five million American Catholics approximated the combined numbers of the mainline

Protestant denominations. Despite lingering ethnic divisions, immigrants fortified existing bases of Catholic political power. In 1928, Alfred E. Smith, the Catholic governor of New York, won the Democratic presidential nomination after narrowly missing out in 1924. Interwar Catholics comprised what we might call a "majoritarian minority," holding majorities in many industrial cities and approaching half of the population in Massachusetts, Connecticut, and Rhode Island even though they totaled under 20 percent of the national tally.[1]

By contrast, American Jews remained a "minoritarian minority" with a tiny demographic footprint, despite dominating a few urban neighborhoods. Eastern European and Russian arrivals quickly outnumbered the older German-Jewish population. Their children swelled the ranks at colleges and universities, leading Protestant administrators to restrict Jewish enrollment in the 1920s. Jews became increasingly prominent in intellectual life and the entertainment industry. Yet their numbers limited their political power; Jews topped out at around 3 percent of the national population in 1937.[2]

In response, Anglo-Protestant nativism spiked in the early 1920s. Influenced by new forms of scientific racism, nativists rejected the "melting pot" assumption that immigrants would assimilate into the dominant culture. The war further aggravated nativism; Irish Catholics and Germans of all faiths faced charges of disloyalty, while Jews were targeted as radicals, especially after the Bolshevik Revolution. After the war, Congress clamped down on Eastern and Southern European immigration. A revived Ku Klux Klan defended WASP purity against Catholics and Jews, as well as African Americans. Like immigration opponents, the "second Klan" aimed to roll back the demographic and cultural clock. Yet the very vehemence of such claims of Protestant cultural hegemony signaled that its days were numbered, and nativists' influence plummeted after 1925.[3]

Still, nativism was only the most dramatic expression of a broader Protestant nationalism that resonated across much of the theological spectrum. Those Protestants who retained the melting pot ideal thought Catholics and Jews would soon join the Protestant fold. Conservative evangelicals endorsed church-state separation but discerned little hope for Americans until they saw the light of Christ. Mainstream Protestants likewise hoped to convert the population through voluntary means. Most followed their nineteenth-century forebears in celebrating religious freedom in a manner that defined their own theologies as simple truths while identifying Catholicism as a sectarian offense against the Constitution.

Yet the numerical pressure of religious minorities could not be ignored, especially in urban schools. Battles over Bible lessons dated back decades, as Catholics disliked the King James translation and Jews rejected the New Testament. Few endorsed the secularization that resulted, and conflicts continued to flare.[4] After 1914, many advocates of religious education embraced the "released-time" model, which reserved part of the school day for religious classes, typically in nearby churches and synagogues. Yet the controversy continued. Although some Jewish leaders thought released time programs would aid the growing network of Jewish day schools, most feared it would turn public schools into theological battlegrounds. They preferred after-school and Sabbath classes, outside school hours and apart from public school facilities. Catholic officials, for their part, called for "every Catholic child in a Catholic school" and rejected any schooling "in which religion is not the foundation of the whole curriculum," although lay Catholics still flocked to public schools in practice. Despite high hopes, the released-time model did not resolve the vexed issue of religion in the schools.[5]

In the 1920s, the released-time controversy fed into a broader debate over how religion, morality, tolerance, and politics related to one another. Education was hardly the only issue on which Jewish and Catholic Americans found themselves opposed. Though united against nativism, they disagreed profoundly over the proper shape of the nation. They allied themselves with different segments of the Protestant establishment, which began to split along theological and political lines.

Vastly outnumbered, Jews stood no chance of turning the culture their way and could hope for little more than tolerance from the Christian (and often anti-Semitic) supermajority. This situation reinforced a strong commitment to a secular public sphere that dated back to the European Enlightenment. Jewish leaders joined naturalists and a number of influential Protestants in seeking to "de-Christianize" American public institutions. These figures developed a pluralistic vision of the nation as a diverse set of belief communities under a formally secular state. Democracy, they argued, required an open public sphere in which a respectful attitude toward individual and group differences would uphold the rights of all and allow the full expression, on equal terms, of all ethnic and religious subcultures. Celebrating religious diversity as a source of national strength, they argued that the cardinal virtue of tolerance for any and all beliefs anchored a democratic culture.[6]

Despite the prominence of naturalists such as the Columbia philosopher John Dewey, believing Protestants and Jews made up much of the pluralist camp. They offered theological arguments for pluralism, insisting that their faiths demanded tolerance and brotherhood, and assumed that open-ended religious tolerance could comport with all particularistic identity commitments. "The way to get together is to work together," not "agree on doctrine," explained the modernist theologian Shailer Mathews. But pluralists feared that some faiths—especially Catholicism and fundamentalist Protestantism, with their exclusive, absolute truth claims—undermined tolerance. Although pluralistic liberals decried intolerance from all sources, they habitually associated it with Catholicism and fundamentalism.[7]

Nonetheless, a fraught but often potent antinativist alliance emerged repeatedly in the 1920s. For the most part, American Catholics, Jews, naturalists, and many liberal and moderate Protestants—especially in industrial cities—bracketed their profound disagreements on the nature of democracy and formed an unsteady coalition for the pressing task of deflecting the nativist offensive.

This coalition was especially visible during the *Pierce v. Society of Sisters* case in 1925 and Al Smith's 1928 campaign. *Pierce* involved a 1922 Oregon law that sought to shut down Catholic parochial systems by banning private education altogether. As the case moved toward the Supreme Court, pluralistic liberals such as Dewey, Columbia president Nicholas Murray Butler, American Civil Liberties Union head Roger Baldwin, and the Jewish legal scholar Felix Frankfurter deplored the ban. The National Education Association backed Oregon's parochial schools, as did the American Jewish Committee, which filed an amicus brief. Although these liberals favored secular education and worried about separatist impulses that cordoned off immigrant communities, they found Protestant nativism far more dangerous than Catholic education. As Frankfurter wrote, the Supreme Court's unanimous rejection of the Oregon ban embodied "the essential spirit of liberalism."[8]

The antinativist alliance emerged in 1928 as well. When Democrats tapped the anti-Prohibition Catholic Al Smith for the presidency, old-stock Protestants mobilized. Nativist bigotry overlapped—how much is hard to say—with principled resistance from Protestant "drys." Yet Smith's nomination itself signaled the limits of nativism among Protestants. Historians have overemphasized the *Christian Century*'s choice of Prohibition over Smith, as if it spoke for all Protestants. In fact, 1920s Protestants adopted divergent cultural and political stances. Those favoring pluralistic liberalism, including secular and Jewish liberals such as Frankfurter, saw in Smith's run a major strike at intolerance. The secular Jewish journalist Walter Lippmann helped anchor Smith's campaign. Even Butler, a staunch Republican and hardly one to rock the political boat, broke ranks to support Smith.[9]

John Dewey outlined the liberal case for Smith in the *New Republic*. Dewey's dislike of Herbert Hoover's laissez-faire approach certainly allayed his suspicion of Smith's Catholicism, but he also agreed with Smith's meritocratic assertion that religious affiliations should neither negatively nor positively impact political careers. Liberals like Dewey saw the Smith campaign as a test of the country's commitment to religious pluralism. When the chips were down in the 1920s, pluralists set aside their concerns about Catholic political influence and defended the rights of all religious minorities.[10]

Lines of Tension

At the same time, this antinativist alliance papered over simmering conceptual tensions that would erupt under the very different political conditions of the 1930s. The main fault line divided pluralistic liberals from the Catholic Church. Although lay Catholics varied in their responses to religious diversity, US Catholic leaders firmly rejected political secularity. They agreed with many liberal Protestants that America's religious self-conception should include non-Protestants, but they followed theologically conservative Protestants in contending that democracy required firm religious foundations. As political winds shifted, Catholics recalibrated their balancing act between the different wings of the Protestant mainstream. In the 1920s, the fierce anti-Catholicism of conservative Protestants usually drove Catholics into the arms of the pluralists. But the changed climate of the 1930s, when nativism waned and struggles over democracy's cultural roots deepened, highlighted Catholic leaders' rejection of a secular public sphere and led a number of important Protestant thinkers to turn against secularism as well.

Scholars have argued that pluralism instantiates a "Protestant secular" by portraying Protestant theories of religion and the church—namely, that both are voluntary and separable from public life—as neutral facts about the world. But the interwar years also birthed a competing perspective—one might call it a "Catholic secular"—that presented Catholic interpretations of the boundaries and public roles of religion as neutral, factual ground on which Protestants and Catholics could meet. In the 1920s, liberal Catholics such as Catholic University's John A. Ryan rested the case for religious toleration on prudence. The Vatican's preference for Catholic establishments remained theoretically valid, they argued, but this was irrelevant in practice. Protestant critics reacted violently, seeing rank hypocrisy in the principle/prudence distinction and fixating on Catholics' theoretical rejection of religious tolerance. By the 1940s, liberal Catholics had come to identify the natural law and the associated definition of religion as shared, secular ground. This shift enabled Catholic leaders to participate in America's Judeo-Christian discourse.

Liberal Catholicism in the interwar United States reflected the powerful influence of neo-Thomistic philosophy. Like Protestant natural theologians and moral philosophers before them, neo-Thomists found embedded in the structure of reality, beneath the flux of everyday life, a spare but comprehensive set of absolute moral principles—the natural law—that transcended temporal experience and could be accessed by individuals of all faiths through "right reason," not biblical revelation. As with the earlier Protestant frameworks, the neo-Thomists' view of natural law as a normative dimension of reality enabled them to argue that the state would simply acknowledge an objective moral order, not impose sectarian tenets, in favoring certain religious commitments.[11]

Of course, many neo-Thomists expected Americans to choose Catholicism anyway. Rejecting the authoritarianism of Europe's Catholic regimes, liberal US Catholics argued that their system could flourish without state support. The "Catholic Action" movement trained a "lay apostolate" to articulate and promote Catholic ideals among the citizenry. Neo-Thomism and Catholic Action seemed to square Catholicism with the American Constitution and render irrelevant the Vatican's insistence on church-state union. The connection of Christianity to American political institutions would be voluntary, running through a citizenry that recognized the primacy of the natural law, not the Church as an institution. Nonetheless, liberal Catholics rejected the idea of a secular public sphere and decried as anarchistic relativists those who questioned absolute truths about God, religion, and the state.[12]

These figures contended that the US Constitution banned a church establishment but rooted governance in divinely ordained moral laws and natural rights that no government could abridge. Any other view of politics made individuals mere "serfs of the state," declared the liberal Catholic journal *America*. Rights either flowed from God or came from the state—which could thus revoke them. With France in mind, liberal Catholics decried a "secularism which makes men creatures of the State and pawns of government" and saw in European history an accelerating descent from the heights of the medieval period back toward paganism.[13]

Over time, liberal Catholics would increasingly identify their assertions about religion and politics as secular and factual, rather than distinctively Christian. Already in the 1920s, *America* compared natural rights to the facts of arithmetic and physics.[14] But for the time being, liberal Catholics raised the ire of pluralists by resting their case for religious tolerance on prudential grounds. For example, Ryan, the dean of interwar liberal Catholicism, aligned the US Constitution with the Vatican's rejections of liberalism, modernity, church-state separation, and "indifferentism" (the error of deeming other faiths legitimate) by making two moves. First, he distinguished the militantly secular "Continental liberalism" of the French Revolution, which denied God's authority over state and society, from American liberalism, a genially tolerant "attitude of mind" whose advocates, Ryan said, joined the Church in denouncing Continental liberalism. On this view, the First Amendment recognized religion's political centrality and favored those religious claims compatible with the natural law. Second, Ryan insisted that the 1864 *Syllabus of Errors* did not reject all forms of liberalism or demand church-state fusion everywhere. Church-state union, he said, applied only to polities with overwhelming Catholic majorities. In mixed societies, Catholics should embrace church-state separation—though out of prudence, not principle. Ryan's critics jumped on his assertion that the First Amendment expressed a "political policy," not full "ethical principle." Ryan identified religious liberty as a practical adjustment to the unfortunate fact of religious diversity, not an expression of Catholic ideals.[15]

Liberal Catholics of the 1920s often buttressed this argument with a historical narrative that traced democracy to medieval Catholic roots. Ryan, for example, traced the ideal of popular sovereignty to Catholicism's teaching that "the ruler derives his right to rule from God" and the "doctrine of the essential equality of human beings, the intrinsic worth of every human soul and every human person in the eyes of God." The Columbia University historian Carlton J. H. Hayes likewise contended that "America is a daughter of the Catholic Church, more literally so than even Europe." Dividing the globe into religiously defined civilizations—Christian, Buddhist, Hindu, Muslim—Hayes argued that the cultural orientation of each guided even inhabitants who disavowed its defining faith. He thus credited the achievements of America's Protestant founders to the medieval Catholic heritage that provided their cultural matrix.[16]

Grounding Western civilization in natural rights derived from "traditional" Christianity represented a halfway house on the path to the Catholic secular. It allowed liberal Catholics to advocate religious liberty while calling for "the revival of the spirit of Christendom as the motive power of civilization." Hayes thus urged Americans to buttress the "foundations of Christian society," even as he favored protection of religious minorities. Indeed, liberal Catholics often identified civic toleration as a tool for rebuilding Christendom, reducing the problem of religious difference to the schism between Catholics and Protestants. Among even the most liberal Catholics of the 1920s, calls for tolerance usually stopped short at Christianity's borders, especially in theory.[17]

The Catholic secular thus remained largely latent in the 1920s. Liberal Catholics mostly identified the platform they held out to Protestants as shared Christian ground, not universal human ground. Still, the Catholic secular was becoming visible. Like its Protestant counterpart, it defined controversial assumptions about religion's scope and content as neutral ground—items of simple truth and common sense rather than theological doctrines. "Religion is the science of the greatest truth in existence," explained one advocate. Thus, *America*'s editors could agree with Protestants, Jews, and even naturalists that "within their peculiar spheres Church and State are supreme," even as they drew a different line between God and Caesar. Meanwhile, the Catholic secular, like the Protestant version, labeled any deviation from its principles "sectarian."[18]

Over time, the Protestant secular slowly lost its iron grip on the American public conversation, if not the legal system. As a result, the political territory disputed between the two frameworks—especially education, but also other matters of moral guidance and socialization, such as censorship and birth control—generated ongoing church-state conflicts in which each side assumed that its own rendering of the church-state boundary reflected reality itself.

For the time being, Catholic commentators identified the Church as "the conserver and only authoritative definer of Christian principles," uniquely able to "draw the line clearly, cleanly and without confusion between politics and religion." They favored a Catholic nationalism rather than the broader, pan-Christian version implied by their call for Protestants to rebuild Christendom by reclaiming the natural law. Indeed, liberal Catholics contended that "the Protestant principle of private judgment" could never anchor democracy because it elevated individual opinion over God's authority, leading even fundamentalists toward moral relativism and atheism. Despite the language of Christian reconciliation and the emerging Catholic secular, most 1920s Catholic leaders predicted the disintegration of American society absent wholesale conversion.[19] For these figures, as for their more conservative Catholic counterparts, Protestantism of any variety represented a slippery slope that inevitably led to the destruction of religion itself.

Such divisions became manifest in a number of instances. Although nativism united opponents of Anglo-Protestant nationalism, other issues of the 1920s highlighted their disagreements and threatened to split the fragile antinativist coalition. These disputes foreshadowed the ferocious battles of the 1930s, when the shared enemy of Protestant nativism had faded. They centered on the scope of state authority, which the *Christian Century*'s Winfred Ernest Garrison rightly identified as the sticking point between Catholics and Protestant and Jewish pluralists.[20]

To be sure, not all intergroup tensions followed that line of division in the 1920s. Prohibition pitted Catholics, Jews, and secular liberals against many

Protestants with otherwise progressive views. Temperance advocates blamed alcohol for myriad social ills and described Prohibition as the linchpin of national regeneration. Many immigrants and religious minorities, on the other hand, experienced Prohibition as an assault on their identities and practices. These tensions mirrored neither the 1920s clash between nativists and their critics nor the 1930s split between antisecularists and pluralistic liberals.[21]

But most 1920s controversies directly prefigured the later divide. On numerous issues, Catholics stood closer to conservative Protestants than to liberals of any religious affiliation. Particularly controversial were Catholic-led censorship campaigns. As civil libertarianism gained ground in the 1920s, liberal Protestants increasingly deemed censorship inimical to democracy. But Catholic leaders enthusiastically took over the task from Protestants where numbers allowed, including many industrial cities and a few northeastern states. Tensions deepened in 1927 when the Vatican, redoubling its campaign against liberalism, embraced censorship. US Catholic leaders such as Boston archbishop William O'Connell—who called Einstein's theory of relativity an anti-Christian conspiracy—urged laypeople to read only Catholic authors. Meanwhile, the Church's campaign to prevent all Americans from using birth control became a particular bone of contention as mainstream Protestant and Jewish leaders began to embrace contraception.[22]

Educational disagreements also foreshadowed later tensions. The expansion and continued secularization of public schooling rankled even so progressive a Catholic as *Commonweal* editor George N. Shuster. Only "a system of denominational schools subsidized and to some extent supervised by the state," Shuster contended, matched "the general American religious outlook, which does not accept any creed as official but which does quite emphatically claim the adjective 'Christian' for itself." Shuster blamed secularization on "the grotesque stupidity of Protestants," whose anti-Catholic rancor reinforced their naïve belief that "the 'public school' would stay Christian" absent religious instruction. Catholic leaders campaigned tirelessly against secularism in American public culture, but especially in the schools.[23]

By contrast, their Jewish counterparts embraced secular schooling precisely because they feared a Protestant-Catholic convergence on Shuster's broadly Christian model. For them, as for liberal Protestants and naturalists, any religious instruction amounted to "sectarianism." It was a matter of simple justice: If "the state has no right to compel me to have my child taught atheism," the Protestant modernist Shailer Mathews argued in 1906, "neither has it any right to compel the atheist's child to be taught my faith." But Catholics argued that secular schools did, in fact, teach atheism, which deserved no tolerance because it rejected the principles of natural morality. Secularism, declared *America*, was a "pagan philosophy from abroad . . . repugnant alike to the spirit of Christianity and to the spirit of the Constitution" because it "rules God out of court, assum[ing] to legislate for the most sacred human relations, striving to bring under its sway parents and children, education and charity, the whole structure of society, and even religion itself."[24]

The 1925 Scopes Trial showed that even the most liberal Catholics protested secular education. Although evolution and the Bible produced the fireworks, Catholic leaders saw the deeper issue: William Jennings Bryan's claim that local majorities should determine school curricula. To Catholics, this portended "an organized movement to set up an established Protestant church in America." But even more important, explained *Commonweal* co-founder Michael Williams, was whether Americans viewed human beings as animals or children of God. Catholic commentators rejected Bryan's majoritarianism but lauded his antisecularism. The participation of the American Civil Liberties Union (ACLU), "the champion of socially dangerous people and causes," bolstered liberal Catholics' perception of "an organized assault upon fundamental Christian principles and social customs" by an "agglomeration of vague, yet violent and destructive, moods and heresies and philosophies allied against revealed religion." For them, the main dispute pitted Christianity against atheism, not Catholicism against Protestantism. Indeed, they admired Bryan's anti-Darwin stance "in so far as it seeks to conserve and to spread the true central doctrines of Christianity."[25]

For Catholic commentators of the 1920s, education represented the main battleground between Christianity and a relentlessly secularizing, authoritarian state. Throughout history, declared *Commonweal*, "the central religious conflict has had to do with the question of pedagogical prerogatives . . . who was qualified to teach, and what was the basis of obedience." The "secularist of today," wrote the Polish-Russian émigré Catherine Radziwill, favored "an omnipotent State, controlling the activities of the citizen from the cradle to the grave, legislating in mass-terms for man's most sacred and intimate relations with his fellows." The school question raised a deeper political issue: Did divinely ordained principles constrain the state, or could it arrogate spiritual authority to itself? Catholics rejected Protestants' approach of subjecting the state to private judgment rather than divine authority. But they feared even more the secularizing tendency of pluralistic liberalism. Indeed, many Catholics saw liberal pluralism and secular education as the American counterparts to Bolshevism, reflecting a paganistic assault on all of Christendom.[26]

Liberal Catholics also saw other evidence of a slide into paganism. Like John A. Ryan, they championed a social safety net but decried the threats to "self-control and local control" from the "modern craze for regulation by a huge centralized government." Ryan deplored a "flood of Socialistic and semi-Socialistic legislation threatening to overwhelm Congress at every session." To *America*, even a proposed child labor amendment portended "a Sovietized United States." As Mark O. Shriver explained, "Education, child-birth, roads, and countless others are first aided and then dominated and controlled and regulated by that authority at the capital." Shriver also saw pernicious centralizing tendencies in Prohibition, the direct election of senators, and even the Reconstruction-era Thirteenth, Fourteenth, and Fifteenth Amendments. As early as 1922, the founders of the National Catholic Welfare Conference (NCWC)—often seen as a source of New Deal liberalism—warned Pius XI that "a thoroughly secularist philosophy" prevailed in the United States. The American state, they wrote, had moved decisively into the Church's sphere. Viewing itself as "the promoter of all public welfare," it "continually trespass[ed] upon the domain of the spiritual" through "educational and social works." Behind Warren Harding's genial conservatism, NCWC leaders saw strong parallels to Bolshevism. In the 1920s, such fears even led many Catholics to reject federal aid to parochial schools.[27]

Developments abroad deepened the gulf between Catholic and pluralist leaders. Mexico's campaign against Church prerogatives and the resulting Cristero War of 1926–29 reinforced Catholic leaders' view of the modern state as inherently anticlerical. So did the casual response of non-Catholics. While Catholic leaders called for a global, pan-Christian alliance against secularism—the Knights of Columbus urged President Calvin Coolidge to invade Mexico and depose its president—most Americans saw in Mexico only the liberation of republicans from clerical oppression. Many pluralists found Catholics' outcry against secularism far more dangerous than Mexico's secularizing moves.[28]

For many pluralists, the warm Catholic response to Mussolini confirmed that absolute truth claims led to absolutist politics. Even antifascist Catholics such as Ryan allowed that Mussolini's "despotic and benevolent compulsion" comported, in principle, with Catholic teachings. "There is no natural right either to vote or to hold office," Ryan wrote in 1926; democracy merely meant protecting human welfare, defined in Catholic terms. If Italians chose fascism, no one could complain. Although Ryan excoriated fascists in prudential terms for abridging civil liberties, his inclusive definition of democracy registered far more loudly with pluralists. Meanwhile, other Catholic writers lauded Mussolini for his "hearty cooperation" with Christianity. Whatever their view of fascism, Catholics drew the church-state line very differently than did pluralists.[29]

These struggles over religion's public role cut through the nascent interfaith movement. Like the Judeo-Christian discourse that followed it (and
partly grew out of it), the interfaith impulse is often treated by scholars as an
expression of pluralistic liberalism but actually reflected multiple, divergent
visions of democracy. The interfaith movement housed a wide array of post-
Protestant conceptions of American identity, uneasily pairing commitments
to tolerance and to substantive religious claims. Some Protestant interfaith
activists feared political secularity as well as nativism, and most of the handful of Catholic participants bitterly decried secularity and liberal pluralism. In
short, the early interfaith movement embodied the tense antinativist alliance,
whose members shared little more than opposition to Protestant bigotry. By
the 1930s, pluralists and exceptionalists in the leading interfaith organization,
the National Conference of Christians and Jews (NCCJ), would scrap over the
legitimacy of secularism and secularists.

Although local issues created small-scale interfaith initiatives in the late
nineteenth century and the Religious Education Association (REA) fostered
interfaith exchanges after 1903, a national movement took shape only in the
1920s. Wartime cooperation between religious agencies serving an increasingly diverse military offered a model for peacetime work. A postwar surge
of xenophobia raised the stakes, as Red Scare leaders identified the "International Jew" as the epitome of the foreign radical. Klan activity, immigration restriction, and bigotry toward Al Smith further heightened interfaith
sentiment.[30]

Founded in 1927, the NCCJ rose to national prominence in the wake
of Smith's campaign and outshone such initiatives as Isidor Singer's Amos
Society (founded in 1923), the Reverend Edward Hunt's American Goodwill
Union (1924), the Inquiry into the Christian Way of Life (1925), the University
of Iowa's School of Religion (1926), and Rabbi Isaac Landman's Permanent
Commission on Better Understanding between Christians and Jews (1927).
The NCCJ, a joint creation of the Federal Council of Churches (FCC) and
the Central Conference of American Rabbis (CCAR), reflected ongoing controversies over Protestant missionizing in Jewish neighborhoods. The groups
resolved to "unite Jews and Christians in goodwill" and ground American
society in "those ideals of justice, fellowship, and peace which are common to
the prophetic traditions of Jews and Christians alike."[31]

Pushing beyond social harmony, the NCCJ identified interfaith relations
as a *political* issue and grounded democracy in religious tolerance and religious diversity. It was soon enmeshed in the antifascist struggle. In 1933,
the NCCJ publicly protested Hitler and launched the first of its famed "trio

tours," sending a Catholic priest, a Jewish rabbi, and a Protestant minister—
here, J. Elliot Ross, Morris S. Lazaron, and NCCJ head Everett R. Clinchy—to
thirty-eight southern and western cities. That campaign and subsequent trio
tours reached some 54,000 people at 129 meetings, and untold thousands
via radio.[32]

NCCJ leaders addressed tensions within the antinativist alliance by dis-
avowing theological discussion. Ross, the group's leading Catholic member, said it pursued "ways and means of being decent with one another," not
"fantastic dreams of unity." Theological divisions had long undermined interfaith efforts; Christians said Jews wanted them to disavow Christ and the
cross, while Jews saw the twin threats of conversion and assimilation behind
Christian-led calls for unity. In 1928, moreover, the Vatican stated that Catholics could not participate in interfaith endeavors addressing theological questions. The NCCJ's rejection of theological debate enabled Catholics to join
what they considered a civic rather than religious organization. Even so, the
Vatican ban kept many Catholics at arm's length and forced NCCJ leaders to
repeatedly insist that they sought no theological common ground, only civic
peace and mutual respect.[33]

Yet political questions still cropped up, revealing the fault lines in the antinativist coalition. Many NCCJ leaders rejected Catholics' understanding of
democracy, although Ross seems not to have protested expressions of liberal pluralism. At a 1929 seminar, for example, Nicholas Murray Butler, citing
the Treaty of Tripoli, argued that "our government was in no wise founded
upon the Christian religion" and that the Founders sought a high "barrier . . .
between church and state" to protect the former from the latter. In the 1930s,
as tensions deepened under the pressures of totalitarianism and state growth
at home, the NCCJ's concern with the political side of intergroup relations
would make it a key site for disputes over religion and democracy.[34]

State Growth and the Charge of Secularism

The events of the 1930s dramatically changed the conditions under which
opponents of nativism addressed political theory and practice, opening bitter
divides between them. The New Deal, like totalitarianism abroad, amplified
fears of the secular state among Catholics, as it did among many conservative Protestants. As earlier, Catholic leaders viewed American developments
through a world-historical lens, discerning a titanic struggle between states
and churches for control over the formation of citizens. They saw the aggressively secular French regime as the quintessential modern state. In the United

States, meanwhile, a shift of power from local to federal agencies, epitomized in the nationalization of welfare provision, convinced most Catholic leaders that a false, "Continental" theory of the state now prevailed.

These developments fostered substantial resistance to state growth and secularization. When the New Deal coalition is viewed through the lens of cultural politics, one suddenly sees theological and philosophical tensions simmering underneath Roosevelt's landslide victories. To most observers, the New Deal went beyond political economy, portending a fundamental shift in American character that many found alarming. Regulatory and welfare initiatives and bureaucratic expansion spawned widespread fears, even among those who preferred the New Deal to Hoover's laissez-faire.

Such fears appeared at many points on the theological spectrum. Conservative evangelicals steeped in the jeremiad tradition viewed the collapse of capitalism in theological terms, seeing in it God's punishment and pegging economic vitality to spiritual rejuvenation.[35] Meanwhile, a surprising number of moderate and liberal Protestants feared a secular, centralized state. So, too, did many Catholic leaders. Al Smith, who disliked the New Deal, charged in a fiery radio speech sponsored by the American Liberty League that Democrats had become Bolsheviks. "There can be only one capital—Washington or Moscow," Smith insisted. "There can be only one flag, the Stars and Stripes, or the red flag of the godless union of the Soviet." Many others likewise viewed the federal welfare state as a portent of state socialism. These critics endorsed Roosevelt's cooperative rhetoric but challenged his interpretation of that ideal.[36]

Criticism accelerated when Roosevelt hiked taxes, recognized unions, and launched Social Security in the "Second New Deal" of 1935–36. Above all, the assumption of responsibility for health and material welfare caused new rifts. The federal government had taken over from local and state agencies and ethnic and religious institutions the task of protecting—and thus defining—the well-being of citizens. Many feared that the secular state had realized its collectivist potential.

Catholic leaders expressed particular concern. Historians usually count Catholics among the staunchest New Dealers, and lay Catholics continued to back Roosevelt. But by 1936, state growth and centralization had soured many Catholic leaders on the president. Though hostile to laissez-faire, they preferred to leave welfare to private institutions, insisted on banning communists from unions, and rejected the narrowly economic approach of many officials. Catholic leaders struggled to reconcile the New Deal with their opposition to both unrestrained capitalism and a secular welfare state.[37]

Many of these Catholics favored "corporatism," which highlighted collective action toward the common good but deemphasized the state. Like the guild socialism of secular progressives such as Lippmann, Dewey, and Britain's Harold J. Laski, Catholic corporatism proposed an autonomous decision-making body in each economic sector that would set the terms of labor and production and provide a social safety net. The state itself would merely offer suggestions to the vocational groups, coordinate their actions, resolve conflicts between them, and enforce their resolutions. Corporatists sought economic redistribution through the voluntary action of citizens, guided by their consciences, not top-down planning.[38]

By 1936, many Catholic corporatists feared the US state had broken its divinely ordained moral tethers, ignoring spiritual reform and simply coercing economic behavior. Up to 1935, many Catholic leaders found much to like in the National Recovery Administration's industrial commissions and other agencies. They stressed the New Deal's continuity with their teachings and even took credit for laying its foundations. Administration officials returned the favor, identifying papal encyclicals as precedents for the New Deal. Liberal Catholics such as Ryan, who directed the NCWC's powerful Social Action Department—ground zero for Catholic corporatism in the United States— worked with the administration to legalize collective bargaining, while urging Roosevelt to attack competitive individualism even more directly. But the sharper teeth of the Second New Deal ran afoul of the corporatist model. After 1935, Ryan and many other liberal Catholics rejected the welfare state and came to share the right-wing charge that Roosevelt portended Bolshevism. Before then, only the Catholic schools competed directly with a state-run counterpart, and many Catholic enterprises enjoyed state and local support. But the federal safety net challenged the vast network of Catholic welfare institutions, including charities, orphanages, nursing homes, and hospitals as well as schools. Equally important, the idea of federal responsibility violated Catholic understandings of social organization and the First Amendment. For Catholic leaders, the tension between private and public welfare systems reflected the global struggle between the Church and secularizing states.[39]

Meanwhile, schooling remained contentious. New Dealers proposed a federal Department of Education to fund secular public education. Many Catholics saw in this goal the administration's true nature—and the direction from which an American dictatorship would arrive. As before, they insisted that "the school 'neutral in religion' does not exist, and has never existed." Every school taught a comprehensive philosophy, whether Christian or godless. To *America*'s editors, the "movement to bring the local schools under the control of a Washington bureaucracy" would "assuredly lead to a Federal dictatorship," for "what the Federal Government subsidizes, the Federal Gov-

ernment controls." In this context, the events of the late 1930s—New Dealers' growing enthusiasm for expert-led planning, the Popular Front alliance
of left-liberals and communists, and widespread Protestant support for the
Spanish republicans—reinforced Catholic leaders' fear that the shadowy hand
of communism lay behind the New Deal. In their view, secularization led
directly to Bolshevism.[40]

Developments after 1935 highlighted political assumptions that most liberal Catholics shared with many Protestant conservatives. Right-wing Protestants echoed Catholics' preoccupation with communism and argued that the
Soviet Union revealed atheism's political tendency. Many conservative Protestants, appreciating the Church's strong anticommunism, sought out Catholic
allies. Despite earlier precedents for this nascent convergence, especially during the Scopes era, Protestant suspicions of ecclesiastical authority rendered
such connections fleeting in the 1920s. But the New Deal fueled new forms of
cooperation between Catholics and theologically conservative Protestants.[41]

On its rightward edge, this impulse generated quasi-fascist movements
combining anticommunism with anti-Semitism. Right-wing critics decried
the "Jewish New Deal" or simply the "Jew Deal." Scattered expressions of admiration for Hitler's racial policies could be heard, most notably from Henry
Ford and Charles Lindbergh. Other conservative Protestants and Catholics sought a Christian alliance, too. Vigorous Protestant support for Father
Charles Coughlin, the firebrand "radio priest" who championed Christian
nationalism after the mid-1930s, suggested that anti-Catholicism had lessened
in conservative Protestant circles. Coughlin had sought since 1931 to unite
Catholics and Protestants in a "war unto death" against communism. What
one historian has called Coughlin's "ecumenism of discontent" employed the
shared Bolshevik enemy to erode the anti-Catholic bigotry separating would-
be Christian allies.[42]

Many right-wing Protestants also sought a cross-confessional campaign
against socialism and atheism. The fundamentalist preacher and anti-Semite
Gerald B. Winrod, who opposed Al Smith's candidacy, came by the mid-1930s
to see Catholics as potential allies in the fight against communism and its cultural root: "*animalism, animalism, animalism.*" In fact, Winrod's base of support overlapped substantially with that of Coughlin, who by 1936 had gained
powerful allies among fundamentalists. Coughlin's turn to anti-Semitism in
1938 aligned him even more closely with Winrod and brought his Catholic
followers into a hitherto largely Protestant campaign against Jewish influence. Right-wingers Gerald L. K. Smith and William Dudley Pelley (who re-
organized his quasi-fascist Silver Shirts as the Christian Party in 1935) likewise
worked to unite Protestants and Catholics behind Christian nationalism.[43]

Calls for Christian unity sometimes attracted liberal Catholics as well. The invitation to a 1936 anticommunist gathering in North Carolina included "35 of the most prominent Jew- and Red-baiters in the country" as signatories. Nevertheless, several Catholics—including John LaFarge, later known for his civil rights activism—also signed the invitation and attended the conference, which quickly split over the organizer's omission of "Christian" from its name and the inclusion of two rabbis. The forty-five anti-Semites that followed Winrod out were comfortable including Catholics but not Jews. Meanwhile, the language of Christian nationalism also reverberated through the main meeting, despite the aim to draw Jews into an anticommunist coalition. William J. Hafey, Catholic bishop of Raleigh, warned Protestants that they would need to choose between Catholicism, backing "the theory and principles of a representative Democracy," and communism, "a religion of death to man as a freeman and to society as a Christian Commonwealth." In the meeting's wake, LaFarge charged that communism held "a fatal attraction for Jews" and identified "Christian principles" as the only response to America's slide toward communism.[44]

Many liberal pluralists feared an American outbreak of Christian fascism. Although Catholic support for Mussolini garnered little public attention in the early 1930s, the Spanish Civil War highlighted profascist sympathies. Much to the dismay of liberal Catholics, General Francisco Franco inspired widespread enthusiasm among Catholic laypeople, journalists, and officials. Of the nearly 250 American Catholic publications, only the *Catholic Worker* and *Commonweal* opposed Franco. Bishops and archbishops openly lauded him. Many said the Depression proved democracy's inadequacy; the struggle pitted fascism against communism, not democracy against authoritarianism. Often, they reduced that clash to the age-old conflict of Christianity against atheism. These Catholics found fascism, which made space for the Church and private property, far superior to any secular regime. Meanwhile, liberal Catholics such as John A. Ryan continued to define their antifascism in prudential terms. Only in the 1940s would Jacques Maritain and John Courtney Murray develop the theoretical armature to reject Mussolini and Franco on principle.[45]

During the late 1930s, groups of mainstream Protestants came to appreciate Catholic views on democracy as well. Here, the main point of connection was a pejorative discourse of "secularism" that identified pluralists as political threats. Widespread among Catholics by the 1920s, the "secularism" label conflated atheism with a strict reading of church-state separation and asserted that political secularity inevitably entailed active opposition to religion. Many Protestants had long argued that separating religion from politics benefited church as well as state. When mainstream Protestants worried about irreligion in the 1920s, they referenced the burgeoning consumer culture and the "rebellion against Victorianism" in personal—especially sexual—morality. But in the 1930s, many came to agree with Catholics that strict church-state separation privileged atheism, perhaps to the point of establishing it as a national faith and threatening all religions with extinction.[46]

Whereas the older terms "naturalism," "atheism," and "materialism" referred mainly to personal beliefs, then, "secularism" brought public institutions and church-state relations under its capacious umbrella. It spoke to international issues, too; many users held that secularism led directly to totalitarianism. No worldly means, they contended, could check states that refused to recognize their dependence on God. The growing identification of secularism as the main threat to religion, and perhaps even democracy, in the late 1930s reoriented the national conversation away from the ethnic and cultural disputes foregrounded by 1920s nativism and toward the philosophical and political dimensions of religious identity. To critics of "secularism," both personal nonbelief and church-state separation represented existential threats to religion as such. Many mainstream Protestants began to fear that they had gone much too far in embracing secular culture. These figures often agreed with liberal Catholics that state growth at home, like totalitarianism abroad, reflected a growing tide of paganism.

This new understanding of secularism conceptually eliminated the longstanding contention of Jews and most Protestants that a high church-state wall actually benefited religion. It undermined the possibility that religious believers could support a pluralistic conception of democracy *for religious reasons*. Catholics and antisecularist Protestants defined political secularity as the establishment of atheism, not an institutional arrangement that could be supported on various grounds, both theistic and nontheistic. The discourse of antisecularism presented a stark choice between "religious and anti-religious first principles," from which flowed "all other views, all other opinions, all other thoughts and, therefore, all the actions which proceed from thought." Either every aspect of a society reflected religious commitments or none did. By the late 1930s, moderate and liberal Protestants began to join Catholics and conservative Protestants in adopting this Manichean framework. In it, Americans had to choose between religion and secularism, not tolerance and intolerance. Rather than competing ways of treating citizens with different views, they faced a choice between competing sources of truth and authority: God or humankind.[47]

Liberal Catholics, who did much to define this discourse, identified secularization as a holistic process that produced laissez-faire capitalism, statist liberalism, and totalitarianism alike. This meant that secularism anchored fascism as well as communism. Secularism, they argued, deified the state in the guise of "the people." Such a system toggled easily from one mode of state-worship to another—for example, from statist liberalism to totalitarianism. Each reflected the socially atomizing tendencies of atheism and the result-ing impulse to officially establish atheism. Liberal Catholics traced Nazism and communism to societal decline at the hands of philosophical naturalists such as John Dewey. Once science's corrosive skepticism had pushed aside God, they averred, Hitler and Stalin had taken charge in the name of massi-fied man. These figures rejected their coreligionists' enthusiasm for fascism, arguing that the struggle between democracy and totalitarianism reflected a deeper conflict of Christianity against secularism. If Americans embraced the philosophical error of the pagan Germans and atheistic Russians, they argued, they would meet the same political fate.[48]

By the late 1930s, the discourse of secularism had reshaped American cul-tural politics. As the antinativist coalition fractured, a new antisecularist al-liance formed, creating spaces where Judeo-Christian rhetoric would soon flourish. In 1936, the University of Chattanooga's Protestant leaders invited Notre Dame president John F. O'Hara to address their semicentennial. De-scribing religious education as the bulwark against dictatorship, O'Hara as-cribed to both Catholics and his Protestant audience a "framework of super-natural religion" that avowed "the existence of God and of the supernatural life, the immortality of the soul, the divine authority behind the Ten Com-mandments, the existence of grace, the efficacy of prayer, the reality of eter-nal reward and punishment, and, for Christians, the historical proof of the Divinity of Christ and the consequent divine authority of Christ's teachings." These principles, O'Hara stated, emerged from Judaism but "reach[ed] their fulfillment and perfection in Christianity." Against totalitarianism, the only "universally effective barrier" was "religion, with its affirmation of the rights of the individual soul."[49]

Many liberal and moderate Protestants retained the pluralist language of tolerance and religious liberty but expressed growing unease about secularism as the Protestant establishment slowly pulled apart. *Christian Century* editor Charles Clayton Morrison lauded church-state separation but insisted that it required neither "separation of religion and the state" nor "separation of religion and politics," nor even "separation of the Church and politics." Such figures increasingly blamed atheism for America's ills and argued that only a religiously grounded public culture could safeguard democracy. Worrying that they had jettisoned too much of Christianity in their search for social and political relevance, these Protestants took seriously the Catholic charge that they had unwittingly helped atheists destroy America's moral fiber. Many were veterans of the fundamentalist-modernist controversy who feared their generation had embraced science too uncritically. William Adams Brown, a leading Social Gospeler, wrote ruefully in *A Creed for Free Men* (1941) that his generation had confidently swept aside traditional doctrines, expecting science to fill the gap. Brown looked back to a time when the Bible was democracy's "textbook," providing an integrative faith and absolute moral standards for all. Though still touting church-state separation, these Protestants thought secularism—especially in schools—threatened the country's demise. They came to fear secularism more than Catholicism, and to suspect that their Catholic counterparts had a sounder view of religion's public role.[50]

This shift accompanied a new definition of religious authenticity that equated genuine belief with active, public opposition to secularism in all forms. On this view, those who denied that religion should anchor public culture were neither democratic nor genuinely religious. A long-standing defense of religious liberty that deemed church-state separation a positive boon to religion lost purchase among those liberal and moderate Protestants who traced secularization to strict separationism.

Even Roosevelt fed the growing perception that religion underpinned democracy. The president's 1939 message to Congress contended that religion anchored both "democracy and international good faith." As would so many others before Pearl Harbor, Roosevelt used the religion-democracy link to urge intervention in the war. Calling democracy "a covenant among free men" and religion the foundation of civilization, Roosevelt challenged Americans to mobilize against "the enemies of our faith and our humanity."[51]

Other international developments led liberal and moderate Protestants toward the discourse of secularism. Missionary work figured especially prominently. In 1928, the Quaker Rufus Jones announced at the International Missionary Council's Jerusalem meeting that Christianity's "real rival" was "not Buddhism or Islam or any other of the great religions, but secularism." William Ernest Hocking's 1932 book *Re-Thinking Missions* brought this understanding to a wider audience. *Time*, summarizing the study, explained that missionaries should now target the "materialism, secularism, [and] naturalism" underlying "the philosophies of Marx, Lenin, [and Bertrand] Russell," not other faiths. "The case that must now be stated," read the Hocking report, "is the case for any religion at all." *Time* agreed: "Should not the churches unite against atheism and secularism?" This view of secularism as the global enemy reinforced fears of its influence at home and led many Protestants to follow Catholics in seeing, beneath 1930s political shifts, a titanic struggle against atheism.[52]

Shifts among Protestant theologians likewise fueled antisecularism. At New York's Union Theological Seminary, Reinhold Niebuhr and the German émigré Paul Tillich spearheaded a renewal of theological reasoning. To them, science explained reality's surface, whereas religion grasped the "nature and destiny of man." The "theological renaissance" enlisted many kinds of Protestants, from Social Gospel liberals such as F. Ernest Johnson of Teachers College to those who joined Niebuhr in emphasizing sin. The common thread was the charge that secular cultures became totalitarian because science eliminated the distinctively human dimension. Epistemologically, Niebuhr and his allies threaded between naturalism and supernaturalism by offering myth as a mediating form of truth. Politically, they provided a religious justification for progressive social policies and made antisecularism palatable to Protestants who had equated supernaturalism with social reaction. These figures hardly endorsed miracles, but they agreed with Catholics and conservative Protestants that naturalism, not supernaturalism, threatened the country. They helped to cement a narrow, desiccated image of naturalism in American public culture.[53]

Patterns of interfaith cooperation reflected such changes in political thought, as old cultural conflicts between faith communities gave way to nascent political alliances cutting across them. Many mainstream Protestants moved away from Jews and naturalists and toward liberal Catholics, uniting with their old theological foes against the threat of secularism. Pluralists, who said intolerance posed the greatest threat to the nation and political secularity fostered religious vitality and political health, found themselves besieged by former allies from the antinativist campaign.

Meanwhile, virtually all Jewish leaders steered clear of antisecularism. One exception was Louis M. Minsky, director of the NCCJ-affiliated Religion News Service. Writing in the Catholic *Commonweal*, Minsky lauded Protestants for turning against secularism. He urged "a united front of religionists— Protestants, Catholics and Jews," aimed at "converting" the United States to "the religious way of life." But Minsky was a lonely voice in the Jewish community, especially before the 1940s. The Chicago rabbi and interfaith activist Louis L. Mann voiced the majority opinion at the 1940 National Conference on Religious Liberty. Every group in the American religious drama, Mann argued, had at some point played the role of dissenter. Only tolerance could protect the interests of all. Like most other Jewish commentators, Mann rooted democracy in the "inviolability of human personality and the right and privilege to be true to one's own inner self." He explicitly included nonbelievers as well. In short, Mann grounded American democracy in religious freedom, not religion itself.[54]

Jewish leaders feared even those theistic conceptions of democracy that included Judaism. They offered ringing endorsements of freedom of conscience and civil liberties. If Americans strayed from their faiths, they insisted, the churches and synagogues, not the state, should bring them back into the fold. Rabbi Norman Gerstenfeld called Jews "historic Protestants," noting their "abhorrence for religious authoritarianism." Jewish pluralists recognized that the antisecularists' definition of religion presented particular obstacles for Jews, many of whom had long since abandoned their ancestral faith. The debate over secularism in the late 1930s helped rejuvenate the charge that Jews were soft on communism, which paralleled a widespread view of Catholics as fascist fellow travelers. Of course, American Jews did favor socialism more often than Protestants and especially Catholics. Yet that fact, Jewish leaders protested, in no way undermined their loyalty to democracy.[55]

As the question of whether communism or fascism represented the greater threat became increasingly urgent, it pitted Catholics against naturalists, Jews, and many liberal Protestants. For Notre Dame's O'Hara, communism added to fascism's prohibitions "the denial of the right to hold property, the denial of the right to worship according to the dictates of conscience, [and] the denial of the family to recognition as the primary unit of society." By contrast, most liberals found fascism's assault on freedom of belief far worse. Democrats, they held, should aid the communists if an uncomfortable alliance became necessary.[56]

Both sides, unsurprisingly, deemed their opponents implicitly totalitarian. Pluralists often parried antisecularism with the simplistic countercharge that Catholics would deliver America into totalitarian hands. Morris Lazaron insisted in 1938 that Catholics sought to browbeat Protestants and Jews into supporting right-wing politics by questioning their loyalty to democracy and God. Catholic censorship efforts likewise fed the image of a totalitarian church, especially when they targeted motion pictures in the 1930s. But above all else loomed the laity's enthusiasm for Franco. Dewey and many other pluralists insisted that defining America in religious terms would foster top-down cultural repression. Each party to this dispute over democracy's foundations tended to articulate its position in a negative manner by labeling its opponents closet totalitarians and silently pinning the label "democracy" to its own particular theory of democracy.[57]

Under this weight, the fragile antinativist alliance collapsed. Yet the pluralistic liberals did not simply win out. In many ways, the opposite is true; the antisecularists' standard of religious authenticity increasingly held sway. As a result, Jews encountered obstacles that Catholics did not face. They would remain deeply suspect in any society where commitment to democracy required belief in God and opposition to secularity. Even as those standards worked to integrate Catholics into the mainstream, they shut out most Jews, many of whom had strayed from the fold and virtually all of whom identified political secularity as the precondition for their freedom. Jews, like naturalists, theological modernists, and other small belief communities, feared not only Protestant nativism but also the broader threat of Christian nationalism: an ecumenical but unofficially established Christian supermajority that imposed its own definitions of religious authenticity and loyal Americanism.

Meanwhile, those defending pluralism on explicitly theistic grounds— mostly liberal and moderate Protestants—found their views defined out of existence in the 1930s. Figures such as the FCC's Samuel McCrea Cavert understood that antisecularism forced them to choose between their faith and a pluralist conception of democracy. Many reasserted their long-standing endorsement of church-state separation for religious reasons. Supporting political secularity, they insisted, did not mean embracing atheism. Rather, that framework offered the soundest protection for all religious beliefs. But this claim was increasingly suspect in American public life.[58]

The rise of antisecularism deeply impacted interfaith organizations, further belying the familiar view of those groups as bastions of pluralism. In the Religious Education Association, for example, the founders' liberal assumptions largely gave way to antisecularism. REA participants increasingly doubted that religion could be taught historically and endorsed released-time programs that allowed a normative approach. REA official Luther A. Weigle went farther in 1936, charging that American schools fostered "irreligion and atheism" by teaching children that religion lacked "truth or value." Protestants' inexplicable support for secular education, Weigle argued, "imperils the future of religion among us," and thereby "the future of the nation itself."[59]

Elsewhere in the interfaith movement, too, Protestants recoiled at secularism and challenged the pluralist theory of democracy. They increasingly sought interfaith amity less to advance civic peace and social justice than to challenge secularism by sustaining a theistic culture. In a common interfaith slogan, Protestants, Catholics, and Jews shared in "the brotherhood of man and the fatherhood of God." Whereas the "brotherhood of man" loomed large in the 1920s, the "fatherhood of God" increasingly took precedence thereafter.

Developments in the NCCJ illustrate this shift of emphasis from a shared struggle against bigotry to a shared struggle against secularism. From the NCCJ's inception in 1927 through 1934, it focused on outreach and education. With Hitler's rise, the group launched its trio tours to damp the fires of anti-Semitism. This emphasis on justice and cooperation characterized NCCJ director Everett R. Clinchy's *All in the Name of God* (1934), which said Americans were coming to embrace religious diversity and toleration. Clinchy's theoretical references—the anthropologists Franz Boas and Clark Wissler and the philosophers John Dewey and Horace Kallen—located him squarely in the pluralist camp.[60]

At the same time, Clinchy's book shows that early interfaith activists already worried about the dissolution of theological differences in a secularizing culture. Clinchy declared that mere toleration—"the fatuous notion that it makes no difference what a man believes"—undermined religious belief and had no place in a pluralistic society. "The more deeply and strongly flows the current of one's distinctive religious faith," he continued, "the more helpful is likely to be his contribution to wholesome human relations with those from whom he differs." Only robust religious frameworks could undergird true pluralism. Interfaith activists, wrote Clinchy, rejected "indifference to religious issues" and sought a "democracy of cultures" in which all would "reverence the right of others to their reverences." Anticipating Will Herberg's classic *Protestant-Catholic-Jew* by two decades, Clinchy portrayed the United States as a religiously tripartite polity wherein each faith constituted a distinct "culture" or "*way of life*."[61]

Still, Clinchy drew freely on social scientists and naturalistic philosophers, rather than blaming them for totalitarianism. Columbia's Carlton J. H. Hayes, who replaced J. Elliot Ross as the NCCJ's leading Catholic voice in 1934, brooked no such middle ground. His ascension both reflected and heightened the growing battle over secularism among interfaith activists. Hayes attacked tolerance more sharply than Clinchy or Ross, seeing in it the tool of imperialistic secularists seeking to impose atheism, not simply a misunderstanding of the preconditions for cooperation.[62]

For reasons that remain unclear, Ross turned down NCCJ speaking engagements after early 1934, abruptly ending the "trio tours" and leaving group leaders in a bind. Although Hayes was the Catholic cochair, Ross had been the most active Catholic member by far. Now, Hayes became much more involved, producing a distinct shift in the NCCJ's tone. Hayes urged an alliance of religious believers against secularists, who sought, he argued, "the abolition of intolerance" through "the abolition of religion." In a widely read volume, he argued that secularism produced far more intolerance than did religion. In fact, "so-called religious persecution" actually reflected "political and economic considerations and ambitions, cloaked in religious guise." Discerning secular nationalism behind all modern ills, Hayes rejected many NCCJ members' desire to cooperate with nonbelievers. To Hayes, it was the "antireligious" forces, not religionists, that sought to impose their outlook on others and create a totalitarian unity.[63]

Hayes's portrait of three faith communities battling religious indifference and atheism made considerable headway among interfaith leaders. This anti-secularist version of the interfaith impulse steadily supplanted an older version centered on tolerance and support for civil liberties. Whereas the cross-confessional ties of 1920s interfaith activists reflected opposition to Protestant nativism, a different set of connections now emerged, defined by opposition to secularism. As elsewhere, that category implied a definition of religion that excluded believers who were friendly to naturalism or even political secularity. To Hayes and his allies, "religion" denoted nonliberal religion. The new understanding turned the vehemence of a group's rejection of everything lumped under "secularism" into a litmus test for its religious authenticity—and its political loyalty.[64]

✳

By the late 1930s, many mainstream Protestants had embraced this view of religion and secularism. But it would prove easier for secularism's critics to identify a common enemy than to define the precise religious content of a genuine democracy. Before World War II, Catholic antisecularists usually identified "Christianity" as the basis of American political culture. Some Protestant antisecularists did, too. Others referred generically to "religion," which evaded the question of whether the term included Judaism but clearly ruled out the pluralists' secular public sphere.

Yet these formulations were problematic for interfaith activists, given their organizational ties to Jewish leaders—not to mention the nation's struggle against an anti-Semitic foe. By the early 1940s, "Judeo-Christian" emerged as an alternative for many antisecularists, even as the term also gained traction among pluralists. Among pluralists, Judeo-Christian discourse captured a long-standing commitment to religious tolerance as the foundation of democracy. For antisecularists, however, the Judeo-Christian language signaled a tripartite alliance against secularism. In this usage, the Judeo-Christian tradition represented the unifying creed sought by William Adams Brown—a simple, ecumenical religious framework, aligned with democracy against naturalism and secular education, in which members of the three major faiths could enlist. On both sides of the increasingly contentious divide over religion's political role, the image of the United States as a Judeo-Christian nation came to the fore during World War II.

3

Democracy's Tradition

THE EMERGENCE OF A RELIGIO-POLITICAL CATEGORY

On December 20, 1931, readers of the *New York Times* opened its pages to find a striking analysis of the global scene by the British writer and frequent *Times* contributor P. W. Wilson. Rather than dividing the world into West and non-West, or democracies, monarchies, autocracies, and colonies, Wilson discerned a battle between Judeo-Christian and authoritarian regimes. He identified the militantly secularizing states founded by Lenin and Ataturk as "alternatives to the Judeo-Christian faith." Grounding political systems in deeper, cultural structures and defining Judeo-Christianity as a comprehensive mode of social and political order, Wilson helped to craft the modern discourse of Judeo-Christianity. In this usage, "Judeo-Christian" marked the antithesis to the political phenomenon that would soon be called "totalitarianism." Even before Hitler's rise—usually seen as the inspiration for America's Judeo-Christian discourse—Wilson not only identified "Judeo-Christianity" as a single religion alongside Buddhism, Hinduism, and Islam but also presented authoritarianism and Judeo-Christianity as mutually exclusive political principles. In this view, secularity, not suppression of dissent, defined totalitarianism.[1]

During the decade after Wilson first used "Judeo-Christian" in this manner, many Protestants and Jews, along with a few Catholics, would join him in describing democracy as a Judeo-Christian alternative to totalitarianism. Yet this discourse did not, as scholars have suggested, function mainly to combat Hitler's anti-Semitism and integrate Jews into the American mainstream. Many did use "Judeo-Christian" in this manner; from 1934 onward, Jewish and liberal Protestant commentators increasingly invoked that term as they called for open-ended tolerance of all belief systems. At the same time, however, Judeo-Christian rhetoric also emerged among others who identified atheism as the root of totalitarianism—and the leading threat at home. As the rift between pluralistic and exceptionalist conceptions of democracy opened up in the 1930s, Judeo-Christian language began to appear on both sides of that theoretical divide.

Thus, the historical record frustrates attempts to trace Judeo-Christian discourse exclusively to American Jews, or to Protestant champions of tolerance. We should instead locate its origins in networks of Jewish and Christian thinkers, mostly centered in New York, who for varying reasons paid special attention to political developments abroad—the rise of totalitarianism, and especially the fate of both Jews and Christians in Nazi Germany—and interfaith relations at home. These figures typically rejected both laissez-faire capitalism and Marxism, along with progressive views rooted in the social sciences, and came to see secularism as their common source. Theologians who drew conceptual resources from multiple faith traditions—the "neo-orthodox" Protestant Reinhold Niebuhr, the Catholic convert and French émigré Jacques Maritain, the Jewish ex-communist Will Herberg—played especially important roles in crafting exceptionalist versions of the Judeo-Christian discourse that identified shared religious principles, rather than religious tolerance, as the cornerstone of democracy.

Although pluralist voices remained strong through World War II, Judeo-Christian exceptionalists would increasingly supplant them by the late 1940s. As Wilson's writings suggest, the emerging discourse of Judeo-Christianity was shot through with anxieties about not only fascism but also secularism and communism. Careful exploration of the Judeo-Christian discourse in its infancy highlights the internal tensions—especially between pluralistic and exceptionalist theories of democracy—that would deepen further as the discourse reached maturity during World War II and flowered in the postwar years.

The Early Judeo-Christian Discourse

Despite his British provenance, P. W. Wilson captured the growing tensions that mainstream American Protestants felt in the 1930s, as they weighed their long-standing commitment to church-state separation against a growing fear that secular thinkers—including many of their own allies, especially in the universities—would undermine religion altogether. Born in 1875 in Kendal, Westmorland, Wilson had paternal ties to a powerful Quaker political dynasty that produced many members of Parliament. He himself joined Parliament as a Liberal MP in 1906 but turned full-time to writing after a failed reelection bid in 1910. Into the 1940s, he not only served as a correspondent for the *London Daily News* but also wrote frequently for American audiences in the *Times*, the *North American Review*, and the *Methodist Review*. (Wilson was connected to the United States through his American wife, Alice Selina Collins, the daughter of a wealthy machine manufacturer.) He also published over twenty well-known books on politics and religion before turning to mystery writing late in life. These books variously explained Christianity's relevance to modern life or chronicled the lives of establishment figures, including politicians and philanthropists as well as religious leaders. Wilson's turn to journalism when his political career foundered helps to explain both the particular subjects he treated and his prolific and passionate engagement in the field. He seemed to view writing as an alternate route to the kinds of cultural changes he had hoped to effect through Parliament.[2]

Wilson's religious commitments elude easy description. Despite the prominence of Quakers in his family, both his mother and his wife were Congregationalists. Meanwhile, Wilson's father was a devout member of the Plymouth Brethren, a nondenominational group of evangelical Christians whose early-nineteenth-century development of "dispensationalism" and the doctrine of "the Rapture" would decisively shape American fundamentalism. As an adult, Wilson exhibited strong Wesleyan influences; he published frequently in Methodist journals and wrote several books and articles on Methodist leaders. However, he attended a Congregational church in London whose minister, Charles Silvester Horne, helped lead the Brotherhood movement. This religio-political initiative brought together nonconformists who aimed to engage and uplift the working class, believing with Horne that religion "must penetrate and permeate all relationships, economical, social and political, as well as family and personal."[3]

As a dissenter from the Anglican establishment, however, Wilson championed religious liberty, even as he called for American-style Prohibition and other regulations rooted in broad religious principles.[4] Like so many American Protestants, he endorsed both the formal separation of church and state and an informal but all-encompassing infusion of broadly shared religious values into all domains of life. Indeed, Wilson put his commitment to church-state separation ahead of his personal beliefs on countless instances.[5] Yet he simultaneously insisted that Judeo-Christian faith should set the collective terms of existence for all peoples.

Despite his pioneering contributions to a discourse that formally included both Catholics and Jews, in fact, Wilson gave Protestantism pride of place in the modern world. In his *New York Times* articles of the early 1930s, Wilson equated Judeo-Christianity with the American principle of "a free church in a free state" and identified two opposing authoritarian threats. On the one side stood the "ancient and comprehensive" regime of Catholicism, which asserted "an authority that claims to be eternal and universal" over all nations and peoples. On the other side were emerging forms of secular authoritarianism. Both the Soviets and the Turkish regime, Wilson argued, pursued ruthless campaigns against religion.[6]

Indeed, Wilson worried more about secular authoritarianism than its Catholic counterpart, because it looked forward rather than backward. The Soviet and Turkish experiments embodied the false, dangerous hope of living without religion, which Wilson saw on the rise around the world. Yet he insisted that all forms of secular thought, from John Dewey's genial assertion of the self-sufficiency of "art, science and culture" to the Soviets' "communal humanism" that divinized Lenin, functioned as substitute faiths and proved that "man is—what he always has been—a religious animal." Wilson's identification of Judeo-Christianity as a political system reflected his belief that all human action took its shape from religious first principles. "Differences of religion affect more than faith and worship," he wrote in 1933. "They are differences of life itself, and life is organized in community." The adherents to different religions, said Wilson, "live side by side but in separate worlds."[7]

How, then, could Wilson so confidently invoke a common "Judeo-Christian" culture? Like so many other Protestants before and after him, Wilson adopted a supersessionist stance that relegated Judaism's contributions to the distant past. To be sure, he defined those contributions expansively. In "the ceremonial and creeds of the Church, including even the 'Logos' or divine word," Wilson declared, one found almost nothing "that cannot be traced directly to Jewish history, law, psalmody, prophecy or ritual." At the same time, Wilson joined many other evangelical Protestants in actively seeking to convert Jews to Christianity. (Here, the childhood influence of the Plymouth Brethren may have lingered, despite his later dismissal of that group as "a peculiar people" who shunned modern politics and culture. As dispensationalists, the Plymouth Brethren championed Christian Zionism—the belief that the prophesied return of the Jews to Israel portended the Second Coming—and missionized among Jews to further hasten that outcome.) Wilson supported the efforts of the messianic Jews in the Hebrew Christian Alliance and penned the foreword to *Why I, a Jew, Am a Christian*, a pamphlet by B. A. M. Schapiro, director of the American branch. His identification of democracy with Judeo-Christianity thus accompanied a deep ambivalence toward Judaism, as well as a near-total rejection of Catholicism.[8]

As Wilson's 1930s writings illustrate, the Judeo-Christian discourse took much of its shape from the emergence of totalitarianism. The public use of Judeo-Christian formulations spiked after Hitler took power in January

1933 and again after 1938, when war loomed in Europe and the question of American intervention pressed increasingly hard. Yet the new discourse held dangers as well as opportunities for American Jews, insofar as they joined some Christians in defining Nazism as an attempt to stamp out the Judeo-Christian heritage altogether. The new language identified the cause of Hitler's Jewish victims with the preservation of Christianity itself. At the same time, arguing that Christians should mobilize against Hitler as a matter of self-defense also threatened to cut Jews, as such, entirely out of the picture. German Jews could easily appear as simply abstract symbols of a larger religious formation—Judeo-Christianity—to which Wilson and many other Christians deemed modern-day Judaism irrelevant.

Many took the risk nonetheless. As early as 1934, and likely earlier, prominent American rabbis began using Judeo-Christian formulations to alert the public to the plight of Germany's Jews and to challenge anti-Semitism at home. Especially decisive were the interventions of Stephen S. Wise and Louis I. Newman, leading Reform rabbis in New York who shared strong ties to the Zionist movement as well as one another. Newman had assisted Wise at the Free Synagogue before being ordained by Wise and Martin Meyer in 1918. The two men stayed in close contact throughout the rest of their lives, as attested by their voluminous correspondence.

Wise made his earliest known public contribution to the emerging Judeo-Christian discourse at the 1934 meeting of the Central Conference of American Rabbis (CCAR). A Quaker speaker had inflamed the gathering by advising Jews to turn the other cheek in the face of Nazi insults, asserting that they could best press their case by "show[ing] good will toward the Nazis and appeal[ing] to the Christian conscience of the German people." In response, Wise led the conferees in signing a resolution that identified Hitler's system as a direct challenge to "the great Judaeo-Christian heritage of our civilization." Unlike Wilson's writings, Wise's resolution embodied Judeo-Christian pluralism; it defined the Judeo-Christian ethic in civil-libertarian terms as "the right of every individual to have perfect liberty of conscience and freedom of utterance in all matters of religious, social, economic and political import."[9]

Although Newman did not use Judeo-Christian formulations regularly until the late 1930s, he did so with gusto thereafter. From 1938 to 1940, Newman frequently invoked "Judaeo-Christian ethics," "Judaeo-Christian morality," and "the Judaeo-Christian way of life" in his sermons. Newman described Christianity as "an Oriental religion based upon the Hebraic ideals of peace, brotherhood, and good-will" and Nazism as a form of neo-paganism rooted in Nietzsche's writings. The Germans' "campaign to destroy the Judaeo-Christian ethics," Newman argued, reflected "a fear of the Hebraic struggle

for peace and goodwill." But he contended that "the Judaeo-Christian morality can shield humanity against the rising tide of savagery."[10]

After 1938, other Jewish leaders joined Wise and Newman in using Judeo-
Christian formulations. The publisher and interfaith activist Roger W. Straus
urged Americans to fight in Europe for "Judeo-Christian principles," especially the core "doctrine of brotherly love." A CCAR resolution of 1939 celebrated "the great Judeo-Christian tradition," which taught democrats to safeguard "the inalienable rights of all individuals irrespective of the blood in
their veins or of the religious creed which they may profess or not profess at
all." And in October 1940, the New York rabbi Samuel Schulman said civilization was in the hands of the "English-speaking peoples into whose soul the
message of the Bible, the Judeo-Christian tradition[,] has been woven."[11]

Wise's invocations of Judeo-Christian rhetoric foregrounded the danger to
Christians as well as Jews. In a November 1940 Carnegie Hall sermon on the
need for "world resistance" to Hitler in "the form of renewed and deepened
loyalty to that morality which, viewing its origin, is Judaeo-Christian," Wise
urged Jews to join Christians in "upholding and magnifying" the "Christian-
Jewish ethic." Wise's rousing January 1941 address "Nazarene and Nazi: Jesus
vs. Hitler" called the war "a conflict between Judeo-Christian ethics and Hitlerism." According to a reporter, Wise declared that the Nazis meant "to blast
out of existence the teachings of Christ relative to the Fatherhood of God,
love of neighbor and the value of the individual life." As we saw in chapter 1,
Wise viewed Jesus as "the embodiment and the supreme teacher" of "Judeo-
Christian ethics." He called the persecution of German Jewry "the spearhead
of an attack on the world-wide Judeo-Christian ethic."[12]

Although Wise had long deemed Jesus a moral paragon worthy of respect
by Jews, his thinking about Nazism was also apparently influenced by Maurice Samuel, a Romanian émigré and well-known platform speaker. Samuel's
1940 book *The Great Hatred* claimed that German anti-Semitism represented a displaced hatred of Christianity itself. As a reviewer noted, Samuel
interpreted Nazism as the product of a "fanatical fear-hatred of the Judeo-
Christian humanitarian morality, not economic or political motives." Another
reviewer credited Samuel with recognizing Nazism as "an assault upon all the
values associated with Judaeo-Christian civilization."[13]

Two syncretistic books by the Yiddish novelist Sholem Asch also influenced Judeo-Christian discourse in these years: *The Nazarene* (1939), trans-
lated by Samuel, and *What I Believe* (1941). Reviewers described the former as
an exposition of "the great central ideals of the Judeo-Christian tradition—
dedication to God, the struggle for a kindly world, respect for personality,
a yearning for righteousness—in vivid contrast to the Nietzschean view

of life," and the latter as "a remarkable and constructive exposition of the Judaeo-Christian ideas from which traditional antagonisms largely have been eliminated."[14]

Wise, however, rejected Asch's postulation of theological continuities—as opposed to shared ethical principles and political interests—between Christianity and Judaism. On the same grounds, he deplored efforts by the Jewish writer John Cournos to make of Jesus "a bridge holding the Jewish and Christian traditions together" and the activities of John M. Oesterreicher, a Jewish convert to Catholicism who aimed to bring Jews into a deeper engagement with Christianity and founded the Institute of Judaeo-Christian Studies at Seton Hall University in 1953. Jews could never follow these men in accepting "the Christ of dogma," Wise declared. "I accept Jesus Christ," he wrote, "not to be safe, not to be saved, but as an enlightened, noble young Jewish teacher and brother who paid the price that Jews have always paid." Though his own emphasis on the Jewish Jesus struck many as overly syncretistic, Wise drew the line at using Jesus to bring Judaism closer, theologically, to Christianity. Other Jewish leaders likewise deplored the work of Asch, Cournos, and Oesterreicher.[15]

Yet the attraction of Judeo-Christian rhetoric remained. By 1940, Jewish commentators followed Wise and Newman in contrasting Nazism to Judeo-Christianity. How better to mobilize Christians against Hitler than to define Nazism as a resurgence of paganism, aimed at stamping out Judeo-Christian principles worldwide? Still, there is reason to suspect that Wise and Newman, unlike syncretists such as Asch, felt ambivalent about the new Judeo-Christian discourse. Indeed, both men abruptly ceased using Judeo-Christian formulations as soon as the United States entered the war. It seems likely that these Jewish leaders regarded the Judeo-Christian discourse as a risky resource, to be mobilized sparingly under extreme circumstances, and deemed it unnecessary once Roosevelt joined the Allies.

The earliest Judeo-Christian formulations by American Protestants likewise reveal the complexity of responses to European developments, in the context of deepening tensions between pluralists and exceptionalists. Among Protestants, Judeo-Christian rhetoric emerged in tandem with the concept of "totalitarianism," designating a form of society that opposed the liberal-democratic model at virtually every point. This was particularly true among German émigrés and others closely attuned to German thought. Thus, Reinhold Niebuhr, who grew up in a German-speaking community and read widely in postwar German theology, was both an early user of the "totalitarian" label and a key contributor to the Judeo-Christian discourse (although he preferred the terms "Hebrew-Christian" or "Jewish-Christian"). As these

figures sought to understand the meaning of Hitler, in the context of developments in the United States, they arrayed Judeo-Christianity against totalitarianism in a manner akin to P. W. Wilson.

Unlike "Judeo-Christian," "totalitarian" was not an older term that took
on new meanings amid the political changes of the 1930s. The Italian theorist
Giovanni Gentile coined the adjective in 1925 to capture the overarching character of the proposed fascist state. Mussolini popularized this adjectival usage
in the late 1920s, and Nazi theorists also adopted the term after 1930, though
they used it more sparingly than Italians. On American shores, the journalist
Walter Lippmann apparently introduced the term to American audiences in
an April 1927 *Commonweal* article, "Autocracy versus Catholicism," several
months before Gentile himself explicated the concept in "The Philosophic
Basis of Fascism," in the January 1928 issue of *Foreign Affairs*.[16]

The appearance of Lippmann's 1927 article in a liberal Catholic journal
signals the domestic conflicts that shaped American uses of the concept of totalitarianism. Lippmann—increasingly a sharp critic of naturalism— offered
a political narrative essentially identical to that of the journal's lay Catholic
editors. The fascists' root word *totalitaria*, he explained, reflected a state that
acknowledged "no rights of man, no rights of the family, [and] no rights of
association, lay or spiritual." According to Lippmann, the whole course of
politics since the Reformation pointed toward this Hobbesian view of the
state as "unitary, omnipotent, and irresistible," even if it featured democratic
decision-making. He favored an alternative, pre-Reformation view of the state
as a "corporation with limited and derived powers, existing among other corporations which were autonomous, and endowed with inalienable rights."
Deeming this "fundamentally liberal doctrine" the only one "consistent with
a free and civilized life," Lippmann credited it to Aquinas and other Catholic
theorists. Lippmann thus contended that true liberalism grew out of Catholic
natural-law thinking and found its contemporary expression in the Anglo-
American constitutional tradition, with its strict limits on governmental
power. By contrast, he argued, the general tendency of the modern state ran
toward totalitarianism.[17]

The concept of totalitarianism did not figure prominently in American
public discourse until after Hitler's ascension, however. Most Americans first
encountered the term in reference to the Nazis, among whom it briefly came
into vogue before falling out of favor. Thereafter, émigré intellectuals such
as the Italian theorist Max Ascoli picked it up. By the mid-1930s, American
commentators increasingly replaced the adjective "totalitarian" and the Italian nouns *totalitaria* and *totalitarismo* with "totalitarianism." Articles in *Social
Research*, launched in 1934 by the New School for Social Research's University

in Exile—a haven for émigré social scientists—gave the term additional currency. After 1935, scholars increasingly used it to distinguish the new governments from traditional dictatorships. In 1938 and 1939, a number of comparative government textbooks followed the economist Calvin B. Hoover's influential book *Dictators and Democracies* (1937) by categorizing political systems as either democratic or totalitarian and equating Stalin's regime with those of Hitler and Mussolini.[18]

Scholars generally credit these social scientists, and especially the émigrés, with popularizing the concept of totalitarianism. Their role should not be minimized; they were far more attuned to the repressive and anti-Semitic aspects of the Nazi and Soviet regimes than most Americans. Yet so too were many theologians, who viewed foreign affairs through the lens of religion's political roles. Among them, the concept of totalitarianism took shape alongside the closely related Judeo-Christian discourse. Liberal Catholics and many of the neo-orthodox Protestants around Reinhold Niebuhr and Paul Tillich mobilized both frameworks against pluralistic liberals, who generally interpreted the fascist regimes as expressions of religious nationalism. In fact, the real danger to the modern West, according to these Catholic and neo-orthodox figures, was not politicized religion but rather politicized secularism of the kind they attributed to pluralists, which in the eyes of these critics represented nothing less than the official establishment of a false, atheistic religion. In their view, totalitarianism offered a new faith that divinized the state and required it to coopt or stamp out all competing institutions.[19]

Tillich, who emigrated from Germany in late 1933, is sometimes said to have introduced American theorists to the concept of totalitarianism in a November 1934 *Social Research* article. But Niebuhr, who likely encountered the concept through his conversations with Tillich, had injected it into a running print conversation about political philosophy more than a year earlier, in the summer of 1933. Niebuhr began to regularly invoke "totalitarianism" as he traveled through Europe and reported back to the mainstream Protestant journal *Christian Century*. Hitler, he wrote, sought an utterly new kind of state that "exercises authority over every type of human association and assumes direct control of all organizations, whether athletic, artistic, commercial, religious or merely social."[20]

Niebuhr's new terminology reflected broader changes in his politics and theology. Though he remained a socialist and a fierce critic of social visions rooted in love and brotherhood, after 1933 Niebuhr increasingly described the needed alternative to liberal Christianity as "Christian orthodoxy" or the "Jewish-Christian tradition." Shortly thereafter, starting in 1934, Niebuhr gradually ditched the Hebraic-Hellenic distinction and began to identify the foundation of Western civilization as "the Jewish-Christian mythos." Niebuhr's biographer attributes his theological shift to an exchange with his brother H. Richard on the problem of grace.[21] But events in Germany also provided a powerful catalyst for his new emphasis on sin and natural law. Like a number of other Protestant leaders, Niebuhr argued that Nazism's rise reflected a fatal theological weakness among German Protestants. He wrote in April 1933 that "the Protestant church in Germany" has on the whole fallen under the spell of Hitlerism." Thereafter, Niebuhr repeatedly charged that neither Social Gospel liberalism nor Karl Barth's version of neo-orthodoxy could arm citizens against the assaults of a totalizing state. Niebuhr sought a flexible, Protestant conception of the natural law that could perform the same cultural and political functions as the much more detailed Catholic version, but with Calvin rather than Aquinas as its starting point. He rejected the traditional Protestant identification of church-state separation as the source of religious vitality and hoped to place American culture on a solid, if ecumenical, theological foundation. In the German case, meanwhile, Niebuhr credited the churches' weakness to "the traditional political realism of Lutheranism, which has always regarded politics as belonging to 'the world'" and thus resistant to the application of moral principles. In the same article that introduced the concept of "totalitarianism" to *Christian Century* readers, Niebuhr called for a reconstruction of Protestant theology so that it could better resist the blandishments of the totalitarians.[22]

Most of the Protestants who spoke of "totalitarianism" in this early period foregrounded the Nazis' alleged secularism or paganism rather than their anti-Semitism. Like Niebuhr, they argued that the totalitarian state sought either to harness or eliminate the churches. As war broke out in Europe in 1939, John A. Mackay offered this argument repeatedly in the *New York Times* and linked it explicitly to anti-secularism. A Scottish-born Presbyterian, former Latin American missionary, prominent ecumenist, founder of *Theology Today*, and longtime president of Princeton Theological Seminary, Mackay was one of the best-known Protestant writers of the mid-twentieth century. For him, the modern struggle was not East against West, or even left against right, but rather "those who believe that the Christian era has . . . come to an end in history, to be followed by a new iron age," against "those who maintain that, whatever be the imperfection[s] of religion and democracy as we have known them in our tradition, both have derived from an everlasting spiritual source where they may obtain renewal."[23]

Totalitarianism, Mackay explained, combined "faith and politics . . . in a crusading unity" by identifying "the State with God," a "jealous and ruthless deity": "The State is divinized and makes demands upon human personality which only God has a right to make." According to Mackay, totalitarian "church-States" had "their own scriptures, their liturgy, their theology, their priesthood, their missionaries, their dream of world dominion." But this dual, religio-political challenge had a silver lining: It had revealed democracy's Judeo-Christian roots. The concept of totalitarianism offered Mackay and many others a way to challenge secularism and assert a firm link between religion and democracy. Arguing that German fascism challenged Christianity as well as democracy, these figures contended that secularism bore the seeds of totalitarian rule.[24]

In such contexts, Judeo-Christian rhetoric began to spread. Although P. W. Wilson used the term infrequently throughout the 1930s, it gained a major new foothold in newspapers in late 1937, when the syndicated columnist Dorothy Thompson told her roughly ten million readers that Hitler's Germany had "officially repudiated Judeo Christianity." Thompson had experienced Nazism firsthand, having been expelled from Germany in 1934. As the daughter of a Methodist minister of British extraction, Thompson shared much in common with Wilson. And she, too, published a spate of popular books on religion, including the religious character of Western civilization. In a 1938 column, meanwhile, Thompson argued that the modern crisis, with Germany at its head, was "not a Jewish crisis" but rather a Western one, threatening "the common civilization that runs from the Greeks to our own day . . . that mixture of Graeco-Roman culture, Judaeo-Christian religion and ethics, and the fearless mentality of the scientific awakening, which all together we call Western civilization." In subsequent columns of December 1939 and 1940, Thompson again argued that the Judeo-Christian heritage underpinned Western democracy, adding its "ethical sanction" to the Greek and French emphasis on "reason and realism."[25]

Protestants also used Judeo-Christian rhetoric in other contexts as well. One was the interfaith movement. A 1938 report by NCCJ director Everett R. Clinchy lauded the emergence of an interfaith alliance against Hitler, Stalin, and Mussolini's "political party machines." These regimes, Clinchy wrote, "deny the sovereignty of God above all else, pour contempt upon the spiritual values of the Judeao-Christian tradition, and refuse to recognize those natural rights of freedom of conscience, freedom of church, press, of pulpit, and of religious organizational work." Another crucible of Judeo-Christian discourse was the contest over religion in the schools. F. Ernest Johnson of Columbia's Teachers College argued in 1940 that "the faith of the Hebrew-Christian tradition to which our culture owes so much" should guide the public schools. The Founders would not have countenanced secular schooling, Johnson contended, for they knew that religious liberty meant "liberty *in* religion, not immunity from it." Finally, the debate around intervention in World War II also led many Protestants to join Jewish leaders in calling for American entry and denouncing anti-Semitism at home. "The Christians of this land share with the Jews the tradition of the prophets," wrote Secretary of Agriculture Henry A. Wallace in a 1940 issue of the *Menorah Journal*. Indeed, Wallace argued, "the Jewish tradition, the Christian tradition, the democratic tradition and the American tradition are all one."[26]

On the Catholic side, it is usually said that the Protestant cast of Judeo-Christian rhetoric led American Catholics to reject it.[27] For some of these figures, ambivalence toward antifascism may have been a factor as well. Unlike most Jews and liberal Protestants, who sharply challenged fascism, many Catholic leaders found themselves in a more ambiguous position. The Church's friendliness to Mussolini and Franco and the support of many American laypeople for the firebrand, quasi-fascist "radio priest" Charles Coughlin further muddied the waters. Moreover, the Church's prohibition on interfaith dialogue likely discouraged some antifascist Catholics from using Judeo-Christian formulations.

Still, these impediments applied less clearly to liberal Catholics than to conservative ones, and less clearly to the laity than to members of the hierarchy. Thus, a handful of lay Catholics did use Judeo-Christian language in the 1930s. A key figure was Jacques Maritain, an increasingly influential liberal Catholic theorist in the 1930s and early 1940s. For the most part, however, Maritain used "Judeo-Christian" to denote either world religions or the moral values associated with Western civilization. For instance, in a 1933 speech that defended "theocentric humanism," Maritain spoke of the West's "Judeo-Christian religions." Likewise, a 1937 article invoked "Judeo-Christian monotheism," and the 1938 book *True Humanism*, based on lectures delivered in 1934, noted the influence of "judeo-christian values" on Marx's thought. Finally, Maritain contrasted the "Indian" and "Judeo-Christian" conceptions of the world in a 1941 *Review of Politics* piece, "The Immortality of Man." Still, Maritain, like most other early Catholic users of Judeo-Christian formulations, did not connect them to democracy until later in the 1940s. Although liberal Catholics such as Maritain were quick to adopt the categories of "totalitarianism" and "secularism," they typically contrasted these to Christianity, not Judeo-Christianity, until at least the mid-1940s.[28]

The leading exception was the prominent Columbia University historian Carlton J. H. Hayes, a convert from Protestantism and a fierce antifascist—and antisecularist. Hayes was one of the earliest Americans to argue that Westerners faced a choice between Judeo-Christianity and totalitarianism. Indeed, he may have been the first academic commentator to explicitly connect those discourses. In numerous books, articles, and speeches, Hayes contended that genuine democracy rested on Judeo-Christian foundations, whereas totalitarianism abroad and liberal pluralism at home represented twin expressions of atheistic materialism.

Intimately familiar with the views of John Dewey and his many naturalistic colleagues at Columbia, Hayes worked to make the liberal Catholic analysis of democracy more palatable to Protestants. He recast Catholic political arguments in a less belligerent style and a more familiar political idiom, associating the Church's position on church-state questions with keywords such as "freedom," "tolerance," "pluralism," and "democracy." As a widely respected historian of modern Europe, Hayes also gave empirical warrant to the claim that totalitarianism reflected the long ascent of secular nationalism. The atheistic tendencies of the modern liberal state, he insisted, had laid the groundwork for totalitarian regimes throughout the West.

Hayes made his scholarly mark with several studies of nationalism, which he deemed the leading cultural and political force in the modern era. Westerners, he wrote in 1926, had been "systematically indoctrinated with the tenets that every human being owes his first and last duty to his nationality, that nationality is the ideal unit of political organisation as well as the actual embodiment of cultural distinction, and that in the final analysis all other human loyalties must be subordinate to loyalty to the national state." In fact, nationalism offered nothing less than a state-centered religion in place of the traditional faiths. Each of the nationalistic religions, Hayes contended, featured "a symbolic patron or personifying figure as its God" and a corresponding "mythology or theology." Through such means, the modern state claimed for itself "the mission of salvation and the idea of immortality."[29]

Hayes's analysis offered several advantages for liberal Catholics. For example, it parried the customary charges against medieval Catholicism by identifying modern nationalism as far more irrational, dogmatic, intolerant, and divisive than earlier religions. According to Hayes, the medieval era featured a diffusion of human loyalties across many levels, including the supranational level of Christianity, not blinkered intolerance. (Elsewhere in the world, he explained, Buddhism and Islam had likewise fostered unification.) Hayes drew on long-standing critiques of Judaism in framing modern nationalism as "a reaction against historic Christianity, against the universal mission of Christ," that "re-enshrines the earlier tribal mission of a chosen people." The god of nationalism, wrote Hayes, "resembles the Jewish Yahweh, in that he is the god of a chosen people, a jealous god, and preeminently a god of battles."[30]

Identifying nationalism as a distinctly modern, highly divisive, and profoundly intolerant form of religion allowed Hayes to blame it for a remarkable variety of ills, including many often traced to the churches. Thus, it was the dominance of nationalism, not the persistence of religion, that accounted for the modern era's "spirit of exclusiveness and narrowness," its "premium on uniformity," the "docility of the masses," and rampant militarism. And it was the nationalists, not the medieval Christians, who had truly sought to keep people ignorant in order to protect an established faith. They imposed their "official theology" on the public schools through "an Inquisitorial Board of Education," complete with "a nationalist Index Librorum Prohibitorum." Meanwhile, the forces of nationalism had colonized the older religious traditions, so that each faith community now offered distinctively tinged variants of nationalism. Hayes thus traced both church-state breaches and "so-called religious persecution" to nationalism, not genuine religion.[31]

Hayes's interpretation also provided crucial resources for the Judeo-Christian alliance against liberal pluralism that would emerge in the late 1930s. When he developed his views of nationalism, in the 1920s, Hayes portrayed Catholics as virtually alone in opposing it. Both Protestantism and Eastern Orthodoxy developed in tandem with nationalism, he argued. Judaism, meanwhile, was "a tribal religion of the Hebrew nationality," not a universalistic world religion, and Jews eagerly embraced other forms of nationalism as well, seeking tolerance by helping Protestants and skeptics fight Catholicism. With such flimsy religious resources at hand, Hayes wrote, the masses had "come step by step to look upon the state, rather than upon the church, as the guardian of the family, the dispenser of charity, and the promoter of education and culture" and to transfer to it tasks such as "the custody of vital statistics, the regulation of family relations, and the conduct of public charities and education." The need at present was to win back the allegiance of the masses to Christianity, understood in Catholic terms as an "organised society."[32]

Yet if Hayes's writings of the late 1920s identified Catholicism as uniquely capable of challenging nationalism, they also opened doors to cross-confessional cooperation. For example, Hayes abandoned the usual Catholic charge that the Protestant Reformation had inaugurated the destructive reign of modern individualism. He identified the Enlightenment, not the Reformation, as the source of the modern world's philosophical deficiencies—especially the moral void that, in his view, led directly to totalitarianism. Hayes also embraced the language of pluralism and freedom, portraying the national state as the great enemy of diversity, hostile alike to "individual differences, class differences, [and] religious differences." These moves paved the way for John Courtney Murray's postwar attempt to align Catholicism with religious liberty without abandoning a theistic conception of democracy.

Hayes's early writings on nationalism showed how to break down obstacles preventing Catholics from participating in joint action against secularism, revealing the terms in which a new Catholic argument could be framed to appeal across confessional lines.[33]

In the mid-1930s, Hayes's view of nationalism as a state-centered religion led him to embrace the concept of totalitarianism. In a 1934 *Commonweal* series on that phenomenon, he identified Hitlerism as the logical endpoint of modern nationalism. The total state, Hayes argued, embodied the total commitment to the collective demanded by nationalists—and no longer checked by the church as an independent object of loyalty with distinctive social functions. By 1938, Hayes focused increasingly on identifying totalitarianism's causes. That system's "utter denial of any moral law superior to the might of dictators," he said, constituted a "revolt against the continuity of historic civilization"; it attacked both the "ideals of spiritual and mental freedom" and "the supernatural and absolute bases of our traditional morality."[34]

Hayes continued to mobilize the concepts of freedom and diversity. As a Catholic, he insisted, "I do not prefer Fascism to Communism. I do not want any totalitarianism. I want to stick to democracy, with its traditional intellectual and spiritual freedom." Identifying "cultural pluralism" as a bulwark against totalitarianism, Hayes credited American democracy to "the traditional cultural differences among our several religious groups." If a secularizing state tried to "fuse" these differences or "blot them out altogether," he warned, "then democracy itself would die in the United States."[35]

In a fall 1939 address to the American Philosophical Society, Hayes developed his analysis in corporatist terms while identifying medieval Christendom as the epitome of pluralism. The medieval order, he explained, featured multiple sources of authority; "semi-public, semi-independent corporations" such as the "church, nobility, guild, [and] university" hemmed in states. Since then, the state had steadily captured terrain due to secularization, liberalism, industrialization, and the elevation of the masses over the "special classes" that had traditionally represented them. ("Cats want to be kings," Hayes lamented, "and, through sheer press of numbers, some of them actually become kings.")[36]

Underneath it all, however, lay religious decline. After centuries in which Christianity had grounded Western institutions and practices, wrote Hayes, "some of the classes, especially the intellectuals," had rejected "our common religious heritage," and the masses had followed. This had upended traditional conceptions of social order by substituting a false "equality of minds or of purses, of talents or of occupations," for Christianity's "equality of souls before God, an equality in dignity of personality" rather than station or attainment. Westerners had also abandoned the "noblesse oblige" underpinning a "Christian consecration of the classes to the service of the masses" and the corresponding deference of the masses. Finally, the "religious void" in Western culture, being "unnatural" and "unendurable," had been filled by demonic secular equivalents. Yet the Judeo-Christian tradition remained a close memory, inspiring totalitarian rulers' quest to "destroy Judaeo-Christianity both in its roots and in its flowers." After Russian Christians and German Jews, Hayes argued, the totalitarian regimes would target Russian Jews and German Christians.[37]

Hayes's analysis produced a distinctive conception of democracy. Because totalitarianism reflected Christendom's disintegration into secularizing nation-states, political procedures could not prevent it. What defined a political system was not the means of choosing officials but rather the underlying distribution of social authority and the conception of moral order that justified it. Unitary structures of political authority inevitably inclined toward totalitarianism; an elected majority could "gather all power in its hands and crush minority dissent" as easily as any dictator. Only the restoration of genuine pluralism, Hayes argued—the recovery of alternative sources of authority beyond states—could check totalitarianism. And this would require, above all, replacing the nationalistic religions with traditional faiths that worshipped the one true God.[38]

Religion and Democracy

On the eve of World War II, American thinkers connected religion to democracy in a variety of ways. One of the most influential approaches emerged among those advocates of "personalism" who joined Hayes in sharply distinguishing religion from secularism and seeing a spiritual battle between the two behind modern political struggles. Personalism, a cross-confessional theological orientation that enjoyed substantial influence by World War II, appealed to Protestants (the British philosopher John Macmurray), Catholics (Maritain), Orthodox thinkers (the Russian exile Nikolai Berdyaev), and Jews (Will Herberg). These figures typically sought a religious alternative to socialism; they embraced Marx's ideal of economic justice but despised the Soviets' militant atheism and abridgement of political freedoms. Personalists argued that Marxists trampled on individual rights because they employed a thin, secular conception of the human person. Offering some of the earliest Judeo-Christian formulations, they identified both secular liberalism and Marxism as outgrowths of atheism and grounded genuine democracy in Judeo-Christian faith.[39]

Personalism identified the dignity of the individual, derived from creation in God's image, as a transcendent standard against which to measure human institutions and practices. This divine justification for individual rights allowed personalists to defend key tenets of liberal democracy against totalitarianism while keeping their rhetorical distance from liberalism itself. It also led them to assert the limited, conditional character of such rights, insofar as they could hinder the recognition of individual dignity. Meanwhile, personalism enabled critics from the political left and right to set aside their policy differences and target the common enemies of Marxism and secular liberalism.

Most importantly, the personalist idiom enabled left-leaning Catholics to unite with Protestant and Jewish socialists, among others, in an antiliberal alliance that took over much of the content of liberal-democratic theory but subtly altered its terms. These groups sought a path between relativism and absolutism in political morality—a theory that was responsive to the liberal value of tolerance without reducing democracy to formal procedures. Although they disagreed on many specifics, they agreed that secular constructions of liberalism gave rise to totalitarianism. Personalist political thought grew out of, and reinforced, a sense that modern liberalism was hopelessly and dangerously secular, a pale imitation of the authentic, theologically rich tradition of the West.

Despite its appeal to some Jewish thinkers, most notably Herberg, personalism's tendency toward declensionist narratives of Western history led many to frame it in Christian terms, even when they employed the new language of Judeo-Christianity or its older counterpart, Hebraism. Supersessionism typically anchored such claims. For example, John Macmurray's 1936 book *Creative Society*, which influenced many Americans, argued that Judaism bequeathed an emphasis on "social righteousness" but remained fundamentally "materialistic"; its "intense and continuous realism" accompanied no "doctrine of immortality," or indeed any form of "other-worldliness." Christianity, by contrast, exhibited a "universal concreteness," a self-critical "capacity to remain fully material and yet to achieve universality." This made it uniquely capable of underwriting a modern civilization based on the personalist ideal of individual dignity. For Macmurray, strengthening Western Christianity represented the only effective response to atheistic communism.[40]

Personalism could authorize intensely coercive political ideals, as well as Christian triumphalism. For many personalists, the expansive interpretation of civil liberties characteristic of liberal pluralists threatened society as surely as Marxist atheism; both embodied moral relativism. This anti-libertarian tendency characterized *The City of Man*, a lengthy 1940 manifesto issued jointly by a rather heterogeneous group that included Reinhold Niebuhr as well as Herbert Agar, Frank Aydelotte, Van Wyck Brooks, William Y. Elliott, Dorothy Canfield Fisher, Oscar Jászi, Alvin Johnson, Hans Kohn, Thomas Mann, Lewis Mumford, William Allan Neilson, and Gaetano Salvemini. Lambasting nationalist divisions and hedonistic individualism, the authors foresaw a "dictatorship of humanity" that operated through "a Universal Parliament" and a "President of Mankind" to enforce a fundamental "law for the protection of human dignity"—namely, that "everything must be within humanity, nothing against humanity, nothing outside humanity." Historically, the volume declared, Western societies had embraced "the Jewish and Christian confessions" and their offshoots. On this basis, they proposed to clamp down harshly on myriad heresies, from nudism to blasphemy to civil libertarianism, as well as any view outside Jewish or Christian auspices and all challenges to the "pillars of family and property."[41]

Like Macmurray's book, *The City of Man* also vacillated between the emerging Judeo-Christian framework and an older Christian nationalism of clearly Protestant inflection. They variously called their ideal polity "a community of persons" and "a wholly Christian society." The authors carefully delineated the failings of Protestantism's rivals, assessing how each fell short of the universal religion of the New Testament. Still, the volume predicted, in a passage not replicated in its critical assaults on Asian religions and Judaism, that "freedom-loving, justice-loving Catholics" would eventually abandon "spiritual totalitarianism" and join clear-seeing Protestants in a purely religious, nonpolitical "allegiance to the City of God." Only Christians, this formulation implied, could truly uphold the ethical tenets of the Judeo-Christian tradition. In *The City of Man*, as in many other instances, personalism reinforced the supersessionist tendencies that often shaped invocations of Judeo-Christianity.[42]

Other kinds of Judeo-Christian formulations also spread widely in the run-up to World War II, however. That compound term became increasingly visible as the debate over American participation unfolded. As early as 1939, an anthology of sacred texts identified "Judeo-Christianity" as a single religion, alongside the rest of the world's great faiths.[43] By 1941, the Judeo-Christian discourse had begun to mature, spurred by calls for the United States to join the Allies. During that fateful year leading up to Pearl Harbor, Judeo-Christian formulations exploded into mainstream parlance. The Judeo-Christian framework proved especially appealing to advocates of intervention, because it equated the European and American causes. In its typical uses, it embedded the United States in a broader "West" under ideological assault by Germany and the Soviet Union and suggested that victory for these totalitarian powers would eventually spell an end to the American way of life. The looming global conflict made Judeo-Christianity a central trope in American public discourse by 1941.

That linguistic tendency masked substantial disagreements on the nature of a democratic society, however. Did democracy require substantive theological commitments? Or did it find its source in religious tolerance instead? Many World War II–era commentators followed an intermediate path between these exceptionalist and pluralist views, arguing that tolerance itself flowed from Judeo-Christian sources. Throughout 1941, as more and more Americans linked Judaism and Christianity with democracy in the cause of intervention, they often glossed over questions about the meanings of those terms. Figures of widely divergent persuasions could agree with the Congregational minister John Walter Houck's declaration that "the Judeo-Christian heritage of faith" constituted "the foundation of all our freedom and liberty in America."[44]

With American intervention not yet assured, many Jewish leaders offered Judeo-Christian formulations that clearly centered on tolerance. In August 1941, for example, Hyman J. Schachtel identified the Allied cause with "the triumph of the Judaeo-Christian traditions of the Western World." Shortly thereafter, Roger W. Straus declared that Hitler challenged "the very basis of the Judaeo-Christian tradition." Similarly, in recommending Abba Hillel Silver's 1941 book *The World Crisis and Jewish Survival*, the Book of the Month Club reiterated Silver's contention that German Jews were persecuted because "they stand as symbolic representatives of the Judaeo-Christian religious tradition, which the Nazis rightly regard as the enemy and antithesis of everything they represent." On December 6, the day before Japanese bombs rained down on Pearl Harbor, Israel Goldstein called the Bible "the source book of Western civilization."[45]

Many Protestant commentators linked Judeo-Christian principles to democracy in a similar manner. In March 1941, the NCCJ's Clinchy argued that Americans came from all the "Old World countries" and "worship[ped] at the altars of all the branches of the Judaeo-Christian tradition." Still, Clinchy asserted, "the foundations of America are spiritual—religious convictions about the dignity of man and his natural rights because he is a creature of God." Like many Jewish commentators, Clinchy argued that attacks on Jews, whether at home or abroad, represented the entering wedge for a broader attack on Christians. Meanwhile, the journal *Protestant Digest* dedicated itself to "the democratic ideal . . . implicit in the Judeo-Christian tradition," in this case by issuing a special publication that countered common anti-Semitic charges.[46]

Other Protestant paeans to Judeo-Christianity in 1941 seemed to suggest a more substantive role for faith commitments in a democracy. The *New York Times* reported that the chemist Harold C. Urey, a Nobel laureate who grew up in the Church of the Brethren, argued at a conference that "the fundamental basis for our way of life is to be found in the Judeo-Christian tradition, which in turn is the mother of democracy." (A Hindu participant, Howard University's Haridas T. Muzumdar, charged Urey with "spiritual fascism or totalitarianism.") Several months later, New York's Episcopalian mayor, Fiorello La Guardia, encouraged all of the city's ministers to sermonize from an outline he provided, calling freedom "the political projection of a religious idea founded in faith in the fatherhood of God and the brotherhood of man."[47]

Catholic responses to these Protestant statements on the religious basis of democracy varied substantially. The influential Catholic journalist Thomas F. Woodlock thought Protestants aimed to impose by force a "religion of democracy" that identified all historic faiths as variants of a suspiciously Protestant "common creed," centered on the existence of divine purpose in the world. By contrast, the Notre Dame philosopher Francis E. McMahon praised Protestant attempts to find a middle way between "the Scylla of an anarchistic liberalism and the Charybdis of totalitarianism," despite the "sloppy thinking" that underlay syncretistic versions of that project. Their statements at least "preserved (and developed) one great truth of the Judeo-Christian heritage, namely, the dignity of the human person," McMahon reasoned.[48]

Still, Catholics were far less likely than Protestants to frame their political ideals in Judeo-Christian terms. At times, they mentioned Judaism and Christianity in the same breath while omitting the hyphen. For instance, in an August 1941 speech before the Williamstown Institute of Human Relations, Carlton Hayes insisted that the West faced an all-determining choice between "the theistic basis of values as taught by Judaism and Christianity" and "the individualistic or selfish basis of values, as incorporated in the nationalistic doctrine of the Nazis." But elsewhere, as in his influential 1941 book *A Generation of Materialism, 1871–1900*, Hayes called for recapturing the West's "historic Christian roots." On the eve of World War II, a veritable chorus of Catholic leaders followed Hayes in emphasizing the twin threats that secularism and totalitarianism posed to Christianity, and thereby to democracy and Western civilization. The bishop of Erie, John Mark Gannon, discerned "an all-out struggle between modern paganism and Christianity": "On the one side are grouped the unbelievers under the banner of secularism, and on the other side, the children of God under the banner of Jesus Christ." Such starkly

Christian rhetoric was the norm in Catholic circles during the early 1940s, and the occasional uses of Judeo-Christian formulations by Hayes and other liberal Catholics constituted the exception to the rule.[49]

Although a wide range of views on the relationship between religion and democracy still circulated in 1941, the Judeo-Christian exceptionalist claim—that only Protestantism, Catholicism, and Judaism possessed the resources to serve as cultural foundations for democracy—could increasingly be heard amid the jumble of Judeo-Christian rhetoric that burst forth that year. Two collective volumes published in 1941 reveal both the complex, charged ideological struggles that underlay wartime invocations of national unity and the growing impetus toward Judeo-Christian exceptionalism in that era, even among strong advocates of interfaith harmony.

Historians often use the first of these books, which was coauthored by three NCCJ stalwarts (Louis Finkelstein, J. Elliot Ross, and William Adams Brown) and published under that group's auspices, to symbolize the World War II generation's embrace of religious pluralism. In fact, however, the book tended to advance the cause of Judeo-Christian exceptionalism—without invoking the term "Judeo-Christian" itself—through its tripartite structure and its very title, *The Religions of Democracy: Judaism, Catholicism, Protestantism in Creed and Life*. The book's preface, by NCCJ secretary Robert A. Ashworth, filled in the outlines of Judeo-Christian exceptionalism. Arguing that religion underpinned democracy and that atheism led to totalitarianism, Ashworth insisted that the First Amendment demanded only neutrality between competing faiths and that religious liberty should not protect actions and utterances that would "offend the consciences" of the pious majority. And two of the three main authors offered versions of exceptionalism, although not necessarily in Judeo-Christian terms.[50]

Ashworth's preface offered the clearest rendering of Judeo-Christian exceptionalism. America's Protestant, Catholic, and Jewish citizens, he declared, all "agreed that, to be permanent, democracy requires the support of religious sanctions." Meanwhile, Ashworth argued that freedom of conscience did not extend to "what is offensive to the consciences of a great many others." Ashworth held that the Constitution allowed a ban on, for example, processions by the Doukhobors, a pacifist sect that rejected state authority. Finally, Ashworth described the struggle between democracy and totalitarianism as the reflection of a deeper conflict between religion and atheism in which members of the Judeo-Christian faiths should all take the same side. "Standing aloof and apart, and mistrusting one another," wrote Ashworth, "Jews, Catholics and Protestants in Europe have been victims of pagan, totalitarian forces." Their American counterparts would have to muster the "mutual respect and appreciation" needed to sustain "each other's and their common rights." In all of these regards, Ashworth's remarks prefigured the mature postwar discourse of Judeo-Christian exceptionalism.[51]

J. Elliot Ross, the Catholic contributor to *The Religions of Democracy*, spoke broadly of belief in God as the foundation of democracy, but he clearly meant the God of Judaism and Christianity. Ross also sounded exceptionalist themes, singling out secular education as a uniquely potent threat to democracy. A population trained in secular schools, he wrote, would reject God, his laws, and the rights they established: "Citizens, in the eyes of such an unbelieving majority, will have *no rights*, but only privileges which the State graciously grants and which at its whim it may revoke." For Ross, as for Hayes, the locus of ultimate authority and loyalty—God or the state—truly mattered, not the distribution of political power. In fact, said Ross, a dictator could follow the theistic principles that democracy requires. "Anything which undermines belief in God," Ross concluded, "endangers human liberty; and anything which tends to confirm belief in the God of Abraham, Isaac and Jacob strengthens the possession of human liberty." Fortunately, according to Ross, the First Amendment prohibited "the subjection of the Church, or religion, by the State" and "its confinement to the sacristy."[52]

The Jewish contributor, Louis Finkelstein, also stressed the importance of substantive religious commitments. In *The Religions of Democracy* and a second 1941 volume, *Faith for Today*, Finkelstein offered an unusual version of exceptionalism that included Islam alongside Judaism and Christianity. Only these three "monotheistic faiths," rooted in the teachings of the Hebrew prophets, could support "Western, Anglo-Saxon democracy," wrote Finkelstein. Long before the Greeks, he explained, the Hebrew prophets had inaugurated the democratic tradition by defining "all human beings as equal persons, clothed by their Creator with certain rights and dignities." According to Finkelstein, only the "traditional religions," which advanced this ancient ethical ideal, could preserve religion and democracy, and then only by joining hands against secularism. "No religious tradition will survive if the adherents of any considerable denomination become a focus for anti-religious propaganda," he wrote; it was crucial "for every faith to help preserve all faiths.[53]

Many of the contributors to *Faith for Today* framed exceptionalism in more familiar, Judeo-Christian terms. Gerald Walsh, the Catholic participant, joined Ross in stressing the divine source of political rights. "We do not believe that a majority, however big, can give us freedom of speech, freedom of press, freedom of assembly, freedom of religion," he wrote, "because if we believed that we should have to believe that the same majority could take away those rights." There was only one real antidote to totalitarianism, namely, "faith in an Omnipotent Creator Who endowed human nature with rights that no human power can take away and with duties that no human authority can destroy." Through "free and rational discussion and debate," Walsh thought, even nonbelievers would come to agree with Catholics, "orthodox Protestants," and "the Jewish tradition" that Judeo-Christianity offered the only possible foundation for political authority and individual rights.[54]

The popular lecturer and radio commentator Stanley High also endorsed Judeo-Christian exceptionalism in *Faith for Today*. Echoing Hayes's view of "Hitlerism" as a new religion, rooted in the worship of Germany as God and Hitler as Christ, High argued that the Nazis were more concerned with eradicating Christianity than with "the purging of the Jews." The proper response for Westerners was to rediscover "the special genius of our faith." The civilization that nourished democracy, wrote High, had

> drawn its seeds and nurture from religious sources. They have been drawn from the Decalogue, from the ninety-first Psalm and the fifty-fifth chapter of Isaiah, from Amos, Hosea, and Micah, from Jesus, from Christmas, Good Friday, and Easter, from the Sermon on the Mount and the Lord's Prayer, from the eleventh chapter of Hebrews and the thirteenth chapter of First Corinthians. All these are not merely a part of the tradition and the literature of Western civilization. Insofar as the West is civilized they *are* civilization.

Although the three major American religions diverged in "the area of personal ministration," according to High, one could discern a common ethical thread, where "at the point of social conduct and social consequences these three great faiths converge."[55]

Although exceptionalist theories figured prominently in *Faith for Today*, other chapters announced a pluralist vision of democracy grounded in tolerance and inclusion. The book, subtitled *Five Faiths Look at the World*, included not only the Catholic Walsh and the Jewish Finkelstein but also two Protestants of different "faiths"—High and the Methodist minister and journalist Frank Kingdon—and a Hindu, Swami Nikhilananda. Based on a series of Town Hall lectures, *Faith for Today* featured a breezy, inviting introduction from Town Hall president George V. Denny Jr. Readers, said Denny, would find in the book "some common denominators for a faith for today, to which you must add your own personal convictions and preferences as you choose that religious way best suited to your own spiritual needs." Within broad parameters, they could mix and match as they saw fit. "We want to believe," Denny imagined a Town Hall audience member imploring, but we "are bewildered by creeds, dogmas, and doctrines" and need "some common denominators that will renew our faith in religion."[56]

Meanwhile, Kingdon and Nikhilananda used their chapters to stress the diversity and equality of all the world's religions, large and small. Portraying Western history as an "adventure of emancipation," driven by "humanity's striving after a free life," Kingdon held that "God beats a unique path to every man's house and enters each heart by a private door." For his part, he meant by "God" simply "th[e] Best that life can be." Nikhilananda, meanwhile, rooted democracy in a perception—shared, he asserted, by all of the major faiths—of the common divinity and ultimate unity of all life forms. Like many exceptionalists, he denied that morality could exist without belief in God and identified the moral law as "the steel-frame foundation of spiritual life." Yet to Nikhilananda, this moral law was neither an exclusive possession of the Judeo-Christian faiths nor the philosophical foundation of democracy. Instead, he rooted democratic freedoms in "positive reverence for the ideals of other religions," Judeo-Christian and otherwise. Although he traced morality to religious belief, then, Nikhilananda equated democracy with an embrace of those who expressed their faith differently, not specific professions of belief in a law-giving God.[57]

*

As the contributions to these 1941 volumes suggest, the loose consensus that began to form around the idea of a "Judeo-Christian tradition" in the late 1930s and early 1940s masked profound and deeply political divisions regarding the content of the Judeo-Christian heritage and its relation to democratic theory. Although World War II–era purveyors of Judeo-Christian formulations tended to agree upon the existence of some fundamental link between the Judeo-Christian tradition and American democracy, they differed in their understandings of what democracy entailed and exactly how the Judeo-Christian tradition sustained it. The competing Judeo-Christian formulations that emerged during this period thus served to advance distinctive and largely preexisting conceptions of democracy.

At the same time, the new language also began to place new boundaries on American political discourse. By the late 1940s, for example, few besides conservative evangelicals would insist that only Christians, let alone Protestants or Catholics only, could be good democrats. That view came to seem needlessly controversial or hurtful, although the sentiment itself continued to lie just below the surface of an increasingly ecumenical public conversation. At the other end of the spectrum, the newfound popularity of the term "Judeo-Christian" increasingly led pluralists to attach that adjective to their pluralistic vision, using it as a shorthand for "tolerance."

As old debates were relocated onto new linguistic terrain, however, the competing political theories began to take firmer shape, as the fight for democracy led Americans to think more carefully about what that political system entailed. The disputes of the World War II era, muted by a shared commitment to defeating fascism, would pave the way for postwar struggles over the source of individual rights, the proper relationship between church and state, the resources and failings of political liberalism, the meaning and impact of secularism, the place of science in a democracy, the problem of toleration in a pluralistic society, and the similarities and differences between the Protestant, Catholic, and Jewish traditions.

PART TWO

Secularism and the Redefinition of Democracy

The Flowering of a Discourse

DEFENDING DEMOCRACY IN WARTIME AMERICA, 1942–1945

Following Pearl Harbor, Judeo-Christian language became central to American public discourse. It now made sense to most Americans when a Houston rabbi identified "the Judaeo-Christian tradition" and "Hitler" as opposing ways of life, rooted in religion and paganism, that had faced off since ancient Rome. Contributors to a 1943 essay contest for women "agreed that the foundation of a lasting peace must be the Judeo-Christian precept of the Brotherhood of Man and the Fatherhood of God." For a growing number of Americans, the phrase "Judeo-Christian tradition" captured their deepest spiritual, ethical, and political commitments. Some Judeo-Christian formulations were humorous; others bordered on the absurd. Many betrayed an empty, sloganeering quality. But one thing was certain: America's Judeo-Christian tradition had arrived.[1]

Underneath this apparent consensus, however, lurked profound disagreements over the intellectual content and political implications of the Judeo-Christian tradition. By 1943, one observer noted, religion's political role provoked intense controversy: "Is it essential to democracy that man be conceived as fashioned in the divine image, or is the philosophy of the Enlightenment with its exaltation of man in his own right a sufficient basis for a democratic faith?" As we have seen, this "crisis of democratic theory" began among leading intellectuals in the late 1930s. During the war, however, the preoccupation with democracy's cultural roots shaped public discourse much more broadly, fueling bitter, freewheeling disputes.[2]

The wartime proliferation of Judeo-Christian theories of democracy posed distinctive challenges to American Protestants, Catholics, Jews, and nonbelievers. Protestants, continuing a trend of the late 1930s, increasingly turned against secularism, appreciating Catholic critiques even as they feared

Catholic political ambitions. Meanwhile, a number of liberal Catholics reached out to Protestant critics of secularization, while seeking middle ground between the Church's support for church-state fusion in contexts such as Spain and what they considered overly licentious understandings of religious liberty in the United States. As many Christians converged on the view that democracy required Judeo-Christian faith, the much smaller groups of religious and secular Jews and nonbelievers fought charges that their heterodoxy and strict separationism endangered democracy.

In each of these contexts, the war fueled conceptual innovations, including the spread of Judeo-Christian formulations. Together, the antifascist campaign and the language of Judeo-Christianity substantially reshaped interfaith relations and the broader terrain of cultural controversy in the United States. But they hardly quelled the long-standing tensions over religion's role in American public culture. Indeed, those tensions flared, as disputants charged one another with aiding the enemy.

Silences and Meanings

Not all commentators embraced the new Judeo-Christian discourse. Indeed, the term raised deep suspicions among many it aimed to include. To most Catholics, Judeo-Christian formulations challenged their claim to universal truth and portended attempts at theological synthesis. Many Jews remained wary, too. Doubting that Christians would set aside what one Protestant called the greatest obstacle to cross-confessional amity—namely, "the Cross"—they saw supersessionism, forced assimilation, or threats to religious liberty behind Judeo-Christian rhetoric. Meanwhile, many Americans of all varieties thought the new discourse overemphasized similarities and ignored equally vital divergences, as well as power differentials.[3]

For these reasons, among others, many wartime commentators employed ecumenical, "tri-faith" conceptions of American identity but not Judeo-Christian language. They identified Jews, Catholics, and Protestants as good Americans without placing them under a single Judeo-Christian umbrella. In the military, for example, officials schooled soldiers in the tri-faith model. (The war also gave that model its first martyrs: the "Four Chaplains" of the *Dorchester*, said to have given their life vests to the enlisted men before going down with the ship, praying together in English, Latin, and Hebrew as they sank beneath the waves.) Yet these leaders rarely used Judeo-Christian terminology. They needed cross-confessional peace, not a theory of democracy or Western civilization. For their purpose, the triad "Protestant-Catholic-Jew" sufficed, and generated far less controversy. Moreover, the military called its

Jewish soldiers "Hebrew" until 1954. Thus, the services implemented a tri-faith understanding without dipping into the well of Judeo-Christianity.[4]

More surprisingly, given many scholars' belief that Jews invented the Judeo-Christian tradition, New York's liberal rabbis—including Stephen S. Wise and Louis I. Newman, who had helped popularize the language of Judeo-Christianity—jumped off that bandwagon after Pearl Harbor. The reasons remain unclear, but the timing suggests the term served an instrumental cause: convincing American Christians to defend European Jews. Still, Judeo-Christian rhetoric might have proven useful as Jewish leaders continued to fight anti-Semitism at home. Outside cosmopolitan New York, figures such as Hyman J. Schachtel sometimes invoked Judeo-Christianity. Yet when Wise edited a 1943 volume, *Never Again! Ten Years of Hitler*, only one of fifty-two contributors (a Unitarian) used Judeo-Christian language. Perhaps recognizing the power of Judeo-Christian exceptionalism, figures such as Wise and Newman avoided Judeo-Christian language while advancing a tri-faith vision rooted in religious tolerance.[5]

Our histories would also lead us to expect Judeo-Christian formulations in publications of the National Conference of Christians and Jews. Yet few appear there, or in the NCCJ's archives. "Tri-faith," "interfaith," and "brotherhood" abound in NCCJ literature and posters, but not Judeo-Christian terminology. Of those uses, moreover, almost all came from director Everett R. Clinchy, who occasionally used Judeo-Christian rhetoric in speeches arguing that anti-Semitism directly threatened Christians as well as Jews. Here, the NCCJ's need to assuage Catholic fears of theological syncretism—indeed, theological discussion of any kind—likely shaped its decision to insulate a tri-faith vision from Judeo-Christian language. The tri-faith model did not require Judeo-Christian rhetoric, which held potentially dangerous connotations.[6]

That language spread widely nonetheless. As anti-Semitism surged at home, some Jewish leaders and interfaith activists used Judeo-Christian formulations to emphasize the self-destructive character of Christian attacks on Jews. And both Hitler's atrocities and the demands of wartime cooperation led a growing number of Christians to verbally include their Jewish neighbors. Meanwhile, Judeo-Christian constructions of Western civilization appealed to many commentators who sought to align the United States with Europe—especially, though hardly exclusively, those suspicious of secular worldviews.

As before, commentators assigned disparate values to the Judeo-Christian tradition. Most of them used vague formulations ("the rights of individuals and the responsibilities of individuals to society") or lists ("dedication to God, the struggle for a kindly world, respect for personality, [and] a yearning for righteousness") that emphasized unity at the expense of precision. But some attached the new term to very specific notions of democracy, ranging from the exceptionalist assertion of the uniquely democratic character of America's three major faiths to an open-ended embrace of all beliefs, including atheism. The pluralist and exceptionalist views of democracy developed in the 1920s and 1930s could each be repackaged in Judeo-Christian language—often with little change to their content. And by 1945, these polar positions drew an increasing number of adherents.[7]

Judeo-Christian exceptionalism appealed to Protestants worried about secularism—including many of those influenced by theological neo-orthodoxy—as well as some liberal Catholics and a small number of Jews. Its Catholic adherents were among those most concerned to distance the Church from fascism, while its Protestant and Jewish supporters were often turning away from an engagement with Marxism. Judeo-Christian rhetoric allowed these figures to choose American democracy over totalitarianism without softening their critique of contemporary forms of political and theological liberalism.

This view strongly implied that religious believers made better democrats than did nonbelievers. Moreover, most Judeo-Christian exceptionalists also questioned, at least implicitly, the loyalty of those favoring political secularity—especially secular public education. Such implications were not lost on the many Jews, liberal Protestants, and naturalists who embraced a pluralistic theory of democracy rooted in free discussion and tolerance. During World War II, some of these figures adopted the language of Judeo-Christianity as a shorthand for the broader project of inclusion. The "Judeo-Christian tradition" thus became a politically multivalent concept as it spread through American public discourse.

Even Judeo-Christian exceptionalism itself could take many forms. The war years witnessed much soul-searching about the ideational content of democracy and how it overlapped with Protestantism, Catholicism, and Judaism. As the discussion proceeded, it increasingly centered on what came to be called "human rights." And those rights were frequently defined in personalist terms, as granted by God, not the state. Pluralists, when they spoke of rights, usually remained agnostic on their ultimate source. What mattered was that they found support in community norms and expression in public policies. But to many exceptionalists, this approach meant that the state itself granted rights to its citizens. And what the state granted, it could take away. For exceptionalists, rights could trump state power only if they came from God and rested on the divinely created status of individuals.

The writings of Jacques Maritain and other personalists helped many exceptionalists answer the pressing questions of what the Judeo-Christian faiths shared and how they sustained democracy by identifying the dignity of the person as a transcendent standard. Framed as a principle of political morality rather than theology, the personalist emphasis on human dignity offered fertile ground for a cross-confessional alliance against secularism. As personalists frequently argued, only in their capacity as God's children were all individuals equal.

Personalism attracted exceptionalists with divergent economic and social views. It allowed left-leaning religious thinkers to defend democracy and seek economic justice without embracing either secular liberalism or Marxism. More conservative thinkers found in personalism a theistic analogue to liberal individualism, one that centered on individual liberties but defined the true essence of human freedom as spiritual, not material. For all of these thinkers, personalism offered strong religious grounds for opposing fascism. To them, totalitarianism violated God's plan by subordinating the individual to society. "Communists and fascists alike assert that only communities know the truth and that it reveals itself only in a collective conflict," wrote the Russian philosopher Nikolai Berdyaev, while noting that he still embraced Marxism's "social demands."[8]

Grounding democracy in the divinely ordained worth and equality of all persons gave distinctive meanings to key political concepts such as "rights." Pluralists often rested their understanding of rights on the assumption that the truth would win out in free and open debate, such that public discussion offered the best way of aligning policies with the public good. Many contended that absolute truth claims threatened democracy by short-circuiting the open-ended exchange of opinions on which it rested. Exceptionalists, however, insisted that such critical discourse itself could undermine democracy by challenging its basic postulates, namely, the God-given nature of rights and the value of the individual as a child of God. To them, citizens needed to recognize that the concept of natural rights, so central to Western political thought, entailed the existence of God as the author of those rights. To deny the absolute value of the individual was to remove the only effective check on the growth of the totalitarian state.

Personalism also offered an alternative understanding of freedom. Rejecting the open-ended freedom of liberals—whether they defined such freedom negatively as the absence of restraints on action or positively as the ability to actually carry out such action—most personalists viewed freedom as inseparable from a higher spiritual authority. In their view, freedom required strong communal norms and corresponding truth claims. Absent these anchors, they believed, procedural guarantees of unfettered public expression would produce an unfree society by dissolving all norms and truths. Indeed, majority rule, unchecked by a firm commitment to human dignity, would devolve into the tyranny of the majority, with the total state claiming to speak for the people.

Personalists often argued that human beings were incurably religious; they always worshipped something. The impossibility of genuine nonbelief left two options: the worship of God or the "deification" of the people, leading inexorably to the deification of the state. Thus, the prevailing views of the human person and the source of rights offered a surer test of a country's democratic character than, say, its protection of dissent—or even its provision of voting rights. Personalists defined democracy primarily in terms of philosophical content, not procedures, policies, or structures. Ultimately, they believed, all policies and institutions reflected underlying ideas.

Protestants and the Challenge of Secularization

"Can Protestantism Win America?" asked *Christian Century* editor Charles Clayton Morrison in a series of postwar articles. By then, Morrison and a growing number of his Protestant counterparts feared the answer was no. Catholics, they believed, were far better equipped than Protestants to ward off secularism. Indeed, Catholics had long charged that features they considered intrinsic to Protestantism, including its emphasis on individual judgment; its institutional fragmentation, decentralization, and denominationalism; and its alliances with nation-states and social scientists, encouraged secularism. Could Protestantism be remade to more effectively combat both secularism and the Catholic alternative? Could it offer something like Catholicism's absolute truths? During the war, growing concerns about Protestantism's weakness in a two-front battle against "Romanism and secularism" helped fuel ecumenical initiatives, the spread of neo-orthodoxy, a campaign to re-Christianize the universities, and changing views of church-state relations.[9]

Of course, many Protestants trod familiar paths. Fundamentalists and other theological conservatives flatly rejected Judeo-Christian language and the tri-faith vision. And many theological liberals and modernists continued to identify religious tolerance as democracy's core and to fear Catholicism far more than secularism. But two other approaches to questions of religion and politics gained ground within the Protestant mainstream. Figures from more evangelical (and often missionary) backgrounds tended to fear secularism and Catholicism equally. Thinkers such as Princeton Theological Seminary's John A. Mackay and the missionary leader M. Searle Bates hoped to strengthen the country's religious fiber while maintaining a sharp church-state divide. A second group, fearing secularism more than Catholicism, increasingly rejected secular public education and strict separationism. This camp included Reinhold Niebuhr and other advocates of neo-orthodoxy, or "Christian realism," but also the progressive Methodist F. Ernest Johnson, the Congregationalist educator Luther A. Weigle, and the Episcopalian political theorist John H. Hallowell, among others. Impressed by the Church's stands against both economic injustice and secularism, these figures began to seek points of overlap with Catholic teachings.[10]

Much of the debate among Protestants centered on religion in education, which opened onto the larger issue of church-state relations. A growing number of Protestants agreed with Catholics that secular schooling would eradicate religion by teaching students to understand the world without any reference to God. But tough questions remained: What kind of religion could the schools in a diverse democracy teach? How should public institutions treat nonbelievers? And how, practically and legally, could Americans create a system of religiously grounded education? Judeo-Christian exceptionalism helped to answer all of these questions by asserting that Americans had historically adhered to three closely related faiths, that these faiths uniquely underpinned democracy, and that the Constitution and other national institutions aimed to promote them.

Critics of secularism devoted considerable attention to higher education, where the 1940s brought an effort by Protestant educators to reground the collegiate curriculum in religion. Although these figures generally looked to Christianity in particular, some also employed Judeo-Christian formulations. Yale's Clarence Prouty Shedd sought to anchor the entire curriculum in "the Hebrew-Christian faith"; another group deemed American democracy "unintelligible apart from the Judeo-Christian tradition." The latter group allowed that they proposed "a form of sectarianism," since "Judaism and Christianity are preferred to, let us say, Buddhism." Yet such faiths were "a negligible influence among us," they continued; any criticism would likely come from militant secularizers. Like Catholics, such Protestants tended to claim educational institutions "cannot be neutral" in religious matters and needed to choose between Judeo-Christianity and idolatry.[11]

The question of religion in public schools raised both constitutional and practical issues. Luther A. Weigle, Shedd's colleague and longtime dean at Yale Divinity School, said secular education violated "the religious liberty of that vast majority of American citizens . . . for whom religion is an essential part of education." Although schools should exempt dissenters from religious activities, Weigle argued, catering to "the pagan few" would "coerce the conscience of the many." Because Americans shared a "basic, elemental faith

which is deeper and more fundamental than any of religion's institutional
or sectarian forms," Weigle continued, church-state separation squared with
a recognition of God's sovereignty over nations. The schools should "manifest reverence for God and respect for religious beliefs," and teachers had
"no right either tacitly to suggest or actually to teach secularism or irreligion." Dismissing practical difficulties that plagued attempts to teach religion,
Weigle proposed that "a careful selection of materials, making use of Catholic
and Jewish as well as Protestant versions of the Scriptures," would rid Bible
training of sectarianism and render it "expressive of our common faith." To
do otherwise was to advance "the sectarianism of atheism or irreligion." A
Weigle-chaired committee advocating Bible training castigated Protestants
for aiding "the new paganism" and strengthening the modern tendency "to
worship the State." It asserted a foundational "right of the citizen to hold the
state itself responsible to the moral law and to God."[12]

While many Protestant critics lambasted the churches' friendliness to
secular education, others thought their individualism aided secularism. Economic progressives often differentiated Judeo-Christian conceptions of freedom and democracy from the possessive, materialistic individualism that in
their view dominated the liberal tradition. F. Ernest Johnson, who worked
alongside John Dewey and his fellow naturalists at Columbia's Teachers College, dismissed his secular colleagues' conviction that tolerance anchored
democracy and aimed to reinvigorate the Social Gospel through a "progressive desecularizing of the mind." Writing in Niebuhr's *Christianity and Crisis*,
Johnson argued that what his contemporaries called "democracy" was merely
a transposition of economic individualism and laissez-faire. Protestantism,
too, had "fallen in with the secular ethic of our age, with its nominalistic emphasis on the ultimacy of the single, private individual" and principle of "inalienable *private* rights," whereas Catholics clearly separated "the Christian
and the capitalist ethic." As a result, fascists were "filling the spiritual void in
men's souls left by an atomistic type of democracy that is powerless to create
organic fellowship." A genuine democracy, wrote Johnson, viewed individuals through their "membership in a corporate spiritual fellowship." He looked
back to medieval Europe, with its "inclusive and unifying moral sanctions
over the whole of man's activities," including economic life.[13]

Johnson, the longtime executive director of the Federal Council of
Churches' Department of Research and Education and the president of the
Religious Education Association from 1944 to 1946, illustrates how criticiz-
ing individualism could turn Protestants away from inherited conceptions
of religious liberty. In a 1944 *Christendom* article, Johnson agreed with John
Courtney Murray and other liberal Catholics that religious liberty was simply

"an aspect of political liberty"; there was "no *sui generis* category of religious liberty which the state can be asked to respect." Like Murray, Johnson empha- sized the qualifier "consistent with public order and public morals" attached to statements of religious liberty and favored significant limits on religious expression. He thus deplored the Supreme Court's 1944 decision that Jeho- vah's Witnesses could proselytize freely. Johnson believed states should up- hold communal beliefs, whether those were Catholic, as in Latin America, or Judeo-Christian, as in the United States.[14]

Yet Johnson, again like Murray, advocated religious liberty on pruden- tial grounds. Denying that the concept of rights had any place in Christian thought, he rooted religious liberty "in *agape*—in the constraint of divine love impregnating the community" and creating a "spiritual obligation . . . to allow every other person a maximum of authentic religious experience." A revelation, he continued, could "acquire finality" only by "fully authenticating itself" in the minds of freely willing believers. In short, the churches could seek converts only in the civil sphere, through voluntaristic means. Johnson thus retained, for policy purposes, a negative definition of liberty as freedom from authority, so long as religious pluralism prevailed. Still, his reasoning created a theoretical opening for dialogue with Catholic theorists, whose starting point he much preferred to the radical individualism that infected both political liberalism and Protestant thought.[15]

Whereas Johnson shared with Catholics a tendency to prioritize religious communities over individuals, John H. Hallowell joined them in discerning absolute moral laws. Indeed, Hallowell identified the legal realism Johnson favored—the premise that the laws of a community should embody its values and interests—as a destructive manifestation of moral relativism. Instead, he sought to reground positive law in the natural law. Hallowell also shared with liberal Catholics such as Carlton Hayes a historical account of the rise of the modern state and the moral bankruptcy of secular liberalism, eventuating in Nazism. Over the centuries, he argued, an "integral liberalism" that recog- nized objective moral laws and defined freedom as the ability to follow them had given way to a "formal liberalism" that jettisoned moral absolutes and left human will entirely unchecked. Into the void stepped the Nazi behemoth, wrote Hallowell, and the liberals, mired in moral relativism, "had no alterna- tive but to accept the arena of force as the final arbiter of 'right' and 'justice.'"[16]

Hallowell was one of many Protestants influenced by Reinhold Niebuhr's thinking during World War II, when he published both his starkest statement of Judeo-Christian exceptionalism and his major contribution to democratic theory. In the former, a 1942 *Fortune* article, Niebuhr argued that Americans could preserve democracy only by recapturing "the Hebraic-Christian tradition, which underlies our Western culture." Meanwhile, Niebuhr's 1944 classic *The Children of Light and the Children of Darkness* opened by calling Christianity's conception of the human person "more adequate for the development of a democratic society than either the optimism with which democracy has become historically associated or the moral cynicism" of the totalitarians. Niebuhr warned his readers that no society could fully embody religious ideals, and indeed anchored democracy in tolerance and humility rather than more substantive theological claims. Yet he insisted that only genuine religion provided the "constant fount of humility" on which democracy's self-limiting system of power relations rested. Secular worldviews, according to Niebuhr, produced either the fatuous optimism of the Enlightenment or the frank materialism of a Hitler or Stalin. And theological liberalism was merely a capitulation to secular thinking. After the war, Niebuhr and his allies would extend this critique of secularism more fully into the contested domains of education and church-state relations.[17]

For their part, mainstream Protestants with evangelical and missionary sensibilities walked a different line between Catholicism and secularism. Although they deemed religion central to American democracy, they reiterated classic Protestant arguments about state neutrality—and the Catholic threat. Some said religion was so important that it could not become entangled with partisan politics. Others argued that religion could not perform its cultural tasks without full freedom of expression. Still others emphasized the practical impossibility of finding a single religious outlook shared by all or even most Americans. Whatever the reasoning, these Protestants identified the maintenance of democracy's Judeo-Christian cultural foundation as a task for the churches, not the state. They urged Protestants to counter both secularizing tendencies and Catholic attempts to breach the church-state barrier.

John A. Mackay combined an exceptionalist theory of democracy with strict separationism in this manner. Mackay lambasted Catholicism as well as secularism, arguing that a religiously vital culture would emerge from religious competition, not state-sponsored religious education. At long last, Mackay wrote in *Heritage and Destiny* (1943), "Christians and Jews realize[d] that what is really at stake in the world is the Hebrew-Christian tradition," and thus stood "in mutual sympathy as they have not done for two thousand years." He urged them to build on that achievement by recovering ancient Israel's "theocratic principle," which defined the life of a people as a divine "vocation" centered on service to God. "The basis of true democracy is still, and will continue to be, theocracy," he declared. Yet Mackay differentiated the principle of theocracy, under which a nation "recognizes its dependence upon God and its responsibility towards God," from the institution of a state church.

The latter was merely one way to implement the theocratic principle, and not always the best choice. In the United States, Mackay strongly opposed state support for religious institutions and saw a marked "upsurge of clerical pretension" among Catholics that portended "the crucifixion of liberty, political fascism, social decadence, revolutionary violence, and anti-clerical revolt."[18]

Many Protestants agreed with Mackay that the campaign against secularism should take place in the civic realm. M. Searle Bates's widely read *Religious Liberty: An Inquiry* (1945), written for the Federal Council of Churches and other mainstream groups, offered the traditional Protestant church-state arguments. Bates, a Disciples of Christ missionary and a professor of history at China's Nanjing University, acknowledged that strict separation frequently fueled "the secularization of the community." But mixing religion and politics was even more dangerous, since the former was properly "voluntary and spiritual" and the latter intrinsically "coercive and secular." Bates challenged Johnson's assertion that Americans shared a common core of religion that could be taught in schools; there were, he said, innumerable disagreements within the shared Judeo-Christian framework. He likewise rejected Catholic calls for public funding of parochial schools. Despite the Church's laudable "service . . . in protecting liberty against state absolutisms," he declared, the "authoritarianism" of Catholic thought "inclines toward a Catholic totalitarianism." Bates, like Mackay, thought the opposing threats of secularism and Catholicism magnified the need for church-state separation.[19]

Still, much had changed in the minds of even these Protestants. Growing fears of cultural secularization brought them closer in spirit, if not strategy, to Catholic critics of godless education and modern liberalism. Few followed Johnson in defining religious liberty as a positive freedom rooted in communal norms, but leading Protestants exhibited a growing respect for Catholics' vigorous antisecularism. These figures questioned the assumption that secular thought and institutions—above all, the social sciences—could buttress religious convictions. The developments of the 1930s and 1940s unsettled long-standing patterns of Protestant thinking about the relationships between the individual conscience, moral law, and public institutions. As the language of Judeo-Christianity spread, it increasingly signaled to Protestants a theologically grounded, exceptionalist understanding of democracy, though one that many still hoped to sustain through nonpolitical means.

Catholics and the Challenge of Pluralism

A number of prominent liberal Catholics also moved toward Judeo-Christian exceptionalism and sought to build cross-confessional ties in the face of secularism. However, they faced institutional opposition from those in the hierarchy who disliked democracy and liberalism, viewed Protestantism and Judaism as little better than paganism, and sustained a strict ban on theological discussion with non-Catholics, which was said to foster "indifferentism": the error of deeming non-Catholic faiths valid. These liberals risked formal rebuke by the hierarchy for using Judeo-Christian rhetoric or participating in interfaith organizations. Yet they persevered, hoping the Church would rethink its positions on pluralism and religious liberty to facilitate a counteroffensive against secularism. As mainstream Protestants increasingly defined themselves in opposition to Catholicism and secularism, then, liberal Catholics sought to avoid both authoritarianism and indifferentism. They did so by developing key theoretical distinctions: first between civic cooperation and theological discussion, and later between the natural law and particular religions.

Even the most politically liberal Catholic theorists rejected secularism out of hand. "We hold the atheist to be the foe of this Republic and we challenge his citizenship," declared Catholic University's rector in 1940. Yet many Catholics chafed at the Church's insistence that only Catholic doctrine could underpin political structures and its corresponding preference for church-state fusion. As perceptions of a global spiritual crisis deepened, American liberal Catholics began to argue that a broader Christianity or Judeo-Christianity could anchor a democratic culture. In any case, bracketing shared political concerns until the other three-quarters of the American population converted to Catholicism was an utterly insufficient response to the challenge of secularism and totalitarianism.[20]

Like Jewish leaders, lay Catholic commentators sometimes used Judeo-Christian formulations to hitch their wagons to Protestantism and prove their democratic bona fides.[21] Despite such phrases, however, Catholic theorists of religion and politics emphasized Protestant-Catholic relations. Most identified the West's traditional faith as Christianity, not Judeo-Christianity. Even the few liberal Catholics who used "Judeo-Christian" tended to do so interchangeably with Christian formulations. This habit implied supersessionism: the view that Judaism mattered only insofar as it had birthed Christianity. But it also reflected a practical concern for Christian unity against secularism. Catholics thought Protestant church-state theories offered no resistance to the threat they saw in secularism.

Could Catholics meet that threat by means other than converting Protestants? A number of liberal Catholics began to argue that it was more important, for now, that Protestants and Jews deepen their own faiths. The fight against totalitarianism led figures such as Carlton Hayes, Jacques Maritain, and John

Courtney Murray to urge cross-confessional cooperation in defense of religion itself, against the secularist threat. Catholics, they insisted, should align themselves with genuinely religious Protestants and Jews—namely, those who held that democracy required belief in divine authority. If Americans could not agree on this point, secularism would sweep the field and all of the faith traditions would be lost, along with democracy itself. Few of these thinkers used the term "Judeo-Christian" regularly. Yet by enabling American Catholics to accept the tri-faith model of American identity, they cleared a path for the ascension of Judeo-Christian exceptionalism. They portrayed tri-faith democracy as a legitimate expression of Catholic political ideals in the current context, if hardly the ultimate realization of the Church's spiritual mission.

One such thinker was J. Elliot Ross, a sharp critic of anti-Semitism. Ross ranked Judaism below Christianity on the scale of world religions (though above all others) and emphasized his desire "to see Jews become Catholics." But, he continued, he would much rather "see those who are racially Jews be good Jews religiously than by agnosticism lose the spiritual values of Judaism without finding those of Catholicism." Catholics could assert their own correctness, Ross explained, yet still believe that the state, like God, should tolerate "the affiliation of creatures with many different religions." Indeed, Ross urged "active, zealous membership in the synagogue" as a contribution to democracy. His Judeo-Christian exceptionalism drew theologically upright Jews into the circle of democrats, while locating atheists, theological liberals, and non-Judeo-Christians beyond the pale. Ross placed Protestantism and Judaism in the conceptual category of "religion" and clearly differentiated them from secularism.[22]

Yet such expressions often brought down the charge of indifferentism, rooted in the traditional view that all non-Catholic beliefs were equally dangerous. Theorists such as the Catholic University theologian Francis J. Connell saw interfaith activity as a distraction from the paramount need to convert Protestants and Jews to Catholicism, while sustaining their own correct belief. The nightmare scenario, for these critics, was the path of Vincent A. Brown, whose participation in the NCCJ's trio tours led him to espouse cooperation not only with Protestants and Jews but also "with upright pagans in India and China" and "even perhaps with atheists at the head of Soviet Russia, provided they are willing to agree on some fundamentals of the natural law."[23]

Carlton Hayes drew the brunt of such criticism in the early 1940s. During those years, Hayes emerged as a leading Catholic theorist of Judeo-Christian exceptionalism. In April 1942, shortly after Roosevelt appointed him ambassador to General Franco's Spain, Hayes traced Nazism to the "debasement of the spiritual values of our Judeo-Christian heritage" and urged the recovery of those values through concerted action against secularism. As part of that effort, Hayes aimed to legitimate Catholic participation in interfaith activism by denying that it involved theological discussion with non-Catholics, or any discussion whatsoever with atheists. Hayes forcefully rejected Vincent Brown's approach, insisting that interfaith work entailed cooperation on the basis of strong confessional boundaries and a shared antisecularism.[24]

Ironically, Hayes's vigorous assault on secularism generated the statements that irked critics such as Connell. Hayes and other liberal Catholics hoped to capture the linguistic banner of pluralism by charging that liberals would reduce all faiths to a single "lowest common denominator" and "pave the way for a new uniformity and thence for a totalitarian state tyranny." Hayes urged instead a vigorous "cultural and religious pluralism," meaning a strengthened "devotion to one's particular religion." He wrote, "The task is not to water down Judaism or Protestantism or Catholicism, but to make Jews better Jews, Protestants better Protestants, and Catholics better Catholics." Noting at a 1940 NCCJ seminar that Americans "differ about religion," Hayes added, "I thank God we do, and I pray that we may continue to respect differences."[25]

Keenly aware of the fine line he was walking, Hayes specified that he endorsed "*Differences*," not "*Indifference*." But he had pushed critics too far. In Connell's rendering, Hayes had essentially said, "We should strive to keep some people outside the Catholic Church. I thank God that there are men and women who reject the one true religion of Jesus Christ." For Connell, the real task was to make non-Catholics into Catholics and existing Catholics into better Catholics. Religious diversity did not change "the basic Catholic doctrine that there is only one true religion," and true charity toward others meant "striving zealously and prudently for their conversion." Connell urged Catholics to recognize that on doctrinal matters they were "narrow, intolerant, and illiberable [*sic*]."[26]

Hayes offered a twofold rebuttal. First, the NCCJ was "a civic organization" promoting "good citizenship," not a common creed. Second, civic amity was not just a moral imperative; it was prerequisite to survival. Connell failed to appreciate the threat of secularism and the need for "allies in the contemporary conflict between religion and irreligion." The Church itself would certainly fare better among practicing Protestants and Jews than among "more and worse pagans"; no religion, Catholic or otherwise, could survive in a culture that rejected religiosity wholesale. To Hayes, the biggest threat to Catholicism and democracy alike was the indifference of so many Protestants, Jews, and their lapsed compatriots to the titanic struggle between religious and materialistic interpretations of life.[27]

But Hayes and his allies needed stronger theoretical armature than the distinction between civic charity and theological discussion. They were not simply seeking intergroup amity; they wanted a specific, substantive alliance of Protestants, Catholics, and Jews sharing an understanding of democracy as a religious phenomenon. Both to win allies among sufficiently orthodox Protestant and Jewish leaders and to assuage suspicion among members of the hierarchy, these liberal Catholics had to establish two points: First, it was an objective truth, not a specific item of Catholic dogma, that rights flowed from God and that democracy would collapse unless social and political institutions actively promoted this understanding among the population. Second, Catholics could adopt this conception of democracy as an item of shared, nontheological truth—and thus the proper object of interfaith cooperation—without endangering their specifically Catholic commitments.

John Courtney Murray, above all, solidified these arguments in the 1940s. He defined an exceptionalist conception of democracy as part of the natural law, identified the natural law as a universal possession based on right reason rather than revelation, and described it as a subset of the broader body of Catholic truth. In short, Murray inscribed an exceptionalist theory of democracy in a "Catholic secular" that he offered as the basis for a tri-faith alliance against atheism and strict church-state separation.

Murray's strategy took some of its shape from the work of the French émigré philosopher Jacques Maritain in the late 1930s and early 1940s. A prominent commentator on Christianity's relationship to Judaism, a major figure in the Catholic Action movement, a widely read political theorist, an influential champion of personalism, and a leader of the Catholic antifascist forces in Europe before spending World War II in the United States, Maritain wielded considerable influence over American Catholic thought. He gained the admiration of many non-Catholics as well, especially for his frank advocacy of Judeo-Christian exceptionalism.

The relations between democracy, natural law, and interfaith cooperation had long preoccupied Maritain, a former Protestant who married a Jewish convert. He offered some of the earliest Judeo-Christian constructions in the United States, starting with his first English-language speech in 1933. During the war, Maritain insisted that the Catholic framework of natural law, discoverable through reason alone, could anchor a democracy that was both "vitally and truly Christian" and fully tolerant of other faiths. Properly understood, Maritain argued, the natural law authorized the universal human rights, including religious liberty, that defined a genuine democracy. Here was common ground on which Catholics and non-Catholics could stand against totalitarianism, without syncretism or indifferentism.[28]

Murray brought philosophical rigor to Maritain's elliptical formulations of this argument. His 1937 dissertation cleared the ground for his later work by defining the supernatural realm as a development, not a negation, of the natural world. This meant that a political order based on the natural law would be both theologically neutral and faithfully Catholic at the same time. Over the next few years, he argued that the challenge of modern secularism could be met only by a well-orchestrated combination of theological innovations and lay initiatives aimed at recovering the religious basis of social and political institutions. Thereafter, as a professor at Maryland's Woodstock College, editor of the American Jesuits' *Theological Studies*, and religion editor of *America*, Murray worked to build both the theological architecture—including a "Catholic conception of co-operation"—and a base of cultural support for a cross-confessional alliance against secular liberalism and totalitarianism. Targeting the gap between lay enthusiasm for interfaith activism and the hierarchy's resistance, Murray made available to American Catholics an approach to cooperation that clearly obeyed the stricture against theological discussion.[29]

In short, Murray crafted a specifically Catholic—or rather, Catholic secular—expression of Judeo-Christian exceptionalism. Although Murray almost never used "Judeo-Christian" and sought mainly to convince Protestants on church-state issues, he dropped the term "Christian cooperation" after his first article on cross-confessional organization and clearly included both Protestants and Jews in his typical phrase "men of good will": those who rejected political secularity and recognized the need to root democracy in natural law. More than any other Catholic theorist, Murray opened up avenues for cooperation with Protestant and Jewish critics of secularism. In the 1960s, Murray's wartime writings would inform the Church's embrace of democracy and religious freedom during the Vatican II reforms.[30]

Murray's writings backed Hayes and other interfaith activists in their struggle against critics such as Connell. He agreed on the need to push Protestants and Jews toward more traditional expressions of their faiths, "not only as a lesser evil, but as a positive value." Catholics, he argued, had a direct political stake in the religious beliefs of their fellow citizens. Although they should eschew religious pluralism as a matter of principle, in practice they should steer Protestants and Jews toward the "common human ground" of the natural law, with its "affirmation . . . of the religio-ethical bases of society." In fact, Murray argued that right-thinking Protestants and Jews already shared the tenets of the natural law, above all its recognition of the religious foundation of the social order; they simply needed to grasp the implications for church-state relations and recognize that Catholics would meet them on that shared ground. (Indeed, "no one can be invincibly ignorant of the first principles of natural law," Murray wrote: "Outside of that unity no one could stand.")[31]

By the time Murray published his famed articles on religious liberty in 1945, he could point to many signs of a thaw between Protestant and Catholic critics of secularism. His work with other liberal Catholics on the Ethics Committee of the Catholic Association for International Peace (CAIP) both reflected and promoted this growing cross-confessional alliance. The Ethics Committee provided the primary initiative for "The Pattern for Peace," guidelines for postwar reconstruction written under Murray's guidance and issued simultaneously in October 1943 by the National Catholic Welfare Conference, the Federal Council of Churches, and the Synagogue Council of America. The text of the statement, to which each group added its own prologue, declared that "not only individuals but nations, states and international society are subject to the sovereignty of God and to the moral law which comes from God." Murray called the statement "a perfectly synchronized three-front attack" on "the dismayingly strong secularist front."[32]

Many Protestants indeed responded warmly to Murray's overtures. "Catholics Will Collaborate!" exulted the *Christian Century* in January 1944, after Murray's piece on intercredal cooperation appeared in pamphlet form. Interpreting the pamphlet as a quasi-official statement, the editors—Charles Clayton Morrison, Paul Hutchinson, Winfred Ernest Garrison, and Harold E. Fey—saw in it evidence that the Church would cooperate in rebuilding "the foundations of a social order grounded on the moral law, natural and divine." All Protestants, they advised, "ought to go along with this program. Many of them have been saying the same thing for years."[33]

Still, even the most antisecular Protestants usually remained suspicious of Catholic political intentions. In February 1944, the *Christian Century* defined the Church's main aims as "security, property, power and prestige." And in August, it contended that Catholics needed to "learn how to collaborate"— although Protestants, in turn, needed to "learn how not to compromise." Deep theoretical rifts persisted as well. Statements such as M. Searle Bates's 1945 volume and Fey's "Can Catholicism Win America?" series in 1944–45 revealed the sticking point: the divergence between Protestant and Catholic views of religious liberty.[34]

Murray targeted this theoretical obstacle to cross-confessional cooperation in his celebrated 1945 articles. Lauding F. Ernest Johnson for his insight, Murray sought to wean Protestants from an "antinomian" conception of freedom they shared with religious skeptics, wherein freedom meant "sheer release, total emancipation, an indefinitely expanding spontaneity." This view, he wrote, obligated individuals and the state to define anything "sincerely experienced" as "authentic" and thus deserving of rights. It allowed a small cadre of militant atheists to hold the believing majority hostage: "One group is not free peacefully to live out its faith, because other groups are free to disturb its peace." Meanwhile, the Protestant theory abetted totalitarianism; understanding freedom as "an Absolute, over against which the authority of law can stand only as an enemy," it undermined the legitimacy of all principles. Murray instead defined freedom as "the privilege of being obedient only to reason." And reason, he continued, revealed freedom's true nature: "the freedom of the person to reach God, and eternal beatitude in God, along the ways in which God wills to be reached."[35]

Murray's 1945 articles extrapolated from the natural law a spare "natural religion," common to all of humanity, which described "the religious and moral universe, as it would be known simply to reason" without the aid of revelation. In this "purely natural order," he wrote, "there is still one true religion," comprising "the sum of truth about God and man which reason can discover from the works of God." That natural religion identified God as "a personal being, the author of all things that are, infinite in perfection, provident over the world and especially over the life of man." It also detailed "man's essential duties towards God, himself, and his neighbor." Finally, it defined religious associations as "purely voluntary in character." In short, Murray's natural religion yoked a Protestant theory of the church to Catholic understandings of freedom and moral obligation. From this starting point, he enumerated the rights and liberties of "the human person inasmuch as it is the image of God, a rational and free moral agent, destined both to the good life on earth and to a supratemporal beatitude, under the direction of the sovereignty and law of God."[36]

Although Murray's natural religion included a voluntary conception of the church, it defined freedom of conscience very differently than most Protestant theories. Because all genuine rights of conscience were actually obligations imposed by God's law, Murray argued, no conscience that rejected that law itself and "demand[ed] respect for every private fancy" was legitimate. "As over against God and the eternal order of reason which He has established for the government of His rational creatures," he wrote, "conscience has no rights, but only the duty of unlimited obedience to God's known truth and will." In short, religious error had no public standing, and its proponents could not legitimately advocate their views. The state could ban both "the propaganda of atheism or secularism" and "the practice of immorality" in any form, which for Murray included proselytizing by Jehovah's Witnesses. This exercise of power represented care or nurture, not repression: "The action of the State is really medicinal; it notifies the individual that his conscience is erroneous, and thus puts the truth within his reach."[37]

However, Murray then set aside principle and turned to prudence, where long experience in pluralistic societies suggested to him that the "evils of re-pression" often proved "greater than the evils repressed." The state, he con-tended, should "choose not to exercise its right to repress atheistic propa-ganda" and should instead assign "the defense of religion and morality" to "the pressure of the common conscience and of public opinion." Murray thus appealed to all "men of good will" to mobilize in a great cultural offensive against both liberalism and totalitarianism. Each elevated human will over divine law: liberalism divinized the individual will, rendering society "an an-archy of atoms," while totalitarianism divinized the collective will, creating "a mechanized army of slaves."[38]

Murray concluded that Catholics, not Protestants, had always been the true champions of religious liberty. In the *Syllabus of Errors* and other nineteenth-century statements—the documents that convinced many Protes-tants the Church hated democracy—Murray saw merely the Judeo-Christian exceptionalism of his day. He predicted dire consequences if Protestants and Catholics could not set aside their differences and cooperate in fighting "the totalitarian authoritarianism that denies the natural rights of conscience" and "the secularist liberalism that denies the natural obligations of conscience."[39]

Thus, while Murray avoided Judeo-Christian formulations, he powerfully aided the cause of Judeo-Christian exceptionalism by clearing theoretical ground for a cross-confessional alliance against secularism and totalitarian-ism. Murray's writings distanced the Catholic Church from authoritarian politics and aligned it with democracy, pluralism, and freedom. In his por-trayal, Catholics were ready to work side by side with Protestants and Jews on behalf of democracy, without seeking to convert their counterparts or touting their own correctness. Indeed, Murray, like other liberal Catholics, said it was actually pluralistic liberals who sought to impose their cultural framework—secularism—on a diverse nation. If interpreted in secularist fashion, Murray argued, church-state separation fostered totalitarianism, via the spiritual des-iccation of the culture. By 1947, when the Supreme Court ruled on this issue in its *Everson v. Board of Education* decision, many Protestants and a few influential Jews had come to share Murray's assessment.

Jews, Naturalists, and the Challenge of Antisecularism

Most Jews and many liberal Protestants, however, joined naturalists in react-ing with alarm to the rise of Judeo-Christian exceptionalism. Nonbelievers, of course, found their views widely pilloried as un-American in the 1940s. But the new view of democracy also identified theological liberals and strict separationists, including most Protestants and virtually all Jews, as witting or

unwitting accomplices of a campaign to destroy religion. In the new exceptionalist framework, opposition to political secularity became a litmus test for
both religious authenticity and democratic commitment. Within each faith
community, warned a Catholic writer in 1941, "the sheep-goat division must
be recognized."[40]

Naturalists and their pluralist allies pushed back on the assumption that
substantive religious commitments underpinned democracy. As the Ethical
Culture leader Jerome Nathanson put it, echoing William James, "there are
many ways of feeling the push and pull of the universe," and "none of them
has been shown to be essential to the democratic way of life." Often they challenged the descriptive claim that all Americans were Protestants, Catholics, or
Jews, portraying a more variegated nation of numerous belief communities,
ranging from "democratic humanists" to theosophists and Confucians, as well
as nonbelievers. For these naturalists, Jews, and Protestants, the "freedom of
the individual to differ" anchored democracy. Yet pluralists struggled to check
the burgeoning tide of Judeo-Christian exceptionalism and the emerging alliance against theological liberalism and secularism.[41]

Although American Jews, like Protestants, split sharply on the question
of democracy's foundations by the 1940s, they inclined much more strongly
toward pluralism. Several factors fostered discomfort with Judeo-Christian
exceptionalism. First, many exceptionalists included Jews only nominally
within the "Judeo-Christian tradition" and stressed the "Christian" half of
the formulation. These figures, as we have seen, alternated between paeans
to the "Judeo-Christian tradition" and the "Christian heritage of the West."
Indeed, many failed to see Judaism as a modern Western faith at all, defining
it solely in terms of its historical role in preparing the way for Christ. John
Mackay, among many others, lauded Jewish inheritances but criticized historical Judaism. Jews, he wrote, had worshipped Caesar since their betrayal
of Christ and needed, with Christians, "to direct a common gaze towards the
Nazarene who, for both, in differing senses, has been the Man of destiny."
Behind the scenes at the Federal Council of Churches, Mackay contended
that democracy was "a product of Christianity" and that its "purity and per-
manence" were "bound up with Christianity."[42]

Polling data likewise showed that most Americans defined their nation as
Christian and downplayed or even denied the suffering of Europe's Jews. In
1938, over half of Gallup's respondents blamed Hitler's persecution partially
or wholly on Jews' own behavior. At home, nearly a quarter would exclude
Jews from government posts, while 20 percent hoped to "drive Jews out of
the United States." Moreover, American intervention in World War II actually heightened anti-Semitism. Meanwhile, many Christians viewed Nazism

as an attack on "Judeo-Christian heritage" in general, not on Jews in particular. Pointing to Nazi ideologues such as Alfred Rosenberg, these Christian commentators identified the war as a struggle between Judeo-Christianity and neo-paganism. A characteristic 1943 article cited Rosenberg's writings to prove that Nazi anti-Semitism stemmed from a deeper "campaign against Christianity."[43]

Opposition to Judeo-Christian exceptionalism took numerous forms. Some Jewish commentators rejected outright, or quickly abandoned, the idea of a coherent Judeo-Christian heritage. Critics such as the biblical scholar Theodor H. Gaster and the New York Public Library's Joshua Bloch blamed "the misguided, irrational and irresponsible zeal of interfaith partisans" for the "fiction of an ill-defined and actually non-existent 'Judeo-Christian civilization.'" And many of the urban rabbis who pioneered the use of Judeo-Christian rhetoric during the campaign for American intervention ditched the term after Pearl Harbor. But most Jewish critics instead challenged exceptionalist uses of Judeo-Christian rhetoric: its mobilization to tie democracy to traditional theologies. These figures saw a logical fallacy in the presumption that democracy was inextricable from the religious beliefs prevailing at the time of its birth. Indeed, pluralists of all persuasions countered the new exceptionalist framework with ringing endorsements of freedom of belief, opinion, and conscience. Many invoked a coherent cultural tradition, variously dubbed "liberal," "humanistic," "democratic," or simply "American," that centered on civil liberties and religious inclusion.[44]

Still, Judeo-Christian terminology resonated so widely with Christians that it offered real, if limited, opportunities to promote an inclusive understanding of democracy that included Judaism. Some Jewish commentators sought to steer Judeo-Christian rhetoric in a more pluralist and inclusive direction by using "Judeo-Christian" as a shorthand for full-blown religious diversity in the public sphere. Horace Kallen's linguistic shift is revealing here. In 1943, he argued that Western civilization was not at all "Judeo-Christian"; Jews were a "small and weak people" with "rights but no power," representing "the traditional scapegoat of the powerholders of the Christian world." By late 1945, however, Kallen began to use "Judeo-Christian" himself. He portrayed the United States as, historically, a tri-faith nation that was slowly moving away from narrow formulations of Judeo-Christianity toward a more inclusive public culture. During the Cold War era, this Judeo-Christian pluralism would allow Jews and other pluralists to challenge exceptionalist models of democracy without describing their own position as secular.[45]

Many pluralists, accused of aiding totalitarianism, countered by insisting that it was actually Judeo-Christian exceptionalism that paved the way for totalitarianism. Pluralists in the universities—many of Jewish extraction—and religious modernists and humanists often argued not only that democracy required open-ended tolerance but also that the practice of tolerance rested on a tentative, fallibilistic understanding of all truth claims. Those who believed in absolute, unchanging truths, the argument ran, would eventually seek to impose those truths by force. John Dewey put the argument simply: "There is implicit in every assertion of fixed and eternal first truths the necessity for some *human* authority to decide, in this world of conflicts, just what these truths are and how they shall be taught."[46]

Philosophers such as Kallen and Sidney Hook pursued this critique with vigor during World War II. Combining fallibilism with varying degrees of anti-Catholic bigotry, they warned that Catholics and fundamentalist Protestants, with their "unscientific and undemocratic principles of Papal and Biblical infallibility," prepared the ground for totalitarian rule. In the face of the antisecularist alliance and its "clerical totalitarianism," *Humanist* editor Edwin H. Wilson called for "a coalition of non-Fundamentalist Protestants, Jews and secular leaders" to defend tolerance. Even pluralists far less fearful of the Catholic hierarchy than Wilson urged champions of tolerance to draw the line at those whose definitions of truth appeared to set them against tolerance itself. They insisted that certain religious commitments, such as a belief in miracles, the literal inerrancy of the Bible, or papal infallibility, undermined the "democratic faith" because they resisted empirical analysis. For these figures, the battle against Nazism was part of a larger struggle between tolerance and intolerance throughout the West.[47]

In intellectual circles, much of the controversy over democracy's cultural requirements swirled around the New York–based Conference on Science, Philosophy, and Religion in Their Relation to the Democratic Way of Life (CSPR). The Conservative rabbi Louis Finkelstein, of Jewish Theological Seminary, launched the group in 1940 to foster intellectual dialogue and thereby catalyze religious revitalization. Like Niebuhr, Finkelstein espoused an idiosyncratic version of Judeo-Christian exceptionalism holding that traditional, monotheistic theologies—including Islam—buttressed democracy by fostering humility and toleration, not specific tenets or creeds. Also like Niebuhr, Finkelstein cultivated a very different set of allies than did his pluralist counterparts. He repeatedly insisted, "There can be no religion in the modern world unless there are traditional religions." Most of the other organizers of the CSPR, including F. Ernest Johnson, George N. Shuster, and John LaFarge, offered more straightforward renderings of the exceptionalist claim that democracy rested on "the firm rock of belief in God."[48]

To pluralist critics, the CSPR epitomized the burgeoning antisecularist alliance. During planning for the first meeting, both Jacques Maritain and Mortimer Adler, a Jewish philosopher committed to neo-Thomism, sought to exclude the logical positivists, philosophers with a science-centered worldview. Unsuccessful in this endeavor, Maritain did convince Finkelstein to reject a paper proposal by the Yale philosopher Brand Blanshard, a sharp critic of Catholicism. The group's initial public statement then contended that democracy could not survive "as a secular phenomenon" and proposed a "disciplined cooperation" of the "traditional faiths." At the CSPR's tumultuous first meeting, exceptionalists repeatedly attacked secularism, with Adler calling "the positivism of the professors" a more potent threat to democracy than Nazism and prompting a bitter response from Sidney Hook. Hard feelings persisted the following day, when Albert Einstein identified the idea of a personal God as the stumbling block to cooperation between religious leaders and scientists. Finkelstein apologized publicly for Einstein's statement— though not Adler's—after the conference.[49]

Pluralists split over how to respond. Hook, Kallen, and many other naturalists and humanists boycotted subsequent meetings of the CSPR, leaving the group with a narrower intellectual range. For these critics, the second gathering offered proof of the group's exceptionalist bias. There, a group of Princeton University professors, including scientists as well as humanities scholars, joined John A. Mackay in arguing that naturalists' "essentially materialistic" philosophy could not sustain a belief in human dignity. Father Gerald Phelan, Nels Ferré, and Luther A. Weigle also urged a theistic basis for democracy, as did the chemist Harold C. Urey.[50]

Those urging a boycott also included the University of Wisconsin philosopher M. C. Otto, the University of Illinois philosopher Arthur E. Murphy, and Edwin Wilson of the *Humanist*. Wilson urged naturalists and humanists to sever all ties with a militantly "Hebraic-Christian" group whose leaders called them "philosophical fifth columnists . . . responsible, both in logic and in history, for Hitlerism." Hook likewise called on "democratic humanists, naturalists, theists, theosophists, Mohammedans, Catholics, Jews, Protestants, pagans, atheists, [and] Confucians" to defend the liberal tradition in their own, alternative forum. Yet the resulting Conference on the Scientific Spirit and Democratic Faith remained marginal and quietly expired after two years, in 1945. By contrast, the CSPR continued into the 1960s, with strong financial support from the Jewish Theological Seminary and the participation of leading thinkers.[51]

A few humanists, however, thought rigorously exclusive conceptions of truth comported with democracy, so long as their adherents could cooperate in practice. After Dewey criticized the philosopher Harry A. Overstreet for remaining in the CSPR, Overstreet lauded the "free and open—and often bitterly antagonistic—discussion" at the group's meetings. "There's something good and American about that," he wrote. "As to Sidney [Hook]'s fear that we—the liberals—are being taken in by these fascist minded theologians, I think that is all nonsense. I get more and more to believe that people can have the most cock-eyed theology and still be fine people. (I've just been teaching Mormons; and, as people—socially minded people—they are tops!) For the most part, theology (like academic metaphysics) doesn't carry down into practical life." Suggesting that the CSPR had quickly abandoned its quixotic search for intellectual unity, Overstreet found its meetings at worst irrelevant and potentially productive of new points of agreement and "much needed courtesies" among conferees.[52]

Among American Jews, disagreements over political theory reflected, in part, the deepening divide between Judaism's branches. Not all Conservative Jews were Judeo-Christian exceptionalists, by any stretch. But Jewish adherence to Judeo-Christian exceptionalism was largely confined to the Conservative movement that took shape in the mid-twentieth century. Indeed, the pattern was sufficiently striking that Joshua Bloch identified the Judeo-Christian concept itself as a dangerous attempt to boost Conservatism over Judaism's other branches. He saw in Conservatism nothing more than assimilationism: conformity to the widespread American belief that traditional religion anchored national life.[53]

Conservatism, albeit in rather heterodox forms, certainly drew the support of the most vigorous Jewish champions of Judeo-Christian exceptionalism: the novelist and literary critic Waldo Frank and the labor intellectual Will Herberg. These figures reversed the charge of assimilation. Leaning heavily on Reinhold Niebuhr's arguments, Frank and Herberg charged that Jewish advocates of strict church-state separation, eager to join the American mainstream, had adopted a shallow, antireligious form of universalism. During World War II, Frank forcefully denied "that Jews become better Americans as they become less Jewish." In truth, he argued, "the Jew cannot belong to the United States dynamically as a Jew unless in an essential way he is distinct." To become authentic democrats, Jews needed to "take themselves seriously as Jews," which meant "to believe truly in the God of their fathers" and set themselves against secularizing forces. Frank thus defined Jewish identity in exclusively religious terms. Meanwhile, he contended that the Founders had enshrined, if sometimes in secularized form, "the implicit premise of the Judeo-Christian tradition"—namely, that "God is [a] potential, absolute presence in every human life" and thus that "the principle of freedom" resided in every individual. Frank accused Horace Kallen and his pluralistic allies of seeking to stamp out religious affiliations and impose on all citizens—in the name of tolerance, no less—a featureless, secular Americanism.[54]

Will Herberg soon became the most prominent Jewish advocate of this antisecularist critique. Like Frank, Herberg developed an exclusively religious definition of American Jewish identity, argued that Jews could stave off anti-Semitism only as a corporate religious body, and took much from Reinhold Niebuhr, who inspired Herberg's shift from Marxism to Judaism between 1939 and 1943. Writing more clearly than Frank, and to a wider audience, Herberg touched off a vigorous postwar debate among American Jews over their long-standing support of a secular public sphere. Secular liberalism, he warned, naturally devolved into totalitarianism; the only antidote was a personalist defense of democracy, rooted in core Judeo-Christian principles and embedded in three traditional faith communities.

Herberg arrived from Russia as a young child and grew up in a poor, nonpracticing household. During the 1920s and 1930s, he championed Marxism and sought a non-Stalinist "democratic socialism" for the United States. After Stalin's purges and the 1939 Nazi-Soviet pact, Herberg set out to discover why Soviet communism had devolved into totalitarianism and to craft a libertarian socialism that would maximize freedom in the United States. The idea of a Judeo-Christian tradition, grounded in a personalist emphasis on the supreme value of the individual, helped Herberg explain why Soviet Marxism had gone awry—and reassured him that Americans could avoid that outcome. Searching for a theistic foundation for democratic socialism, Herberg apparently considered Catholicism, which as late as May 1940 he called "the mother of totalitarianism." Convinced by Niebuhr to turn instead to Judaism, Herberg explored his natal faith through classes at Jewish Theological Seminary. Yet it was a close reading of Reinhold Niebuhr's *Moral Man and Immoral Society* in May 1940 that truly lit his path. That book suggested to Herberg that humanity's sinfulness would lead every organized group to betray its ideals and promote its own survival at any cost. He concluded that the shortcomings of both capitalism and totalitarian socialism reflected a primal will to power that constantly undermined the struggle for justice. Herberg now defined Marxism as a misguided religion, with a cult of the prophet and a priesthood engaged in abstruse, quasi-theological hairsplitting.[55]

With the aid of Niebuhr's writings, Herberg found the final piece of the puzzle by 1944: a rendering of Judeo-Christian faith that combined a flexible, constructive attitude toward political means with a firm commitment to the permanently valid ends of freedom and justice. He argued that a unitary religious culture (which Herberg variously labeled "the Christian heritage" or "the Judaeo-Christian tradition") dominated Western thought so thoroughly that even nonbelievers reflected its presuppositions. But only the genuine article, Herberg argued—the authentic Judeo-Christian tradition, consciously recognized and upheld—could prevent corruption by the imperatives of organizational survival and struggle. Following the Russian philosopher Nikolai Berdyaev, Herberg dubbed his Judeo-Christian outlook "personalist socialism" and argued that it alone could avoid the temptations of power by constantly holding unrealizable but potent ideals "over us as an eternal judgment reminding us that the best we can do is none too good and warning us against converting the inescapable necessities of practical life into standards of right and good." The inner check of the moral law, combined with the outer checks of institutional pluralism and decentralization—each a logical derivation from Judeo-Christianity, Herberg argued—would keep the power of men over men to a minimum in political and economic affairs. "This," Herberg concluded, "is democratic socialism."[56]

Herberg thus saw in the modern era an essentially religious struggle. "Totalitarianism is not a political system," he wrote, but rather "a spiritual regime, a way of life." As such, it was not confined to regimes abroad and could not be fought piecemeal; democrats needed to target its philosophical roots directly. Like other antisecularists of his day, Herberg traced modern liberalism and totalitarian socialism to a common source: a secular, utilitarian ethical theory that reduced human beings to mere tools, dissolved ideals in a sea of materialism, and thereby elevated "collectivism into an end-in-itself and source of value." In 1945, Herberg called liberals the "special victims and carriers of the disease" of totalitarianism in the United States: "eager advocates of government control in every sphere" and "arrogant zealots intolerant of disagreement." He highlighted "the pluralistic corporatism of the Middle Ages," when the church, guilds, and other bodies exerted their own forms of authority against that of the central state. Although the medieval system opposed "individual self-determination," Herberg wrote, it upheld the crucial distinction between society and state. In the modern world, with its absolute, undivided conception of sovereignty, Herberg held that "only the personalist *mystique* of vital religion" could keep socialism true to itself by supplying it with "the spiritual resources to resist totalitarian diabolism."[57]

By 1945, Herberg was on his way to becoming the leading Jewish exponent of Judeo-Christian exceptionalism. Fusing personalism with Niebuhrian neo-orthodoxy, he identified liberalism and totalitarian socialism, rather than fascism, as the major threats to American democracy. Over the next few years, Herberg would turn to implementing his vision. Venturing into theology, he would articulate a version of Judaism compatible with the neo-orthodox conception of sin and the personalist emphasis on the value of the individual.

Meanwhile, Herberg would consider the institutional dimensions of a personalist socialism, grappling with thorny questions of education and church-state
relations. As he did so, he would gravitate toward liberal Catholics' church-
state views and mobilize the language of pluralism against the secular state
and public schools.[58]

*

The efforts of Frank and especially Herberg convinced many Christians that
Judeo-Christian exceptionalism reflected core Jewish commitments, even
as the vast majority of American Jewish leaders insisted that only tolerance,
freedom of expression, and strict church-state separation could protect them
against the increasingly powerful view of democracy as an outgrowth of traditional theologies. Despite this pluralistic undertow, Judeo-Christian exceptionalism would largely dominate American thought after World War II. The
shift toward exceptionalism, already well under way during the war, would
accelerate in the late 1940s and early 1950s. Mainstream Protestants—the de-
ciding factor in struggles over the meaning of democracy, due to their numerical and cultural dominance—would increasingly conclude that defeating
totalitarianism required understanding democracy in religious terms.

From World War to Cold War

JUDEO-CHRISTIAN EXCEPTIONALISM
ASCENDANT, 1945–1950

The decade after World War II is rightly remembered as the period of the most rapid growth in the popularity of the notion of a Judeo-Christian America. By the mid-1950s, the concept of a Judeo-Christian tradition was so taken for granted and so closely linked to democracy that one speaker felt compelled to remind her listeners, "Our Western civilization owes much to Greek thought as well as to Judaeo-Christian belief." Most commentators skipped the non-theistic sources altogether: "The origins of our democracy may be found in the Judeo-Christian religions."[1]

The postwar spread of such arguments, and the precise political meanings that commentators assigned to the Judeo-Christian tradition, owed much to political and geopolitical changes. By 1947, it was becoming clear that the military struggle against fascism had not brought global peace but had rather given way to a standoff between the "free world" and the forces of communism. The battle to eradicate totalitarianism, many Americans concluded, would need to continue indefinitely. Anticommunists, moreover, often saw totalitarianism as a threat at home as well as abroad. They thought a network of communist sympathizers and fellow travelers had extended its reach into key American institutions. Many anticommunists further believed that advocates of secular worldviews or strict church-state separation powerfully aided the enemy.

That fear drew in part on a pair of Supreme Court decisions in 1947 and 1948 that dramatically altered the terrain of church-state relations and alarmed many religious believers and leaders. In 1947, *Everson v. Board of Education* permitted indirect aid, in the form of busing, to Catholic school students. The decision's true import, however, lay in the wording of the majority opinion, which enshrined Jefferson's "wall of separation" metaphor in First Amendment jurisprudence, sharpened the meaning of church-state separation to prohibit any promotion of religion, even on an equal basis, and brought state laws under the aegis of the establishment clause. In short, *Everson* ruled out both an "accommodationist" reading of the First Amendment—the view that it allowed aid to all religions equally—and local control over church-state policies. As Justice Hugo Black summarized the court's stance, "Neither a state nor the Federal Government . . . can pass laws which aid one religion, aid all religions, or prefer one religion over another." A year later, the *McCollum v. Board of Education* court used the new principles to uphold a complaint by the parents of an atheist child and ban released-time programs for religious education during the school day and on school property.[2]

Taken together, the Cold War and the church-state cases gave a major boost to Judeo-Christian exceptionalism. Even as Judeo-Christian language spread, the divide between advocates of exceptionalist and pluralist theories of democracy deepened and the relative power of the exceptionalists grew. Scholars have often noted this postwar flourishing of the Judeo-Christian discourse but have rarely recognized it as in part an attack—often implicit but usually quite vehement—on secularists, primarily of Jewish and Protestant origin. In many hands, the Judeo-Christian idea functioned as a device of inclusion to bring religious Jews into the national community, marking an important step in the development of a more inclusive polity and culture. But the remarkable growth of Judeo-Christian language between 1946 and 1955 also reflected a very different dynamic. Judeo-Christian exceptionalism reached its high-water mark in the decade after World War II, becoming a pillar of Cold War ideology in those years. Judeo-Christian exceptionalists routinely depicted those who did not profess Christian or Jewish religious beliefs—and even those friendly to nonbelievers and advocates of strict church-state separation—as carriers of ideologies inimical to the flourishing of American democracy.[3]

During those years, Judeo-Christian pluralists did their best to expand the "circle of 'we'" implicit in the Cold War equation of Judeo-Christianity with democracy. But they could not stop exceptionalism's meteoric rise and were thrown back on the defensive by the widespread belief that democracy required Judeo-Christian religion for its continued health and vitality. Judeo-Christian exceptionalists wielded tremendous cultural influence in that period, due to the Cold War–era obsession with "godless communism." This widespread belief that democracy took its motive force from Judeo-Christian religion cemented the strong association of the "Judeo-Christian tradition" with American democracy that was forged in World War II. The postwar ascent of Judeo-Christian exceptionalism would culminate during President

Eisenhower's first term, just as McCarthyism reached a fever pitch. In this su-percharged ideological context, exceptionalists warned with ever-greater stri-dency that secularism and atheism would erode democracy from within. As it became increasingly easy to portray defenders of a civic definition of national belonging as a dangerous fifth column bent on subverting democracy, the antisecularism of the early Cold War years presided over the ascendance of Judeo-Christian exceptionalism, and thus the spread of Judeo-Christian lan-guage more broadly.

Defining and Contesting Judeo-Christian Exceptionalism

The postwar years witnessed a sharp increase in the use of Judeo-Christian formulations by Catholics, especially laypeople and converts. Several histo-rians have claimed that mid-twentieth-century Catholics almost universally rejected the Judeo-Christian language because it encoded a liberal attack on their faith or violated prohibitions on interfaith dialogue.[4] In fact, however, many postwar Catholics contributed significantly to the Judeo-Christian discourse, though on their own terms and for their own purposes. A few such uses, especially in the context of civil rights work, focused on human dignity and bracketed the question of democracy's foundations.[5] But most of the Catholic commentators who mobilized Judeo-Christian formulations highlighted the dangers of an overweening state, asserted a strong causal rela-tionship between secular liberalism and totalitarianism, identified secularism and atheism as threats to national security, and insisted that political equality was only possible under God.

The postwar shift in national focus from fascism to communism enabled the emergence of a robust Catholic discourse of Judeo-Christianity. The ear-lier contrast of Judeo-Christianity to fascism had created significant stum-bling blocks. Although most American Catholics rejected German Nazism and anti-Semitism during the World War II era, many were ambivalent or even enthusiastic about Franco—who garnered the support of 58 percent of Catholics polled in 1938—and Mussolini. This fact, coupled with the Vati-can's prohibition on cross-confessional theological dialogue, discouraged all but the most avant-garde Catholics from using Judeo-Christian formulations prior to 1945. After the war, however, the scales tipped decisively from those who viewed fascism as the greatest threat to American democracy to those who worried about communism. Many lay Catholics from across the political spectrum, as well as a few renegade priests, now joined Jacques Maritain in celebrating the Judeo-Christian roots of democracy and viewing Soviet totali-tarianism as the outcome of a secular public sphere.[6]

As early as October 1945, commentators such as Catholic War Veterans head Edward T. McCaffrey saw the Cold War on the horizon and identified "Judeo-Christian belief in God" as the needed defense against communism. McCaffrey allowed that even "our God-fearing fellow-citizens who, professing no formal religion, still believe in a Supreme Deity" could advance the cause of democracy. But the struggle against communism would have to rest on Judeo-Christian theism. In 1947, as it became increasingly obvious that the United States would take a strong anticommunist stance, the Catholic journalist Anne O'Hare McCormick framed the Cold War as a spiritual conflict between "the totalitarian religion that man is the creature of the state" and "the religion of individual free will and responsibility." The West, wrote McCormick, "is not so much a geographic as a religious conception; it is a culture, a system of values, a principle of development, an emphasis on the person, growing out of the Judaeo-Christian teaching and tradition." Even professed nonbelievers, she argued, "live under the laws shaped by the Ten Commandments and social compulsions emanating from the Sermon on the Mount."[7]

Not all postwar Catholics employed Judeo-Christian rhetoric, by any means. Figures such as Clare Boothe Luce, the wife of the powerful magazine publisher Henry Luce and a recent convert under the guidance of John Courtney Murray and the philosopher-turned-radio host Fulton J. Sheen, defined the core democratic principle that "each man has a value as a sovereign being" as a Christian inheritance. Luce aimed primarily at "scientific materialism" rather than statism, contrasting the Soviets' view of "an animal without a soul," governable only by force, to "the Western concept of man as a child of God, a creature with a sovereign soul . . . who is, or rather should be, obedient to God's laws." And she held that the needed "concept of the nature of man" was firmly "Christian" in origin. Skipping the supersessionist invocations of Judeo-Christianity offered by some Catholics, Luce equated the West with Christianity. Luce reiterated this Christian-exceptionalist theory of democracy in a widely read account of her conversion the following spring.[8]

Some postwar Catholics still claimed specifically Catholic roots for democracy. As late as 1955, one Jesuit traced that system back to Augustine and Aquinas. But most liberal Catholics employed a broader account of democracy's lineage. Luigi Sturzo called democracy "the fruit of Christian civilization" and traced it to "the Judaeo-Christian tradition of thought." Carlton Hayes used Judeo-Christian language more consistently, defining Western civilization as the result of the "fructifying" influence of "the Judeo-Christian tradition" on "the Greco-Roman tradition."[9]

Of course, exceptionalism and antisecularism united Catholics across such linguistic divides. Even more than the secularity of Soviet leaders, they

blamed nonbelief at home for the Western predicament. "Maybe the very secularism from which we suffer is a reaction against our own spiritual infirmity,"
Fulton Sheen suggested in March 1946, "and the growth of atheism and totalitarianism, the measure of our want of zeal and piety and the proof of our un-
fulfilled Christian duties." A Knights of Columbus leader declared in 1948 that
the struggle against "the unsatiated red monster of Moscow" and its domestic
agents was "badly handicapped by the indifferentism, secularism and materialism that have changed a God-fearing people to a Godless people." And a
Fordham professor, writing in the *New York Times* in 1950, traced modern
"hedonism" to the "repudiation of the Judaeo-Christian tradition on which
our Western civilization rests." Invoking the Roman example, he warned, "We
must return to the virtues of our earlier days or ultimately perish."[10]

On the Jewish side, meanwhile, Will Herberg worked valiantly but largely
unsuccessfully to turn his coreligionists toward Judeo-Christian exceptionalism. "A Protestant by theological inclination, a Catholic by temperament, and
a Russian Jew by birth," according to his biographer, Herberg attacked secular liberalism with increasing frequency and vehemence after 1945. Although
he would continue to call himself a socialist into the 1950s, he now advocated a "pluralistic and libertarian" socialism that featured a strictly limited
state and a decentralized, pluralistic structure of authority. Indeed, Herberg
identified his "democratic collectivism" as a version of the "Anglo-American
liberal tradition," emphasizing "personal and minority rights" and "individuality, self-help, and voluntary group effort." In Herberg's rendering, secular
liberals had warped the concept of democracy beyond recognition, equating
it with "the mass-state, a ruthless uniformitarianism, [and] the exaltation of
the collectivity," all justified in the name of "the deified People." No individual
or group, he said, could assert rights against the modern liberal state, which
aggressively stamped out all nonstate organizations and "minorities." Herberg
particularly feared that the New Deal state would gain control over the religious and educational institutions needed to check its grasping tendencies,
although his writings of the late 1940s focused mainly on political theory and
the nature of Judaism, not education as such.[11]

Herberg rooted his conception of democracy, both philosophically and
historically, in Judeo-Christian faith. He drew on Niebuhr's concepts of "prophetic faith" and "biblical realism" to define democracy as "the institution-
alization of permanent resistance to human sinfulness in politics." Herberg
then traced the limited-power state to the Calvinism of the Puritans, the
source of the Founding Fathers' "somber theological realism." Throughout
the late 1940s and early 1950s, Herberg sought to ground democracy in an "ultimate" or "total commitment" capable of "protect[ing] it from inner corrup-

tion as well as from external attack." He believed that only "prophetic religion" could serve this function, preserving democracy by revealing "that nothing in this world is absolute and worthy of worship, that everything stands under the judgment of a holy God." As before, Herberg also took inspiration from the Christian personalists' emphasis on the God-given nature of human dignity, identifying persons as the only legitimate "ends in themselves" and all else—"social institutions, society, and the state"—as mere supports of human dignity.[12]

Meanwhile, secularism failed because it portrayed man as "the supreme power in the universe, entirely sufficient unto himself." Herberg identified secularism—the common intellectual denominator between Marxism and a debased modern liberalism—as the spiritual source of totalitarianism. Adopting a historical account common among Catholics, Herberg traced the origin of totalitarianism to the "disintegration of the medieval social order," wherein a "pluralistic corporatism" had given way to the "absolute unitary state" of the sixteenth and seventeenth centuries and the "popular absolutism and modern mass-democracy" of the eighteenth century. He also advanced a theory of secularist false consciousness, explaining that although many secular and religious liberals were democrats, "their democratic and humanist convictions are the fruit not of their secularist philosophy but of the religious tradition, whose moral values they have absorbed but whose spiritual foundations, which alone can give power and meaning to these values, they have rejected." Secular and religious liberals, he argued, naturally exalted "the 'social-welfare state' as an omnicompetent agency for the total control of social life." In his mind, this stance portended a reprisal of the "revolutionary terror" of the French and Russian Revolutions. The slippery slope might begin with welfare liberalism, he wrote, but it always ended in totalitarianism—the pure political manifestation of a secular worldview.[13]

In the United States, Herberg contended, "secularism" had become the "official voice" of American culture. Theological modernists had transformed their churches and synagogues into "glorified social and adult education centers" while fundamentalists had ceded the public sphere entirely, retreating into cloistered spaces of "legalism or moralism or pietism." True religion, by Herberg's definition, meant "*total* obedience to God in the *totality* of existence," and it demanded public action as well as private observance. Niebuhr, he said, had done an invaluable service by translating the "pluralism and social relativism" of democracy into Judeo-Christian terms while excising the modern liberals' divinization of humanity and the state.[14]

Herberg was particularly dismayed by the tendency of American Jews to affirm their identity in secular terms, via "*ersatz*-Jewish faiths" such as "Jewish nationalism, culture, social service, [and] 'anti-defamation.'" The authentic Jew, he wrote, was "a man of two souls," not fully at home "even in Zion." But individuals and groups sought to "'normalize' Jewish life" by wishing away the existential predicament created by the "objective though supernatural fact" of "covenant-existence." Most frequently, Herberg charged, American Jews fetishized survival by turning the Jewish community itself into a false idol to be defended at any spiritual cost. Thus, he complained, the Reform tradition regarded the Jewish covenant as merely "a 'creedal union,' a voluntary associa- tion along the lines of a Protestant denomination." Meanwhile, Reconstruc- tionists and secular Jews adopted ethnic or cultural definitions of Judaism. Finally, Zionism was merely "political nationalism," the "most radical perver- sion of the idea of Israel." The common denominator between these "ersatz- Jewish" movements, according to Herberg, was their overriding emphasis on group survival—the same emphasis on institutional self-preservation that he thought plagued Marxist labor unions and secular democracies. Herberg pro- posed instead an exclusively religious definition of Jewishness, arguing that Jews lived under the covenant whether they liked it or not.[15]

Herberg worked doggedly to turn American Jews away from secular con- ceptions of both democracy and Judaism. He believed that the Jewish com- munity was strategically important to the democratic project because Jewish identity contained a tension between "the Jew as son of the Covenant and the Jew as natural man and loyal citizen of his secular community." By creating a perennial state of "self-alienation," Herberg wrote, this inner division made religious Jews ideal democrats, always on guard against the state's tendency to deify itself. If Jewish self-alienation offered critical distance, however, it also fostered a susceptibility to secularism. Echoing Niebuhr's critique of liberal Protestantism, Herberg blasted contemporary Judaism, decrying "the routine reiteration of inherited formulas, the ostentatious parading of meaningless idealistic platitudes, and the serving up again of the stale commonplaces of yesterday's humanist philosophy." In his view, a "hidden liberalism" infected even Orthodoxy. Lamenting the absence of a "Niebuhr or Tillich to 'shake the foundations'" of Judaism, Herberg called for a Jewish theological renaissance akin to Niebuhr's neo-orthodoxy, in support of a democracy understood in the terms of Judeo-Christian exceptionalism.[16]

Herberg's efforts notwithstanding, calls for a unified political culture based on belief in a Judeo-Christian God fueled steadfast resistance from plu- ralists. That group included many liberal Protestants, whose commitment to freedom of conscience led them to defend the rights of dissenters. It also in- cluded non-Christian believers, especially Jews, who suspected that attempts to forge closer ties between religion and the American state would benefit mainly the Christian churches. Moreover, given the well-established tradition of secular Judaism, the Cold War impulse to divide the believing sheep from the nonbelieving goats threatened to drive a political wedge through the Jewish community.[17]

Pluralists repeatedly raised the alarm in the late 1940s, as the religious logic of the Cold War emerged. It simply was not true, insisted a frustrated reader of Clare Boothe Luce's article, "that one who is an atheist must also be a Communist"; there were "tens of millions" of Americans who were neither theists nor communists. Edwin H. Wilson of the American Humanist Association (AHA) likewise decried the postwar call for "a unity of religious peoples" against secularism. According to Wilson, such attacks targeted "all liberal religion, theistic or humanistic," and aided "the ideological drive of Rome to promote a Holy War, not only against Russia, but against all liberalism." Although the AHA had little interest in communism, wrote Wilson, it likewise rejected "the cry for unity of the so-called 'Three Faiths' in behalf of a 'Holy' War against Russia because of Russia's advocacy of the Brotherhood of Man without the Fatherhood of God."[18]

At the same time, some pluralists found Judeo-Christian language useful in liberal reform efforts, especially those related to civil rights for African Americans. In the influential 1944 book *An America Dilemma*, the Swedish social scientist Gunnar Myrdal had argued that all Americans shared a consensual "American Creed": a set of core social and political values that ruled out racism and segregation if properly understood. Civil rights workers quickly framed that creed in Judeo-Christian terms—not least to stave off charges of communist sympathizing. In December 1946, A. Philip Randolph warned African Americans against communism and argued that democracy "stems from the Judeo-Christian ethic," with its "fundamental affirmation of the value and worth of the individual." A few years later, a speaker at Fisk University's Race Relations Institute declared, "One of the greatest things in the Judeo-Christian religion is that there has always been someone who has raised his voice against tyranny and oppression." A reporter summarized the speaker's message thusly: "Final victory over race prejudice and totalitarianism is assured by America's Judeo-Christian cultural heritage."[19]

Whether or not they used Judeo-Christian language for their own purposes, however, pluralists decried the antisecularism associated with Judeo-Christian exceptionalism. As before, many of them linked democracy to a fallibilistic, pragmatic understanding of truth that they associated with science. The philosopher Arthur E. Murphy denied that "the liberal tradition, the American creed, the Judeo-Christian heritage of Western civilization," or any other set of tenets represented a precondition for democracy. Rather, democracy took its shape from *how* citizens believed, not what they believed. When arguments "that can operate only within the unity of a particular faith" were presented as absolute truths, Murphy wrote—singling out Catholic neo-Thomists and Marxists in particular—there were "no possible peace terms short of unconditional surrender." In "a free society," he explained, "ideas are reasons, not by authoritative fiat, but in their capacity to justify themselves in the open, to the common sense and purpose of co-operative life."[20]

Pluralists of this variety often viewed the question of democracy's foundations in a global perspective. In June 1946, Horace M. Kallen marveled that American commentators lauded "democratic Christian society" or "Judaeo-Christian culture" when the United Nations featured a majority of "black men and brown men and red men" and various "Communists and Confucians and Buddhists and Mohammedans and Parsees and Sikhs and Bahais and agnostics and atheists and many other faiths and cultures, as well as Judaism, Catholicism, and the Protestantisms." Kallen extended this critique in a 1950 essay on human rights that identified "religion" as an honorific rather than empirical label: "The thoughts and things to which it is applied receive thereby a certain privileged status, and are endowed with unique powers" said to derive from their transcendence of the merely human world. Yet there were hundreds of competing faiths in the United States alone, Kallen wrote.

> The Protestant Christians of today's United States are diversified into more than one hundred different and distinct communions. The Catholics, in spite of an unremitting and relentless sacerdotal resistance, are divided at least as Roman and English, Polish National and Old Roman; the Orthodox are Greek and Serbian and Ukrainian and Syrian. The Judaists are divided into Orthodox and Reformed and Conservative. And these name only the major variations within the Judeo-Christian cults. There are enough lesser ones to bring the total number of these units of religion in the United States up to two hundred and fifty. When we count the others—the Mohammedans, the Parsees, the Brahmanists, the Sikhs, the Shintoists, the Taoists, the Confucians, the Fascists, the Nazis and other racists, the Spiritualists, the Communists—and so on to no end—each having its variants and dissenters, we cannot help realizing that although the grammarians would hold *religion* to be a noun, singular, third person neuter, it is in fact a portmanteau word, a singular sign for a multitude of supernaturalist communions. The men and women of the world have religion*s*, not religion.

Of course, "when the protagonists of any cultus say 'religion,'" Kallen continued, "they mean their own and only their own." He sought to distinguish all such faiths from secularism. As "the principle of equal rights for different faiths to life and liberty and growth," secularism offered an umbrella under which all faiths could coexist, if they set aside dogmatic claims. To Kallen, secularism meant the provision of basic human rights to adherents of the world's myriad theistic and nontheistic faiths.[21]

Schooling and the Church-State Question

Kallen's definition of secularism found relatively few adherents in the early Cold War context, however. Battles over religion's role in education revealed the growing power of Judeo-Christian exceptionalism, even as the Supreme Court's decisions on that question heightened fears of secularization in the United States. An ever-larger group of Americans wondered how democracy could survive if its schools failed to teach core Judeo-Christian tenets.

Concern for the spiritual dimensions of American schooling could be heard at the highest levels. Americans, declared Commissioner of Education Earl J. McGrath in 1950, "want a world in which the ideals of the Judeo-Christian conception of life prevail." But how could they create such a world? Catholics and many conservative Protestants had a clear answer: The schools should teach Christian or Judeo-Christian doctrines. Mainline and liberal Protestants, by contrast, diverged sharply from one another. Although most Protestants rejected direct aid to parochial schools, and many defended the public schools against charges of godlessness, they disagreed on the need for religious education and the various means of providing it. Some viewed religion as either too important or too divisive a topic for the public schools. Others joined Catholics in decrying the secularization of public schooling and championed some form of religious education within the public system—either a "common core" model centered on shared Judeo-Christian principles or the released-time approach wherein students received instruction from their own religious leaders during part of the school day.[22]

The Supreme Court's decisions in *Everson* and *McCollum* dramatically altered the terms of the debate by ruling out both of these forms of religious education and rejecting as well the accommodationist view that the First Amendment authorized the state to favor religion over atheism by aiding all religions equally. Predictably, Catholics reacted with outrage. So, too, however, did a surprisingly large number of Protestants, including theological moderates and even liberals. These figures likewise worried that the court had twisted the long-standing and legitimate meaning of church-state separation into an aggressive secularism.

On the Catholic side, John Courtney Murray responded to *Everson* and *McCollum* in an uncharacteristically direct and public manner. He took his case to wider audiences and even led a rally of religious leaders against secularism, in Wilmington, Delaware, after *McCollum*. Calling that decision "a legal victory for secularism" and "a radical departure from our Federal constitutional tradition," Murray urged all members of America's Judeo-Christian faiths to unite behind a "common cause—the defense of the 'established habits' of our people, which are religious habits, and habits of cooperation between church and state within the wise constitutional guarantees of personal liberties." They should, he insisted, "make common cause against a common enemy—secularism, which strikes not only at our respective religions, but at our common American freedom."[23]

Since 1945, Murray had continued to target what he considered the two key Protestant misunderstandings that shaped church-state debates in the United States, while writing increasingly frequently in the lay journal *America* as well as his own specialized *Theological Studies*. His first target was a faulty conception of "freedom of religion" as an unbounded and purely subjective phenomenon rather than a strictly political deference to "the demands of the religious conscience." The second misunderstanding had to do with Catholic pronouncements on liberalism; Murray sought to establish that the Church's unqualified condemnations of liberalism in the nineteenth century applied only to the secular French version, not to the religion-friendly American model. All true liberals, he asserted, could surely agree on the disastrous effects of nineteenth-century liberalism's "militant secularism," its "systematic denial of the relevance of religion to social life." Characterizing "those who deny the sovereignty of God over human society" as "the most dangerous enemies of human liberty," Murray repeatedly insisted that the Church's campaign against secularism should be "the cause of all men of good will."[24]

Emboldened by Pius XII's Christmas messages of 1944, which exhibited a newfound warmth toward democracy, Murray argued that a form of democracy rooted in the natural law offered the best possible fit with the character of the human person, as embodied in Christian teachings. He urged Protestants to replace the question "How shall religion be made free in society?" with "How shall society itself be made religious?" At the same time, however, Murray increasingly turned his attention toward the practical dimensions of implementing his vision, including concrete issues regarding First Amendment history and jurisprudence. During the late 1940s, the main focus of Murray's writings shifted from the natural law, a set of philosophical principles, to an organizational model he called the "lay state." Murray believed that this model was clearly articulated in the Bill of Rights and made American liberalism friendly to religion. As Cold War tensions deepened and the Supreme Court widened the church-state gap, he urged Americans and Vatican officials alike to recognize the true meaning—and genius—of the US Constitution.[25]

Murray began to spell out the lay state model in November 1946. Like other Catholic leaders, he followed the *Everson* case closely as it wound its way through the courts. After the oral arguments, he charged that the Supreme Court interpreted the First Amendment as "a theological document" that "canonizes Liberal Protestant ecclesiology in an extreme form, and anathematizes as un-American all dissenters." In particular, the court read into the First Amendment "the doctrine that all churches are simply voluntary societies, of equally human origin and of equal value in the sight of God, each of them offering man an equally good way to eternal salvation." In so doing, Murray continued, the court "makes the First Amendment do the very thing that Congress is forbidden by the First Amendment to do, namely, to play the theologian and promulgate articles of faith." Properly understood, he argued, the First Amendment did not define religion; it simply defined the state by "guaranteeing the equality of all religious consciences . . . before the law." Because the American state is not itself a religious authority, Murray explained, it "respects whatever religious authority is accepted by any of those whose temporal good it serves" with the goal of serving them "all, impartially, regardless of their religion." At the same time, it could not be atheist or agnostic; lacking any theological authority, the state could not "deny or doubt that there is a religious authority" operating among its citizens.[26]

Murray told his Catholic readers that "many thinking Protestants" rejected efforts by "the secularist educators and clerical Protestantism" to write their anti-Catholic bigotry into law. Unfounded fears that Catholics sought to control all of education, he argued, threatened to produce a wall between church and state that would ensure the "legal suppression" of Catholic schools by deflecting "all governmental aid singly and solely towards the subsidization of secularism, as the one national 'religion' and culture, whose agent of propagation is the secularized public school."[27]

When the *Everson* decision arrived in February 1947, Murray responded cautiously. He praised the court for upholding New Jersey's busing laws but wished it had clarified the relationship between the First Amendment's free-exercise and establishment clauses. These stood in a hierarchical relationship, he argued, with the establishment clause operating solely to insure free exercise. Church-state separation was thus "subordinate to, and a means toward, the effective realization of religious freedom and civic equality." The First Amendment, Murray summarized, "'requires the State to be neutral in its relations with groups of religious believers; it does not require the State to be their adversary.'"[28]

Other Catholic writers expressed their criticism of *Everson* more forthrightly. A leading voice was James M. O'Neill, a speech professor at Brooklyn

College and chairman of the American Civil Liberties Union's Committee on Academic Freedom. Writing in the American Jewish Committee's journal *Commentary*, O'Neill numbered the "so-called 'great American principle of *complete* separation of church and state'" among the worst of the myths littering debates on civil liberties. He identified only one authoritative principle in church-state relations—that "there shall be . . . no organic union between the state and *any one church.*" Nowhere did the Constitution prohibit aid to multiple religious institutions on an equal basis, argued O'Neill. Like Murray and the Jesuit Wilfrid J. Parsons, but with the additional freedom afforded by his lay status, O'Neill contended that Protestants, blinded by anti-Catholicism, completely misread the First Amendment.[29]

Such reactions by Catholic writers helped to inspire the formation of Protestants and Other Americans United for the Separation of Church and State (POAU) in January 1948. The group represented a tense alliance between fiercely antisecularist evangelicals and committed secularists of various stripes, who found common cause in opposition to Catholic calls for federal aid to parochial schools. Many of these figures saw behind the outcry over *Everson* a concerted campaign by Catholics against secular institutions in the United States. Murray, in response, insisted that there was no threat of Catholic authoritarianism, which in any case paled in comparison with the danger posed by secularism. He urged Protestants to "wake up—return to reality—see an analyst—at all events, give up the scare techniques, the appeal to fear," and recognize that democracy stood in grave peril from "the secularism that bears within itself the seeds of future tyrannies." At the same time, Murray reminded his Catholic readers that "even nightmares are constructed from the fragments of the day"; Catholics bore some responsibility for not explaining their position clearly enough. They would need to extend the olive branch to Protestants in order to receive goodwill in return: "We need to go down into the City and prove by more deeds than we have hitherto shown that we are the friends of its liberties, that our progress is its progress, that our power is in its service, that no man has to fear from us infringement of any of his rights." Murray sought to make that case himself in a March 1948 article, explaining to the mostly secular and Protestant readers of the *Annals of the American Academy of Political and Social Science* "what the Catholic Church is" and "what the Catholic Church wants."[30]

However, Murray's cautious, even conciliatory tone vanished with the *McCollum* decision that same month. In his Wilmington speech, Murray challenged the religious authenticity of the decision's Protestant supporters and dismissed them as a fringe group of nativist bigots. He now described *McCollum* as the work of "a few, a very few, radical Protestants" who had joined "a strange assortment of Masons and secularist educators" in an anti-Catholic crusade. The case, in his view, represented a total victory for "the secularists" over "the thoughtful, religious men—Catholic, Protestant and Jewish." Murray concluded his Wilmington speech by directly addressing Protestants: "You boast of your primary contribution to the formation of American culture as a religious culture; then you cannot shrink from primary responsibility for the defense of this heritage. If the myth of democracy as a religion is triumphant, and achieves its "establishment" as our national religion, the triumph will be over you. Your God will have been supplanted by an idol." As "the largest religious force and the most powerful in the country," Murray argued, Protestantism bore a heavy "obligation of leadership" in the cultural struggle against secularism.[31]

Yet mainline Protestant organizations continued to fear Catholic influence. From 1946 to 1950, national leaders and groups battled over the prospect of federal aid to education. Few denied either the propriety or the desirability of such aid, as the war had brought both neglect of educational facilities and a new appreciation for the practical impact of education—not least on military capacity. Moreover, the wildly popular GI Bill of 1944 underwrote higher education for millions of former soldiers as the nation shifted back to a peacetime economy. But the battle lines over equivalent support for K–12 education hardened quickly and prevented any congressional action until the early 1960s. The issue was simple: Catholics argued that their schools deserved support, noting that they were taxed twice and that no one had complained when students used GI Bill funding to attend religious colleges. Such arguments, however, often accompanied strong criticism of secular education. Even when they did not, they reinforced Protestant fears that Catholic leaders aimed to drive the public schools out of business and break down the church-state barrier more generally.[32]

Against this backdrop, Murray published a spate of articles in 1949 that captured his ongoing study and reflection on the church-state issue. "Reversing the Secularist Drift" moved beyond vague references to "secularists" by analyzing "the myth of 'democracy as a religion,' a secularist faith, created without reference to God or any transcendent law, claiming to be the successor to sectarian Christianity, a more peaceful creed and a more operative one, with a higher, more unifying mission, and more totally salvific resources." Meanwhile, he clarified that the historical situation facing Western Catholics had three main elements: first, "the dechristianization of society"; second, "the emergence of the threat of the totalitarian state"; and third, "the corresponding struggling effort to validate the right of the human person to be the center, source and end of the social order." Murray explored the historical

provenance of the First Amendment as well. Madison, he argued, had shared
the view of religion as "a 'wholly private' interest" now held "by education-
alists like Kilpatrick, Thayer, and Hook et al.; by jurists in the tradition of
Holmes and by jurisprudents of the positivistic schools; by a variety of Protestants; by secularists *en masse.*" Yet the court was wrong to ground its decision in this "sectarian idea of religion," even if Madison had harbored such a
view. In "the effort to prove that 'no establishment of religion' means 'no aid
to religion,'" Murray summarized, the Supreme Court had proceeded "to establish a religion—James Madison's." Madison's intentions notwithstanding,
Murray argued, strict separationism was "an irredeemable piece of sectarian
dogmatism" that was forbidden by the First Amendment.[33]

Nevertheless, Murray saw considerable hope for the United States. Despite the "mounting sea of misunderstanding and prejudice and fear" between
Catholics and their critics, he told a group of Jesuit missionaries, "on the
farther shore there are men of good will who wait for you, ready for collaboration with you on terms of civic equality" and "ready even to accept the
leadership which your Christian principles make you responsible to give."
Looking around him, Murray saw a growing recognition "that the problem
of democracy in all its phases is at bottom a religious and moral problem"; he
also perceived "a new openness to the role of religion in society, in education,
in the direction to all human affairs."[34]

Murray elaborated on this argument in an October 1950 memorandum
to the Vatican. Over the past decade, he wrote, Protestantism had been replaced by "articulate, organized, and doctrinal secularism or naturalism" as
the Church's main enemy. Even as secularists fostered "a newly intense fear,
distrust, and hostility," Murray discerned among Protestants a growing "challenge to religious liberalism" and an accompanying "interest, curiosity, and
sympathy" regarding Catholicism—even renewed interest in "the political
ideas of the Middle Ages." Moreover, the secularists themselves were not "cynical" but "idealistic," open to "what are called 'spiritual values.'" Reiterating his
Wilmington argument, Murray argued that American secularism took the
form of a seductive "quasi-religious belief . . . in 'democracy'" that had become
"a widely popular 'religion' in America." Under these conditions, it was crucial
to overcome suspicion of Catholicism in "the intelligent Protestant," who "also
recognizes this naturalism as 'the enemy'" and "feels that he should make
friends with the Catholic in a common struggle against it." Murray urged
his superiors to recognize that the American lay state derived from medieval
roots, by way of "the Anglo-Saxon political tradition." The First Amendment,
he argued, meant that "the lay State is subject to the sovereignty of God" and
"recognizes that its acts and legislation ought to be in harmony with the law of

God," even though "the political form of the State requires that this harmony be effected by the people." In short, "the State has a duty to cooperate with the Church." Through "the medium of democratic institutions," Murray elaborated, "the people themselves bring the demands of their religious conscience to bear upon the acts and legislation of government."[35]

Murray urged Church leaders to develop further the ideas broached in the 1944 Christmas message by offering "a clear statement of certain simple, fundamental, leading ideas that will meet and satisfy the legitimate demands of the democratic political conscience." Referring specifically to Reinhold Niebuhr's overtures, Murray argued that "intelligent Americans" accepted the Church's theory of itself as "the one true Church"; the real sticking point was the belief, fostered by the Church's friendliness to dictators in Spain and elsewhere, that it "must and will, wherever possible, make this tenet of her faith the premise for a program of political intolerance and civil inequality." In short, Murray urged the Vatican to base its policy, at least in American-style democracies, on prudence rather than principle. No doubt referencing his own experience, Murray explained that the statement "Error has no rights" was "unintelligible to the American thinker, who associates rights only with persons, and regards judgment on the truth or error of religious beliefs as beyond the competence of the State." The Vatican had to demonstrate to sympathetic Protestants that it would act on prudential considerations, rather than translating its theory of the church into "a determination . . . to use the coercive power of secular government to deny legal existence to beliefs which the Church regards as erroneous."[36]

Murray was right that many Protestants had begun to appreciate the Church's position on the danger of secularism and the need for religion in the schools. *Everson* and *McCollum* fueled intense polarization between the neo-orthodox and modernist wings of American Protestantism, as Niebuhr and his allies argued that the court's decisions were morally bankrupt and unsupported by legal precedent. The sympathies of some liberal Protestants also swung in that direction after the court handed down its verdict on religion in the schools. Anxieties about both communism and the bureaucratic state at home—anxieties increasingly refracted through the school question—fueled a belief that Americans needed to mobilize on behalf of Judeo-Christian values against an increasingly powerful tendency toward secular nationalism.

Niebuhr had issued a comprehensive and widely read statement of his political philosophy in the 1944 book *The Children of Light and the Children of Darkness*, which he subtitled *A Vindication of Democracy and a Critique of Its Traditional Defense*. Democracy, he argued there, required citizens to steer a course between the "optimism" of secular and liberal Protestant thinkers (the children of light) who thought perfect justice could be attained in the human world and the "moral cynicism" of the totalitarians (the children of darkness) who knew no moral judgments whatsoever. As a political system, democracy embodied both the human obligation to strive toward justice and the recognition that all such human efforts fell short of God's perfection—and fell under God's judgment. But it could persist, Niebuhr argued, only if the children of light became thoroughgoing realists who recognized "the power of self-interest in human society" and worked to "beguile, deflect, harness, and restrain self-interest, individual and collective, for the sake of the community." As before, Niebuhr held that prophetic faith offered unique political resources by serving as a potent source of humility, teaching adherents "that their religion is most certainly true if it recognizes the element of error and sin, of finiteness and contingency, which creeps into the statement of even the sublimest truth." Throughout the book, Niebuhr's fallibilism clashed with his apologetic insistence that the Judeo-Christian tradition was the primary source, and perhaps the only source, of that spirit of contrition and humility underpinning democracy.[37]

Well before Murray's Wilmington speech, Niebuhr had concluded that the main form of secularism in the United States—and thus the leading threat to religion and democracy—was a "religion of democracy" that divinized the democratic process itself. In a 1946 article, "The Religious Level of the World Crisis," Niebuhr contended that "various forms of political and social religion"—specifically, liberalism, Marxism, and fascism—had rushed into the "vacuum" created by Christianity's abdication between the wars, claiming to offer "ultimate answers to the ultimate issues of human existence." In the United States, he clarified the following year, the main threat was "democracy as religion," on display in "the current American devotion to democracy" over and against totalitarianism. As a temporal phenomenon, he emphasized, democracy was neither "a worthy object of unqualified loyalty" nor an "adequate religion," because "man is only partly fulfilled in his social relations." Here, as elsewhere, Niebuhr warned, idolizing human institutions "accentuates their vices and makes them incapable of adjusting themselves to new situations."[38]

By 1948, Niebuhr's influence was such that *Time* placed him on its cover, noting that "Niebuhr has restored to Protestantism a Christian virility" and "even Roman Catholic theologians respect Dr. Niebuhr." The converse also held true; Niebuhr closely followed, and often admired, Catholic leaders' pronouncements and writings. He wrote three largely favorable reviews of Maritain's work between 1936 and 1942 and cited Maritain frequently thereafter. More generally, Niebuhr admired the Church's "consistent attitude" on the nature of property and other theoretical issues and was impressed by its organic unity and capacity to fashion powerful, persisting norms of justice. In the winter of 1945, reviewing Francis E. McMahon's *A Catholic Looks at the World* for the *Nation*, Niebuhr urged Protestants to recognize the political contributions of "socially progressive Catholics" and noted the capacity of democracy to foster cooperation "on various cultural, religious, and political levels" between those who disagreed fundamentally on other issues.[39]

In the run-up to the Cold War, however, Niebuhr remained sharply critical of what he considered Catholicism's pretensions and hypocrisies. He lambasted Church officials for hewing to "a papal system in which democracy has been sacrificed for the sake of unity," although Niebuhr acknowledged that "Protestant democracy" faced, and often succumbed to, the opposite danger of "anarchy." Niebuhr's concern about the willingness of Catholics to subordinate democracy to unity grew by the spring of 1946. One source was the rhetoric of Fulton Sheen, the popular Catholic leader. While asserting that "the world is rapidly being divided into two camps of the comradeship of Christ and the comradeship of anti-Christ," Sheen had also raised the charge of communist infiltration in the United States. Meanwhile, the Knights of Columbus in St. Louis took out a newspaper advertisement claiming that American policy toward Franco's Spain reflected communistic tendencies and "hatred of Christ." In truth, Niebuhr insisted, both communism and Catholicism reflected the same "self-righteous fanaticism," rooted in the assumption that "sinlessness" could be achieved in human history.[40]

As the *Everson* case progressed, however, Niebuhr shifted his attention to Catholicism's positive aspects. "Is it really right," he asked in the summer of 1947, for Protestants to "insist so absolutely on the separation of church and state" or to "become so excited about the possibility of Catholic parochial school children riding in state school buses?" Niebuhr warned that the danger of secularism far outweighed that of Catholics gaining some slight advantage. The "American solution of absolute separation," he wrote, "requires that we pay a very great price in the secularization of our culture." The real threat was that Protestants would let their faith "degenerate into mere anti-Catholicism" and church-state separation would be "interpreted too rigorously."[41]

Niebuhr had argued for some time that American liberals fetishized individual liberty and missed the need for "a sufficient fund of common loyalties" in a healthy society. Although liberty offered "the only basis for harmony in a pluralistic society," such a society also needed a set of "common convictions" and "overarching loyalties" to temper "the conflict of economic interests and party passions." But the scholars' progressive, humanistic naturalism fell short; it failed to grasp "the height and depth of man's existence." Meanwhile, religious liberalism was "so pathetically anxious to prove itself intellectually respectable that it [was] in peril of sacrificing all that is unique and important in the Christian faith." The only solution lay in a return to "the classical religious faiths of the past." As Niebuhr explained in "The Religious Level of the World Crisis," the "charity and forbearance which are required to solve our domestic and international problems must come from the sense of a divine majesty which stands over and against all the pretentious majesties of human existence, mitigating their pride; and of a divine judgment more final than all historic judgments, thus restraining their false claims to finality; and of a divine fulfillment of life which offers us peace when we see that all human fulfillments and realizations have new touches of evil in them." Only a strong sense of human sin and divine judgment could orient a democratic society toward justice, precisely by tempering the expectation of its imminent and total achievement.[42]

Niebuhr was just as clear, however, that the solution would involve treating individuals as parts of groups, rather than isolated atoms. The community, Niebuhr wrote in *The Children of Light and the Children of Darkness*, "requires liberty as much as does the individual," and "the individual requires community more than bourgeois thought comprehended." And a diverse society required diverse religious communities. Niebuhr celebrated religious differences—"cultural variety and social pluralism"—as a positive good. Yet religion was potentially also a source of division that every religious tradition would need to help temper by inculcating the proper spirit of humility. Understood properly, each tradition could, by instilling this profound humility, foster a "genuine universalism" that would "establish harmony without destroying the richness and variety of life." Although secular thought always fell short, many forms of religious belief did so as well, by failing to grasp the human capacities for both good and ill.[43]

By the fall of 1947, Niebuhr had largely shifted his focus from criticizing Catholics for their lack of humility to criticizing Protestants for their excessive individualism and lack of appreciation of Catholic critiques of secularism. He called opposition to busing parochial school students "hysterical," warning Protestants not to "make a fetish" of church-state separation but rather to adopt a prudential stand, recognizing that Catholics "pay school taxes and tax themselves in addition to maintain[ing] their parochial schools." Besides, he noted, every other democracy in the world went "further than we in the use of state funds for the support of religious instruction."[44]

In a major September 1947 article, "Our Relations to Catholicism," Niebuhr found fault on both sides for the "scandalous" tension between the two confessions. Catholics, he said, contributed through their "unqualified identification of Christ with the historic church." On the Protestant side, "we fail to appreciate the real concern for religious values which underlies the Catholic insistence on religious instruction." The present push for a high church-state wall, Niebuhr wrote, reflected both "the prevailing secularism of our culture" and "the Protestant fear of Catholicism." Such sentiment was partly legitimate, but also reflected

> an effort to cover up[,] by political action, the weakness of Protestantism in the field of religion itself. The anarchy of Protestantism, its lack of spiritual discipline, its ridiculous tensions between obscurantist versions of Protestantism on the one hand and of liberal versions on the other, its half-secular sentimentalities, all these weaknesses are more responsible for its sense of insecurity than anything that Catholicism may do politically. Let us defend ourselves against any political actions of Catholicism which tend to encroach upon our liberties; but let us achieve a greater consciousness of our own weaknesses and our tendency to cover our weaknesses by our apprehensions about a religious foe or competitor.

On the matter of the First Amendment, meanwhile, Niebuhr wrote that the Founders "quite obviously and quite rightly wanted to prevent the establishment of religious monopoly," but added "it is not at all clear that they sought to prevent the state's support of religion absolutely, provided such support could be given equitably to all religious groups." Lauding the Supreme Court's "decisions over a period of decades and centuries," Niebuhr clearly favored the accommodationist view. He also believed, based on his proximity to the Deweyan faculty of Teachers College, "that the prevailing philosophy which is pumped into our public schools day after day is itself a religion. . . . It preaches the redemption of man by historical development and by the illusory 'scientific objectivity.'" In short, Niebuhr contended, the public schools had officially established a religion of secularism.[45]

The Supreme Court's decisions spurred Niebuhr and his neo-orthodox allies to action on behalf of their accommodationist views. In the wake of *McCollum*, the National Conference of Christians and Jews sponsored an "off-the-record meeting" that brought Niebuhr, John Courtney Murray, and many like-minded figures together to discuss church-state questions. The eight participants (four Protestant and four Catholic) in the March 25, 1948, planning session included two of Niebuhr's close colleagues, John C. Bennett of Union Theological Seminary and F. Ernest Johnson of Columbia's Teachers College, as well as the Catholic theorists Murray and Wilfrid Parsons. The full meeting, held on April 26, 1948, at New York's Biltmore Hotel, included sixteen Catholics (including the three leading Catholic proponents of accommodationism, O'Neill, Parsons, and Murray); Niebuhr, Bennett, NCCJ director Everett R.

Clinchy, and ten other Protestants; and three Jewish leaders, at least one of whom—Louis M. Minsky of the Religion News Service—had sharply criticized secularism.[46]

At the meeting, Murray and Niebuhr framed the discussion by delivering prepared remarks on the recent decisions and church-state matters more broadly. According to the minutes, Murray not only described *McCollum* as fostering "the secularization of education" and making "the child a creature of government" but also warned of the decision's tendency "to make an idol out of democracy." As he would put it at the Wilmington rally a few days later, "I am concerned about the rising religion of democracy, whose church would be the public school. The Supreme Court exists in order to protect the U.S. citizen from any establishment of religion in our democracy; it would be a curious irony if it somehow assisted the establishment of the religion of democracy." At the NCCJ gathering, Murray expressed fear that secularists might use the schools to promote "secularized democracy as an end in itself," against a proper understanding of democracy as merely "a means for the realization of spiritual and moral ends." As for Niebuhr, the NCCJ minutes indicate that he, too, warned of a "religion of democracy" and called it "either a vacuum or a pseudo-religion." He also argued that "the Constitution does not require the *absolute* separation of Church and State" and echoed Murray's claim that *McCollum* aided "secularism in education."[47]

Niebuhr's comments at the 1948 meeting probably resembled his published writings on church-state relations from the spring and summer of that year. Concerned about both the tendency of secular commentators to blame democracy's ills on religion in general and the tendency of Catholics to target secularism, Niebuhr nevertheless joined Catholics in worrying about secularization. Criticizing the concurring opinion of his good friend Felix Frankfurter in *Everson*, Niebuhr challenged the elevation of the "wall of separation" metaphor into "a constitutional principle" and questioned whether singling out children who did not participate in voluntary religious observances undermined the school community. In "trying to preserve our unity at the expense of the vitality of our culture," he contended, Americans were creating a "spiritual vacuum" that would prove more perilous than would disunity. Niebuhr noted ominously that "modern secular surrogates for historic religions have a free course in our public schools" and "do not have to worry about the 'wall of separation,'" since they were "only implicitly and not explicitly religious."[48]

Niebuhr sought to distinguish himself from Catholic critics of secularism such as Murray by suggesting that "the true test of the Christian faith is not so much whether we believe in God" as whether we know God to be "our Judge as well as the Judge of our enemy." For all of its faults, Niebuhr observed, secularism also registered "a protest against the simple identification of God with, let us say, Franco's social system, or any other relative political idea which the church cherishes." Of course, he emphasized, the secularist belief that "the best way of getting rid of religious fanaticism is to get rid of religion" produced a "vacuum" that gave rise to "even more pagan idolatries" such as "the worship of a state, or a nation or of some relative value such as freedom or democracy." Niebuhr hoped that Protestants would carve out a position of their own, fighting both the tendency of "all traditional religion" to claim "the majesty of God or the sanctity of Christ" for secular ideals and "a secularism which empties life of meaning" and makes an idol of man. He argued that a "genuinely Biblical faith" could "render a greater service to 'democracy'" than either Catholicism or secularism, because it could "penetrate through all the pitiful pretenses which men practice in the name of both religion and irreligion." According to Niebuhr, the secularist view "that all men should have the right to believe anything or nothing" would turn a vibrant democracy into "a culturally empty association of empty individuals." Niebuhr called upon Protestants to reject "the illusions of modern secularism" while remaining vigilant "against the sins which are the characteristic corruptions of religion." Yet, at every turn, Niebuhr concluded that religion's shortcomings paled in comparison to the threats posed by secularism.[49]

A memorandum on the Biltmore meeting by one participant, Father William E. McManus, to the National Catholic Welfare Conference confirms the points of agreement between Murray and Niebuhr but also notes several bones of contention that emerged. The meeting, McManus begins, aimed to explore "the possibilities of formulating a Catholic-Protestant statement of policy concerning the right relationship of church and state in the United States." Murray aimed at the meeting to rally the "'anti-secularists' . . . around . . . a theory of church and state that will allow religion to be a vital force in American life." But Niebuhr, while troubled by the "philosophy of secularism latent in the McCollum decision," also criticized Murray for failing "to give due consideration to the contribution which secularism as a way of life has made to the development of American democracy." At the same time, McManus observed, Niebuhr blamed John Dewey for convincing the vast majority of Protestants that "religious differences are vestigial" and are "destined to disappear as democracy becomes the religion of the people." According to McManus, Niebuhr held Dewey responsible for "the temper of the American people, the majority of whom today are religious individualists." Niebuhr then argued that these individualistic convictions "allow most American citizens to accept rather good naturedly the drastic theory of sepa-

ration of church and state advanced in the *McCollum* decision." In short, wrote
McManus, Niebuhr contended that Dewey-inspired "religious individualists"
had "secularized American society." In fact, McManus claimed that all of the
conference participants embraced two tenets: "that the philosophy of secularism latent in the *McCollum* decision constituted a threat to organized religion
in the United States," and that "in the practical order—here in the U.S.—the
so-called principle of separation of church and state is not an absolute."[50]

At the close of the Biltmore meeting, according to McManus, participants
urged "the so-called moderate Protestants, i.e., those who are anti-secularists,"
to "prepare a statement representing a moderate Protestant view and to coopt
a considerable number of moderate Protestant leaders to sign such a statement." The statement, McManus specified, would likely "endorse released
time religious instruction, employment of chaplains in the Army and Navy
and possibly furnishing of services for nonpublic school pupils," based on
"a denial that the separation of church and state is an absolute that forces
all Americans to accept the secularist position." According to McManus, the
group also recommended further meetings across the country in which "men
of good will" would "mobilize the forces of religion in a frontal attack on the
secularism that all deplore."[51]

The Protestant statement, signed by a somewhat different set of figures
than had attended the Biltmore meeting—most of them Niebuhr's neo-
orthodox allies and/or Union Theological Seminary colleagues—was released
on June 17, 1948, and published soon after in Niebuhr and John Bennett's
journal *Christianity and Crisis*. It defended the accommodationist position
and described it as the traditional American understanding of church-state
relations, as well as the intent of the Founders. The signers warned that the
court's "hardening of the idea of 'separation'" would foster "the secularization of our culture" and undermine "the religious foundations of our national
life." In an accompanying editorial, Bennett—the only person to attend both
NCCJ meetings and also sign the statement—argued that the court's position favored "aggressive secularism," in the form of a "tendency to make the
institutions and assumptions of American democracy into a religious faith or
into a substitute for religious faith." Bennett blamed anti-Catholicism for the
Protestants' embrace of strict separationism, which would "destroy all types of
cooperation between Church and State which the American people have long
taken for granted from the military chaplaincy to tax exemption for church
property." He argued that, "as a nation, we should recognize that Christian
standards have a claim upon us and that as a nation we need the guidance and
the power that come from God through Christ." The "place of the Jewish faith
in American life," Bennett continued, required a somewhat broader formula-

tion at the national level, but that needed to be attained "without cancelling the fundamental idea that, for the vast majority of our people, any sense of our standing under God's judgment and mercy as a nation must be expressed in Christian terms or, in effect, denied."[52]

Among mainline Protestant leaders, however, such arguments largely fell on deaf ears. The *Christian Century*'s editors indignantly summarized the *Christianity and Crisis* statement: "Protestants Take Catholic Line." Among these Protestants, and other pluralists suspicious of Catholic educational arguments, the events of 1948 simply deepened fears of an impending assault on the very principle of public education. By 1949, a heightened sense of crisis could be felt on all sides of the school debate.[53]

The increasingly bitter tenor of the public conversation reflected, in part, the writings of Paul Blanshard. A left-leaning, muckraking journalist who had long ago abandoned his Congregational faith, Blanshard levied a ferocious critique of the Catholic Church's political stance in a series of *Nation* articles that were originally published in 1947 and 1948 and then republished as *American Freedom and Catholic Power* in 1949. Intermingling sober analysis with crass stereotypes, Blanshard proved to his satisfaction—and that of many readers—that Catholic officials aimed to overthrow democracy and install a regime of clerical fascism. Blanshard's call for a "resistance movement" against the "antidemocratic social policies of the hierarchy" struck a nerve; the book sold like hotcakes and went through edition after edition.[54]

The combination of disputes over education and Blanshard's writings spawned a series of fierce controversies. After the *Nation* published Blanshard's articles, many bishops urged boycotts of public libraries carrying that journal, provoking vigorous outcries against censorship. Catholic officials increasingly spoke out publicly on the education issue as well. In 1949, New York's sharp-tongued Cardinal Francis Spellman called North Carolina congressman Graham A. Barden, who had sponsored a bill to prohibit federal aid to private schools, an anti-Catholic bigot. Eleanor Roosevelt, who had also protested the *Nation* boycott, responded in her "My Day" column by defending "the original traditions of our nation," ruling out aid to "denominational" schools. Spellman then wrote a long letter accusing Roosevelt, too, of bigotry. The controversy escalated to a point where Vatican officials stepped in and urged Spellman to moderate his tone.[55]

Liberal Catholic intellectuals responded to Protestant opposition with greater equanimity, though their frustration was palpable as well. James M. O'Neill spent the next three years crafting his response: the 1952 book *Catholicism and American Freedom*. Murray, in his review of *American Freedom and Catholic Power*, influentially dubbed Blanshard's position "the new nativism."

The book confirmed Murray's sense that the Church's primary adversary was secularism; it offered nothing like the "ranting, redfaced, mid-nineteenth century Nativism" of Protestant yore. Rather, Blanshard's "cold, cultured" approach reflected a "secular positivism that deplores bigotry, at the same time that it achieves a closure of mind and an edge of antagonism that would be the envy of a Bible-belt circuit rider." In Murray's reading, Blanshard identified "the democratic social-welfare state" as the sole legitimate authority in all domains: "science, medicine, and social welfare, culture, the family, education and information, politics, economics and law." Meanwhile, that state followed no higher norms; its policies reflected only the will of the majority. Murray charged that Blanshard, by deeming Catholics un-American, had used "the terms 'American' and 'un-American' as categories of ultimate value," in keeping with "the contemporary drift toward a cultural monism, the idea of the democratic state as All There Is, and a colossal national self-righteousness." In short, Blanshard peddled a soft, secular form of totalitarianism that cloaked itself in claims of tolerance.[56]

Even the steady-handed Murray did not always maintain his cool amid the turmoil of 1949, however. Late that year, he became embroiled in a high-profile spitting match in the *American Mercury* with one of Niebuhr's colleagues, W. Russell Bowie. The Union Theological Seminary dean had provoked Murray's ire by drawing a familiar contrast. "Roman Catholicism," he wrote, "as it impinges on the community and the State, is totalitarian, and Protestantism, which believes in the dignity of all human souls and in the liberty of mind and spirit as the only guarantee of truth, is bound to recognize and reject totalitarianism, no matter how much it covers itself with religious garb." Murray shot back that "Catholicism is not tense, not polarized against Protestantism" at all, "except in so far as this or that Protestant position manifests an alliance with secularist tendencies." But he added that Protestants were "wounded and angry because the Catholic Church considers Protestantism to be a second-class religion."[57]

Protestants of all varieties responded sharply to Murray's contention that they suffered from an inferiority complex. The *Christian Century* editorialized, "Protestants think much worse things about Roman Catholicism than that it is 'second-class.'" Yet, the journal insisted, "anti-Catholicism" was ultimately "incidental" in Protestant thought: "It derives from the necessity of fighting for a standing ground on which to hold and practice the Christianity of free men without compulsion or restraint." Reinhold Niebuhr, noting his admiration for Murray, nevertheless deemed the Jesuit's accusation highly uncharitable. Protestants harbored no "secret fear that they might be second-class Christians," wrote Niebuhr; instead, they feared "becoming second-class citizens in America," at the hands of Catholics who constantly urged even their staunchest Protestant friends to "join the true church." According to Niebuhr, "the wide advances of Catholicism since the war have made Catholics even more confident than hitherto that Protestantism is a heresy or defection which must ultimately disappear, since its dismal anarchy compares unfavorably with the impressive inclusiveness and unity of the Roman church." A few months earlier, Niebuhr had likewise pinned the blame firmly on Cardinal Spellman in his spat with Eleanor Roosevelt. The latter's column, he said, expressed "an honest difference of conviction," whereas Spellman's response indicated that he would treat anything other than total agreement as "proof of 'anti-Catholic prejudice.'" Still, Niebuhr reminded disputants on both sides that democracy required "respect for the motives of people who differ with us seriously."[58]

Positioning himself as a mediator, Niebuhr explained to separationists that "the sense of injustice which the Catholic taxpayer feels" reflected a recognition "that there are democratic nations in which public funds are used for the support of religious schools or for religious education in public schools." Niebuhr also urged Catholics to abandon their superciliousness toward Protestants and posture of infallibility; he stressed "how much patience is required when our own convictions are constantly challenged as obvious violations of the natural law, and as, therefore, in conflict with the expressed will of God." And Catholics should also do more to reassure Protestants that the American Church would favor the lay state endorsed by Maritain and Murray over Spanish-style church-state fusion. (Official Catholic denunciations of toleration had "hardened the hearts of non-Catholics in this country," Niebuhr wrote, in a passage that Murray quoted directly in his memo to the Vatican.) Yet Niebuhr saw a simple solution to the school question at hand: a policy akin to the GI Bill, with federal money flowing directly to students rather than schools. If non-Catholics would follow that precedent and Catholics would openly disavow "direct tax support" as a future goal, the controversy could be quickly put to rest. One thing was clear, Niebuhr warned: If the theologians failed to get it right, the secularists would step in with their own solution.[59]

Despite his irritated tone and lingering suspicion, then, Niebuhr's writings of 1949–50 revealed that the intellectual architecture was in place for an alliance of liberal Catholics and many Protestants against secular theories of democracy and strict separationist readings of the First Amendment. The following year, in fact, the Catholic journal Ave Maria reported enthusiastically on a Cleveland College speech in which Niebuhr urged Americans to follow European democracies in providing tax support to parochial schools. Protestants simply needed to give up their "formally legalistic" objections and provide "health and welfare benefits" to parochial school students. The Founders wanted no "absolute impregnable wall," Niebuhr asserted; they were "religious men themselves" and "believed that religion was part of education." In the end, it was largely Protestant prejudice that kept the controversy alive: "The whole problem of government support would have been settled a long time ago if we had been willing to give our Catholic friends a break."[60]

*

One striking feature of the debate over federal aid to education was the invisibility of American Jews. To be sure, Jewish groups themselves sought to influence the conversation. Leo Pfeffer and the American Jewish Congress, among other groups, pushed hard for strict separationism. But the leading Protestant and Catholic contributors identified only three parties to the dispute: Catholics, Protestants, and "secularists." Bennett's editorial alongside the *Christianity and Crisis* statement was extremely unusual in acknowledging the complicated issue of Jewish Americans—and entirely typical in turning immediately to the question of how to assure Christians that national institutions reflected their faith commitments. Meanwhile, Will Herberg, the leading Jewish critic of strict separationism, held his tongue on the school question until the early 1950s.

As the Judeo-Christian discourse continued to expand after World War II, then, it intersected with a church-state debate that saw growing numbers of Protestants rail against the inroads of secularism and line up with liberal Catholics on the side of accommodationism, even as the Supreme Court embraced strict separationism. To say that the postwar transformation of the country's self-conception entailed merely the replacement of a narrowly Protestant or Christian framework with a tri-faith sensibility is to miss the full significance of that change. The coming of Judeo-Christian America accompanied the emergence of the Cold War against "godless communism" and a sharp spike in antisecularism at home, as well as growing discontent, among Catholics and many Protestants, with the federal government's evolving approach to church-state questions. As the United States took the helm of Western civilization and sought to beat back totalitarianism, many cultural commentators insisted that it could fulfill its appointed tasks only if Americans rejoined the religious fold, trading skepticism, secularism, and religious liberalism for more traditional forms of theism and greater church-state cooperation.

6

Fighting Godless Communism

RELIGION AND SECULARISM IN
JUDEO-CHRISTIAN AMERICA, 1950–1955

With the Cold War under way and open conflict breaking out in Korea, the early 1950s brought the most confident and widespread uses of Judeo-Christian rhetoric that the nation would see. That era witnessed a remarkable upsurge in religious affiliation and attendance, along with unprecedented forms of cultural visibility—especially in motion pictures—for Catholicism and, to a lesser extent, Judaism. As the federal government acknowledged God on currency and in the Pledge of Allegiance, the revivalist Billy Graham and other popular religious leaders led tens of thousands of Americans back to Christ. Religious participation meshed easily with celebrations of American prosperity; works such as Norman Vincent Peale's *The Power of Positive Thinking* (1952) joined Rabbi Joshua L. Liebman's earlier *Peace of Mind* (1946) on the bestseller lists.

Religious celebrities such as the Catholic bishop Fulton J. Sheen, who made the jump from radio to television in 1951, often promoted exceptionalist visions of democracy and characterized the Cold War as a global spiritual struggle between Judeo-Christianity and paganism or atheism. As Senator Joseph McCarthy ramped up his campaign against subversives in Hollywood, the universities, and the federal government, both liberal and conservative anticommunists feared the influence of communist fellow travelers at home. With these worries came heightened concerns about godlessness. A belief that secularism and secularists would undermine democracy lay at the heart of Cold War ideology. "There is a tendency to regard all people who are not committed to one of the three great faiths as being disloyal to American principles and traditions," complained the Ethical Culture leader Sidney H. Scheuer in 1954.[1]

Of course, nonbelievers attempted to fight back, as did other pluralists

who believed that democracy rested on tolerance rather than substantive religious teachings. Indeed, both nonbelievers and pluralists could become quite
hostile toward religious groups—above all Catholics—with exclusive truth
claims. In recent years, historians have foregrounded figures of this ilk, especially the circle of naturalist philosophers around John Dewey and the notori-
ous polemicist Paul Blanshard. Horace Kallen, too, combined his expansive
rhetoric of inclusion with aggressive and sweeping criticism of Catholicism.
But scholars have generally ignored the many powerful commentators who
expressed analogous views of the "secularism" of naturalists, humanists, and
religious liberals. Indeed, it was Judeo-Christian exceptionalists, with their
shrill warnings about the dangers of secularism, materialism, and atheism,
who generally controlled the tenor of public debate in the 1950s, although
they faced opposition within the universities and could not necessarily count
on the Supreme Court to defend their views. As always, the inhabitants of
each pole on the Judeo-Christian spectrum saw those on the opposite side as
dangerous enemies who threatened the body politic. The continuing potency
of the charge of secularism in American political life reflects this powerful
legacy of the early Cold War period, an era that turned theologians into
public intellectuals—and presidents into theologians.

Religion and the Cold War

Through the early 1950s, public commentators continued to frame Judeo-
Christianity's contributions to democracy in various ways. A common catch-
phrase was "the fatherhood of God and the brotherhood of man": "The concept of the Supreme being as our father in heaven is essentially democratic,"
declared one Presbyterian minister, "because it means that we on earth are
brothers and sisters, children in a family." A second writer added the meritocratic ideal of "equality of opportunity to work regardless of creed, race,
or color" to the list of Judeo-Christian values. *Time* listed four tenets of "a
Judeo-Christian heritage with which men of all faiths may agree" and which
defined Western civilization: "1) the fatherhood of God, 2) the brotherhood
of man, 3) the essential dignity of man, and 4) the right of the individual
to hold and administer private property, subject to his responsibilities to his
fellowmen." Another list included "the belief that man is created in God's
image and is son of God," and thus "has worth in and of himself"; the idea
that "man is encompassed in a brotherhood that includes his fellowman";
"the general ideal that we call integrity" (encompassing "truth, honor, service,
beauty, justice, mercy, courage, temperance, sympathy, compassion, kindli-
ness, [and] love"; "freedom of mind and spirit" ("not the pseudo freedom of

license, but the responsible freedom of brothers that respects the rights and needs of others as it does those of self"); and "reverence for life as creation and gift of God."[2]

Many Judeo-Christian formulations deemed individuals innately selfish and immoral, absent religious sanction. "Men who start out to do good for others, because it is a pleasant pastime" rather than a religious obligation, argued Boston University president Harold C. Case, "end up by doing well for themselves because it is a profitable enterprise." The Catholic philosopher Samuel I. Clark likewise deprecated "a non-theological charity": "The brotherhood of man, when separated from the fatherhood of God, becomes a Dale Carnegie society where charity is employed to win friends and influence people—in other words, a society of pleasant, mutual exploitation."[3]

Commentators routinely attributed totalitarianism to the loss of a religious foundation for morality. "We have no choice but to arm," declared *New York Times* publisher Arthur Hays Sulzberger, "if we would preserve our way of life and the Judeo-Christian concept of pity, decency, justice, and humanity." The venerable liberal Protestant Harry Emerson Fosdick also called the Cold War a spiritual battle and traced democracy to "major elements in the Judeo-Christian faith concerning God and man, backed by the insights of the Greek seers." To Fosdick, the ever-expanding grasp of the American state represented an alarming symptom of religious decline. RCA head David Sarnoff, a Russian-Jewish émigré, termed the Cold War "a deep-reaching contest between our Judeo-Christian civilization and a Godless way of life and thought." And the Catholic journalist Anne O'Hare McCormick, labeling 1952's Christmas festivities a "victory" over totalitarianism, said Santa Claus embodied the altruism "that distinguishes the Judeo-Christian code from the pagan creeds that preceded or now aspire to succeed it."[4]

Postwar thinkers increasingly considered the dynamics of spreading democracy to non-Western countries as well. Although Westerners viewed "the Judeo-Christian beliefs in the dignity of man and the sacredness of human personality" as "the common aspiration of men," warned University of Iowa president Virgil M. Hancher, these "have never been known in Russia or in much of Asia." Waldo Frank traced communism to the "crassness" and "explosiveness" of "peoples never tinctured . . . by the social justice and the tenderness of the Judaeo-Christian tradition." Indeed, Frank found that cultural maturity in Europe but only rarely in the United States, which "despite its Judaeo-Christian tradition and its churches" followed "materialist and pragmatist values."[5]

The tumult of decolonization led those with "Third World" sympathies to employ both Judeo-Christian formulations and unusual alternatives.

The African American scholar and minister C. A. Chick Sr. told a group of black Baptists that Americans could keep Africans "within the fold of the Free West" by treating them in accordance with "the noble principles and high ideals of the Judeo-Christian religions," especially "liberty, equality, and fraternity." Writers of Middle Eastern origin, touting their home countries' democratic bona fides, reiterated late-nineteenth-century assertions of links between Islam and Judeo-Christianity. One traced Egyptian culture to the "Greco-Roman and Judaeo-Christian-Islamic civilizations," adding that Egyptians were "firm believers in God and private ownership." The Syrian-born Presbyterian minister Edward J. Jurji invoked instead "the Judaeo-Christian tradition with which Mohammedanism is linked." Although these formulations skirted the question of democracy's precise institutional contours, in the Cold War context they tended to strengthen the dominant, exceptionalist view of religion's political role.[6]

Attacks on secularism flourished accordingly. Although McCarthyism fueled a shift in focus toward domestic subversion, it also reflected longstanding fears that apostasy at home fueled totalitarianism abroad. "The cancer of secularism which is impregnating our lives is far more than dangerous than the atomic bomb," asserted Robert J. Slavin, the Catholic president of Providence College. "The real fight today is for God and the things of God." Another Christian educator agreed: "Secularism and ethical humanism are everywhere apparent, and must be supplanted with the theism found in the Judeo-Christian conception of life." The "nation's basic struggle," held Queens College president John J. Theobald, pitted "the Judeo-Christian tradition" against "those who are trying to substitute neo-paganistic ideas and practices," wherever they resided. A Valparaiso University professor rebutted secularists who said principles derived historically from "the Judeo-Christian tradition" could survive without it. Christianity, he wrote, taught that "secularized standards of value repeatedly become distorted and are robbed of their dynamic power when divorced from their basis in Christian love." In its fierce antisecularism—and its lingering supersessionism—this formulation captured the leading tendencies in postwar Judeo-Christian discourse.[7]

As the Cold War picked up steam and anticommunism's political center of gravity shifted rightward, such arguments became powerful tools in domestic political struggles. The African American editors of the *Pittsburgh Courier* announced that America's "Judeo-Christian civilization" was "being disparaged and UNDERMINED by a Fifth Column of our OWN citizens." The Brooklyn Republican leader John R. Crews, arguing that communism "threatens the destruction of our Judeo-Christian civilization itself," went ahead and named names. Since 1932, he charged, "the Democratic party has furthered the sapping of our body politic by moving ever nearer that statism, the ultimate of which is communism."[8]

Heterodox theists bore much of the criticism. Given their political prominence, liberal Protestants found themselves tarred and feathered as communist sympathizers in the early 1950s. The Methodist bishop G. Bromley Oxnam's July 1953 appearance before McCarthy's committee symbolized, to many fellow liberals, a systematic attempt to "discredit progressive, liberal churchmen who have a concern for social progress." The Unitarian pastor A. Powell Davies flung Judeo-Christian rhetoric back at Oxnam's critics. Contending that "Congressional committees are moving in on the churches," Davies said McCarthy sought "the substitution of enforced conformity for independent judgment, and of anti-Communism for the Judeo-Christian ethic, and of authoritarianism for the American founding principles."[9]

The charge that newer theologies threatened democracy also emerged from struggles within religious organizations. The Episcopal rector John Ellis Large charged that theological liberalism and modernism had rendered the United States helpless against the Soviet juggernaut by replacing Christian principles with atheistic views of the person as "a deluxe monkey" and God as a "celestial bellhop." To safeguard democracy, Americans would have to recapture the image of "a created creature whose fulfillment lies in seeking and trying to do the will of his Creator." Characterizing "the *denial* of God" as a religion in itself, Large argued that "morality, cut off from the primary worship of God, will be as short-lived as a cut flower."[10]

This cut-flower image undergirded much American thinking about the Cold War. George M. Docherty relied heavily on that argument in the February 1954 sermon to President Eisenhower and others at the New York Avenue Presbyterian Church that inspired the addition of "under God" to the Pledge of Allegiance. The Cold War, he said, pitted "the view of man that comes down to us from the Judao-Christian [*sic*] civilization" against "modern, secularized, godless humanity." Docherty sought to encompass Muslims, but he deemed an "atheistic American" a "contradiction in terms." He explained that "ethical seculars" were usually model citizens but remained "'spiritual parasites' . . . living upon the accumulated Spiritual Capital of a Judaio-Christian [*sic*] civilization."[11]

Although scholars have been slow to recognize the antisecularism at the heart of much Cold War rhetoric, those targeted at the time recognized its significance. The iconoclastic journalist and lecturer Henry Geiger neatly dissected the logic behind FBI director J. Edgar Hoover's mantra that "Communism is Secularism on the march": "All Communists are atheists. Therefore, all atheists are either Communists or potential Communists." In the hands of "demagogues," Geiger continued, this assumption justified the conclusion that "our only defense against Communism is to identify Democracy and Christianity." Geiger called "the ideological war against the 'secularists'" a "dishonest and anti-democratic campaign to destroy the very 'way of life' . . . it sets out to defend."[12]

Some critics of anticommunist initiatives turned Judeo-Christian rhetoric to their own ends. A letter in the *New York Times* declared that the "Judeo-Christian heritage of the value of the individual and respect for his liberty" should foster confidence in the capacity of American culture and ideals to overwhelm a few communist agitators hawking a "material self-seeking philosophy (if it warrants the name)." A. J. Muste of the Fellowship of Reconciliation went further, proposing "a pacifist policy" toward the Soviets in the face of "mounting evidence that military power and war under modern conditions cannot possibly provide security or help to save our democratic and Judeo-Christian values."[13]

Others sought to debunk the protean concept of secularism. As the wave of McCarthyism crested in 1954, the modernist theologian Edwin E. Aubrey pushed back with *Secularism a Myth: An Examination of the Current Attack on Secularism*. Aubrey contended that "secularism" had recently become "a rallying cry for religious forces, much as paganism was in the early Christian church, or 'the infidel' in the Middle Ages, or 'popery' in seventeenth-century Protestantism." As in earlier days, "secularism" provided a "convenient slogan" to "arouse the loyalty of a group against a common enemy" by differentiating the "in-group from the out-group." And like most such terms, Aubrey continued, "secularism" was remarkably vague, referring to an enormous range of phenomena disliked by more orthodox believers. Likening "secularism" to the constellation of epithets, including "ecclesiasticism, dogmatism, absolutism, pessimism, credulity, conservatism, cynicism and moral indifferentism," that were directed at various theologies, Aubrey urged his readers to resist using the term to foster "a spurious sense of crusading unity."[14]

Behind the growing use of the discourse of secularism in Protestant ecumenical pronouncements, Aubrey detected the deleterious influence of neo-orthodoxy on Protestant thinking about the relationship between the church and the world. A longtime participant in New York's Theological Discussion Group, alongside the leading lights of neo-orthodoxy, Aubrey judiciously directed the brunt of his criticism toward that movement's European theorists and portrayed its American interpreters as moderating forces in ecumenical discussion. Yet he took issue with the overall movement's underlying "determination not to succumb to contemporary culture," which struck Aubrey as a mere rationalization for an "imperious attitude toward society" that mistook "ecclesiastical pride" for "loyalty to God" and turned "fear of social impotence" into "strident defiance." Aubrey counseled church leaders to stop alienating potential allies and "focus on their real enemies—human sins such as greed and hypocrisy—rather than constructing a mythological common enemy out of secular movements as such." A truly humble believer, he wrote, would recognize that "there have been spiritual values in secular movements which Christianity cannot claim to have originated and which should, in plain justice, be acknowledged."[15]

Even Aubrey, however, placed some viewpoints beyond the pale. He embraced scholars, social reformers, humanists, agnostics, and other nontheistic idealists but rejected "the atheist or the morally indifferent person" who harbored no ethical—and thus potentially spiritual—commitments whatsoever. Horace Kallen, whose *Secularism Is the Will of God* also appeared in 1954, challenged such distinctions and sought to put all belief systems on a level plane, even as he contended that each constituted a religion because it rested on nonscientific articles of faith. Kallen aimed to subvert the typical categories of "believer" and "unbeliever" without reinscribing the pejorative distinction by contending that nontheists followed a false religion.[16]

Since the war, Kallen argued, all of the modern ills frequently "lumped together as 'materialism'" had been "concentrated and transformed into the figure of an overweening power menacing all freedoms—the Soviets with their 'godless Communism.'" In response, Kallen continued, most commentators offered an "infallible remedy," namely, "'belief in God'—of course 'God' as their faith, and not another's, defines 'God.'" But the truly American approach was secularism, a kind of metafaith that "neither competes with any other religion nor displaces any other" because it "takes for its business the relations between faiths, not the creeds they assert." Secularism, Kallen continued, entailed not just "abandoning conversion," as Jews had long since done, but also "gladly accepting diversity and liking persons of different faiths just the way they are." In short, it jettisoned the distinction between true believers and infidels.[17]

Kallen rooted his vision of secularism in American history, challenging the exceptionalist claim that rights required a divine source. The Declaration of Independence, he wrote, recognized that rights "are not a grant from without by some superior external power" but rather flowed from the consent of the governed. On the basis of this understanding, said Kallen, the Founders had instituted a regime of secularism, a "collective guarantee that everyone may safely believe, change his belief and speak his beliefs to whomsoever would listen."[18]

Looking around the world of 1954, however, Kallen saw Americans rapidly falling away from their long-standing tradition of secularism. As always, he pinned blame on the Catholic hierarchy. The Church, wrote Kallen, would stand against democracy until it joined other religious groups in replacing "clericalism" with secularism as an approach to intergroup relations. Instead, however, Catholic leaders waged a worldwide campaign to discredit those who dared think differently about religion as intolerant bigots and dangerous subversives. Kallen portrayed the Cold War itself as a global "war of religions" launched by "the present Czars of Russia" against "the Romanists" and pitting the communists' "red authoritarianism" against the Catholics' "black authoritarianism." Each party, he contended, sought to abridge the free and open competition of faiths characteristic of secularism by imposing its own exclusive claim to truth. The hierarchy's policy, everywhere and always, was "unfailing aggression against all that is diverse and will not yield its integrity of conscience."[19]

Kallen's extravagant fears of Catholicism aside, *Secularism Is the Will of God* indicated a key point of disagreement in debates over religion and politics. At stake was not simply whether democracy rested on religion but also the degree to which religious traditions could change their contours over time. Kallen held that Jews worldwide, and mainstream American Protestants, had eschewed missionizing and embraced difference. (At various points, Kallen invoked "the social gospel" and the "religions of the Enlightenment" in characterizing the shift toward secularism in various traditions.) He also took for granted that every religion could embrace an inclusive, fallibilistic conception of knowledge without losing its essential character. Under the umbrella of secularism, he explained, every religious leader "endeavors to persuade, not compel, everybody else to bet their lives on his faith and not another's." Kallen assumed that, absent coercion, all believers in diverse societies would move over time toward open-ended tolerance, associated with the image of "a God who is a perfect being whose substance is love" and a functionalist understanding of truth as merely "the trust we put in a belief as it manifests superior operational worth in a competitive field among rivals as freely and safely attempting on equal terms to do a better cognitive job." Needless to say, most of his contemporaries disagreed.[20]

Educational Controversies

Although federal aid was off the table after 1949's fireworks, *Everson* and *McCollum*, and religion's role in education more generally, continued to fuel controversy. The jurist Paxton Blair called the court's decisions "historically indefensible" and equated democracy's Judeo-Christian character with scientific facts. To "inform pupils that our nation was founded by men who believed in God, and that it is based squarely 'on the Judaeo-Christian ethics and concept of God,'" said Blair, was like teaching "the chemical components of the air we breathe, or the water we drink." Yale Divinity School dean Luther A. Weigle neatly captured the implications: public schools "may be neutral as to the strife or sects; but they cannot be neutral as to God." As earlier, John Bennett and other neo-orthodox Protestants took this accommodationist approach as well.[21]

Similar arguments circulated in the universities, where the postwar years witnessed a concerted effort to reground the undergraduate curriculum on religious principles. This effort was notable for its Christian tenor; proponents hardly mentioned Judaism and used Christian and Judeo-Christian language interchangeably. A typical advocate, the Methodist philosopher Russell J. Compton, argued that "the Judeo-Christian religious heritage," having long "provided Western man with intellectual and practical order for his life," should become the "unifying framework for contemporary education." Compton then reiterated the point in Christian terms: The "most important fact" about the West was that it was "a Christian civilization." Even the substantial Greek element, Compton averred, came in through "its assimilation into the living stream of Christianity."[22]

In April 1952, the Supreme Court took a significant step back toward accommodationism. The *Zorach v. Clauson* decision allowed released-time religious education during school hours, provided it took place off school property. As in *Everson*, the decision's impact stemmed mainly from the majority opinion's wording. The court called Americans "a religious people whose institutions presuppose a Supreme Being" and whose government "respects the religious nature of our people and accommodates the public service to their spiritual needs." It denied that the Constitution required "callous indifference" or even "hostility" toward religion; those approaches privileged nonbelievers over believers.[23]

Mainstream Protestants continued to adopt this accommodationist view in the early 1950s. In January 1953, the Episcopalian philanthropist Anson Phelps Stokes noted a "growing awareness," in the face of the Soviets' "crass materialism," of "the need for emphasis on religion in our life to strengthen moral standards and true democracy." Like many of his Protestant forebears, Stokes thought it possible to find a nonsectarian form of religious education—now, a Judeo-Christian form—that no right-thinking American could reject.[24]

Even some Protestants who favored separation in the wider public sphere advocated religious education. John A. Mackay, for example, advocated "full religious freedom" for all believers and atheists but saw in secular education "a prelude to, and a basic preparation for, a totalitarian system in both education and government." Mackay wanted the schools to teach "the Hebrew-Christian religious tradition," which had been "the dominant spiritual influence in Western civilization" and "shaped the culture of this country in the most creative period of our national life." The teacher, Mackay stipulated, should "introduce his students, in an objective manner, to the facts and supreme values of religion, very especially as they are exemplified and set forth in the Judeo-Christian tradition."[25]

Catholics welcomed such tendencies but deemed "nonsectarian" approaches theologically inadequate and secularizing in their effects. The Catholic historian John Tracy Ellis took Anson Phelps Stokes to task for endorsing religious education, the *McCollum* decision, and John Dewey's educational philosophy all at once. Vashti McCollum was "a professed atheist," Ellis objected, and Dewey had inspired "the annihilation of the supernatural element in education." Samuel I. Clark decried the "secular humanism" of the American schools, where a "belief in the perfectibility of man by means of education" had supplanted "the Judeo-Christian concept of sin and salvation." But no "lowest common denominator" model could work, especially if it accommodated secular thoughtways. Clark denounced initiatives based on "moral and spiritual values dissociated from traditional theological thought," insisting "religion is too significant and integral a part of American culture to be treated in any other fashion than directly and vigorously."[26]

Many pluralists argued just the opposite. The progressive educator and Ethical Culture leader V. T. Thayer contended that morality could only be taught adequately in secular schools because they alone refrained from grounding it in "one religious orientation, be this narrowly denominational, or, as vague and general as the Judaeo-Christian affirmation." Noting that even Catholics rejected the "common core" approach, Thayer argued that morality would fare best when it was recognized as a shared possession of the entire population and not associated with a specific theology.[27]

A few weeks before the *Zorach* decision, Harvard University president James B. Conant added fuel to the fire. In 1950, Conant had used his baccalaureate address to warn that "zealous proponents of religious schools" threatened the country's culture of tolerance. Secular schools were neither "amoral" nor "Godless," Conant argued; they taught the "common moral judgments" underlying each religious faith. In April 1952, Conant sharpened his critique of "dual" (public-parochial) education in a controversial address to the American Association of School Administrators (AASA). At the same meeting, AASA president Kenneth E. Oberholtzer called private schools "divisive," while the group's executive secretary claimed "denominational schools build prejudices, they build little Iron Curtains around the thinking of people." A third AASA official identified parochial education as a form of segregation akin to Jim Crow.[28]

But it was Conant's speech that made waves. The influential Episcopal minister James A. Pike and Richard J. Cushing, the Catholic archbishop of Boston, contended that secular schools were hardly neutral; they taught the religion of secularism. Where Conant saw a conspiracy of sectarians to stamp out public education, these figures saw a conspiracy of secularists to stamp out religion. In an Easter sermon before Boston's mayor and the governor of Massachusetts, Cushing charged that Conant's speech would aid the accelerating "campaign of secularism against independent schools, above all religious schools." Pike held that Conant used "the smear tactic of shouting 'un-American'" for "totalitarian" purposes: to establish "a monolithic educational philosophy." And both identified religious education as a political resource, upholding "the independence of the mind and soul of a person in the face of the omnipotent modern state." For such critics, religious education offered virtually the last remaining defense against a grasping, implicitly totalitarian state.[29]

The controversy continued after the *Zorach* decision in late April. At the National Education Association meeting in July, Agnes Meyer, a member of President Truman's Commission on Higher Education, advocated a constitutional amendment against public funding for private schools. Otherwise, Meyer contended, Catholics and fundamentalists would "tear our Nation into irreconcilable factions," destroying "all hope of religious amity and of community solidarity" and leaving the nation "so torn by hostile groups that we would become an easy prey to the Communist foe." On the other side, Fulton Sheen, like other Catholic leaders, said it was the secularists who were "fostering disloyalty in our nation" by denying Americans knowledge of God and making them "illegitimate children who know not their parentage." Among Protestants, the National Council of Churches (NCC) warned in a "Letter to the Christian People of America" that the United States would become fully secularized, and thus criminally dangerous on a global stage, unless it restored religion to its "rightful place." The letter, written under the guidance of John A. Mackay, argued that any country elevating secularism to the status of a religion "tends to assume divine prerogatives and commits satanic crimes."[30]

In this regard, at least, the authors of the NCC letter closely and consciously followed the American Catholic bishops' statement of the previous month. As they had after *Everson* and *McCollum*, the bishops argued that civic association existed "only when justice and charity, universal in their binding force because imposed by God himself, are embodied in law." Because "religion is important to good citizenship," they continued, the state was obligated "to help parents fulfill their task of religious instruction and training." Here, however, the NCC leaders diverged. Rejecting aid to parochial schools, they argued that public schools could heighten "awareness of God" through "reverent reading" of biblical texts, supported by the school's "moral and cultural atmosphere" and "the attitude, the viewpoints and the character of the teachers." In short, they favored a "common core" approach.[31]

Theorizing Democracy

Meanwhile, theorists of various persuasions continued to debate broader questions about democracy, religion, and secularism, as anxieties about national unity in the face of communism ratcheted up. Indeed, the need for cooperation led at least one Catholic citizen to reject the exceptionalist claim that nonbelievers threatened the nation. Writing to the *New Republic* in 1952, Charles Stinson credited Western civilization to a "predominantly Judaeo-Christian moral and ethical atmosphere" but held that atheists, too, embraced that system of "natural morality and ethics." Catholics, he asserted, knew that the natural law "ultimately draws its authority from the supernatural truths underlying it (i.e., dogmatic theology)" but also recognized "that in the temporal order it is possible to live this morality in its basic forms without accepting or even knowing anything about those underlying truths." As a result, nonbelievers could join the ethical consensus of the West. Stinson held that even disagreement on the central question of God's existence in no way prevented "our getting together as people of good will in order to defend our cherished temporal way of life." Implicitly rejecting the cut-flower argument that morality required religion, Stinson diverged from Murray by arguing that the shared teachings of the natural law did not include the tenet of God's sovereignty over human affairs.[32]

A much more prominent figure, *Commonweal* editor John Cogley, pushed the boundaries of Murray's approach in a different way. A former Catholic Worker radical, Cogley prefigured sensibilities that would become widespread after Vatican II and expanded the theological and political boundaries of liberal Catholicism for a generation of progressive "*Commonweal* Catholics." In the early 1950s, Cogley rejected the anticommunist crusade that so many Catholics pursued. Indeed, he seemed to question the very idea of democracy as a religious phenomenon.[33]

Cogley's antisecularist credentials were actually unimpeachable. *Commonweal* joined Murray in distinguishing two forms of liberalism. One, addressing "pure economics or pure politics," was fully compatible with Catholicism. But when liberalism offered ultimate truths, it became "a rival religion," namely, "dynamic secularism." Cogley thus responded fiercely when "Paul the Apostle of Secularism" published a sequel, *Communism, Democracy, and Catholic Power*, in 1951. Blanshard's tome, wrote Cogley, illustrated a common pattern among liberals: It "exalted what he chooses to call Democracy but is properly known as dynamic Secularism, to the status of a pseudo-religion."[34]

But Cogley drew the line at anticommunism. "Throughout my entire adult life," since the mid-1930s, he lamented, "opposition to Communism" had been the milieu in which "we Catholics lived and moved and had our being." That negative imperative had "colored almost everything we said and did," becoming "the one unfailing constant, the touchstone by which we made our judgments and determined to a great extent the political line we followed." Cogley saw the whole project as a colossal waste of time and resources: "an anti, largely rhetorical enterprise" that drew energies away from "genuinely Christian social reconstruction."[35]

Cogley's view led him to agree with the civil-libertarian constructions of democracy offered by fellow "anti-anti-communists." In the spring of 1954, shortly before McCarthy's fateful Army hearings, Cogley stepped into a hornet's nest. Horace W. B. Donegan, New York's Episcopal bishop, had challenged the oft-heard defense that McCarthy's "aims are good, though his methods are bad," by calling democracy "a method," not "a content." Cogley agreed: The term "un-American" applied only to "method and procedure"; there was "no body of political dogma or any full-fledged philosophy of life to which all Americans are bound." Indeed, democracy bracketed philosophical and theological convictions entirely: "We do not require immigrants to subscribe to capitalist economics, progressive educational theories or even basic Judaeo-Christian religious beliefs before they are permitted to become citizens of the United States." Americans judged each other by whether they used the democratic method—setting aside ultimate commitments and discussing concrete policies—rather than asking about a citizen's "philosophical and religious views, even his political philosophy." This was too much for the editors of the Jesuit weekly *America*. Cogley's view, they wrote, mirrored that of "positivistic jurists and political theorists" and contradicted "both the Christian and the Anglo-American traditions." Understood as a method, they emphasized, democracy devolved into majoritarian tyranny, whereas genuine democracy "acknowledges as its standard of right and wrong a 'higher law' which is the only safe repository of freedom and justice."[36]

The exchange highlighted the distance between the leading liberal Catholic journals on questions of political strategy. Cogley's approach positioned

Catholics as an unpopular minority threatened by mainstream American leaders—both McCarthyists and secularists—who aimed to "'ideologize' democracy" and thereby write them out of the polity. From that perspective, the civil-libertarian notion of democracy as a method promised to keep Catholics within the democratic fold by convincing their opponents to bracket truth claims and agree to disagree. By contrast, *America*'s editors—Murray among them—set aside McCarthyism and viewed the question of religion and politics from the standpoint of a broad Christian majority threatened by a secular minority that had seized control of key institutions. Although the two sides converged in the ideal of a lay state that refrained from imposing religious tenets on its citizens, *America* sought to vanquish "dynamic secularism" in a very different manner from Cogley, by anchoring its conceptions of democracy and liberalism in religion.

In the context of the early Cold War, this argument that democracy (and liberalism, properly understood) comported with Christianity fit better with prevailing attitudes than did Cogley's civil-libertarian stance. As Murray put it, Catholics needed to work toward "restoring both the idea and the institutions of democracy to their proper Christian foundations." Although Cogley's call for state neutrality also found adherents, a growing number of Protestants agreed that the Constitution reflected a comprehensive, theistic "public philosophy." No state could be neutral, Murray agreed; each was "inescapably on the side either of good or of evil." With evil now taking the form of secularism, government agencies either promoted "the new rationalism" or the natural law, providing "a more profound metaphysic, a more integral humanism, a fuller rationality, [and] a more complete science of man in his nature and history." Even on a sociological level, Murray contended, "stable political unity" required "perduring agreement on the common good of man at the level of performance."[37]

But how did the American Constitution embody Catholic principles? In the federal aid controversy of the late 1940s, Murray had argued that the First Amendment created a lay state with no competence to judge between competing faiths but an obligation to aid them equally. This raised a key question: How could that state be impartial, yet embody a theistic public philosophy? Meanwhile, critics such as Catholic University's Joseph C. Fenton, Francis J. Connell, and George W. Shea challenged Murray's deviation from the principle of Catholic establishment. Once again, he was torn between his quest for an antisecularist alliance and his need to assuage Catholic theologians— this time on the central church-state question, not just the issue of interfaith activity.[38]

In the early 1950s, Murray walked this tightrope by further developing

themes from his work of the early 1940s. He again identified a populace
steeped in the natural law as the means through which God's sovereignty
would find political expression. But Murray now added important new arguments: First, the Bill of Rights reflected an underlying popular consensus on
the nature of the state and its relation to God. Second, his consensus ("the
American proposition") reflected the political principles of the medieval
Church (the "ancient liberal tradition"), transmitted to the colonists through
English common law. Third, Catholic theorists, over the centuries, had consistently heeded a particular principle of social and political organization: "the
Gelasian thesis of the two powers and the two societies," attaining harmony
between the sacred and secular, the spiritual and the temporal, by ensuring
the primacy of the former. Finally, applying that dualistic, Gelasian principle
in changing historical contexts produced divergent but equally legitimate
models of church-state relations.[39]

In the pluralistic American context, Murray stressed, the First Amendment's lay state represented the proper application of Catholic political teaching. Church-state separation of the American variety, as opposed to its secularist ("Continental") counterpart, represented a full, sufficient expression
of Catholic principles—not just a prudential accommodation but a positive
good, justifiable in both theory and practice. Catholics embraced religious
toleration due to "moral principle," not mere "political expediency." Indeed,
the First Amendment gave the Church, under American conditions, the same
freedom and authority afforded by the Spanish Concordat.[40]

Murray thus distinguished between the Church's timeless, eternal, dogmatic teachings and the contingent, historical, human institutions through
which it sought to achieve its goals. Each deserved assent, but on a different
level. The First Amendment's religion clauses ("articles of peace," Murray
came to call them) had "no religious content; they answer[ed] none of the
eternal human questions with regard to the nature of truth and freedom or
the manner in which the spiritual order of man's life is to be organized or
not organized." Yet they met the moral criteria of "rationality and goodness,"
which was the most that one could ask of any human law. In short, the First
Amendment represented the best available strategy, in a particular historical
context, for promoting the Church's eternal principles.[41]

For the time being, however, Murray could not convince his superiors.
Not that he failed to try; Murray penned a series of six articles asserting
continuities with Leo XIII's foundational church-state statements in the late
nineteenth century, which he described as polemical responses to a particular
historical context rather than absolute principles in themselves. In the last
piece, Murray pulled together his arguments in a strong—if supersessionist—

statement of Judeo-Christian exceptionalism. "A society that is religiously pluralist, but that knows itself to stand within the Judaeo-Christian tradition," he sought to assure readers, "will still recognize its duty of public worship, and will fulfill it in a manner suited to its pluralist texture." Murray urged, as usual, cross-confessional cooperation against the secularism that had created Nazism and communism and remained "latent in the enormously powerful and positive, centralized, bureaucratic, social-service and social-welfare state that has succeeded the negative, laissez-faire, 'umpire' state of nineteenth-century theory." But that article would not appear for decades, as Vatican officials prohibited its publication and forbade Murray from writing further on religious liberty.[42]

That high-level opposition may help explain Reinhold Niebuhr's assumption that the Church had not changed its tune, despite his knowledge of Murray's arguments linking Catholicism to the Anglo-American liberal tradition. Liberal Catholics recognized Niebuhr's interest in their views; when Cogley's *Commonweal* reached out in 1953 for articles on Protestant and Jewish conceptions of Catholicism, it chose Niebuhr and his admirer Will Herberg as the authors. But Niebuhr continued to cast aspersions on both sides, as he steered his usual course between secularism and Catholicism. In the *Commonweal* article, Niebuhr attributed two main tenets to the Church: first, an overly detailed understanding of natural law as a body of fixed doctrines that prescribed correct modes of behavior in all situations; and second, a belief in "the duty of the state to teach not only religion but the 'true religion.'" Nevertheless, he believed that the Church could, "without sacrificing any important claims," adopt the democratic view "that the state is responsible for the general welfare but not for the salvation of souls."[43]

Meanwhile, Niebuhr challenged "stereotypes which identify Catholicism with the political structure of Spain." Such images, he said, missed the Church's many contributions to "the free societies in America, France, Germany, and Western Europe," where its appeal to workers and doctrine of "the superiority of political authority over the economic process" had helped those polities steer a course between laissez-faire economics and revolutionary Marxism. Non-Catholics in the United States, Niebuhr asserted, failed to "appreciate the tremendous difference between the Church in an unreconstructed medieval social setting and the Church finding a creative place in the moral and political reconstruction of a modern industrial society." If these critics were going to challenge Catholic political ideals, Niebuhr insisted, they should at least take care to understand them.[44]

On the matter of natural law, Niebuhr essayed an alternative in 1952. His earlier publications, such as *Moral Man and Immoral Society* and *The Chil-*

dren of Light and the Children of Darkness, had argued that human institutions could achieve, at best, a rough approximation of justice by balancing power between competing groups. Now, Niebuhr posited a deeper "law of love." There could be no more than this minimal and rather vague principle, he warned Catholics: "This is the only final law, and every other law is an expression of the law of love in minimal or proximate terms or in terms appropriate to given historical occasions." And yet, Niebuhr saw in the law of love the "final dyke against relativism."[45]

In terms of political theory, Niebuhr carried forward his distinctive, indirect form of Judeo-Christian exceptionalism that grounded democracy in the humility taught by Christianity and Judaism. Indeed, the early Cold War years brought some of Niebuhr's sharpest and best-known blasts against the secular mindset of the universities. Although Niebuhr's *The Irony of American History* (1952) drew immediate and widespread acclaim from numerous quarters, including a group of mainstream scholars the philosopher Morton White famously dubbed "Atheists for Niebuhr," others chafed at his dismissive portrayal of the social scientist as arrogant, manipulative, and utopian, along with his clear admiration for what he deemed the more realistic—and thus implicitly Christian—attitude of the practical statesman and even the businessman. Through the early 1950s, Niebuhr insisted that "when we use our common sense, we are more 'Christian' in the analysis of the human situation than when we apply our scientific theories." Modern culture glossed over the clear lessons of everyday experience, whereas the "historic Hebraic and Christian interpretation of our human situation" captured those lessons in its conceptions "of both the dignity of man as creator and the misery of man as destroyer and sinner."[46]

Yet, even as the logic of Niebuhr's intellectual project led him to insist that modern society could not survive without insights about human nature derived from the Christian faith, he felt increasingly ambivalent toward the Cold War crusade against "godless communism." Not long after he spoke out against secular education in the wake of *Everson* and *McCollum*, Niebuhr began to soften the edges of his antisecular polemics. For the time being, he did so mainly by heeding his brother H. Richard's warning that identifying Christianity as a source of democratic commitment threatened to reduce it to a handmaiden of politics. Niebuhr increasingly stressed the caveat to his longstanding refrain about Christianity's political contributions: namely, that an attitude of overweening pride toward the resources of the Christian faith would actually lead to diminishing political returns. Paradoxically, he wrote in 1950, "the more Christians seek to commend their faith as the source of the qualities and disciplines required to save the world from disaster, the less does that kind of faith prove itself to have the necessary resources." *The Irony of American History* likewise held that faith buttressed democracy only if it was faith in God's judgment rather than faith in man's capacities. A "purely utilitarian justification of Christianity," Niebuhr repeatedly insisted, undermined all "genuine engagements between the soul and God, or between the nation and God."[47]

In Jewish circles, Will Herberg issued similar caveats about utilitarianism but harbored far fewer qualms about describing the Cold War as a religious conflict. He interpreted neo-orthodoxy's political implications in starker, more Manichean terms than his mentor Niebuhr. Indeed, Herberg's writings of the early 1950s clearly prefigured his move toward the political right. (Herberg would take up with the New Right leader William F. Buckley Jr. in the late 1950s and become the religion editor of Buckley's *National Review* in 1961.) Weaving Niebuhrian themes into a political-theoretical framework closer to that of Fulton Sheen, Herberg had developed the outlines of his mature conservatism by the early 1950s.

Herberg codified his theology in *Judaism and Modern Man* (1951), adopting a neo-orthodox and existentialist stance. Yet his interpretation of Judaism had a Christian cast that limited its influence. At the same time, Herberg began to craft the less normative, more descriptive strategy of persuasion that he would employ, to far greater effect, in his iconic 1955 book *Protestant-Catholic-Jew*. He began to insist that his substantively religious, antisecularist definition of Judaism meshed perfectly with American social and political conditions, offering the path to assimilation and survival.[48]

"There are growing signs," Herberg wrote in May 1950, "of a reaction against the pervasive secularism of the past century." If secularism represented "the mark of the modern mind," he continued, then a "post-modern" outlook was emerging amid recent crises. Herberg thought younger Jews, especially, were abandoning the long-standing "Jewish-secularist alliance," and Reform and Orthodox Jews were converging on the middle ground of Conservatism. Herberg contended that even secular Jews, recognizing the "'survivalist' utility of Jewish religion," were tempering their personal skepticism with a "pro-religious attitude."[49]

Yet Jews could not reclaim their authentic identity and find social acceptance until they renounced strict church-state separation. A secular culture did not treat religions equally, Herberg contended; instead, it enshrined secularism as an official faith. "The believing Jew will not want to help speed the secularization of American life," he wrote pointedly, while the "responsible" nonbeliever "will see the folly of giving the impression, particularly at this time, that American Jewry is aligned with the anti-religious, secularizing forces." Herberg concluded that Jewish survival "is ultimately conceivable only in religious terms," because "a thoroughly 'de-religionized' society would make Jewish existence impossible."[50]

Herberg did not apply his church-state analysis to education until November 1952. But thenceforth, beginning with a *Commentary* article that drew praise from John Bennett and others, Herberg hammered away at the secular public schools. Herberg took the accommodationist view that the First Amendment allowed "aid on an equal basis to all religious groups" and actively favored "the propaganda of theism," whereas "non- or anti-religion has never enjoyed and does not now enjoy the same public status as religion." But "secularist educators" in universities had now imposed the continental European view of public education as a "'natural' activity of the state designed primarily to inculcate a common doctrine and create a uniform mentality among the citizens," rather than a mere "device for making up the inadequacies of individual or group effort." Herberg warned that "the secularist counter-religion of naturalism," leading to totalitarian rule, filled the void wherever "religion—that is, Jewish-Christian religion—is deliberately excluded from education." Herberg believed that Catholics had much to teach Jews about religion and politics and worked to popularize John Courtney Murray's interpretation of religious liberty. Meanwhile, American Protestants demonstrated to Herberg the consequences of failing to heed the danger of secularism; blinded by anti-Catholicism, they had simply "surrendered intellectual leadership to non-religious forces."[51]

Herberg levied the same charge of anti-Catholicism against Jewish supporters of strict separationism. These figures were wrong to fear anti-Semitism, which had "virtually ceased to exist" in the United States. In the American context, said Herberg, an individual's "'separateness' as a Jew is no longer regarded as a mark of his foreignness but rather as a sign of his Americanness." Herberg promised Jews that if they simply embraced their faith, properly understood, they would become integral partners in American religious life and attain full social acceptance.[52]

Herberg's writings on religion and politics, coupled with the upsurge of Judeo-Christian formulations during the early years of the Cold War, helped to precipitate a sharp conflict among American theologians and other commentators about the legitimacy of Judeo-Christian terminology. A key figure was Robert Gordis, a Conservative rabbi and Jewish Theological Seminary professor. Gordis, along with Herberg and Milton R. Konvitz, cofounded *Judaism*, launched by the American Jewish Congress in 1952. One of *Judaism*'s primary agendas under Gordis's leadership was to encourage religious thinkers to scrutinize carefully the popular understanding of the Judeo-

Christian tradition. Herberg's dogged insistence that democracy flowed from Judeo-Christian faith exacerbated long-standing tensions between Herberg and Gordis. The latter had used "Judeo-Christian" in the 1940s but challenged simplistic, homogenizing readings of that term in 1947. Responding to Herberg's "From Marxism to Judaism," Gordis wrote that "the Hebraic tradition rarely appears in its integrity in organized Christianity," due to its Hellenistic and pagan elements. Gordis contended that reductive readings had "led others to deny the similarities *in toto*," preventing genuine interfaith cooperation.[53]

The second number of *Judaism*, in April 1952, featured a heated debate in which Niebuhr's neo-orthodox ally Paul Tillich took Herberg's side. Judaism and Christianity, wrote Tillich, shared commonalities "so strong that in comparison with the other religions Judaism and Christianity belong to each other." Those of other faiths would find themselves "astonished at the identity of structure at all points, and at the identity of content in most." Like Herberg, Tillich adopted a global standpoint akin to that of the world religions framework.[54]

The Reform rabbi Bernard Heller rejected that broad perspective. How could one equate "the recognition of the abiding value and validity of the ever-evolving Torah" with "the affirmation of the divinity of Jesus and the power of belief in Christ to effect atonement and salvation"? That stark choice, said Heller, produced vastly different "spiritual and ethical aspirations, social habits, forms and institutions." Decrying millennia of Christian persecution and ongoing supersessionism, Heller argued that Judaism inspired a "quest for justice, for human brotherhood, for genuine equality," whereas Christianity fostered bigotry and hatred.[55]

Elsewhere, Herberg reiterated his arguments. He bristled when an English professor attacked Judeo-Christianity's advocates for homogenizing the religious landscape, ignoring other faiths, and claiming for religion a commitment to tolerance that actually stemmed from humanistic sources, especially the literary tradition. This was "quite unacceptable" to Herberg "as a believing Jew": only the Bible, "mediated through the Judaeo-Christian tradition," could explain "the religious problem of existence." Herberg then elaborated in a 1953 article, emphasizing the need for a world-historical perspective that clearly revealed "the profound likeness of the two religions." Indeed, they were "virtually identical in their structure of faith."[56]

Much of Herberg's article actually stressed the distinct roles of Judaism and Christianity in "the divine economy of salvation." Each rested on a covenant that distinguished the saved from the unsaved and defined how the believer would "meet God and receive his grace": either through "the covenant-people Israel" or through Christ. Both anchored human history in "a redemptive, revelatory, and community-creating event" and pledged "to stand witness to God amidst the idolatries of the world." Yet they fulfilled their respective vocations differently, Jews by "staying with God" and Christians by "'going out' to conquer the world for God." God had assigned Jews a "semi-detached" space within Christian-dominated societies and a status— "*in* the world, but never quite *of* it . . . an unassimilable element in any culture engaged in deifying itself"—that Christians could attain only through specifically religious protest. Citing Franz Rosenzweig, Herberg underscored "'the divine mission of Christianity' as 'Israel's apostle' to the nations"; "only through Christianity" could Israel "bring the world to God." Meanwhile, he followed Tillich in ascribing to Judaism "the corrective against the paganism that goes along with Christianity." The two covenant communities needed one other, Herberg summarized, even as jealousy tempted each to deny God's relationship to the other.[57]

At the same time, Herberg contended that this relation of "interdependence" was less important than the participation of Judaism and Christianity in an epistemological relation of "difference in unity and unity in difference." There were three kinds of people in the world, Herberg explained; "man is either a pagan or a Jew or Christian." Jews and Christians each possessed part of God's universal truth, but those human truths were "confessional and conditioned by one's covenantal position." Recognizing this fact would prevent each community from idolizing its own faith or proselytizing the other; they had "irreducible differences which must persist until the final clarification." Yet the two were locked in an embrace: "The unity far transcends the separation, for we are united in our common allegiance to the living God and in our common expectation of, and longing for, the One who is to come."[58]

Gordis now intervened himself, arguing that historical ties and a common scripture paled in comparison to "the far-reaching variations that have developed in the treatment of the same sources." Gordis foregrounded the question of human nature. Challenging what he considered Herberg's crypto-Christian standpoint, he highlighted Christianity's emphasis on the Fall and original sin. By contrast, "Rabbinic thought, with its strong ethical bent, sought to minimize the importance of the Fall" and described "man's nature" as "neutral" or perhaps even "good, actually or potentially."[59]

Bernard Heller offered a different rebuttal. Recent scholarship, he said, showed that the medieval and modern periods had given Christianity a strong pagan overlay, drawn from "the alluring mystery cults of the Orient" and the "ideas, forms and patterns of Graeco-Roman culture." Meanwhile, the remaining Jewish elements had been decisively "revised and reinterpreted," transforming them into something else entirely. There was simply no "fund of common professions and practices." Rather, Heller discerned a pathetic and counterproductive attempt by American Jews to beg for humane treatment on the grounds of likeness. Genuine religious liberty, he argued, was owed to human beings as such; it did not involve "even an implied condition that the tolerated faith conforms or is similar to the one which is dominant and acceptable to the majority."[60]

Herberg did find a Jewish ally in the Detroit rabbi Leon Fram, however. The concept of a Judeo-Christian tradition was not a Jewish defense tactic, Fram asserted. It had emerged among Christians who sought to "give the cause of democracy the powerful support of a faith" in the face of totalitarianism, and it struck the correct balance between inclusion and specificity. Democracy, Fram asserted, "has reached its fullest development in those countries where the Bible has enjoyed its greatest popularity." Unless Jewish critics wanted to define democracy in secular terms, they would need a label for its religious roots, and "Judeo-Christian" fit the facts. Like Herberg, Fram believed that Judeo-Christian rhetoric reflected the waning of anti-Semitism as well. For this reason, he was far more comfortable than most other American Jews with the claim that democracy required religion.[61]

National Politics

On the national scene, that claim of religion's political centrality reached its apogee in the early 1950s. As secretary of state under Eisenhower, John Foster Dulles consistently used Judeo-Christian rhetoric and presented the Cold War as a battle between rival philosophies. Before coming to Washington, Dulles was a top official at the Federal Council of Churches and a leading voice of ecumenical Protestantism. In 1948, he told military chaplains that an unbridgeable gulf separated "advocates of a society based on the Judeo-Christian moral tradition," viewing "man as a creature of God endowed with certain inalienable rights," from "exponents of a materialistic philosophy." Lamenting that "the societies of Christendom have lost the faith and conviction that gave them supremacy for so many years," Dulles argued that success in the Cold War would require "a revival of dynamic, contagious faith in American institutions" and their religious underpinnings.[62] Throughout the 1950s, Dulles consistently framed the Cold War as a religious battle, reflecting his conviction that "American institutions" had been "profoundly . . . influenced by the moral conceptions of the Judeo-Christian faith."[63]

It is easy to assume that Eisenhower took the same approach. No presidency in American history has been more closely associated with the fusion of religion and politics than Eisenhower's. In national lore, the United States under Eisenhower's watch became a self-consciously Judeo-Christian polity—a God-fearing democracy that united Protestant, Catholic, and Jewish Americans in unwavering opposition to "godless communism." Eisenhower's first term brought not only his baptism in office at the behest of the popular evangelist Billy Graham but also the addition of prayers to cabinet meetings, "under God" to the Pledge of Allegiance, and "In God We Trust" to stamps and money. As we have seen, all three branches of government contributed to the atmosphere of public piety: "We are a religious people whose institutions presuppose a Supreme Being," declared the Supreme Court in 1952. In these years, America became a "religious" nation par excellence.[64]

Supporters and critics alike remarked on the strongly religious tenor of Eisenhower's speeches and public statements. True, many doubted the depth of the president's personal piety. Political rivals such as Adlai Stevenson, the Democratic nominee, set the stage for such doubt on the campaign trail. Stevenson attempted to deflect attention away from his own Unitarianism and divorce by highlighting Eisenhower's unchurched status and almost religious devotion to golf: "Some of us worship in churches, some in synagogues, some on golf courses," he quipped. "Yet we are all children of the same Judaic-Christian civilization, with very much the same religious background." Likewise, the historian William Lee Miller famously dubbed Eisenhower "a fervent believer in a very shallow faith." However, even such skeptics could see that Eisenhower's words and actions cemented in the national consciousness a close association between democracy and religion.[65]

At the same time, Eisenhower's complex religious background, coupled with the many different figures who helped craft his speeches, produced a welter of idiosyncratic formulations, even as he insisted that democracy had spiritual foundations. It is true that Eisenhower's awkward invocations of Judeo-Christianity through 1954, when he stopped using the term, gave a major boost to that discourse. Yet his usages often subtly challenged supersessionism and the broader framework of Judeo-Christian exceptionalism along with it. Looking more closely at Eisenhower's words and the contexts behind them reveals some of the key complexities of the discourse of Judeo-Christianity as it flourished in mid-twentieth-century America.

For one thing, Eisenhower seems to have taken the "Judeo-" prefix quite seriously. He repeatedly described American Jews as the West's moral standard-bearers. Eisenhower's references to contemporary Jews as important actors distinguished him from the many Christians who viewed Judaism in the past tense. Moreover, Eisenhower frequently asserted that not only Jews and Christians but also "all others who have come to this land" embraced democracy's spiritual underpinnings.[66]

Eisenhower's earliest invocations of Judeo-Christian rhetoric departed subtly but importantly from its typical uses. For example, Eisenhower spoke of "our Judeo-Christian traditions" in the plural, rather than the singular, before an overwhelmingly Catholic audience at the annual Alfred E. Smith Memorial Foundation dinner in New York on October 17, 1952. Democracy, Eisenhower explained, was "not a mere sentimental mood, nor some casually inherited persuasion," but rather "a doctrine of life and a definition of man." He equated democracy with "the idea of human freedom" and called it "the glorious gift of our Judeo-Christian traditions."[67] A few months later, in December 1952, Eisenhower employed a different but equally unorthodox formulation, speaking of "the Judo-Christian [sic] concept" in an address to the Freedoms Foundation in New York. The Declaration of Independence, he contended, held that Americans gained their rights not through "the accident of birth" or "the color of their skins" but rather directly from God. "In other words," he famously continued, "our form of Government has no sense unless it is founded in a deeply felt religious faith, and I don't care what it is. With us of course it is the Judo-Christian concept, but it must be a religion that all men are created equal."[68] Here, Eisenhower's awkward "Judo" and his implication that other faiths could also buttress democracy departed from the prevailing norm.

On a handful of occasions over the next two years—especially when speaking to Jewish audiences—Eisenhower invoked the "Judeo-Christian" or "Judaic-Christian" roots of democracy. Unlike most other commentators, however, he located the Judeo-Christian tradition deep in the past, describing it as an inheritance from classical times that just happened to have provided the American founders with their understanding of equality. Other faiths, he implied, could provide the same political foundation. And Eisenhower never used Judeo-Christian rhetoric in major speeches such as his inaugural or State of the Union addresses.

Indeed, he gave up that term entirely after 1954. In 1957, Eisenhower made his misgivings about the limitations of Judeo-Christian terminology clear in a letter to his brother Milton. Critiquing a speech Milton had delivered to a gathering of Freemasons, Eisenhower wrote, "You speak of the 'Judaic-Christian heritage.' I would suggest that you use a term on the order of 'religious heritage'—this is for the reason that we should find some way of including the vast numbers of people who hold to the Islamic and Buddhist religions when we compare the religious world against the Communist world.

I think you could still point out the debt we all owe to the ancients of Judea and Greece for the introduction of new ideas." Milton forged ahead, continuing to use Judeo-Christian rhetoric after such formulations had disappeared from the president's own public statements.[69]

Eisenhower's abandonment of "Judeo-Christian" reflected, in part, his administration's overtures to Muslim countries in the Middle East, whose interests he and Dulles sought to balance against those of Israel.[70] However, it also fit with his own background, and perhaps the commitments of his speechwriters as well. In terms of his upbringing, Eisenhower was hardly a conventional Protestant, whether mainline or conservative. He was not born into the powerful Protestant establishment, whose members still occupied most positions of cultural and political leadership in the United States during the 1950s. As a young child, Eisenhower had attended the Sunday school of the River Brethren, a Mennonite sect to which his father's family belonged.[71] Yet the leading religious influence on the family during most of his youth had been the Watchtower Society, the group that became known as the Jehovah's Witnesses in the early 1930s. (Eisenhower's parents were "deeply religious people," he observed, but also "rebels in religion."[72]) Eisenhower would later reject many central tenets of his childhood faith, including the Witnesses' pacifism and fierce anti-Catholicism. But he continued to bear marks of his Watchtower past, despite his postelection conversion to his wife's natal Presbyterianism. In short, Eisenhower was hardly the political counterpart to Billy Graham, as so many accounts of postwar America suggest.[73]

It is difficult to say with certainty how many parts Watchtower sectarian, Bible-believing Christian, Presbyterian elite, wartime ecumenist, probusiness evangelical, apocalyptic Cold Warrior, and crass political opportunist made up Dwight Eisenhower as a religio-political actor during the 1950s. But one thing is clear: Unlike most establishment Protestants, Eisenhower never felt wholly confident positing a singular religious "we." This reluctance clearly stemmed in part from his role as president at a time when foreign relations dominated policymaking. Eisenhower's formulations usually acknowledged the importance of those outside the Judeo-Christian faiths, both at home and overseas. The Cold War struggle for hearts and minds in decolonizing areas of Asia and Africa clearly figured in here. But the president's personal experiences mattered greatly as well. Though exceedingly comfortable with biblical stories and texts, Eisenhower often balked when discussing religion's theological and institutional dimensions. He routinely traded specific religious labels—including "Christian" as well as "Judeo-," "Judo-," or "Judaic-Christian"—for vague descriptions of the nation as "religious" or "spiritual." Moreover, he clearly preferred "spirituality" and "spiritual" to "religion" and "religious," perhaps reflecting the tendency of Jehovah's Witnesses to distrust organized religion—indeed, to view religious institutions of all kinds as conspiracies. Eisenhower's ambivalent use of Judeo-Christian discourse reflects, in part, the fact that he, much more than most other presidents, struggled personally with the question of how to describe the religious beliefs of the American people.

It should give us pause that Eisenhower, the public figure most widely associated with the postwar ascendance of "Judeo-Christian America," used the Judeo-Christian framework rhetoric only sporadically, in minor addresses, during his first term and then eliminated it from his public speeches during his second. Of course, the breadth of Eisenhower's description of the religious roots of democracy does not invalidate his belief in their importance. National Security Council documents show that his administration explicitly aimed to spread religious ethics around the globe. One memo on "basic United States foreign policy objectives" included "the realization of a world order based on the fundamental moral and spiritual values inherent in our Judeo-Christian tradition and shared by other Deistic faiths." In speech after speech, the president emphasized "those spiritual weapons which forever will be our country's most powerful resource, in peace or in war."[74]

Moreover, Eisenhower's awkward but ubiquitous invocations of religion did leave the impression that Judaism and Christianity had a special political role, at least in the United States. A *Life* article featured Eisenhower telling a Russian commander that American democracy flowed from "the Judeo-Christian tradition, resting on belief in a God who holds all men of supreme worth." Eisenhower also followed his famed assertion that "our form of Government has no sense unless it is founded in a deeply felt religious faith, and I don't care what it is," by saying, "With us of course it is the Judo-Christian [*sic*] concept." And in an October 1952 campaign speech, he called democracy "the glorious gift of our Judeo-Christian traditions." Globally, meanwhile, Eisenhower singled out monotheistic ("Deistic") religions, referencing "God" or "the Supreme Being." He often listed specific ethical teachings: the tenet "that all men are created equal," or "the principle of human dignity" and "the ideal of peace." But the heart of Eisenhower's conception was the repeated conviction that democracy was "a spiritual conviction, a conviction that each of us is enormously valuable because of a certain standing before our own God."[75]

Yet a careful study of Eisenhower's religious invocations reveals hitherto unrecognized dimensions of American public culture after World War II. Recent scholarship has emphasized the president's ties to evangelical Protestants imagining a narrowly Christian America, including the revivalist Billy

Graham and right-wing groups such as Spiritual Mobilization. In fact, however, when Eisenhower crafted his public statements on religion, he looked mainly to his brother Milton and to his on-and-off speechwriter, the young liberal Catholic editor Emmet J. Hughes.

Milton, the last of the five Eisenhower boys, was raised in much more conventional religious settings than his considerably older brother Dwight. Milton attended a Presbyterian Sunday school during his youth and eventually became a devout Episcopalian. Unlike the president, then, Milton Eisenhower spoke with ease as a lifelong member of the Protestant establishment, repeatedly invoking his nation's Judeo-Christian roots and character. Like Dulles, he felt entirely comfortable postulating a single Judeo-Christian framework for American culture. Milton Eisenhower confidently defined the Cold War as a battle between advocates and critics of "our Judeo-Christian heritage." Throughout his career as a college and university president, from the 1940s to the 1970s, he delivered countless anticommunist speeches, peppered with Judeo-Christian rhetoric, before packed campus audiences.

By contrast, Hughes, like his fellow liberal Catholics, avoided Judeo-Christian language, which captured their exceptionalist theory of democracy but courted indifferentism. Hughes was close to Carlton Hayes, John Courtney Murray, and Clare Boothe Luce. (Hughes and Murray socialized with the Luces through the 1950s and golfed with Henry while Clare was away as ambassador to Italy.) Like them, he favored more concrete, specific expressions of religion's political contributions than Eisenhower ventured in his off-the-cuff remarks. Although the extent of Hughes's influence awaits further research, it is clear that he penned many of Eisenhower's best-known words about religion and brought the language of American liberal Catholics into the rhetorical heart of the presidency during crucial moments in the 1950s. Eisenhower recognized that Hughes had a knack for helping him find the right phrase to galvanize a Republican constituency that increasingly included Catholics alongside Protestants of various persuasions.[76]

Hughes, a former aide to Hayes during his time as ambassador of Spain, moved back and forth between Time-Life's offices and Eisenhower's administration in the 1950s. He penned Eisenhower's "I shall go to Korea!" declaration—the original, election-cinching "October surprise"—and key speeches from the president's first year, including the inaugural address and the 1953 State of the Union. Eisenhower continued to seek Hughes's counsel after he returned to Time-Life in September 1953, and the two worked closely behind the scenes with NCCJ leaders to discredit McCarthy and ensure his censure by the Senate in 1954. Eisenhower then summoned Hughes again as the 1956 election neared.[77]

At pivotal moments in the president's first and second terms, the Eisenhower brothers and Hughes locked themselves away for hours on end, toiling on major speeches. The resulting proclamations revealed the strong, and often conflicting, commitments of both presidential wordsmiths. Milton's influence, alongside that of Dulles, may account for the president's early tendency to use Judeo-Christian formulations, if awkwardly, during his first term. But a close reading of Eisenhower's invocations of religion, combined with archival evidence, suggests the equally strong influence of Hughes. Indeed, the president's use of Judeo-Christian formulations waned as Hughes's role in his speechwriting process waxed.

With Hughes on board, Eisenhower's public invocations of religion became much more concrete and substantive. Hughes later complained that the president, in his impromptu remarks, spoke vaguely, if rather constantly, of American democracy's "spiritual" character. When drafting and editing Eisenhower's major speeches, Hughes consistently replaced the president's individualistic tenor and watery invocations of spirituality with a historically specific and theoretically rigorous claim: The Declaration of Independence proved that the Founders viewed religion—in particular, a set of rights granted by God and unabridgeable by any political edict—as the foundation of democracy. After Hughes's changes, for example, Eisenhower's first inaugural address argued that democracy rested on a sturdy foundation of natural rights and natural laws that could be understood only as divinely ordained. In 1950s America, this view of democracy was largely Catholic in its provenance. Many lay Protestants accepted this political theory as well, but Protestant leaders, when speaking on religion and politics, typically invoked a broad vision of the spiritually free individual rather than a specific set of God-given rights. At the level of major public pronouncements, then, the Catholic Hughes more directly shaped Eisenhower's religious message to American audiences during his campaigns and early in his first and second terms than did the popular religious figures most often cited by historians, such as Billy Graham.

By late 1954, the Foundation for Religious Action in the Social and Civil Order (FRASCO) drew together the multiple strands of Judeo-Christian exceptionalism. Created in 1953 by a group including the Episcopal clergyman Charles W. Lowry, the prominent Quaker D. Elton Trueblood, and Eisenhower's pastor, the Presbyterian Edward L. R. Elson—FRASCO sought, with Eisenhower's support, to "unite all believers in God" against an "atheistic Communism which aims to destroy both religion and liberty." The group counted Murray and Will Herberg—then completing *Protestant-Catholic-*

Jew—among its members, while the advisory board included Billy Graham. Lowry, FRASCO's spokesman, described democracy as the political application of the "Judeo-Christian religious tradition" and argued that liberals who resisted an explicitly religious defense of democracy could not be trusted as allies. Indeed, Lowry asserted that "secularism is a far graver danger in America than the erasure of walls of separation between Church and State." Not surprisingly, FRASCO struggled to find support from liberal Protestants and Jews, let alone the "Other Americans" of POAU's title.[78]

Herberg's engagement with FRASCO highlighted his distance from the American Jewish mainstream. Speaking immediately after Eisenhower at the first meeting in November 1954, Herberg explicated "the biblical basis of American democracy" in a paper later published by the Catholic journal *Thought*. Although Herberg's paper was received warmly, FRASCO leaders worried about the reticence of official American Jewry toward the group. Noting the "presence of so many high-ranking Catholics" at the inaugural conference, they speculated privately that members' near-unanimous criticism of the "secularization of American life," the "lack of religious influence in the public schools," and the "exaggeration of separation between Church and State" explained both Catholic overrepresentation and the dearth of Jews and liberal Protestants. (Jewish delegates were opposed to religion in public education, the report noted.) A less openly discussed reason for the strong Catholic presence was that Lowry, seeking to circumvent the Church's prohibition of official Catholic involvement in ecumenical ventures, had tailored FRASCO's articles of incorporation and even the group's name to Catholic specifications and given Father John F. Cronin of the National Catholic Welfare Conference veto power over all decisions. Although Cronin's influence remained secret, Lowry's public concessions to Catholic leaders fueled suspicions that both men wielded disproportionate power in FRASCO, leading many Jews and liberal Protestants to doubt the group's commitment to full inclusion.[79]

Moreover, many of FRASCO's leaders treated Judaism as an afterthought, despite their stated aim to build an interfaith alliance against communism. Lowry's 1952 book *Communism and Christ* acknowledged Judaism as the historical "progenitor of Christianity" but quickly dismissed it as "a particularized religion, linked with a single race and tradition, without the potential creativity and universal appeal of Christianity." In a memo to his superiors that recounted FRASCO's genesis, Cronin said that Lowry had sought "the aid of American Catholics in a common struggle to protect the foundations of our Christian civilization."[80]

Meanwhile, Cronin used his veto power to restrict membership to those defining communism as "atheistic and diabolical"—meaning those "who believed in God and who practiced their religious faith." In the "offensive to capture men's minds," Cronin worried especially about religious and secular liberals, who "share somewhat the mentality of the Socialist and similar parties of Europe" and who might prove "too ready for a compromise." Cronin portrayed FRASCO as fighting not just communism abroad but also secularism at home by promoting public confidence in "religious truth as the prime support of human freedom." Similarly, FRASCO's articles of incorporation pledged the organization to resist all domestic activities "which may tend to destroy confidence in religion"—a category that for many members included secular public education.[81]

Archival evidence reveals a sharp divergence between Catholic and Jewish responses to FRASCO. On the Catholic side, Cronin, Murray, and other Church leaders harbored doubts about Lowry's judgment and his larger political aims, but they displayed a genuine enthusiasm for FRASCO. They favored limiting the group to "Protestants and Jews who will go along with our approach, rather than risking incidents by broadening the base too much." By contrast, many Jewish participants viewed FRASCO with alarm. Rabbi Eugene J. Lipman attended the first meeting to gather information for the Union of American Hebrew Congregations (the umbrella organization for Reform Judaism). His report expressed deep misgivings about FRASCO in general and Herberg in particular. He deplored the group's dogged emphasis on "the need for absolute spiritual values" and sarcastically identified Herberg as "the star of the sessions." Herberg, he reported, was "clever, quick, and delighted all the Catholic[s] and Protestants present. He should have," Lipman added, for "he spoke in their terms and presented their philosophy."[82]

Lipman described FRASCO as a heavily Catholic initiative, noting that "Catholic sources" contributed much of the funding and the "hierarchy and laity" figured prominently at the conference. He charged that FRASCO's Protestant and Jewish members would do virtually anything to keep the Catholics on board. Underscoring that the "total recognizable Jewish attendance was very small," Lipman declared that FRASCO's Jewish leaders were "neither representative nor strong either in the Jewish or general communities," being willing "to kow-tow completely to the Christian groups." Summing up, Lipman called FRASCO "so absolute, so anti-liberal, so rooted in the idea of total dichotomy between the free world and the Communist world, that it is almost frightening." Indeed, Lipman suggested alerting the National Community Relations Advisory Council, which could then dissuade Jews from joining FRASCO. Elsewhere, he warned that FRASCO would "bear watching by democratically oriented religious and community organizations."[83]

*

Conspicuously absent from FRASCO's meetings, however, was Reinhold Niebuhr. Lowry repeatedly sought to draw in Niebuhr, offering to share confidential planning documents with him.[84] In the wake of *The Irony of American History* and his stroke, however, Niebuhr had retreated more fully from his wartime defense of democracy in terms of prophetic faith. The dogs of McCarthyism had grown ever louder, and Niebuhr was troubled by the reception of his book, which many of his former liberal allies regarded as a dogmatic Cold War text. Niebuhr had long criticized Catholic leaders for identifying their church with the will of God; now he found his country doing the same thing. A final factor was the vehemence and increasing conservatism of Will Herberg, arguably the most ardent postwar defender of Niebuhr's wartime stance on religion and democracy. As we have seen, Herberg ratcheted up his Cold War rhetoric in the early 1950s, stripping away all of the nuances and qualifications from Niebuhr's analysis and increasingly arguing that Niebuhr was actually a conservative.

Niebuhr resisted Herberg's brand of anticommunism and found the mobilization of his writings by conservatives exasperating. Niebuhr criticized conservatives for valuing religion primarily as a source of social stability and stressed that, as individuals, secularists often proved better than their philosophies. As early as March 1953, Niebuhr also began to experiment with a considerably looser framing of the relationship between religion and democracy. Assessing the long-standing debate as to "whether democracy is the product of the Christian faith or of a secular culture," he answered with an unequivocal "both." Whether one looks at "political institutions" or "cultural resources," Niebuhr wrote, one finds that "free societies" emerged from "the confluence of Christian and secular forces." In the case of American political thought, for example, Niebuhr credited "New England Calvinism and Jeffersonian deism" equally for their contributions. It was true, he wrote, that the "totalitarian regimes to the left of free societies" proved "that secular doctrine can, under certain circumstances, furnish grist for the mills of modern tyrannies." Yet he also stressed "that the Christian faith does not inevitably yield democratic fruits," as evidenced by the existence of "traditional non-democratic Christian cultures to the right of free societies." Neither side had the market cornered on democracy, Niebuhr insisted, and the secular roots of democracy were as important as its religious roots.[85]

Niebuhr's shift of emphasis, slight though it may have seemed at the time, portended deeper divisions in the late 1950s. Among presidents and ordinary citizens alike—including many Protestants, Catholics, and even a few Jews—the postwar surge of public piety accompanied a widespread tendency to argue that those three faiths bore a unique relationship to democracy and that only their active and more traditional practitioners could uphold the American form of government. But this Judeo-Christian exceptionalism, which yoked democracy to theism and excluded both nonbelievers and strict separationists, would come under increasing fire in the late 1950s and early 1960s, even as it continued to powerfully shape American political culture.

PART THREE

From Tri-faith to Multireligious America

Secularism Reconsidered

FINDING EXCEPTIONALISM'S LIMITS, 1955–1965

Throughout the second half of the 1950s, Judeo-Christian exceptionalism retained its hold on American public culture. Among intellectuals, however, harbingers of a pluralist revolt began to appear late in that decade; that movement flowered in the early 1960s. Decolonization represented one challenge to the Judeo-Christian framework. With Senator Joseph McCarthy's censure in early 1954, the political spotlight shifted to the intensifying fight for democracy in Africa and Asia. "Republican and Democrat, Protestant, Catholic and Jew," observed the *New York Times*, "are all engaged in a world struggle over areas dominated not by white Protestants but by Mohammedans, Hindus, Buddhists, Brahmanists and a vast variety of other believers, most of whom are neither white nor Christian." How could democracy find a hearing in those areas if its defenders asserted, like one missionary to Africa, that democracy had only taken root "in nations with a Judeo-Christian basis"? Likewise, the legitimacy of the United Nations suffered when its defenders described it as an expression of "the Judaeo-Christian ideal of mutual responsibility."[1]

Like the push for human rights abroad, the accelerating civil rights movement at home raised thorny questions about the meaning and sources of rights and how best to assert and defend them. Meanwhile, the stark and increasingly conservative religious nationalism reflected in many Judeo-Christian formulations caused some liberal thinkers to reconsider their understandings of religion's role in a democracy. So, too, did the continued presence of prominent nonbelievers in the ranks of democracy's defenders. These developments, which fueled various laments about the religious inauthenticity of the postwar surge of public piety, also inspired a reassessment of the cultural costs of the intense antiliberalism and antisecularism of the early Cold War period. By the mid-1960s, a trickle of literature on humanists, skeptics, and unbelievers in the United States had grown to a steady stream, though the validity and implications of secularism remained up for debate.

At the same time, new groups joined the Judeo-Christian fold and, in so doing, jettisoned narrower conceptions of American national identity. William F. Buckley Jr.'s "New Right" consciously adopted a tri-faith strategy, abandoning the Christian nationalism of the old Protestant right. Conservative evangelicals such as Billy Graham embraced Judeo-Christian language for rather different reasons, as they protested a pair of early 1960s Supreme Court decisions that eliminated prayer and Bible reading in public schools. Finally, Catholics continued adopting Judeo-Christian rhetoric as well. Although theorists such as John Courtney Murray still stressed the Catholic roots of Western civilization, Catholics became increasingly comfortable—especially during John F. Kennedy's presidential campaign—with a tri-faith image of American democracy. By the mid-1960s, America's Judeo-Christian discourse remained powerful. Indeed, it arguably enlisted more groups than it had at any other moment in American history. At the same time, however, Judeo-Christian conceptions of American democracy and national identity—whether exceptionalist or pluralist in tenor—now jostled with a series of more inclusive competitors, especially among liberals, where the turn to multiculturalism was beginning. The abandonment of Judeo-Christian rhetoric by pluralistic liberals was already visible on the horizon, to those who cared to look.

National Contexts

Through the late 1950s and into the early 1960s, a chorus of voices continued to distinguish Judeo-Christian democracy—with its "anti-materialistic, anti-communistic, anti-nihilistic philosophy"—from Marxist atheism. Specific formulations varied, of course. G. Bromley Oxnam, targeted by McCarthy a few years earlier, rooted democracy in "two basic Judaeo-Christian concepts," namely, "the importance of the individual and the orderliness of the universe." Oxnam contrasted these to "the Marx-Lenin belief that man is incidental to history." Meanwhile, a *Boston Globe* article, titled "Why Marx Had No Luck in America: There Is No Class Distinction Here, Thanks to Our Belief in Community of All," traced that belief in community to Judeo-Christian roots. The Judeo-Christian tradition did not always figure as a source of strength in public commentary; one lamented that "the ethics of Judeo-Christianity" impeded swift retaliatory action against Fidel Castro in Cuba. And some commentators, including the Episcopal bishop James A. Pike, still identified

Marxism itself as a "Judeo-Christian heresy" whose architects had secularized key religious tenets. But most commentators continued to root communism firmly in secularism and laud "the rugged rock of our Judaeo-Christian spiritual heritage." (Supersessionist slippage persisted too, as when the *Washington Post* used "Christian Heritage" in the title of an article about a call to preserve the nation's "Judeo-Christian heritage.")[2]

Judeo-Christian rhetoric remained a common device for condemning religious bigotry during these years. Brotherhood Week, celebrated since 1934 under the auspices of the National Conference of Christians and Jews, provided an opportunity to remind Americans of their civic duty to respect other faiths. During the 1958 observance of Brotherhood Week, for example, Vice President Richard Nixon called discrimination "contrary to the principles of our Judaeo-Christian heritage and to the ethical principles of the major religions of the world." (Nixon added, for good measure, that the nation benefited from mobilizing the skills and raising the incomes of minority groups.) Others emphasized "the Judaeo-Christian concept that all men are joined in kinship under the Fatherhood of God" and called Americans back to "the ideals of our Judaeo-Christian heritage and the democratic values upon which our nation was founded." In 1961, new NCCJ head Lewis Webster Jones waded into deeper waters when he argued that democracy's global fortunes would depend on Americans finding agreement on divisive questions such as "public support for parochial schools, birth control policies, [and] Sunday closing laws." Without such agreement, Jones argued, "the strength and unity which America has drawn from the common acceptance of the Judaeo-Christian tradition will be weakened and dissipated."[3]

Civil rights activism, which accelerated in the wake of the Supreme Court's 1954 desegregation decision in *Brown v. Board of Education*, provided another forum for Judeo-Christian language. "We are morally obligated," declared NAACP leader and Talladega College president Arthur Gray in April 1956, to uphold "democratic and moral principles" by "confront[ing] ourselves and our southern brothers with the requirements of our Judeo-Christian faith." The following year, the Richmond Ministers Association urged Virginians to comply with the *Brown* decision, reminding them that they had long defined democracy as "the political expression of the Judeo-Christian faith." As the civil rights movement picked up steam, activists also used Judeo-Christian rhetoric to defend themselves from those who saw Stalin's hand behind calls for racial equality. After Georgia's attorney called the NAACP a communist front, its secretary, Roy Wilkins, responded that "man's struggle for justice, equality and freedom" had been "part of every civilization the world has known." Moreover, Wilkins continued, the United States had been "founded upon the Judeo-Christian concept of morality," and all should seek its full realization.[4]

Martin Luther King Jr., who came to the forefront of the civil rights movement in the wake of the Montgomery bus boycott, repeatedly urged Americans to live up to their Judeo-Christian ideals. In his 1958 book *Stride toward Freedom*, King employed the Jewish philosopher Martin Buber's language, deeming segregation "utterly opposed to the noble teachings of our Judeo-Christian tradition" because it "substitutes an 'I-it' relationship for the 'I-thou' relationship." King and his fellow ministers in the Southern Christian Leadership Conference drew heavily on Reinhold Niebuhr's *Moral Man and Immoral Society*, with its recognition of entrenched group interests and the need to array power against power in order to achieve justice. (Indeed, in private conversations with his advisers, King described nonviolent resistance as primarily "a Niebuhrian stratagem of power" rather than an inheritance from Gandhi.) At the same time, however, King urged his fellow Americans to act for principled reasons. The point of desegregation, he told NAACP leaders in September 1960, was neither to meet "the Communist challenge" nor "to appeal to Asian and African peoples": "The primary reason for uprooting racial discrimination from our society is that it is morally wrong. It is a cancerous disease that prevents us from realizing the sublime principles of our Judeo-Christian tradition. It relegates persons to the status of things."[5]

The sit-in movement that emerged in 1960 also brought numerous assertions that equality for African Americans was a cardinal instance of "the Judaeo-Christian principles of brotherhood" underlying American political institutions. "Our Judaeo-Christian heritage and our democratic principles," one newspaper wrote, "emphasize reverence for life, the equality of all men in the sight of God, and the infinite worth of the individual." Catholic commentators, among others, saw the fruit of Judeo-Christian ethics in the growing civil rights movement.[6]

Top government officials, led by Secretary of State John Foster Dulles, continued to employ Judeo-Christian formulations through the late 1950s as well. In 1956, Dulles told a B'nai B'rith group that "the Judeo-Christian conception of the spiritual nature of man" had infused Western civilization with "individual resourcefulness and a sense of mission and of adventure in the world." Two years later, preaching at the Washington Cathedral, Dulles struck a more somber tone. Communism, he warned, portended "a dark age" that would "erase the great humanitarian gains slowly and painfully won over the centuries by our Judeo-Christian civilization." For his part, UN ambassador Henry Cabot Lodge Jr., speaking at a September 1959 luncheon in honor of Nikita Khrushchev, paid a backhanded compliment to the Soviet premier for sensitizing Americans to "the great ideals which come to us in our Declaration of Independence and from our Judeo Christian heritage."[7]

By contrast, Eisenhower, as we have seen, largely abandoned Judeo-Christian rhetoric after November 1954 and warned his brother Milton in 1957 that Judeo-Christian formulations were too narrow to express American character and purposes. He framed democracy's religious underpinnings more broadly—or vaguely, many said. In some instances, Eisenhower identified "the principles and convictions that have bound us together as a nation," including "personal liberty, human rights, and the dignity of man." These values, he explained, "have their roots in a deeply held religious faith—in a belief in God." Elsewhere, Eisenhower identified "the great concept of the dignity of all men, alike created in the image of the Almighty," as the nation's guiding star. A third formulation located two "mutually dependent . . . liberties" at the core of American democracy: "the freedom of a citizen and the freedom of a religious believer."[8]

On occasion, Eisenhower continued to seek Emmet Hughes's guidance on how to emphasize "the predominant influence of spiritual values" in the democratic nations. Absent Hughes's adept wordsmithing, however, Eisenhower tended to emphasize religion or spirituality in general, rather than to enumerate the specific intellectual contributions of Christianity or Judeo-Christianity to American political theory. Of course, he joined his subordinates in repeatedly stressing that democracies elevated the spiritual over the material, in keeping with foundational principles of religious ethics. He thus gave considerable support to those who ascribed a specifically Judeo-Christian character to the spiritual orientation of the United States and its citizens. But Eisenhower refused to equate democracy with Judeo-Christian religion, and he presented religion as a matter of personal faith rather than of shared intellectual commitments.

Many factors likely help to explain the president's rhetorical tendencies when discussing religion. No doubt Eisenhower's own dissenting background played into his linguistic choices and conceptual formulations. So, too, did his leadership of a country dedicated to spreading democracy to the peoples of Asia and Africa, who stood by and large outside the Judeo-Christian fold. This was the burden of Eisenhower's 1957 letter to his brother Milton: that democracy had to be made conceptually available to Buddhists, Muslims, and other global faith communities. But it is possible that Eisenhower's relationship with Hughes also shaped the specific decision to abandon Judeo-Christian rhetoric after 1954. Catholics were becoming a small but important part of the Republican coalition during the 1950s, and Hughes surely passed on to Eisenhower the misgivings that he and other liberal Catholic allies harbored about Judeo-Christian terminology. Yet Eisenhower's private views on religion continued to diverge from those of Hughes and his Catholic allies. By 1960, and possibly much earlier, Hughes's ambivalence about serving a Republican president had given way to intense annoyance at Eisenhower's proclivities. In 1963, Hughes penned a bitter tell-all that portrayed Eisenhower as profoundly anti-intellectual and morally compromised, indifferent to ideas and hopelessly equivocal when genuine ethical commitment was needed.[9]

Debating the Revival

Among many liberal and moderate Protestants, meanwhile, the militant religious nationalism of FRASCO and Joseph McCarthy prompted soul-searching about how far to go with the antisecularist campaign. These worries fed into broader anxieties about the inauthenticity of the postwar religious revival itself. Critics such as Niebuhr saw two essentially secular dynamics behind much of the era's ostentatious piety. The first, exemplified by FRASCO, was a simplistic anticommunism that collapsed religion into a triumphalist Americanism by contrasting godly Americans to godless Soviets. The second was the dramatic acceleration of consumerism and suburbanization in an increasingly affluent society. To Niebuhr and many others, these dynamics, and the relentless self-congratulation that accompanied them, violated Christian ideals. It increasingly seemed that antisecularism was serving less to challenge the nation's sins than to obscure them by celebrating American piety and decrying Soviet atheism.

This skepticism about the postwar revival, which came from many quarters, focused on its capacity to ease, rather than rouse, American consciences. (Perhaps unsurprisingly, lay interpreters proved more enthusiastic about the revival than religious professionals, and conservatives were more optimistic than liberals.) Articles such as "Is Our Religious Revival Real?" and "The Unreal Revival" captured the mood. The Methodist minister Ralph W. Sockman rejected "attempts to sell religion as a means to health, happiness and prosperity." Likewise, the famed psychoanalyst Erich Fromm dismissed the revival for "trying to combine the ideas of the Judeo-Christian religion with the ideas of Dale Carnegie." And the Jewish educator Judah Pilch described "the almost complete congregationalization of the American Jewish community" in recent years as "a means of conforming to a dominant pattern in American middle-class society." By the early 1960s, the flood of writing on the revival's character had produced a series of important books, many based on earlier articles that had drawn considerable attention. These included A. Roy

Eckardt's *The Surge of Piety in America* (1958), Stanley J. Rowland's *Land in Search of God* (1958), Martin E. Marty's *The New Shape of American Religion* (1959), Gibson Winter's *The Suburban Captivity of the Churches* (1961), and the sociologist Peter L. Berger's classic *The Noise of Solemn Assemblies* (1961).[10]

Some commentators rebutted these dismissals. Edward L. R. Elson, Eisenhower's minister at National Presbyterian and a FRASCO founder, detected sour grapes in the "rash of articles and public utterances denouncing or at least minimizing the religious renaissance of our times." Critics should not be so quick, Elson argued, to dismiss "emotionalism in religious experience," the notion that religion should provide "self-confidence and inner assurance," or even the prospect that social pressure and a desire for belonging might inspire church attendance. "Men do not have to get religion in the same way," Elson wrote, "nor serve Christ in the same office, to have the marks of authentic Christianity." The Harvard sociologist Talcott Parsons likewise averred, "This revival is religiously genuine." To Parsons, postwar developments reinforced the conclusion that "ours is a religiously oriented society" rooted in "a theistic Judeo-Christian belief complex," wherein other religious groups could find tolerance but "do not seem to have gained any serious foothold" as of yet. At New York's famed Riverside Church, the Reverend Robert J. McCracken likewise saw in the revival a salutary emphasis "on the beliefs common to the three communions, on the basic spiritual ideals and values which all share, on the Judeo-Christian tradition which has gone to the making of the American way of life."[11]

But Niebuhr spoke for most of the religious leaders and intellectuals who commented on the postwar revival when he discerned something profoundly amiss at its heart. In 1950, he had presciently predicted that views about the authenticity of the revival would depend on the vantage points of the observers. Two years later he offered his own, divided verdict: The United States was simultaneously "one of the most religious and most secular of nations." More specifically, the popular revival was hopelessly degraded, even as its intellectual counterpart offered some cause for hope. Niebuhr thus attacked the revival's "perversion of the Christian Gospel" in several religious journals in 1955. On the popular level, he explained, postwar piety had "little to do with the Christian faith." Instead, it promoted "faith in faith" or "faith in oneself," stances that fostered "complacency, rather than repentance" and amounted to rank idolatry: "self-worship rather than the worship of God." Niebuhr likely worried that his own efforts to infuse democracy with an explicitly religious rationale during the World War II era had created the preconditions for the crass religious nationalism of the 1950s.[12]

Niebuhr decried the activities of the revival's "false prophets," including

the televangelism of the Catholic leader Fulton Sheen, the stupendous sales of
books by figures such as Rabbi Joshua L. Liebman and Norman Vincent Peale
promoting "peace of mind" and "positive thinking," and the meteoric rise of
conservative evangelicals such as Billy Graham. Although Niebuhr preferred
Graham to "the success cults," he deplored the revivalist's "simple religious
moralism," which tended to suggest that personal conversion to Christianity
could solve all the world's ills. In short, as Niebuhr saw it, the leading religious
figures simply cloaked "the discredited pagan gods in Christian disguises."
Indeed, throughout American public culture, Niebuhr discerned an idola-
trous "faith in ourselves, or in mankind, or in civilization, or in America"—
anything but the "Biblical faith" that would shatter such complacencies and
enable truly effective engagement with domestic and global problems. At the
same time, however, Niebuhr also saw a "real revival of interest in, if not
adherence to, the historic Christian and Jewish faiths." Intellectuals and students, especially, recognized that recent history had decisively refuted the
tenets of secular liberalism and Marxism, proving that only "Biblical faith"
could grasp the complexities and ambiguities of the human condition.[13]

In this context, with charges and countercharges about the revival's authenticity flying, Will Herberg published the blockbuster sociological work
for which he is remembered today: *Protestant-Catholic-Jew* (1955). As one astute reviewer noted, that book portrayed a struggle between an inauthentic
revival, in the spirit of Constantine and Eisenhower, and an authentic revival,
in the spirit of Augustine and Niebuhr. Typically read as a staunch defense of
liberal tolerance, *Protestant-Catholic-Jew* actually incorporated, in subtle but
powerful ways, Herberg's ferocious critique of secular liberalism as a threat
to democracy. In a revealing passage, Herberg accused liberal scholars of
"proceed[ing] from 'the religions of democracy' to 'democracy as a religion'"
by "erect[ing] 'democracy' into a super-faith above and embracing the three
recognized religions." To his mind, this "civic religion" made "a radical break
with the fundamental presuppositions of both Judaism and Christianity" and
amounted to "a particularly insidious kind of idolatry." Herberg's antipathy
to Judeo-Christian pluralism occasionally shone through at other points, too,
as when he wrote off Horace Kallen for advocating a watery, nontheistic "religion of democracy." The vast majority of Herberg's book, however, adopted
a flat, descriptive tone. Herberg's earlier works portrayed a world groan-
ing under the yoke of secularist hegemony and urged the saving remnant
of Americans to align themselves with forms of Protestantism, Catholicism,
and Judaism that rejected secularity in every domain of public life, including
the public schools. Now, Herberg wrote his Judeo-Christian exceptionalist

vision—and the conditions for an antisecularist turn—into the past and present of the United States.[14]

Protestant-Catholic-Jew famously characterized the United States as a "triple
melting pot." Rather than converging on a single culture, Herberg argued,
newcomers became American Protestants, Catholics, or Jews as they lost their
ethnic identities. This interpretation challenged the equation of Americaniza-
tion with Protestantization and made religion appear uniquely impervious to
the acids of assimilation. Herberg naturalized a tripartite model of national
identity by declaring that the "primordial conditions" of American life had
always favored a system of religious pluralism where Protestants, Catholics,
and Jews became Americans within the boundaries of their respective religious traditions. Even as he urged Americans to embrace prophetic faith,
Herberg also insisted that they were already doing so, as witnessed by the
postwar upsurge of religious belief. Indeed, he contended that "militant secularism" was almost dead in the United States. The message was clear: "Self-
identification in religious terms" was expected in 1950s America. As Herberg
summarized elsewhere, the "Jew can integrate himself into American society"
only "in terms of a religious community." Invoking the powerful normative
weight of a purported American consensus stretching back to the founding,
Herberg's book positioned Catholics and practicing Jews within the religious
mainstream while prodding other Jews and liberal Protestants to rethink their
embrace of strict church-state separation.[15]

Protestant-Catholic-Jew provided a new focal point for the burgeoning
conversation on the American revival's authenticity. That book took its overall frame directly from Niebuhr's "most religious and most secular of nations"
observation. Like his mentor, Herberg offered a two-pronged assessment of
the revival, denouncing "pervasive secularism amid mounting religiosity"
but also finding "authentic stirrings of faith" in the United States. Nearly all
of the reviews likewise connected Herberg's book to issues of consumption,
suburbanization, and mass culture. Indeed, while Herberg is sometimes mis-
remembered today as a celebrant of postwar religiosity, most reviewers emphasized his critique of the revival's authenticity and ignored his recognition
of its latent spiritual possibilities. Some even denounced Herberg's book on
this score. One reviewer called him "a devotee of the gloomy existentialist
theology of Kierkegaard, Paul Tillich, Reinhold Niebuhr and Martin Buber"
who "greatly underrates the religion of ordinary people who pile into their
station wagon on Sunday morning and take the children to church." Others
seconded what they saw as Herberg's pessimism about postwar religiosity.
The Episcopal priest and poet Chad Walsh recognized that Herberg saw some

authentic elements in the revival but focused his review on the warning that American Christianity was fast becoming "a confused but warm blend of real religion and patriotism, with God and nation not clearly distinguished." Walsh agreed with Herberg that this path would end in "sudden and violent disillusionment."[16]

For his part, John Courtney Murray drew out a different theme from *Protestant-Catholic-Jew*: Herberg's implicit campaign for religion in the schools. In a 1956 article, Murray used Herberg as his authority in contending that, "from a socio-religious point of view, American society has assumed a new pluralist structure." This shift, he continued, had "invalidated" conceptions of the public schools as "vaguely Protestant" or "purely secular," or as vehicles for inculcating either "'democracy' as a quasi-religious ideology" or "spiritual and moral values in some non-sectarian sense." Instead, as Murray recognized, the logic of Herberg's tri-faith model pointed toward public funding for schools run by each of the three major faiths. As Murray put it, the nation's "pluralist religious-social structure" called for "aid to the religious school." The "good of a pluralist society has to be defined in pluralist terms," he explained, and "the social equality of these three communities entitles each of them to require that the public service should accommodate itself to its particular needs." Catholics, Murray contended, were no longer "a small eccentric group, existing on the periphery of American society, whose needs might possibly be overlooked in the interests of some greater good," but rather "a segment of our society, fully integrated into its pluralist structure, which has now become so large that its educational needs and interests have become public needs and interests." Murray closed by warning that the state ignored such needs at its own peril, for democracy's survival depended on "a religiously informed and virtuous citizenry."[17]

Herberg, too, continued to address the school question more directly in other forums. In April 1955, just as he finished *Protestant-Catholic-Jew*, he penned an article urging American Jews to embrace the explicitly Judeo-Christian anticommunism of FRASCO and like-minded organizations. Herberg again leveled the charge of anti-Catholicism against American Jews. Although he allowed that much Catholic anticommunism had been "crude and uncritical," he nevertheless lauded Catholics' "unequivocal and effective opposition to Communism." He presented Catholic anticommunism as a middle way between the conservatives' simple equation of God's will with the national interest and the liberals' single-minded obsession with "the 'Red-baiting' and 'witch-hunting' presumed to be devastating our civil liberties." Liberal Protestants and Jews, Herberg charged, had not taken up anti-communism in a manner commensurate with their vocal condemnation of right-wing movements. He suggested that a deep-seated anti-Catholicism had quickened their opposition to fascism in the 1930s but now blunted their "witness" against communism, the sworn enemy of Catholicism. The self-styled defenders of tolerance, he believed, had fallen into the trap of bigotry.[18]

Notwithstanding Herberg's efforts, FRASCO and the accommodationist approach its supporters championed made little headway among liberal Protestants and Jews. Herberg likely hurt his cause, quixotic though it already was, by labeling himself a conservative in the late 1950s. For a number of years, drawing on Niebuhr's growing appreciation of Edmund Burke, Herberg had contended that his mentor was a conservative. A number of other commentators, led by Russell Kirk and Clinton Rossiter, echoed Herberg in that regard. After Niebuhr rebuffed those advances, Herberg continued journeying rightward across the political spectrum, eventually becoming the religion editor of William F. Buckley Jr.'s *National Review* in 1961. Like Buckley, Herberg would criticize civil rights activists for breaking the law and abridging states' rights in the early 1960s. Although Herberg is seen today as a progenitor of Jewish neoconservatism, he did not succeed in moving American Jews en masse toward his accommodationist understanding of church-state relations or his affinity for a limited, decentralized state.[19]

Debating Secularism

John Courtney Murray and other liberal Catholics worried about FRASCO as well, though for very different reasons. Of course, Murray, like Herberg, was heavily involved in that group. He and his Woodstock College colleague Gustave Weigel served as FRASCO's primary Catholic advisers and considered the organization far superior to the NCCJ. At the time, wrote the *Priest*, it was "well known" that Catholics were split on the NCCJ, whereas FRASCO had secured "enthusiastic Catholic participation." Yet while Murray and his liberal Catholic allies welcomed FRASCO on principle, they still worried about its Protestant members' syncretistic tendencies and lack of intellectual rigor in the face of the communist threat. It did not help when FRASCO's Protestant leader, Charles Lowry, announced that American Christians and Jews were coming to "realize that they are bound together in a single, indissoluble religious tradition and that, in the mysterious and inscrutable providence of God, they complement and re-enforce one another." This statement captured neither the unity of the Church, as Catholics understood it, nor the purely civic mode of cooperation dictated by official Vatican guidelines.[20]

Catholic participants were wary of Judeo-Christian language for precisely this reason: its tendency to suggest a common theological denominator between the three faiths. Indeed, that concern may explain why FRASCO's leaders, despite the intensity of their Judeo-Christian (or perhaps Christian) exceptionalism, largely avoided Judeo-Christian language itself. President Eisenhower used the term in his opening address to the group, but only in the context of bracketing questions about democracy's deep historical roots. And Lowry also rooted democracy in "the Judeo-Christian religious tradition" at that meeting. But that formulation ignited an extensive discussion in which Murray, among others, raised "the problem of a theological interpretation of democracy." Thereafter, Judeo-Christian rhetoric gradually disappeared from FRASCO leaders' writings. Liberal Catholics such as Murray and Gustave Weigel preferred to avoid Judeo-Christian constructions, lest they be mis-interpreted as believing that Protestants, Catholics, and Jews shared a single superreligion. Although Judeo-Christian exceptionalism provided FRASCO's rationale and defined its identity, the use of Judeo-Christian terminology could endanger the alliance behind that political theory. As elsewhere, the ubiquity of tri-faith language barely masked potent conflicts over the nature and sources of American democracy in the early Cold War years.[21]

In other contexts, Catholics used Judeo-Christian terminology more freely. An important initiative of the 1950s was the Institute of Judaeo-Christian Studies at Seton Hall University in New Jersey. Founded by John M. Oester-reicher, an Austrian émigré and a convert to Catholicism from Judaism, the institute aimed to break down mutual suspicions between Catholics and Jews. It targeted Catholic anti-Semitism, on the one side, by encouraging Catholics to understand and appreciate Judaism. Meanwhile, it also sought to reveal the gifts of Christianity to Jews—and thereby hasten their conversion. Although writers for the Institute's journal, the *Bridge*, argued that they expected no "mass movement of conversion" and simply hoped to "permit Jews as Jews to be nourished from the manifold sources of Christian wisdom," Oesterreicher had devoted his entire career to the goal of making Jewish apostates by lead-ing them down the path to Christ that he had followed himself. The institute and the *Bridge*, reflecting "the intellectual predilection of the Jews," aimed to make converts through intellectual means: namely, promoting scholarship on Jewish-Catholic relations. The journal's name itself reflected a desire to promote movement across the boundary between the faith communities. As one advocate put it, the institute aimed "not to remove the stumbling block of the cross, but to reveal it as the very bridge over which Israel must pass in order to enter the promise." After centuries of resistance, Oesterreicher's 1954 book declared hopefully, "the wall of separation from Christ is crumbling." Although the institute would confine itself to ecumenical work by the 1960s, its earliest incarnation aimed in large part to speed Christ's return by convert-ing Jews.[22]

Meanwhile, more conservative Catholic commentators became increas-ingly comfortable using Judeo-Christian rhetoric to signal a set of traditional social norms. In 1958, the New York Chancery's office argued that birth con-trol violated "the teaching of our Judaeo-Christian heritage." By 1960, the National Legion of Decency routinely slapped a "C" rating ("condemned") on films such as "The Private Lives of Adam and Eve" for their "blatant viola-tions of Judaeo-Christian standards of modesty and decency." Meanwhile, a Catholic sociologist warned that any child lacking a robust Judeo-Christian faith would slide toward one of two extremes: either total "conformity" to social pressures or "a beatnik beard or leotard."[23]

Liberal Catholics, however, generally steered clear of Judeo-Christian for-mulations. Murray, for example, followed that pattern in the articles—mainly written between 1956 and 1960—that constituted most of his 1960 master-work *We Hold These Truths* (and inspired Murray's friend Henry Luce to put him on the cover of *Time* in 1960). In that book, Murray famously argued that America's religiously pluralistic and voluntaristic character had created favor-able conditions for Catholicism's growth. That fact, he said, undercut those Church leaders who thought democracy inimical to Catholicism. However, Murray also contended that Catholicism had a unique gift for Americans: the natural law. He believed that the natural law could provide a nonsectarian structure for American public culture, accommodating its pluralistic char-acter while providing "a common universe of discourse." At present, Mur-ray held, Americans lacked a "public philosophy," being bound only by a "negative American consensus, anti-Communism." But they could develop a proper philosophical basis for their culture by returning to the natural law, on which their political institutions had originally been founded.[24]

Even as liberal Catholics sought such an interfaith alliance against secular-ism, however, they avoided Judeo-Christian language, lest they be accused of asserting theological common ground with Protestantism and Judaism. Mur-ray, at least, also believed that Judeo-Christian formulations overestimated Judaism's contributions to Western thought. At the 1955 Kent Seminar on the Christian Idea of Education, where Murray spoke alongside figures such as Niebuhr and Jacques Maritain, he challenged the physicist-priest William G. Pollard's use of Judeo-Christian terminology. Murray first asked Pollard, rather skeptically, whether "Judaism has been creative of a culture" at any point in history and, more specifically, whether "the Jewish community of America today is creative of something that would be called the American culture." Of course, he noted, the "synagogue is part of the American way of life," but "our pluralist society" also contained "ethical humanists," and "philosophical naturalists, and all the rest of them." For merely demographic purposes, "Judeo-Christian" was actually too narrow.[25]

In another sense, however, that term was too broad: Murray did not believe that Jews had contributed to American culture. Pressed to clarify his own position, Murray contended that the "culturally creative" elements in the Jewish tradition had been "absorbed into the Christian tradition" as part of the "medieval synthesis," along with Greek, Roman, and Germanic elements (especially the "Germanic idea of law"). Medieval Catholicism had then given rise to Western civilization, as "the one root from which our culture at the moment flowers." For Murray, "Judeo-Christian" failed to capture any of the phenomena to which it was routinely applied: the complex mixture of elements that fed into the medieval synthesis, the type of civilization that had resulted from that synthesis, or the religious demographics of the contemporary United States. Murray's analysis thus echoed the supersessionist tendencies of so many of his Christian contemporaries.[26]

Continuing his historical excavations from the early 1950s, Murray now located the liberal tradition's roots even earlier than the medieval period, in the "great confluence of Greek, Roman, Germanic, and Christian ideas about society, law, and government." The core of that "ancient tradition," he explained, was the natural law: "the existence of a rational order of truth and justice, which man does not create, since it is the reflection of the Eternal Reason of God, but which man can discover, since he is himself made in the image of God." And democracy, forged under the Christian canopy, could not long survive without it. Perhaps rebuking John Cogley as well as secular liberals, Murray argued that reducing democracy to a "method of doing things, independently of any judgment on the rightness or value of what is done, is to abandon the public philosophy and the political tradition which launched our Republic." He saw hopeful signs in the postwar revival, with its newfound recognition "that the sovereignty of God is the first principle of American politics." Yet Murray believed that the Christian public philosophy continued to deteriorate, as citizens steadily lost "the body of mediating principles in terms of which the sovereignty of God becomes operative as the dynamic basis of the freedom and the order of our constitutional commonwealth." In short, Protestants failed to grasp the proper relationship between church and state in a tri-faith democracy.[27]

Murray was one of many theorists in the late 1950s who took increasing account of nonbelievers in American society, even as they typically decried secularism as a public philosophy and a social and political condition.

That period brought an increasingly overt—and, in some cases, increasingly positive—engagement with secularism. A growing number of American thinkers began to confront the full extent of their country's religious diversity, recognizing that America was no longer the tri-faith nation that Herberg so deftly conjured in *Protestant-Catholic-Jew*. Some of these commentators, most notably Reinhold Niebuhr, began to look more favorably on the contributions of nonbelievers to their nation's history. Others argued that religious organizations operated in a "secular age" and aimed to formulate the possibilities and limitations of that condition. The relationship between secularism and pluralism drew considerable attention as well, along with the lingering issue of the postwar revival's secularizing tendencies. And various skeptics, humanists, and religious liberals touted the importance of non-religious modes of thought—or, in Horace Kallen's case, the metafaith of secularism—to the American project. By the early 1960s, these debates about secularism and unbelief fed into a resurgence of pluralistic conceptions of democracy. They also prefigured the expansion of American religious pluralism to include non-Western faiths after the Hart-Celler Act of 1965 renewed immigration from Asia, Africa, and elsewhere.[28]

Among mainstream Protestants, the spectacle of McCarthyism and the example of groups such as FRASCO led a number of Murray's erstwhile allies to back away from their vigorous antisecularism in the late 1950s. Chief among them was Niebuhr, whose influence continued to grow even as his health waned. Herberg's interpretation of the political meaning of neo-orthodox theology had highlighted the ease with which Niebuhr's writings could be placed in the service of a forthright—and increasingly conservative—religious nationalism. Niebuhr responded to Herberg's provocations by actively rejecting the conservative label, although in a more scholarly context he distinguished the "kind of conservatism I espouse," centered on "an increasing appreciation of the organic factors in social life," from the "decadent liberalism" of America's so-called conservatism. Meanwhile, he foregrounded the fundamentally liberal elements of his intellectual project.[29]

Niebuhr had already begun, in the early 1950s, to qualify his characterizations of the relationship between religion and politics. For instance, in July 1952, he declared it wrong "to regard every political decision as simply derived from our faith," because "political issues represent various grades and levels which range all the way from clear moral issues to problems of strategy and means." That same month he wrote, "Every political decision requires dozens of subordinate and relative judgments which cannot be derived from, or sanctioned by, our faith." A few years later, in a poignant April 1955 piece entitled "About Christian Apologetics," Niebuhr grappled more openly with his own apologetic approach and qualified his earlier denunciations of secularism. Meditating on the pitfalls of the apologetic task of "commending the Christian faith to those who do not believe," Niebuhr observed that, all too often, believers simply trumpeted "the superior virtues of Christians" while "holding 'secularism' responsible for every moral failure of our culture." Indeed, Niebuhr now suggested that those who advocated religion without sufficient humility could be worse in certain respects than nonbelievers. He also conceded that, through experience, secularists could achieve greater virtue than hypocritical defenders of religion, a sentiment that mirrored his habitual caveat that secularists' practices often proved better than their philosophies.[30]

Still, Niebuhr's writings of the mid-1950s continued to give as much ammunition to the antisecularist, increasingly right-wing Herberg as to the political progressives he hoped to inspire. Thus, his 1955 reflections on the apologetic task culminated in the classic Niebuhrian admonition that "more humility on the part of Christians would make way for the witness to Christ to our unbelieving friends." Niebuhr still could not fully abandon the invidious comparison of secularists to Christians. For all their insights, he wrote, the former had "not confronted in any ultimate way the judgment and mercy of God," and therefore lacked the "saving grace" needed to accompany the "common grace" arrived at through collective experience. For now, this was as much as Niebuhr would distance himself—at least publicly—from Herberg's assertion that Judeo-Christian fallibilism meant nonbelievers could never fully appreciate the true nature of humanity or the genius of democracy.[31]

Behind the scenes, however, Niebuhr's views had begun to shift more substantially. When Herberg's *Protestant-Catholic-Jew* appeared in 1955, Niebuhr praised the book in his two reviews and other writings, but his daughter, Elisabeth Sifton, recalls him wondering privately how Herberg could ignore Buddhists, Muslims, and other religious minorities. Over the next few years, he reconsidered the relationship between Christian and secular ideas in the history of American democracy. Although Niebuhr still saw most forms of secular thought as hopelessly optimistic about the possibility of overcoming human limitations, he now left open the possibility that some secular thinkers could adopt a more realistic stance. Niebuhr also began to attribute modern spiritual ills to consumerism—"the preoccupation of the American culture with the comforts of this life"—rather than science and technology. Although Niebuhr flirted with attributing consumerism itself "to the remarkable efficiency of our technics, of our industrial enterprise, and ingenuity of our applied sciences," he admitted that "such wealth could not have been accumulated without straining after the comforts of life."[32]

Niebuhr fleshed out his new analysis in *Pious and Secular America* (1958), which can be read as a response to Herberg's book. He returned to the "paradox" from which Herberg had begun: Niebuhr's own 1952 observation that the United States was "at once the most religious and the most secular of Western nations." But Niebuhr carefully distinguished "a practical secularism" centered on "the pursuit of the immediate goals of life" from "a theoretic secularism" that "dismisses ultimate questions about the meaning of existence." It was "usually" the case, Niebuhr argued, that secularists of the latter, theoretical type ignored "the 'misery of man.'" But that "usually" signaled an important opening: Niebuhr's condemnation now applied to most, not all, forms of secular thought. Indeed, Niebuhr stressed the historical importance of certain forms of secularism. Western civilization had "profited by the historical dynamism of the Judaeo-Christian religious tradition," he declared, using the more familiar term instead of his usual "Hebraic-Christian." But that civilization had ultimately resulted from "cooperation between secularism and piety," in which "each side possessed more common virtue than the opponent was willing to admit." Moreover, Niebuhr added, the "unique virtues" of each strand of thought had checked the other by "prevent[ing] the other side from pursuing its characteristic virtues so consistently that they degenerated into vices." Secularists, in this new portrait, had not simply managed to hang on to values of Judeo-Christian origin. Rather, they brought distinctive contributions of their own, unavailable through the religious traditions. By 1958, then, Niebuhr had stopped dismissing secularism in its entirety and had begun describing the dialectical interaction of religion and secularism as the source of America's cultural genius.[33]

Another set of writings challenged or modified Herberg's tripartite description of American identity by identifying a "fourth faith" that operated alongside the other three in the United States. A number of traditions vied for this label, but the phrase emerged particularly frequently in the debates around the Unitarian-Universalist consolidation of the late 1950s. (A major bone of contention was the proposed description of the new denomination as "Judeo-Christian.") In 1964, the Unitarian minister Duncan Howlett's *The Fourth American Faith* described the alternative to Protestantism, Catholicism, and Judaism as a tradition that positioned itself in opposition to the other three. The fourth faith, wrote Howlett, "rejects on principle the claim of any religion to priority, pre-eminence, divine authority, truth, and revelation." That tradition had resurged in the mid-twentieth century, Howlett contended, "because Protestantism primarily, and Judaism secondarily, have reverted to a new emphasis on orthodoxy."[34]

A New Era

By the time Howlett's book appeared, many of the factors that had made Judeo-Christian exceptionalism so powerful in the early Cold War years had disappeared. After the Cuban missile crisis of October 1962, tensions between the Americans and the Soviets lessened significantly. Anticommunism waned accordingly, especially in liberal circles. John F. Kennedy's presidency and the Vatican II reforms within the Catholic Church also signaled a significant liberalization of the Catholic position on church-state issues, even as they directed Catholic officials' energy away from the fight against communism. By 1965, the Vatican had embraced John Courtney Murray's arguments about pluralism and religious liberty, dramatically altering the Church's place in the American political landscape. Meanwhile, the school prayer and Bible-reading decisions of 1962–63 led some conservative evangelicals—most notably Billy Graham—to adopt Judeo-Christian rhetoric, prefiguring the rightward shift of that discourse in the late 1960s and early 1970s.

Although Kennedy's campaign reignited suspicion of Catholic political aims in many quarters, his famed Houston speech of September 12, 1960, in which the candidate warmly embraced church-state separation and declared his faith thoroughly private and personal, assuaged many of those fears. It is fitting that John Cogley prepared him for the tough questions that followed his speech, because Kennedy, too, argued that the American state was religiously neutral and Americanism was a matter of method rather than a comprehensive philosophy. Seeking to convince wary Protestants that his Catholicism would not unduly influence his decision-making, he declared in Houston that "I do not speak for my church on public matters—and the church does not speak for me." Presenting religion as a purely private matter, Kennedy called for "absolute" church-state separation and an end to religious bigotry, bloc voting, and religious understandings of Americanism. Kennedy stressed, especially, "my declared stands against an Ambassador to the Vatican, against unconstitutional aid to parochial schools, and against any boycott of the public schools (which I have attended myself)."[35]

Not that Kennedy ignored religion during his presidency. Like Eisenhower in his unscripted moments, Kennedy infused his rhetoric with broad religious claims while largely avoiding Judeo-Christian terminology. In his January 1961 inaugural, for example, Kennedy argued that Americans shared a commitment to human rights, embodied in "the belief that the rights of man come not from the generosity of the state, but from the hand of God." This claim, of course, had been a staple of Judeo-Christian exceptionalists for more than two decades. Yet Kennedy's religio-political rhetoric widened the spectrum of permissible religious belief. He closed the inaugural address by invoking God's aid but also appealing to those with a more human-centered conception of religion: "With a good conscience our only sure reward, with history the final judge of our deeds, let us go forth to lead the land we love, asking His blessing and His help, but knowing that here on earth God's work must truly be our own."[36]

By the early 1960s, with a Catholic president in office, some Catholic commentators had come to accept the need for secular public schooling in a religiously pluralistic nation. In a 1963 book, Gustave Weigel, the Jesuit theologian and pioneering Catholic ecumenist who had helped oversee FRASCO's activities, adopted a much warmer stance toward the public schools. Although Weigel continued to decry "secularism as an ideology," he called secularism in politics and education "a pragmatic form of coexistence," necessary for civic peace in a multireligious context.[37]

A few Catholic leaders also joined Niebuhr in stressing the secular, as well as religious, sources of American political institutions. John Cogley, in a February 1958 *New Republic* essay, argued that two sources had "mothered" American democracy: "the tradition we call Judaeo-Christian" and "the political philosophy which owes its beginnings at least to the philosophes of the Enlightenment." Each of these "has been proudly proclaimed parent by its own partisans," Cogley noted, "but as Reinhold Niebuhr has argued, American democracy can actually be traced back to both; neither has full claim." To Cogley, the American political system was "neither Jacobin nor 'Christian'" but possessed "a genius all its own."[38]

Meanwhile, officials in Rome were reassessing their own position on church-state questions. Between 1962 and 1965, the series of reforms known as Vatican II changed the Catholic Church's stance on innumerable questions, ranging from the position of the priest during Mass to the Church's relation to political systems. On the latter issue, Murray played a key role in the deliberations after being called to Rome in 1963 by, of all people, Cardinal Francis Spellman. He drafted numerous documents during the group's bitter deliberations, which stretched through all four sessions. In the end, Murray's position largely prevailed, despite lingering differences of wording. The statement on religious liberty, *Dignitatis humanae* (1965), left room for the Spanish model of a national church but strongly emphasized religious liberty and the rights of conscience, which it rooted in the principle of human dignity.[39]

At the same time, the African American struggle continued to generate robust assertions of the country's Judeo-Christian character, though these formulations identified the Judeo-Christian tradition with liberal ideals such as tolerance and justice. At the 1963 NCCJ conference where Martin Luther

King Jr. first met his (and Reinhold Niebuhr's) Jewish friend and ally Abraham Heschel, King issued "A Challenge to the Churches and Synagogues" to "affirm that every human life is a reflex of divinity, and every act of injustice mars and defaces the image of God in man." King insisted that "all the dialectics of the logicians" could never square the "undergirding philosophy of segregation" with "the undergirding philosophy of our Judeo-Christian heritage." King was hardly naïve about the capacity of Judeo-Christian teachings to become tools of oppression. He knew full well that Christian concepts such as the "curse of Ham" had been mobilized against racial equality. Yet King deemed those interpretations fundamentally wrong and routinely mobilized Judeo-Christian rhetoric as he appealed to the consciences of white Americans, North and South. He urged church leaders to declare "that segregation is morally wrong and sinful, and that it stands against all the noble precepts of our Judeo-Christian tradition."[40]

The Birmingham "Children's Campaign" of spring 1963 was a fertile source of Judeo-Christian rhetoric. At the start of their nonviolent struggle, Fred Shuttlesworth and other African American activists declared, "We act today in full concert with our Hebraic-Christian tradition, the laws of morality and the Constitution of our nation." After the campaign began, King expressed his appreciation that "the nonviolent movement in America has come not from secular forces but from the heart of the Negro church," adding that the movement's "great principles of love and justice" were "deeply rooted in our Judeo-Christian heritage." A particularly potent formulation appeared in King's "From the Birmingham Jail," where he reflected on the impact of the sit-in movement: "One day the South will know that when these disinherited children of God sat down at lunch counters, they were in reality standing up for what is best in the American dream and for the most sacred values in our Judeo-Christian heritage." Here, as elsewhere, King linked the movement for civil rights to the struggles of the Israelites and early Christians. "As the Apostle Paul carried the gospel of Jesus Christ," he explained, "so am I compelled to carry the gospel," championing "the more excellent way of love" against the Scylla and Charybdis of "complacency" among whites and "bitterness and hatred" among black nationalists.[41]

Specifically exceptionalist uses of Judeo-Christian rhetoric persisted in the early 1960s as well. After the Supreme Court outlawed prayer and Bible reading in the public schools in 1962–63, religious leaders of many persuasions charged that the court had dynamited the cultural pillars of American democracy. When school leaders in North Brookfield, Massachusetts, bucked the court's decision and continued reciting the Lord's Prayer, a supporter declared that such actions "prove that we Americans look not to the Supreme

Court as the supreme measure of conduct, but rather to God and the Judaeo-Christian code as that measure." Pluralists pushed back on these claims. The ACLU sued to remove "under God" from the Pledge of Allegiance, and a skeptical Unitarian Universalist charged that Christians rewrote history when they imagined that the Founders were orthodox Christians: "If we are to believe that America's 'essential consensus' is embodied in the ideas of Jefferson and his friends, we must admit this nation is not and never has been rooted in the Judaeo-Christian tradition." But many commentators shared the Methodist bishop Gerald Kennedy's amazement that the Supreme Court, "in a nation built on the foundation of the Judeo-Christian tradition," had favored "a very small minority's atheism" over "the majority's faith."[42]

Those decisions also gave the Judeo-Christian framework a purchase among conservative Protestants, who would become its most devoted users by the 1970s. Most importantly, the wildly popular revivalist Billy Graham slowly began to incorporate Judeo-Christian language in the era of the court's prayer and Bible-reading decisions. As early as 1962, Graham invoked "the Judeo-Christian concept" in a newspaper column, in reference to a body of moral principles that ruled out, among other things, Hitler-style euthanasia. Although conservative evangelicals continued to foreground Christ, they would gradually come to appreciate the combination of flexibility and specificity that Judeo-Christian language provided.[43]

*

In a sense, the early 1960s saw Judeo-Christian rhetoric reach its widest distribution among the various religious communities in the United States. With Catholics and conservative evangelicals increasingly joining the fold, few kinds of commentators categorically rejected that language. And yet the portents of change could be seen clearly in the late 1950s and early 1960s. Even the most vociferous antisecularists grappled with the palpable fact that the country featured a significant contingent of nonbelievers, and their less vehement counterparts often reassessed the capacity of atheists, agnostics, and humanists to support a democratic culture and institutions. In short, Judeo-Christian exceptionalism came under increasing fire, even as Judeo-Christian language continued to find expression in American public culture. And bigger changes lay just ahead.

Judeo-Christian Visions under Fire

NEW PATTERNS OF PLURALISM, 1965–1975

The mid-1960s, like the Gilded Age period and the mid-1920s, brought a dramatic change in the patterns of immigration that defined American demographics. The Hart-Celler Act of 1965 liberalized immigration policy and reestablished the flow of non-European immigrants to American shores over the ensuing decades. That policy had tremendous symbolic significance in itself, especially when viewed alongside Justice William O. Douglas's statement of the same year that the United States had already become by 1948 "a nation of Buddhists, Confucianists, and Taoists, as well as Christians." Moreover, the impact of the new immigration policy would transform the United States in a few short decades. The immigrants of the post-1965 period were, like their predecessors of the decades around 1900, religiously as well as culturally different. The country's religious diversity, hitherto largely limited to the tri-faith pantheon of Protestants, Catholics, and Jews, now expanded far beyond the confines of Judeo-Christian terminology. As we have seen, the term "Judeo-Christian" spoke both to the historical past and the demographic present during the World War II era and immediate postwar years. But as the 1960s wore on, its power to describe religious life in contemporary America started to wane. At the same time, new scrutiny fell on the term's use as a descriptor of historical realities as well. Once these seeds of doubt had been planted, the overlapping historical and demographic consensus that had propelled Judeo-Christian accounts of democracy and national identity into American public discourse started to become unmoored, exposing a deep chasm in the nation's culture.

As usual, however, cultural changes lagged beyond demography. Hart-Celler's full significance would not become apparent until the 1990s, when the convergence of demographic and political developments undermined the image of a tri-faith America. Nonetheless, the uses and resonances of Judeo-Christian rhetoric changed substantially in American public life during the tumultuous decade from the mid-1960s to the mid-1970s. By the end of that period, the widespread postwar belief that the United States was in some sense Judeo-Christian had fractured, though for reasons mostly unrelated to the nascent demographic shifts. Debates about secularization, the social and political movements of the 1960s, the Vietnam War, and the political developments of the Watergate years all contributed to that transformation. Although Judeo-Christian formulations continued to appear with great frequency throughout this period and beyond, they took on a remarkably broad array of new meanings, most of which bore little relation to the big questions of political theory—questions about the philosophical roots of democracy and totalitarianism—that had predominated in the early Cold War years. Where such claims had once seemed to indicate consensus, moreover, they now fueled the ongoing social conflicts.

Indeed, the decade after 1965 brought an even deeper conceptual change, beyond the scope of Judeo-Christian discourse itself. After an era characterized by assertions of public consensus, many American commentators stopped asserting that all Americans shared a common framework of values. A growing number of Americans replaced consensus with conflict as their main narrative lens for understanding their country's public life. As social movements spread and political crises unfolded, some of these figures positioned themselves as champions of Judeo-Christian values against a soulless political establishment. Others held that the establishment itself followed Judeo-Christian values and that both were morally bankrupt. But these and other new approaches all tended to challenge, in one way or another, the assertion that the United States not only had been but continued to be a Judeo-Christian nation. Some lamented this transformation; others celebrated it. But it was clear on all sides that something fundamental had changed in American culture in the 1960s—and that it might not be possible, even if it were desirable, to go back.

Portraits of American Public Culture

Scholarly commentators on religion's role in American public life were slow to abandon the image of a shared consensus but quick to recognize that all was not as it had been in Eisenhower's day. In the mid-1960s, even as social and political movements began to inspire challenges to the normative authority of Judeo-Christianity as a guide to action, a number of key theorists emphasized the descriptive flaws of simplistic images of the United States as a Judeo-Christian nation. Earlier discussions of secularism, the authenticity of the postwar revival, and a potential "fourth faith" flowered into broader debates over the existence and meaning of secularization—and perhaps the possibility that the United States was already becoming "postsecular." Theorists also fleshed out the concept of a "civil religion" as a possible descriptor for public piety in the United States and elsewhere.

The intellectual ferment in this area brought together a host of scholars interested in religious pluralism, secularization, and national identity, launching arguments that continue today. Many argued that the apparent revival actually masked a deeper secularization process. For some, the moral shallowness and consumerism of much postwar religiosity reflected a tendency toward secularization within the faith traditions themselves. Other scholars viewed secularization more positively as a condition with which religious groups could fruitfully engage and which would eventuate in more robust and fulfilling forms of faith. Still others contended that what looked like secularization actually signaled the emergence of new religious forms, such as civil religion. Although the disputants did not always use Judeo-Christian rhetoric themselves, they developed their thinking in direct response to the tri-faith, Judeo-Christian constructions of national identity that had flourished in the 1950s. Their iconic writings captured a growing perception that American public culture was undergoing an epochal change in the 1960s.

These writers came to national attention as early as 1963, when *Time* identified a group of young Protestants—"prophets of post-Christianity"—who called for "the churches to answer the new challenges of secular times" and provided "a stream of criticism from within." Chief among them was the Lutheran pastor and historian Martin E. Marty. In a series of books and articles after 1958, Marty picked up and developed Will Herberg's argument that the 1950s revival of religion had unfolded on two parallel tracks, one featuring an inauthentic deification of the "American Way" and the other authentic Judeo-Christian faith. A perennial question had reemerged in new forms, Marty wrote: "Does or should a nation, a culture, or a society have a single integrating and supporting societal religion?" Referring to this "societal religion" as a "common faith or religious consensus," Marty rejected the usual descriptions of the United States as Christian or Judeo-Christian, on the one side, or dominated by "a kind of creedal secular religion," on the other. Instead, he portrayed a decisive shift from Protestantism to "religion-in-general"—"a temporalized national religion" that drew on the old Protestant establishment but also many other sources—as the nation's cultural lodestone in the mid-twentieth century. Marty developed his argument further in *The New Shape of American Religion* (1959) and *Second Chance for American Protestants* (1963), where he famously described the overarching "religion-in-general" as an "American Shinto," akin to the state-centered religion of modern Japan.[1]

In 1967, the sociologist Robert N. Bellah applied the term "civil religion," originally coined by Jean-Jacques Rousseau in *The Social Contract*, to Marty's "religion-in-general." A student of Japanese religion, Bellah was inspired to turn his attention to American phenomena by the appearance of Marty's "American Shinto" phrase in Harvey Cox's 1965 blockbuster *The Secular City*. Stressing that the national faith existed alongside more traditional religious institutions but had been ignored by scholars due to Western assumptions about the singularity of religious group membership, Bellah explained that American civil religion's "elaborate and well-institutionalized . . . beliefs, symbols, and rituals" buttressed Émile Durkheim's assertion that "every group has a religious dimension." Although Bellah later complained that he hated "religious nationalism" and should not have been read as an uncritical supporter of civil religion, he held that "this religion—or perhaps better, religious dimension—has its own seriousness and integrity and requires the same care in understanding that any other religion does." Mainstream journalists picked up Bellah's concept immediately. To one *New York Times* writer, Bellah's theory meant that "the elimination of all religious symbolism from schools and official documents would be as dangerous to the state as its identification with a particular religion through compulsory sectarian Bible reading or prayer."[2]

As figures such as Marty and Bellah sought an analytical framework for understanding religious expressions in American public life, another group of scholars asserted that the United States was actually becoming thoroughly secularized. The surge of theoretical interest in secularization quickly coalesced around two influential books: Cox's *The Secular City* and Peter Berger's *The Sacred Canopy* (1967). Cox, a Baptist minister who taught theology and ethics at Harvard Divinity School, was another of *Time*'s "prophets of post-Christianity." In *The Secular City*, he picked up Marty's claims about the "post-Protestant" character of the United States but departed from Marty in celebrating secularization as a positive boon to the churches. Cox argued that many American Protestants had found the same "relief" in the coming of a post-Protestant era that many of their European counterparts had found in a "post-Christian" one. Such a climate allowed them "to stand free enough of their culture to be against it or for it selectively, as the guidance of the Gospel suggests."[3]

Unfortunately, Cox continued, "just as this promising possibility has emerged, the sly temptation of a new sacral society has also appeared," in the form of the "American Shinto" delineated by Herberg and Marty. Attacking the "myth" that Americans shared a "common religious heritage," Cox welcomed the end of an imposed "Protestant sacral culture" and contended that "Christians should continue to support the secularization of American society, recognizing that secularists, atheists, and agnostics do not have to be second-class citizens." For Cox, an American Shinto would mean outright oppression, not to mention the loss of religious authenticity: "It would be too bad if Catholics and Jews, having rightly pushed for the de-Protestantizing of American society and having in effect won, should now join Protestants in reconstituting a kind of tripartite American religion with Americanized versions of Moses, Luther, and Saint Thomas sharing the haloes in its hagiography." Cox's Baptist heritage, among other factors, attuned him to the dangers of any "sacral society," whether Protestant or Judeo-Christian.[4]

By contrast, the Lutheran émigré sociologist Peter Berger deemed secularization an unmitigated disaster and equated what he called Cox's "new secularism" with the era's "death of God" theology. In an earlier book, Berger had echoed Herberg's claim that secularization was occurring within the churches themselves. The import of this argument became clear in *The Sacred Canopy*, where it enabled Berger to compare European and American developments. In the United States, he explained, "the churches still occupy a more central symbolic position," but "they have succeeded in keeping this position only by becoming highly secularized themselves, so that the European and American cases represent two variations on the same underlying theme of global secularization." Berger declared that "the task of the churches today is to call back our society to what is best (I would even say to what is God-given) in its values, including its political ideals."[5]

Another young commentator on public religiosity, the Catholic priest, sociologist, and novelist Andrew M. Greeley, gained fame in 1966 for arguing that secularization had already reached its end and a "post-secular" future was dawning. Like Herberg, who from 1950 forward had repeatedly identified a "post-modern" mindset emerging among the youth of his day,[6] Greeley saw in phenomena such as the student movements evidence that a "post-Christian age" was giving way to a "post-secular age." As both a liberal Catholic and a parish priest, Greeley was centrally concerned with making Catholicism relevant to a new generation. He welcomed many of the reforms adopted by the Vatican II council, in which he saw a decisive move from "a feudal and renaissance world" into "the modern world." At the same time, however, he worried that Catholic spirituality had lost some of its richness and saw among the young Catholics of his day a deep hunger for mystical, personalized forms of religious experience. Although modernization had brought "freedom and abundance," Greeley believed a new, "post-secularist" or "post-post-Christian," phase was opening, as "man determined that it was humanly and psychologically possible to have the best of both, to combine the freedom and affluence of a technological society with the warmth and fellowship of a tribal society." Behind the "personalist revolution" of his day, Greeley saw a broader "revolt against the detribalized society": a search for contemporary alternatives to the old, communal ties of "blood, land, and soil." A postsecular society would combine the inner resources of the faith traditions with the external trappings of the modern world.[7]

Jewish thinkers continued to grapple with religion's roles in American public culture as well. It was not a Lutheran or a Catholic thinker but rather the Reform Jewish theologian Eugene B. Borowitz who relied most heavily on the "post-secular" concept as the 1960s gave way to the 1970s. Borowitz's writings centered on a single contention: Jews were already postsecular, while Christians were still grappling with the original secularization process. In 1970, for example, Borowitz identified a host of contemporary religious tendencies as evidence that Christians were finally coming to grips with modernity. He saw this accommodation, for example, in both "Catholic calls to democratize the church and increase the role of the laity" and "Protestant pleas to live out religion in the streets and through politics." Borowitz agreed with Cox that "urbanization and higher education are the keys to participating in the new secularity," but he insisted that Jewish thinkers, having engaged with such secular phenomena long ago, were now "fundamentally postsecular." "For those who have not been immersed in secular modernity," Borowitz declared, Cox's work and related movements represented "an important step forward." But Jews, he continued, "came through the alliance with secularity some time ago." As a result, there was now "a significant minority in their midst who know that beyond secularity lies the need for grounding in the transcendent. Being modern has made tradition a living option."[8]

Much of the discussion among Jewish theorists continued to address the concept of a Judeo-Christian tradition, which had profound effects on their cultural status. During the 1960s, Herberg's critic Robert Gordis became a much more overt proponent of the Judeo-Christian tradition, primarily in the context of the renewed interest in Jewish-Christian relations brought about by Vatican II. Yet Gordis, while himself a Conservative leader, feared that Herberg's attempt to streamline American Judaism along neo-orthodox lines would do violence to the inherently pluralistic character of the Jewish tradition—and the wider society around it. In *Judaism in a Christian World* (1966), as in his earlier book *The Root and the Branch* (1962), Gordis recounted the career of Judeo-Christian discourse and identified "religious pluralism" as "not merely a reality in modern life but an ideal to be cherished in a free society." Only a pluralistic approach, Gordis declared, "can serve the needs of the emerging world community of the future, which will include countless varieties of religious belief and unbelief." In an extended meditation on Judaism and religious liberty, Gordis argued that "biblical and rabbinic Judaism are the seedbed for a religious theory of freedom of conscience."[9]

Even as Gordis warmed to the Judeo-Christian language, other Jewish thinkers cooled on it. The most direct attack came in *The Myth of the Judeo-Christian Tradition* (1970), a collection of essays by the Jewish humanist Arthur A. Cohen. In the first of those essays, dating back to 1959, Cohen lambasted John M. Oesterreicher's efforts at Seton Hall's Institute of Judaeo-Christian Studies. Entitled "The One-Way Bridge," Cohen's essay read the contents of Oesterreicher's journal as a sustained attempt to win Jews for Christ: "*The Bridge*, as it is and promises to remain, is open only for one-way traffic." A few years later, in 1962, Cohen had denounced Herberg for having "done more than any other modern Jewish thinker to justify that questionable phenomenon 'the Judeo-Christian' tradition." The 1970 book pulled together Cohen's numerous critiques of that concept, which he said "obscures the vast chasm of being which separates the two faiths."[10]

At the same time, however, Cohen argued that Jews and Christians, after acknowledging their "essential theological enmity," could turn to the points of commonality between them. Above all else stood their shared "conviction about the need to work within history to make the way smooth for the Kingdom." Concerning "the magnitude of creation and the grandeur and misery of man," at least, Jews agreed with Christians. "Out of such agreement," Cohen concluded, "an authentic community, a viable consensus, a meaningful cooperation"—what Cohen termed "a Judeo-Christian humanism"—might still emerge.[11]

Social Movements

The social and political movements of the 1960s, however, offered little evidence of convergence on any shared ideals, Judeo-Christian or otherwise. Indeed, the turmoil of that era led many commentators to abandon the very assumption that consensus could or should prevail. As visions of consensus gave way to portraits of conflict, so, too, did the assertion that the United States had always been, and must continue to be, a Judeo-Christian nation. In its place, a vast array of descriptive and normative visions emerged. The resonances of Judeo-Christian rhetoric varied wildly in this time of flux, to the point where that terminology often functioned in directly opposing ways for different interpreters.

Yet, despite the changes afoot, the familiar dichotomy of Judeo-Christian America and secular totalitarianism persisted in some quarters, especially as challenges to the status quo mounted. A *Wall Street Journal* author lamented that "the substitution of secular humanism for the Judeo-Christian ethic is resulting in a steady decline in the quality of human civilization," by "destroying the inner discipline and character of the American people." The writer called for "a return to the authoritarianism of the Old Testament combined with the love and compassion of the New Testament." The charge of atheism continued to carry practical consequences as well; a dispute arose in 1967 as to whether a self-professed atheist and pacifist could be naturalized as an American citizen.[12]

At times, broad-gauged fears of science and technology also filled the gap left by the ebbing of Cold War tensions. One commentator lamented that the right to privacy, once "part of the Judeo-Christian heritage of Western man," was now under assault from "recent, extremely rapid advances in technology, particularly in the development of large, high-speed electronic digital computers." Similarly, the Catholic psychiatrist and psychopharmacologist Frank Ayd Jr. said the greatest struggle of the day was not "religion vs. Communism" but rather "Christianity vs. Science." He wondered aloud, "Which philosophy will dominate—the Judaeo-Christian or the scientist's utilitarian concept of man?" Ayd predicted a showdown between the "scientists who believe man has control over his destiny" and "those who believe that man exists for God, not for [the] race, and that the glories are not only in this world." A *Los Angeles Times* editorial identified "scientism" as the "new religion" of many "scientists and humanists" who had rejected Judeo-Christian faith as unworthy of a scientifically mature species.[13]

For the most part, however, Judeo-Christian rhetoric emerged in relation to the burgeoning social movements of the day: civil rights activism, the antiwar movement, environmentalism, feminism, and many others. Amid the struggles to define and interpret these movements, participants and commentators routinely disagreed on whether the challengers or the establishment stood for Judeo-Christianity. Either way, however, Judeo-Christian rhetoric became enmeshed in the arguments for and against particular protests and social-cultural agendas rather than standing for entire political systems in a dichotomous global conflict.

The counterculture of the late 1960s inspired conflicting interpretations of the social resonances of Judeo-Christianity. Clearly, the hippies engaged in religious experimentation. Journalists fixated on the question of whether the youth's rejection of "the religion of their fathers" in favor of "yoga" and "atheism" meant that "God is dead for young people today." In 1968, *Time* declared outright, "One thing hippee [sic] religion is not is Judaeo-Christian in outlook." Jesus "may be revered as the hip guru of his time who preached a primitive form of love power," the article explained, but the hippies largely rejected "Western churches . . . as irrelevant and square." Instead, it continued, they gravitated toward "the occult" with its emphasis on "levels of spiritual consciousness" lying "beyond man's reason." More sympathetically, Reinhold Niebuhr's biographer June Bingham explained that "the hippies stretch for spiritual meaning beyond the Judeo-Christian tradition," which had "led some to study Hinduism and Buddhism, ancient philosophies too long spurned by the West." At the same time, however, an evangelical strand of the counterculture flourished: the "Jesus people" or "Jesus freaks." And Brotherhood of the Sun, a new religious movement and commune, called itself "Judeo-Christian" even as it incorporated Native American elements. These examples notwithstanding, the city council of Torrance, California, shut down a community course in astrology because it "violates the Judeo-Christian ethic." Many fretful elders insisted that those "questioning religion" still needed to "understand something of the Judeo-Christian tradition," since it remained "the foundation of our Western culture."[14]

On the other hand, some in the older generation legitimated youth activism by describing it as a straightforward expression of Judeo-Christian ethics despite the widespread rejection of traditional religion. A campus chaplain explained, "The average activist is one whose roots are deep in Judeo-Christian ethics. He learned the philosophy of brotherhood and concern for humanity at home, and what he criticizes so ruthlessly—and also inaccurately sometimes—is what he knows so well." A journalist observed that all the "clenched fists and red flags" attest to the fact that "politics is 'in' on campus," but the tone of the demonstrations remains that of "good old Judeo-Christian idealism." Even the sociologist Nathan Glazer, no friend to student radicals, agreed with this assessment. Despite the rejection of "institutional religion" by "today's idealistic, protesting collegians," Glazer suggested in 1966, "their ideals are founded on traditional Judeo-Christian concepts."[15]

In the African American struggle, a clear divide opened up between nonviolent activists in the vein of Martin Luther King Jr. and black nationalists who deemed Judeo-Christianity intrinsically white, practically ineffective, or both. King continued to harness the power of Judeo-Christian rhetoric, although he increasingly emphasized non-Western religious resources after 1965. In the wake of Selma and the Voting Rights Act, King turned his attention to socioeconomic issues and became more vocal in his opposition to the Vietnam War. In a December 1965 speech, King justified his antiwar work in terms of his role as "a clergyman" within "the prophetic Judeo-Christian tradition." Yet King's rhetoric was always rather open-ended, in the style of Judeo-Christian pluralism rather than exceptionalism. By April 1967, in fact, he identified the first epistle of Saint John—"Let us love one another, for love is of God. And every one that loveth is born of God and knoweth God. He that loveth not knoweth not God, for God is love"—as a summary of "the Hindu-Muslim-Christian-Jewish-Buddhist belief" concerning the power of love.[16]

For the most part, however, King's allies and admirers continued to use more conventional, Judeo-Christian rhetoric in the years before and after his 1968 assassination. By contrast, those inclined toward black power and black nationalism identified Judeo-Christianity as a primary source of their oppression. A writer in the *Baltimore Afro-American* explained that he preferred "Black" to "Negro" because it highlighted the African "cultural heritage" and "reject[ed] the usurious, corrupting influence which characterizes Judeo-Christian 'civilization.'" Another commentator urged African Americans to "cut the umbilical cord" tying them "to White Europeans, Judeo-Christian society and its philosophical and cultural imperatives." In 1968, activists in Chicago argued that the black churches were "not giving us a religion we can relate to," while the white churches were impotent: "America simply does not respond to the Judeo-Christian ethic." After African American students demonstrated at a school in Boston's Roxbury neighborhood, the *Globe* identified the underlying cause as the distance between the students' "social moral ethos" and "the middle-class white ethic of administrators and teachers," with their "Judeo-Christian moralism." Black radicals such as Ossie Davis likewise arrayed themselves against "White Western Judeo-Christian Capitalist Civilization."[17]

For many of these radicals, the needed alternative to the Judeo-Christian tradition lay in Islam, whether of the traditional variety or the uniquely American variant developed by the "black Muslims" of the Nation of Islam (NOI). Malcolm X and other NOI leaders identified Christianity as the white man's religion and Islam as the answer to its lies, its colonization of African Americans' minds. So, too, did Amiri Baraka (formerly Leroi Jones), whose call for a "post-American" reconstruction of religion, culture, and the arts signaled the degree to which he and other black nationalists equated Judeo-Christianity with the cultural norms of what they called "white America." Drawing a stark line between the races and their affiliated religions, these activists excoriated mainstream African American leaders such as King for working with the white establishment and adopting its pacifist Christian injunction to turn the other cheek and love one's enemies. Malcolm X deemed the ideal of nonviolence undignified and even inhuman, counter to the natural instinct of self-preservation that whites, in his view, had developed into a fine art while suppressing its expression among black Americans. Malcolm's claim to have named his first two children after Attila the Hun and Kublai Khan, the scourges of Western civilization, signaled his fierce rejection of everything associated with Judeo-Christianity and whiteness. "African American Muslims," the historian Melani McAlister has written, embraced "a symbolic countercitizenship, an identity that challenged black incorporation into the dominant discourse of Judeo-Christian Americanness."[18]

Not all black radicals rejected the Judeo-Christian tradition, however. One African American socialist rooted his position in "the word of the Judeo-Christian ethic: Man is his brother's keeper!" Armed self-defense could be also be justified in Judeo-Christian terms—in this case, "the ancient Biblical prescription: an eye for an eye, a tooth for a tooth. That's the only law uncivilized white racists understand and respect." Meanwhile, the theologian and ethicist Preston N. Williams and a number of other black leaders sought to convince the young radicals that "the Judaeo-Christian tradition is or can be the genuine religion of the black man." Having made that tradition their own over the centuries, they would sacrifice nothing in authenticity or self-respect by following its tenets. But J. H. Jackson, head of the national organization of black Baptists, argued that even King's nonviolent resistance subverted religious tenets. "The Judeo-Christian concept of life is encompassed in the Federal Constitution," Jackson explained, "and a move to civil disobedience in the face of the laws of the land is an insult to all who abide by the law." Only "an increase in moral strength," rooted in a nationwide commitment to "the Judeo-Christian concept of human life and fellowship," would resolve racial conflict, according to Jackson. As these examples suggest, the main line of division in the African American struggle pitted King's Judeo-Christian followers against black nationalists critical of that faith, but alternative formulations often appeared as well.[19]

Among antiwar activists, the pattern was clearer: Virtually all agreed that the Vietnam debacle represented a comprehensive violation of Judeo-Christian teachings. A few said the nation's vaunted "Judeo-Christian tradition" was really a straitjacket that condoned imperialism and needed to be thrown off. But the vast majority of antiwar critics lined up with the prominent religious leaders in CALCAV (Clergy and Laymen Concerned about Vietnam). As opposition to President Johnson's policies intensified, commentators routinely framed such activism as an act of loyalty to the Judeo-Christian tradition. Episcopal bishop James A. Pike told Stanford students that antiwar activism was "more moral now than going to church." Lamenting the country's betrayal of its stated values, Pike described the "'increasingly rapid alienation of belief in the Judeo-Christian tradition'" as a "'personal protest at the immorality of Christian culture." Similarly, William Alberts of Boston's Old West Church, who worked alongside young radicals, saw nothing less than a "religious revival" in the movement: "The whole Judeo-Christian ethic is here in the anti-war demonstrations." By 1968, a *Christian Century* article discerned a "growing consensus among mature, morally sensitive people" that "the spiritual integrity of the United States, rooted as it is in the Judeo-Christian tradition, cannot be secured by our present policy in Vietnam."[20]

As the war dragged on into the early 1970s, the center of gravity in the movement shifted from college and university campuses to the nation's churches and synagogues. CALCAV doubled in size between 1968 and 1972, and commentators in that vein repeatedly decried American policy in Judeo-Christian terms. "I cannot justify what we are doing in Indochina in terms of the Judeo-Christian ethic," one outraged parishioner declared. Describing the war as a costly tragedy wrought by American hubris, Princeton president Robert F. Goheen hoped that candid recognition of its blunders might reorient the country toward "the great humanitarian ideals of our Judeo-Christian heritage."[21]

At the same time, many commentators on foreign affairs asserted the superiority of Judeo-Christian faith to the traditions prevailing in other parts of the world. The African American editors of the *Chicago Defender* asserted the "clear philosophical superiority" of Western ideals, even as they decried the routine flouting of Judeo-Christian principles. Others stressed more clearly the lack of Judeo-Christian faith across Asia. "Compassion, in the Judeo-Christian sense of the word, is not part of the Oriental heritage," asserted a 1967 article on a Catholic mission to Korea. Another author explained that racial conflict in places such as Malaysia was "probably insuperable" due to the lack of a proper work ethic: "The Malays simply do not subscribe to the Judaeo-Christian tenet that hard work is central to life—and the accumulation of material goods its reward." Vietnam appeared as a hotbed of corruption in a third article. "Like so much in this ancient society," the author explained, "the Vietnamese sense of public morality has little in common with the traditions of the Judaeo-Christian world." But a missionary to Japan found cause for hope in "the ancient touch of the Judeo-Christian faith in Japanese culture, buried for thousands of years, but still distinguishable."[22]

The language of Judeo-Christianity found far less support among environmentalists. Indeed, leading theorists described the Judeo-Christian tradition as an unmitigated disaster for the natural world. As far back as 1934, the conservationist Aldo Leopold had arrayed the "new science of ecology" against the "biblical" teaching "that it is the destiny of man to exploit and

enslave the earth." At the December 1966 meeting of the American Association for the Advancement of Science, the medievalist Lynn T. White Jr.
renewed that charge—and inadvertently launched the field of ecotheology in
the process—in his widely noted paper "The Historical Roots of Our Ecologic
Crisis." Adopting the myth of the "ecological Indian," White contrasted Native
American spirituality to the "anthropocentrism" of the Judeo-Christian tradition. Another activist blamed the Garden of Eden story for "our despoiling
of the world about us" and contrasted "a Judeo-Christian ethic that views
the world as put here for our benefit and enjoyment" with "Oriental philosophies" that "see man as a part of nature, called upon to live in harmony with
it." Some commentators identified "the Judeo-Christian injunction that man
'have dominion over the land and subdue every living thing'" as not only the
root of environmental destruction but also the long-standing justification for
scientific and technological innovation. Even an article lauding the impact of
Judeo-Christian faith said it produced "supreme arrogance," an "endless quest
to conquer, subdue and rule all of creation."[23]

Native American activists also began to challenge the moral authority of
the Judeo-Christian tradition. In the fore here was Vine Deloria Jr., a lawyer
and onetime Christian seminarian who penned *Custer Died for Your Sins: An
Indian Manifesto* (1969). His "four years in a seminary," he explained there,
taught him that "Christianity has been a sham to cover the white man's shortcomings" and that Indians should "return to their old religions wherever possible." In a 1972 "plea to the churches," Deloria called for an unmasking of the
mythology of "manifest destiny" that portrayed God as a mere booster for
the United States: "We would no longer have a God busily endorsing and ap-
plauding the things we are doing. We would have to be on God's side in our
dealings with other peoples instead of being so sure that God is automatically
on our side." Deloria also described the Wounded Knee uprising of February 1973 as an attack on Western theological principles. Like White, Deloria
argued that Indian religion was ecologically sounder, in his case because it
revolved around "space" rather than "time," and traced the long history of
conflicts between Indians and European Americans to their contrasting religious perspectives.[24]

Feminism offered fertile ground for criticism of the Judeo-Christian tradition as well. Activists and theorists routinely took aim at the patriarchal assumptions and retrograde views of women found in the Judeo-Christian faiths
and the cultures they influenced. "The philosophy that brought you here,"
one speaker at a 1969 conference told her audience, "is the Judeo-Christian
theory of the dominance of the male, the implication that a woman is a bit
subordinate, a bit inferior." Feminist psychologists likewise attacked "Freud's

Judeo-Christian view of woman as 'the damaged reflection of the male.'" Even *Time* magazine contended in a 1972 article that the religious tenets undergirding Western civilization had long been both racist and sexist: "Judaeo-Christian theology has intermittently taught white superiority over black and consistently taught male superiority over female." The main characters in the Christian narrative told the tale: "God is the Father. Jesus Christ is the Son. Even the Holy Spirit, in the New Testament, is 'he.' And women? Women are the daughters of Eve, the original temptress."[25]

A vigorous school of feminist theology emerged in the early 1970s, with members blasting the patriarchal character of their faith traditions even as they retained an allegiance to them. Catholics figured most prominently, led by Mary Daly of Boston College. In the early 1960s, pioneers such as Rosemary Lauer had hoped that the Vatican II reforms would give women substantial roles in the Catholic Church. When that did not pan out, Daly and others took up the campaign. On November 14, 1971, Daly became the first woman to preach in Harvard's venerable Memorial Church. She famously followed her sermon, "The Death of God the Father," by leading a walkout that helped to catalyze the emerging movement. Two years later, Daly's *Beyond God the Father: Toward a Philosophy of Feminist Liberation* catalogued the "history of antifeminism in the Judeo-Christian heritage." Daly singled out "the myth of the Fall" and "the theology of 'original sin'" as especially pernicious in their effects. She added that Judeo-Christianity's errors ramified in more secular realms of thought through "its hideous blossom, Freudian theory."[26]

Feminist theologians distinguished the historical Judeo-Christian tradition from genuine Judeo-Christian faith, however. As Sheila D. Collins explained in *A Different Heaven and Earth* (1974), the women's movement was both "profoundly religious" and "anti-Christian" in its opposition to "that set of assumptions, priorities, methods and experiences" that had "dominated the Judeo-Christian world since the time of the patriarchs." Collins sought to isolate "the biblical view of man in relation to God" from "the cultural accretions that have grown up around this view." Meanwhile, she attributed the persistence of stereotypes about men and women to the fact that, "until today, the basic values and assumptions of the Judeo-Christian cultural tradition have never been fundamentally challenged in the Western world." As "the founder and preserver of this culture," Collins continued, the church bore much of the blame for its "ungodly view of women." Like so many users of Judeo-Christian discourse before her, though in a much more critical vein, Collins postulated a singular "West" and traced its cultural characteristics to an equally coherent "Judeo-Christian tradition."[27]

Political Shifts

For many Americans, however, it was neither the Vietnam War nor protest movements that raised the question of Judeo-Christianity most forcefully. The Watergate scandal and other developments in national politics inspired numerous Judeo-Christian formulations, as faith in American institutions nose-dived amid fierce debates over how to set the country aright. Still, the commentary on elections and congressional actions took much of its shape from underlying cultural concerns. As Watergate unfolded, many saw in it signs of a deeper cultural malady that they tied to the historical fortunes of Judeo-Christian faith.

Nixon, of course, had taken office calling for a restoration of law and order in the wake of 1968's upheavals. Many Americans likewise associated the Judeo-Christian tradition with the rule of law and feared that both were dissolving amid the chaos. In 1967, a group of Southern California mayors dedicated a week in honor of an organization called Christians and Jews for Law and Morality. Its director believed that the "entire community must be re-educated," in line with "the rule of law and the moral values of the Judeo-Christian heritage." A few years later, an ecumenical statement decried the "unholy trinity" of violence, drugs, and pornography, which had all flourished as young people turned away from Judeo-Christianity. This tendency, the statement warned, could produce "dehumanizing slavery, or perhaps the tyranny of some new Hitler." By 1974, a *Boston Globe* editorial asked, "Where are all the rules to live by?" Although Judeo-Christian ethical principles persisted, they had no backing: "Even supernatural authority has evaporated in a world that assures itself God is dead."[28]

Yet Judeo-Christian rhetoric could be used in multiple ways on questions of crime and policing. In 1972, the attempted assassination of presidential candidate George Wallace led one ecumenical group to urge renewed attention to "fundamental Judeo-Christian ethical guidelines." But another commentator complained that the oft-heard cries of "we are all guilty" were "moral copouts": "By denying that men have even the most fundamental control over their behavior, the notion of collective guilt rejects the very essence of our Judeo-Christian tradition." Meanwhile, more liberal voices discerned violations of Judeo-Christian ethics in police brutality—especially in Richard J. Daley's Chicago—and the punitive character of American prisons.[29]

Above all, however, Judeo-Christian rhetoric revolved around the cluster of issues—abortion, birth control, sexual morality, sex education, family structures, childrearing habits, and gender norms—that social traditionalists would come to call "family values." Conservative evangelicals had been swapping out "Christian" for "Judeo-Christian" since the early 1960s; a growing chorus decried the godlessness of American culture in the wake of the school prayer and Bible-reading decisions. The sexual revolution that came on the heels of those decisions reinforced conservative fears of moral breakdown. Thus, one commentator blamed the combination of the birth control pill and "the disintegration of the Judeo-Christian ethic" for an uptick in co-ed fraternizing in college dorm rooms.[30]

To be sure, many commentators believed that Judeo-Christian principles were outdated, and perhaps on the decline. A psychologist quoted in the "Dear Abby" column held that "the biblical injunction that placed coveting one's neighbor's wife on the same moral level with actual adultery" was "one of the most psychologically destructive heirlooms that the Judeo-Christian moral tradition has bequeathed to us." Another writer decried the Judeo-Christian "prudishness"—"a morass of Middle Ages thinking . . . a stifling blanket of ancient morality"—that fueled opposition to pornography. Lawyers in 1972 argued that "oral copulation" should be decriminalized because the ban rested solely on "the Judeo-Christian ethic" and had "no basis in secular common law." The historian Martin Duberman identified the "model of 'normal' behavior" that prevailed in the scientific literature as a "Judeo-Christian" inheritance and "not a scientific construct." As early as 1967, a group of ordinary citizens likewise dismissed "the declining prudish 'Judeo-Christian ethic,'" responding to plans for a "girlie movie house" in their Cleveland neighborhood with a blasé "If the people want to see it, let them."[31]

This was hardly a consensus view, however. On another instance, in April 1973 in the Boston neighborhood of Allston, a group of residents banded together to push out a pornographic bookstore. "We'll make our own laws if we have to," declared the group's leader. "This is a Judeo-Christian neighborhood and we intend to enforce our standards." The previous year, a community college instructor in California had been fired for reading a poem "that contained a number of Anglo-Saxon obscenities and profane references to Jehovah and the Christ," in violation of Judeo-Christian norms. Sex education in public schools was a common flashpoint for controversy, as it was widely seen as "undermining the Judeo-Christian ethic." The *Los Angeles Times* reported that many parents "fear what they call outside influences, the New Morality, the situation ethic, seizing their children's minds, turning them away from the Judeo-Christian ethic." (The right-wing John Birch Society, meanwhile, labeled sex education "a 'filthy communist plot' to weaken the moral fibre of the young.") The Equal Rights Amendment also drew the ire of conservatives. One critic described American women as the "most privileged" class in human history, by virtue of their participation in a

"Judeo-Christian civilization" that required of each man the "physical protection and financial support of his children and of the woman who bears his children."[32]

Above all, Judeo-Christian rhetoric found a hearing in the early 1970s in the context of bitter debates over abortion. Through the 1960s, abortion was widely regarded as an exclusively Catholic issue; conservative Protestant organizations would not argue that life began at conception or that abortion should be banned in all instances until after *Roe v. Wade* in 1973. Still, many conservatives had grave doubts about legalizing abortion. President Nixon, for example, declared his opposition to abortion in April 1971, calling it "unacceptable" and destructive of the "sanctity of human life" and the rights of the unborn. "Ours is a nation with a Judeo-Christian heritage," he asserted, and it would surely "open its hearts and homes to the unwanted children of its own, as it has done for the unwanted millions of other lands."[33]

Not all positions on abortion were so straightforward. The *Boston Globe*, noting that "high regard for individual life has been a mark of the Judeo-Christian tradition," nevertheless cautioned that "consideration must be balanced and extended to the living as well as to the yet unborn." But so many disputants applied that principle exclusively to the fetus that one commentator concluded that legalizing abortion would require abandoning the Judeo-Christian emphasis on human dignity. Letter after letter to newspaper editors stated the case: "Anyone who belongs to the Judeo-Christian belief should, in conscience, be against abortions. We believe they are immoral and that no amount of civil law legalizing them can supersede the law of God." Numerous commentators—not least Catholic clergy—argued that opposition to abortion was not a Catholic position but rather a shared, Judeo-Christian principle. And many tied abortion to other policies favored by "the slick seculars" peddling a "biological ethic," including "mercy-killing, genetic engineering, and all social or scientific 'reforms' that alter the centuries-old Judeo Christian tenets of reverence for life."[34]

Although abortion consistently generated controversy, almost any policy question could be discussed in terms of Judeo-Christianity. Economic issues inspired a welter of competing Judeo-Christian formulations. A number of commentators spoke of a "Judeo-Christian work ethic" rather than linking that fabled trait to Protestantism. Meanwhile, the head of the Investment Bankers Association announced, "There is no area of man's business activity in which moral values, the heritage of the Greco-Judeo-Christian culture, are more manifest than in the market place for securities." There, above all, he explained, "mutual trust and confidence are essential prerequisites."[35]

Conservative critics of the welfare state sometimes disagreed on the relation of their small-government principles to religion. One letter to the editor argued that unfettered capitalism delivered pure "justice," whereas "Judeo-Christian ethics" preached the communistic principle of "sacrifice to the needs of others" and had no relation whatsoever to American ideals. Others, however, argued that compulsory retirement violated "the Judeo-Christian doctrine of the inherent dignity and worth of the individual." Secretary of Defense Elliot Richardson insisted that American values called for Judeo-Christian charity, not "big government." In 1972, a remarkable article contended that the *Wall Street Journal*'s philosophy reflected Reinhold Niebuhr's *Moral Man and Immoral Society*.[36]

Liberals, meanwhile, frequently rooted welfare-state policies in Judeo-Christian principles. One complained about the *Wall Street Journal*'s slant, arguing that a profit-driven economy "conflicts with the needs of the people and government is the only instrument available to check the imbalances." Welfare liberalism, he explained, "embodies those humanistic ideals which are rooted in our Judeo-Christian ethic and which address themselves to the ultimate dignity of the individual." A group of African American leaders called Nixon's cuts to poverty programs "an offense to the sensibilities of justice which lies at the heart of our Judeo-Christian faith." And after Gerald Ford took office, his "favoritism to the rich" was called "stupid and contrary to Judeo-Christian ethics."[37]

Various other issues likewise generated Judeo-Christian rhetoric in the early 1970s. Opponents of the death penalty, for example, called it "an immoral act of violence which completely denies our Judeo-Christian belief in the dignity and value of human life." US relations with Israel, not surprisingly, also generated Judeo-Christian formulations. Yet here, too, that language could be mobilized in numerous ways. A letter to the *Boston Globe* complained that media coverage tended to "uncritically expand and re-affirm my Judeo-Christian heritage" by failing to include Palestinian perspectives. And some statements reprised the classic postwar equation of democracy with Judeo-Christianity by arguing that the United States and Israel shared two kinds of bonds, one cultural and religious, in the form of the Judeo-Christian tradition, and the other political, in their common commitment to democracy.[38]

In this context, a number of politicians were notable for their widespread use of Judeo-Christian terminology. A *Boston Globe* reporter covering the 1968 presidential race complained that Republican candidate Nelson Rockefeller "can scarcely speak of anything from paving-blocks to world peace without reference to 'our Judeo-Christian heritage.'" The statement said as much about the prevailing political climate—in which Judeo-Christian language had become unusual, and to many a bit ridiculous, rather than taken for granted—as it did about Rockefeller.[39]

For his part, the New York governor hardly shied away from religiously inflected formulations. It is likely no coincidence that former Eisenhower speechwriter Emmet J. Hughes had begun working for Rockefeller in 1967. On the campaign trail, Rockefeller argued that the government's policy of "placing life over personal property" in cases of urban unrest properly reflected "human dignity, which is inherent in our Judeo-Christian heritage." At the same time, Rockefeller saw some danger in the country's Judeo-Christian character, which led to government overspending: "We are a generous people by nature. We want to help those in need at home and abroad. It's part of our whole Judeo-Christian heritage and it's a wonderful quality. But we can't do it all at once. And we, as a people, are close to being dangerously overcommitted." In the early 1970s, Rockefeller repeatedly called attention to the need to promote human rights abroad, another "fundamental, basic, Judeo-Christian concept." At the same time, he continued to blame Judeo-Christianity's emphasis on charity for the excessive largesse of the welfare state.[40]

Judeo-Christian principles found a more consistent champion in the Catholic Democrat Sargent Shriver. American Catholics of all varieties used Judeo-Christian terminology in the wake of Vatican II, which loosened the formerly strict prohibitions on interfaith cooperation. In 1969, a new church in New Jersey took the form of a dove, with one wing dedicated to each of the testaments "to reflect the Judaic heritage of Christianity." Catholic universities and local officials repeatedly framed programs for racial and economic justice in Judeo-Christian terms. And in 1974, the United Catholic Parents Association commended the cause of "civil rights for gay New Yorkers" to "all those who believe in democracy and the Judaeo-Christian tradition of the worth and value of the individual." For his part, Shriver, the former Peace Corps head and brother-in-law to John, Robert, and Ted Kennedy, repeatedly invoked religion in his vice-presidential campaign of 1972. When Nixon celebrated the work ethic, Shriver countered with "the Judeo-Christian humanist ethic that says we should all try to do what we can for our fellow men" and called for applying that principle in foreign as well as domestic policy. Shriver's Methodist running mate, George McGovern, likewise sought to base foreign policy on "the Judeo-Christian ethic," while the Jesuit priest and Massachusetts representative Robert Drinan urged religious organizations to take a larger role in politics and hold government officials to "those moral norms that are enunciated by the Judeo-Christian tradition."[41]

Watergate and Beyond

In this context, Richard Nixon's drawn-out demise raised a host of cries about the moral dimensions of politics. Yet opinions varied on the political contributions of religious leaders, especially those in and around the White House. Minnesota senator Walter F. Mondale urged churches to multiply their lobbying efforts, as the "moral and human concerns of our Judeo Christian faith are not very effectively asserted in Congress." But a sharply worded *New York Times* editorial saw little of substance in what it called a "cult of the Potomac" that "equates America's role with God's will": "Hand-picked clergymen who preside over isolated home worship inside the White House" hardly reflected "the Judeo-Christian tradition, its sacrifices, and its impolite prophets from whose throats the voice of anger rises in a call for truth."[42]

Nixon's inner circle of religious advisers included W. Clement Stone, a self-made man who had parlayed a modest investment into a hugely successful insurance business. A prominent New Thought advocate, Stone became a major Nixon donor in 1968. Prior to that, he had championed the PMA (Positive Mental Attitude) concept of his mentor Napoleon Hill, author of *Think and Grow Rich*, calling his own book *The Success System That Never Fails*. Stone had also founded an interfaith group, the Washington Pilgrimage, in 1951; it advocated adding "under God" to the Pledge of Allegiance and later became the Religious Heritage of America. In 1970, that group named Nixon—who was intimately familiar with its operations from his days as vice president under Eisenhower—its Churchman of the Year. (Ironically, one observer ridiculed that award on the grounds that Nixon exhibited a "transcendent optimism" and ignored genuine faith's recognition of "a tragic flaw in the human character.")[43]

The heart and soul of Nixon's team, however, was the revivalist Billy Graham. The close relationship between the two rankled many progressive Christians. "Organized religion in the Judeo-Christian tradition must maintain a prophetic stance toward the state," one Episcopal priest warned. "Silencing the Church's critical function in regard to national leaders is alien to American ideals." But Graham and Nixon found much to agree on—including, as a secret 1972 tape later revealed, the "stranglehold" of Jews over the American media and the need to "do something" about it. Vietnam was another area of shared concern. Indeed, Graham soon came to advise Nixon on all manner of issues. And when "the sordid Watergate affair" first broke in 1973, Graham simultaneously traced it to "a deeper moral crisis" ("America has condoned amoral permissiveness that would make Sodom blush") and warned readers against rushing to judgment about the guilt of particular individuals.[44]

Although Graham's faith was soon tested by the release of Nixon's secret tapes, he ultimately decided in the wake of the president's resignation that Nixon had grown spiritually. Other conservative evangelicals took a tougher line. "The transcripts," wrote *Christianity Today*, "show him to be a person who has failed gravely to live up to the moral demands of our Judeo-Christian heritage." Other commentators traced Watergate to the fact that the United States, though "theoretically a Judeo-Christian social state," was thoroughly "paganistic" at its core. "Watergate is a product of our modern world and demands a renewal, review, and re-evaluation of our basic ideals, principles, goals, and objectives," ran a characteristic response.[45]

Yet, for those who discerned a collapse of society's moral foundations behind the political and social developments of the day, Nixon's resignation hardly improved matters. New first lady Betty Ford raised a firestorm in August 1975 when she suggested that she would condone a premarital relationship for her daughter and argued that such relationships could bring down the rate of divorce. "I am ashamed for my country, the President, responsible parents and all who hold the Judeo-Christian ethic sacred," one respondent declared. "What kind of hypocrisy was Mrs. Ford foisting on the American public last year as she held the Bible in her husband's oath of office ceremony? She obviously flouts the basic tenets it contains." This commentator went on to blame women's liberation for society's maladies. Another letter to the editor agreed: Ford's views would "undermine the family system which has been so central in the Judeo-Christian culture."[46]

Similar concerns came to light a few months later, after Charles Manson follower Lynette "Squeaky" Fromme attempted to assassinate President Ford in September 1975. Clare Boothe Luce, then serving on the president's Foreign Intelligence Advisory Board, traced the episode to the abandonment of "traditional Judeo-Christian moral values" by "liberal intellectuals" after World War II. She and other critics made much of Fromme's cryptic statement "If you have no philosophy, you don't have any rules." At the *Chicago Tribune*, "Living Faith" columnist Harold Blake Walker, who continued to contrast Judeo-Christian democracy to "godless communism" into the 1970s, identified Fromme as the epitome of modern society's moral relativism. "God is dead and the Judeo-Christian ethic is merely a hangover from an archaic past," Walker summarized.[47]

*

By the mid-1970s, the religious right was beginning to take shape and Judeo-Christian rhetoric was becoming more and more strongly associated with the traditional social norms favored by the likes of Graham, Luce, and Walker.

Conversely, its appeal waned among those who embraced liberation from such norms, or who resisted the easy equation of secularism with moral relativism that the religious right inherited from postwar Judeo-Christian exceptionalists. Indeed, younger Americans increasingly associated Judeo-Christian discourse with the hypocrisies of their elders, who had condemned the moral laxity of the children even as they sent them off to fight and die in Vietnam.

This critical mood found illuminating expression in December of 1974, when the cover of the cutting-edge humor magazine *National Lampoon* portrayed the Virgin Mary as an unwed mother, baby Jesus in arms, being cast from her parents' house. "The Judeo-Christian Tradition: The Joy of Sects," ran the irreverent title. A consummate visual expression of the growing disdain for Judeo-Christian pronouncements among many in the rising generation, the cover indicted the moral bankruptcy of those who would cast out the Son of God in the pursuit of personal rectitude. But the image contains a subtler lesson as well. The *National Lampoon* expressed not only its own skepticism toward pious platitudes but also the new centrality of personal morality in Judeo-Christian rhetoric. No longer did Judeo-Christian rhetoric refer primarily to questions of political theory and the foundations of democracy; now, the main referent points involved conservative constructions of "family values." And among many who disliked that brand of conservatism, America's vaunted Judeo-Christian tradition had become an object of ridicule and scorn.[48]

Multireligious Possibilities

JUDEO-CHRISTIAN DISCOURSE IN A MULTICULTURAL AGE

Never in the long and winding career of America's Judeo-Christian discourse has its existence signaled a stable consensus around either the meaning of democracy or the religious identity of the United States. Yet, from more distant vantage points, we can see that the mid-twentieth century did witness relatively widespread agreement that the country was in some sense Judeo-Christian. In the half century since the upheavals of the 1960s and 1970s, this tri-faith paradigm, touting the equality of Protestantism, Catholicism, and Judaism in American life, has declined precipitously, as a growing number of Americans have rejected Judeo-Christian discourse. Beginning in the mid-1960s, mounting cultural fatigue with the postwar era's habitual paeans to Judeo-Christian democracy began to reach a breaking point. Of course, individual critics had questioned Judeo-Christian terminology at various points since its emergence in the 1930s and its meteoric rise in the 1940s. But never before had there been such widespread disillusionment with the religio-civic language that had shaped America's postwar understanding of its role in the world. Capturing the new spirit perfectly, a 1979 review of a poetry collection by Ishmael Reed highlighted its emphasis on California's "colorful gumbo culture" and concurrent "turning away from the workhouse of Judeo-Christian ethics with its worn-out myths and exhausted ethos."[1] This mounting critique of Judeo-Christian terminology, coupled with a developing multicultural sensibility, was hardly confined to avant-garde artists on the West Coast as the 1970s drew to a close.

Yet, as we now know, Judeo-Christian rhetoric was not receding but changing. In the late 1970s and early 1980s, Americans heard the adjective "Judeo-Christian" applied in novel and consequential ways, as the term began to do new kinds of cultural work. To the extent that those on the political left continued to use Judeo-Christian formulations, growing demographic diversity inclined them to interpret "Judeo-Christian" as a time-bound descriptor of a particular period in America's cultural and political past. At the same time, conservatives increasingly used the term "Judeo-Christian" to identify a set of traditional norms regarding family structures and sexual behavior. In the era's increasingly pitched battles over cultural and social issues such as abortion and gay marriage, conservatives identified Judeo-Christianity with a specific set of moral guidelines for personal behavior as well as the broader political norms—among them, freedom, equality, rights, and dignity—that so many postwar commentators had emphasized. Lamenting the apparent decline of Judeo-Christian morality since the 1960s, conservatives joined progressives in portraying America as having—for better or for worse—departed from the Judeo-Christian principles that dominated 1950s public life.

In short, Judeo-Christian discourse became caught up in what are now called the "culture wars" during the late 1970s and the early 1980s. However, while scholars often argue that political and theological conservatives "co-opted" Judeo-Christian formulations in the 1970s and 1980s, the language of capture implies that Judeo-Christian rhetoric had earlier belonged primarily or even solely to liberal defenders of tolerance. This book has challenged that assumption by showing that the term "Judeo-Christian" was always deeply contested and served a wide range of political and religious purposes. From its inception, the new discourse belonged not only to the likes of Eisenhower but also to figures such as Will Herberg and P. W. Wilson who saw the threat of totalitarianism looming in the secular welfare state. Only from the vantage point of the 1980s and 1990s, when Judeo-Christian terminology became intensely polarized along political lines, did scholars come to see it retrospectively as an uncomplicated bid for tolerance during earlier decades.

New Chronologies

As new uses and interpretations appeared, more and more commentators located Judeo-Christian America in the past. Although some liberal and progressive Americans found the term "Judeo-Christian" hopelessly narrow, others sought to square America's Judeo-Christian past with its growing tolerance for diversity in the present. Among moderate and conservative Americans, some rejected the term for being too broad, but many others attacked the moral relativism they associated with the embrace of difference by calling for a rebirth of Judeo-Christian values in the present day. From the 1930s to the 1970s, Judeo-Christian discourse had elided the past with the present because demographic realities on the ground—the existence of a "tri-faith America" composed almost entirely of Protestants, Catholics, and Jews—mirrored the contours of the term. But by the 1970s, demographic and cultural changes were steadily eroding this perceived correspondence between past and present and convincing many Americans—especially outside the South—that they lived, for better or for worse, in a new era. In terms of culture and language, as well as demographics, the tri-faith America of the World War II and postwar years was no more. And in the increasingly polarized tug-of-war over American values, Judeo-Christian formulations no longer appeared as naturalized features of mainstream public discourse, but rather as markers of a conservative project to reverse recent changes in American culture and politics.

This rhetorical shift heralded a new phase in both Judeo-Christian discourse and American religious history more broadly. Outside conservative circles, a new paradigm I term "multireligious America" increasingly replaced the old tri-faith understanding that had held sway during the middle decades of the twentieth century.[2] Much remains to be learned about this transition, but some of the broad outlines are clear: By the late 1970s and 1980s, liberals, progressives, and urbanites of various political persuasions could see the vast cultural and demographic changes afoot. Of course, the 1960s had fostered a remarkable proliferation of ways of life and conceptions of individual and collective identity. Meanwhile, the Hart-Celler Act of 1965 had opened up immigration from non-European countries and gradually swelled the previously tiny communities of Buddhists, Hindus, Muslims, and other groups understood as outside the Judeo-Christian fold. Members of these faiths had long lived in the United States, to be sure, but they had most often figured in the popular imagination as distant, Orientalized others. Now, they began to push for—and in some cases receive—recognition as part of the American mosaic.[3] Meanwhile, the emergence of a multicultural, multireligious perspective acknowledged the newfound visibility of these growing religious minorities and offered them a seat at the national table. Similarly, the persistence of secularism also challenged the use of "Judeo-Christian" as a descriptor of America's religious identity during these years. Demographically and culturally, many commentators concluded, America was no longer—and perhaps had never been—the tri-faith nation that Will Herberg portrayed in *Protestant-Catholic-Jew*.

However, across much of the rest of the country, in places remote from its cosmopolitan centers, multireligious America was slower to arrive. Many Americans simply ignored what they did not see happening in their own small towns and suburban tracts, while others hoped to reverse the changes under way in the nation's urban centers. For myriad reasons, those unwilling to see the forces of diversification at work pulled the blinds shut at the dawning of multireligious America. It was in these precincts that the new, more thoroughly conservative versions of Judeo-Christian discourse architected by Ronald Reagan found a hearing.

Still, the coming of multireligious America opened up new imaginative possibilities. It marked a decisive shift from the tri-faith America paradigm of the early 1940s through the early 1970s, when Americans heard "Judeo-Christian" applied to their nation's existing political and civic institutions with striking regularity and in a manner that routinely elided past and present—and ideals with reality. During the mid-twentieth century, commentators with divergent understandings of democracy and religion had tended to conflate three different versions of the claim that American was a Judeo-Christian nation. The first version was historical: The United States *has been* a Judeo-Christian nation. The second centered on present configurations: The United States *is* a Judeo-Christian nation (culturally, politically, demographically). And the third version was frankly normative: The United States *should be* a Judeo-Christian nation. The mid-twentieth century featured persistent slippage between these three ways of understanding Judeo-Christian constructions of American identity.

These patterns of usage began to change in the 1970s, not least because American political debates began to focus more heavily on competing visions of personal morality and the character of the American past than on global ideological struggles. The locus of dispute shifted away from the character of a tri-faith democracy toward battles over "family values," especially after *Roe v. Wade* legalized abortion in 1973. In response to that decision, conservatives redoubled their efforts to reassert the traditional social norms they associated with religion. To be sure, other political issues, including anticommunism and economic policy, remained important. But fierce conflicts over "family values" from the 1970s forward, followed by pitched contests over the intentions of the Constitution's framers in the 1980s, dramatically reshaped the use of Judeo-Christian terminology.[4]

Of course, even in the 1950s, Americans had disagreed on what "Judeo-Christian" signified. Yet at that time, contests over the meaning of Judeo-Christianity mostly took place on a subterranean level, through interior struggles to capture the term itself. The 1970s and 1980s saw much more overt conflict over the term's validity than in previous decades. Rather than waging a war from within by subtly inflecting Judeo-Christian discourse with exceptionalist or pluralist assumptions, disputants now contested the very legitimacy of the Judeo-Christian framework.

It is no coincidence, then, that in 1980, when Judeo-Christian rhetoric first appeared in a party platform, Republicans were the ones to use it. (It has appeared in five subsequent Republican platforms, but never in a Democratic platform.) At precisely that moment, the party began to realign itself with the new brand of conservatism represented by Ronald Reagan. As a candidate, and then as president, Reagan skillfully layered the "family values" framework onto the deep-seated anticommunism and aggressive free-market economics that underpinned his policies. The platform did the same, locating the United States within the age-old tradition of Western civilization: "Steeped in the Judeo-Christian ethic and in Anglo-Saxon theories of law and right, our legal and political institutions have evolved over many generations to form a stable system that serves free men and women well." During Reagan's watch, then, political and social conservatives cemented a powerful alliance under the banner of Judeo-Christianity. As the multireligious era opened, cosmopolitan or multicultural visions of American identity squared off against socially, economically, and politically conservative versions of the Judeo-Christian discourse.[5]

The Judeo-Christian Right

The fusion of Judeo-Christian discourse and conservative "family values" took place during the Reagan years, but early expressions of that new sensibility could be heard throughout the 1970s. Although President Nixon eschewed Judeo-Christian rhetoric himself, developments during his presidency led many Americans to conclude that the nation's deepest moral commitments stood under ferocious assault from the left. In the post-*Roe* political climate, religious and political conservatives increasingly used "Judeo-Christian values" to mean conservative "family values" on hot-button issues ranging from women's rights and abortion to homosexuality and same-sex marriage. Often, they also meant such values, alongside broader political ideals such as dignity or equality—when they referred to the nation's Judeo-Christian "tradition" or "heritage."

Indeed, many uses of Judeo-Christian rhetoric asserted a direct connection between personal morality and the survival of the nation. Conservatives contended that the 1960s had ushered in an era of total moral relativism, in which ordinary citizens followed skeptical intellectuals in denying the reality of moral truths. For these figures, as we have seen, a parade of events in the late 1960s and early 1970s demonstrated the depth and rapidity of relativism's spread. Where some conservative critics discerned an alarming absence of standards, others saw the spread of a comprehensive, well-defined worldview: that of "secular humanism."

Throughout the tri-faith era, of course, numerous commentators had contrasted "secularism" to the "Judeo-Christian tradition"—often linking the former to totalitarianism as well. But the enemy of "secular humanism" was something slightly different. When postwar critics referred to secularists, they typically had in mind the likes of John Dewey and his followers: a group of idealistic thinkers who attempted to ground their moral commitments on a pragmatic, naturalistic foundation. By contrast, secular humanism, as a target of criticism, was largely detached from actual people. A faceless enemy, secular humanism was everywhere and nowhere at once. And it did not signal a faulty mode of moral idealism, but rather the outright rejection of any attempt to assert ideals. Whereas postwar critics asserted that secularism inevitably devolved into relativism and egoism, their successors of the 1970s and 1980s charged that secular humanists actively championed relativism and egoism, without any reference to goals higher than individual pleasure: "If it feels good, do it." Secular humanism, to these critics, was not a moral stance at all; it was a concerted assault on the very idea of morality itself.[6]

By the time Jimmy Carter won the presidency in 1976, the political insurgency among conservative Protestants and Catholics had begun to reshape national politics. Commentators often remark on the irony that the first evangelical president of the modern era was a Democrat who disappointed the nascent religious right at every turn. Less noticed is the delicate terminological balancing act Carter performed within Judeo-Christian discourse. As both a Southern Baptist and a liberal advocate of tolerance, Carter was no stranger to prophetic faith: "The Judeo-Christian ethic and study of the Bible were bonds between Jews and Christians which had always been part of my life," he later observed. Yet Carter helped to craft new ways of invoking Judeo-Christianity that could accommodate recent social changes and the increasing diversity of American religious life. He squared the older discourse of Judeo-Christianity with the new celebration of difference by distinguishing between America's Judeo-Christian past and its more variegated present.[7]

Carter's formulations reflected both genuine personal commitment and an emerging tendency among Democratic politicians to emphasize the intrinsic value of cultural and religious diversity. The Democratic Party's 1972 platform celebrated the "mosaic" of America in a section entitled "The Right to Be Different." Indeed, even Richard Nixon's speeches on immigration and desegregation called America "richer for our cultural diversity" and challenged the assimilationist "melting pot" ideal:

America has often been called a melting pot, perhaps because it has forged the cultures and traditions of many lands into a strong new alloy—an American alloy. But let us never forget that one of the finest things about our country is that it does not force its people into a narrow mold of conformity. America is a rich mosaic of many cultures and traditions, strong in its diversity. Each new immigrant has added another piece in the mosaic of American life—a fresh perspective and a fresh appreciation of what it means to be an American.

Unlike Carter, however, Nixon proved inconsistent, even opportunistic, in his references to diversity. On one occasion, Nixon even listed "pluralism" among the anomic, disintegrating features of modern life. "The increasingly urbanized, technological, crowded, pluralistic, affluent, leisure oriented society which America has become in these final decades of the 20th century," he warned in a 1972 radio address, "poses complex new dangers to our traditional concepts of personal safety, human dignity, [and] moral values." Here, Nixon sounded more like a culture warrior—albeit one with an unusually nuanced understanding of the threats to traditional moral norms—than a champion of religious difference.[8]

Carter, by contrast, emphasized both religious diversity and his own Christian faith. His ringing endorsement of America's "pluralistic heritage" harked back to former presidents, including many who had helped usher in the vision of a tri-faith America prior to the revolutions of the 1960s. In particular, Carter echoed the first Catholic president, the Democrat John F. Kennedy, who had regularly invoked America's "pluralistic society." For instance, Kennedy had used the ideal of pluralism to challenge the logic of the Cold War in a powerful speech at Berkeley in March 1962:

> No one who examines the modern world can doubt that the great currents of history are carrying the world away from the monolithic idea towards the pluralistic idea—away from communism and towards national independence and freedom. No one can doubt that the wave of the future is not the conquest of the world by a single dogmatic creed but the liberation of the diverse energies of free nations and free men. No one can doubt that cooperation in the pursuit of knowledge must lead to freedom of the mind and freedom of the soul.

Although Kennedy, like almost all other pre–Vatican II Catholics, shied away from Judeo-Christian rhetoric, his pluralistic defense of democracy dovetailed with the groundbreaking interventions of John Courtney Murray, whose writings on religious freedom had convinced Catholic officials that democracy and pluralism could be powerful allies.[9]

Yet Carter had a much broader understanding of the scope of American religious diversity than any of his predecessors. Indeed, Carter's electoral appeal in 1976 partly reflected a belief he might prove uniquely capable of bridging a widening cultural gulf. As a Bible-believing Democrat from Georgia, Carter fused traditional religious rhetoric with liberal politics in a manner that seemed to offer something to everyone amid the cultural crisis of the age. Accepting the nomination in July 1976, Carter channeled the iconic folksinger Bob Dylan by contending that America in the 1970s was "busy being born, not busy dying." Religious diversity figured prominently in Carter's vision of national rebirth. "We can have an America that encourages and takes pride in our ethnic diversity, our religious diversity, our cultural diversity," he declared, "knowing that out of this pluralistic heritage has come the strength and the vitality and the creativity that has made us great and will keep us great." In September 1978, Carter became the first president to use the term "religious pluralism" itself, while writing, "Human solidarity is based on profound respect for the right of each group to be itself and to be true to its own heritage and culture."[10]

Carter's pluralistic approach and efforts to expand the contours of Judeo-Christian discourse to accommodate it raised the prospect of quelling the brewing conflicts over "family values." His inaugural address sought to unite Americans around a vision of their nation as "the first society to define itself in terms of both spirituality and of human liberty." Citing that "unique self-definition" as the reason for America's "exceptional appeal," Carter highlighted the "moral duties" attendant to this special calling. In particular, he emphasized the need for Americans to "create together a new national spirit of unity and trust."[11]

Although Carter did not use Judeo-Christian rhetoric in his inaugural, he knit that language into speeches on many later occasions. In November 1977, Carter lauded the efforts of the World Jewish Congress "to promote human rights in a universal way." He contended that "the beginnings of the modern concept of human rights go back to the laws and the prophets of the Judeo-Christian traditions." As someone "steeped in the Bible since early childhood," Carter located the basic premises of human rights in the Hebrew Bible: "the idea of equality before the law and the supremacy of law over the whims of any ruler; the idea of the dignity of the individual human being and also of the individual conscience; the idea of service to the poor and to the oppressed; the idea of self-government and tolerance and of nations living together in peace, despite differences of belief." This morally robust conception of America's Judeo-Christian tradition set Carter apart from the less overtly religious presidents of the 1960s and 1970s.[12]

At the same time, however, Carter's subtle terminological innovations

conveyed his awareness of religious diversity's impact on Judeo-Christian discourse. Take, for example, a speech at Emory University in August 1979, just
weeks before the Iranian hostage crisis that likely cost Carter a second term
and elevated Reagan into the presidency. There, he rooted the "conscience of
America" in "its institutions and . . . in the ethics of the Judeo-Christian tradition." For Carter, that tradition was complex, finding "many expressions" both
"within our religions" and within "our secular life as well." Thus, the "gap"
between the religious and the secular could "constantly be bridged by human
beings who search for the correlation" between these two indispensible and
complementary realms. In other words, Carter continued, the "varied expressions" of the Judeo-Christian tradition "are as diverse as we American people
ourselves." However, he emphasized, "underlying that diversity is a basic unity
of belief and purpose." Having identified both "a crisis of confidence in this
country and a need for unity," Carter described Americans as rightly "proud
of our diversity" and referred to the nation's "pluralistic society" as "an important source of vitality and creativity of American life." Yet, even if "American
society is the most diverse in the entire world," he concluded, "we must not
permit diversity to degenerate into division."[13]

Carter thus went far beyond Nixon in his rejection of the melting pot
ideal. Echoing the 1930s "cultural gifts" model as well as the emerging language of multiculturalism, Carter described America as "a beautiful mosaic, with different kinds of people involved in freedom, individuality, pride,
cooperation, understanding, searching for answers to difficult questions in
their own way, each contributing, hopefully, the strongest single characteristic of their background and heritage and special sensitivity to a common
purpose." The Democratic Party platform of 1980 featured a condensed
version of this message: "President Carter has stated that the composition
of American society is analogous to a beautiful mosaic. Each separate part
retains its own integrity and identity while adding to and being part of the
whole." Thus, like so many politicians since his day, Carter declared repeatedly that "the United States draws its strength from the diversity of the people
who live here."[14]

In his efforts to combine Judeo-Christian terminology with assertions that
religious diversity represented a positive good, Carter was ahead of his time.
He clearly recognized that America's "religious diversity" no longer meant
solely Protestants, Catholics, and Jews, as it had during the 1940s and 1950s.
By the late 1970s, that diversity included myriad faiths from both within
and outside the Judeo-Christian fold, as well as secular perspectives such
as humanism and naturalism. Carter's allegiance to a religiously pluralistic
America did not, in his mind, undercut the importance of America's Judeo-

Christian tradition. Yet while political moderates and conservative evangelicals could take comfort in Carter's facility with Judeo-Christian language, his statements about diversity and pluralism likely dampened their enthusiasm for his vision. In this sense, the same qualities that helped propel Carter into the presidency—his dual emphasis on Judeo-Christian values and religious difference—put him out of step with the religious right as it gained strength in the late 1970s.

The disappointment of conservative evangelicals burst into the open with the White House Conference on Families in June of 1980. Having promised such a gathering to his Catholic supporters in the 1976 campaign, Carter held off for years but finally delivered as his reelection campaign accelerated. In his opening remarks, he once again invoked both the nation's Judeo-Christian past and its open-ended present:

> When we think of families, ordinarily we think of brothers and sisters and a father and a mother, with grandparents and uncles and aunts and nephews and nieces and cousins, perhaps. That's a standard that's been held up by many traditions, including of course the Judeo-Christian tradition, and also by thousands of years of human experience. But that same tradition and that same experience teaches us that there is really no such thing as a perfect family or one that should be used as a standard for all other families.

Similarly, the conference organizers sought to represent the full range of American families and employed inclusive language that conservatives deemed hostile to "traditional Judeo-Christian values concerning the family." Alabama governor Fob James boycotted the conference, and the Southern Baptist Convention called it a threat to "traditional Judeo-Christian family values." The momentum behind this conservative opposition to Carter's conference helped to put Reagan in office and fueled the creation of groups such as James Dobson's Family Research Council and Beverly LaHaye's Concerned Women for America.[15]

Nonetheless, Carter continued to tout the benefits of diversity to the bitter end. A few weeks after his November 1980 defeat, he championed diversity before a group of religious leaders gathered for National Bible Week: "Diversity is an integral part of life, in a democracy in particular. Diversity is not something of which we need be afraid. Our Nation has grown strong, not in spite of it, but because of it, and the pluralistic elements of our society in every respect give it strength." In other words, Carter emphasized, "we need not fear debate, exploration, or argument." But fear them many Americans did. Both the content and the complexity of Carter's vision proved harder to sell than Democrats anticipated in what was still a strongly Cold War–inflected context. Moreover, Carter's hopeful words about religious diversity and pluralism clashed with the frightening images of the hostage crisis that flashed across television screens daily. That crisis defined the final year of Carter's presidency, sealing his fate and clearing the way for Reagan's ascendancy.[16]

It is perhaps less of a coincidence than it might seem that the Iran situation and the White House Conference on Families controversy overlapped during Carter's final months as president. The historian David Farber has called the hostage crisis "America's first encounter with political Islam," which of course degenerated into sharp conflict. Farber links the climate of fear the crisis spawned to the burgeoning crusade for "family values." Among American conservatives, he argues, much of the anxiety and hostility generated by black activism and the broader changes of the 1960s and 1970s came to focus on LGBTQ persons in the United States and on Muslims the world over. These groups, of course, remain prominent among the perceived threats to Judeo-Christian values in today's cultural conflicts.[17]

Carter did not improve his case by consistently extending his vision of diversity to the whole globe and calling for tolerance toward the "Muslim world" even as the fifty-two hostages remained imprisoned in the Tehran embassy. "Our task is to build together a truly cooperative global community," Carter told the World Affairs Council in May 1980, creating "a kind of global mosaic which embraces the wealth and diversity of the Earth's peoples, cultures, and religions." On the domestic front, meanwhile, the 1980 Democratic platform urged that all Americans "must learn to live, communicate, and cooperate with persons of other cultures" and that all "public policies and programs must reflect this pluralism." Such inclusive—and, to critics, relativistic—visions, at a time of perceived national decline, helped to set the stage for the conservative backlash that Reagan rode into office. American voters preferred Reagan's Manichean, Cold War–infused rhetoric to Carter's conviction that Judeo-Christian terminology comported with full-blown religious pluralism.[18]

Reagan turned out to be an adept wielder of Judeo-Christian rhetoric, though not the party-line culture warrior that many of his supporters craved. Neatly folding the new focus on personal morality into the broad, familiar style of Judeo-Christian anticommunism, Reagan combined both with a hefty emphasis on free markets. In a characteristic speech of November 1986, he repeatedly invoked the country's "timeless moral principles, principles rooted in the Judeo-Christian ethic." Defining the Cold War standoff as "fundamentally a moral and ethical conflict," Reagan argued that America and its allies faced "a challenge to our Judeo-Christian ethic, to our belief that man is a creature of God and so precious in himself." And Americans, Reagan continued, simply by holding fast to their moral heritage—by "proclaim[ing] our faith in God and the dignity of man, our love of freedom, and our fidelity to our Judeo-Christian values"—offered "hope to every freedom-loving soul that truth is strong and that the hollow shell of totalitarianism may one day crack and let its people go." Americans could best serve other peoples, Reagan emphasized, by recommitting themselves to their own Judeo-Christian inheritance, not by welcoming new ways of being and extending Carter's olive branch of inclusion and tolerance.[19]

That seamless use of Judeo-Christian rhetoric by political conservatives had been a long time in the making. By the time of Reagan's 1986 speech, contributors to journals such as William F. Buckley Jr.'s *National Review* and Russell Kirk's *Modern Age* had worked for three decades to purge the bigotry of the old Protestant right and broaden the conservative movement's base to include Catholic and Jewish "white ethnics." This tri-faith cadre of Judeo-Christian conservatives had sought to separate conservatism from nativism and create an ideological stance more consistent with the religiously pluralistic character of the modern United States. But it was only under Reagan that they finally realized their vision of a new right that united white ethnics and native-born Protestants in a powerful Judeo-Christian alliance. Even then, a lingering fondness for Christian nationalism sometimes frustrated conservatives' quest for terminological consensus. But by the 1980s, much of the Protestant right had finally made its peace with tri-faith America.

A key turning point was the adoption of Judeo-Christian language by the Southern Baptist leader Jerry Falwell in early 1985. A charismatic televangelist, Falwell cofounded the Moral Majority in 1979 and soon helped make it the most visible mouthpiece for the religious right. It had never been entirely clear that the conservative Catholics and evangelical Protestants who joined forces on issues such as abortion and women's rights in the 1970s would adopt the Judeo-Christian frame, despite the presence of some theologically and politically conservative Jews in the movement. Falwell himself stated his position in exclusively Christian terms for a number of years after the Moral Majority took shape. As late as the 1984 Republican National Convention in Dallas, he described the United States as a Christian nation. Indeed, Falwell's followers flocked to the convention in droves, passing out copies of the New Testament and likely foiling Reagan's plan to bring more Jews into the Republican Party. Just six months later, however, Falwell publicly repudiated Christian nationalism and hailed evangelicals' new "spirit of pluralism" in a speech before the rightward-leaning Rabbinical Assembly. "Twenty-five years ago many of us were saying this is a Christian republic," Falwell declared. "Now we say Judeo-Christian republic." Falwell's linguistic conversion marked the consolidation of a Judeo-Christian right in the mid-1980s. It reflected both the Republican Party's desire to avoid perceptions of anti-Semitism and the growing prominence among evangelicals of Christian Zionism: a pattern of staunch commitment to Israel that combined the hope of hastening the Second Coming with a more general tendency to interpret the Cold War and other international matters "in broad moral and civilizational terms."[20]

Indeed, one could argue that the 1980s, not the 1950s, represented the heyday of Judeo-Christian rhetoric in the United States. Judeo-Christian constructions became a staple of the religious right, as its leaders became political kingmakers and sought to define the contours of their movement more precisely. The use of such terminology by Reagan and many followers did not simply reflect their hope that Judeo-Christian norms would prevail in the future; the religious right also assumed a Judeo-Christian past. In their view, American history featured a sturdy, unbroken Judeo-Christian consensus, stretching from time immemorial up to the left-wing assault of the 1960s. The 1950s represented a particular point of focus; nostalgia for a postwar golden age of civic-religious agreement and traditional values figured prominently in Reagan-era conservatism.

Not all conservatives marked their commitment to traditional values this way. Alexander Haig, the Catholic former general who became Reagan's first secretary of state, was one of several commentators who employed the idiosyncratic alternative "Christian-Judeo." At the 1980 Republican convention, Haig framed the question of American foreign policy as a matter of whether the nation would "continue to seek a world order hospitable to the Christian-Judeo values and interests of today" or abandon the field to foreign ideals. Upon joining Reagan's cabinet, Haig reaffirmed his commitment to "a world structured on the Christian-Judeo values that you and I cherish today." Like the term "Judeo-Christian," the "Christian-Judeo" formulation helped shore up Reagan's coalition of Christian conservatives and largely Jewish neoconservatives. One of the latter, *Commentary*'s Norman Podhoretz, endorsed both Haig and his "Christian-Judeo" phrase in a widely reprinted editorial. Several other conservative activists also employed the term in discussing issues such as the Equal Rights Amendment and religion in the schools. The conservative writer William Safire, for his part, deemed "Christian-Judeo" a grammatical monstrosity and favored "Judeo-Christian" for its consistency with "the flow of history" from "the Old Testament to the New." But "Christian-Judeo" enabled some conservatives to acknowledge Judaism's historical influence while identifying Christianity as the dominant thread in both Western civilization and American history.[21]

Reagan, however, favored the "Judeo-Christian" approach and played a key role in cementing that framework to social conservatism. The former actor and California governor used Judeo-Christian terminology far more frequently than any other president in American history, including Eisenhower. Eschewing the linguistic sensitivity to religious diversity displayed by Carter, and on some occasions even Nixon, Reagan habitually identified "our nation's Judeo-Christian tradition" as the cornerstone of American freedoms. On occasion, he mentioned the "diverse cultural and religious traditions which our forefathers brought to America's shores." Yet Reagan still contained these traditions within the boundaries of "our Judeo-Christian heritage." For Reagan, as for so many of his followers, the nation's strength derived from its religious past, not the diverse thoughtways and cultural expressions of the present. "All of us here today," he told a group of Jewish leaders in 1984, "are descendants of Abraham, Isaac, and Jacob, sons and daughters of the same God," sharing "the guiding light of our Judeo-Christian tradition."[22]

Reagan's use of Judeo-Christian rhetoric reflected the continuities between his strong support for Israel and his appeal to Protestant evangelicals—many of them fervent Christian Zionists themselves—at home. From the start of his campaign, Reagan aligned himself with the surging religious right. Wrapping up his acceptance speech at the 1980 Republican convention, he went off script to claim a divine purpose for the United States and call for a moment of silent prayer. A month later, on August 21, Reagan took the stage before a packed house of fifteen thousand conservative Christians in Dallas, including a veritable Who's Who of the religious right. There, as elsewhere, Reagan peppered his remarks with religiously coded language designed to win evangelicals' trust and whip up their enthusiasm. He brought the crowd to its feet by declaring, "I know you can't endorse me . . . but I want you to know that I endorse you and what you are doing." Reagan then connected his own conservatism to that of the religious right. "Traditional Judeo-Christian values, based on the moral teachings of religion," he contended, "are undergoing what is perhaps the most serious challenge in our nation's history."[23]

Upon his election, Reagan chose a number of religious conservatives for cabinet posts, including Secretary of the Interior James G. Watt, Surgeon General C. Everett Koop, and Secretary of Education William J. Bennett. These figures, who led the charge for "family values," enabled Reagan to appeal to evangelicals without alienating other groups of conservatives and moderates by appearing overly wedded to the religious right. During Reagan's second term, the Catholic Bennett became a particularly vocal advocate of traditional morality, consistently identifying the United States as a Judeo-Christian nation and fighting the courts on behalf of public funding for parochial schools.

Conservatives such as Bennett also contended that excluding religion from the nation's public schools privileged the rights of minorities over those of the majority.[24]

So, too, did Reagan, who kept up the linguistic drumbeat of Judeo-Christian conservatism. He told a group of women who he said championed "Judeo-Christian values" that the First Amendment had been "twisted to the point that freedom of religion is in danger of becoming freedom from religion." In the United States, he contended, "government isn't supposed to wage war against God and religion." Elsewhere, Reagan wrote that the Founders designed the "wall of separation between church and state" to "protect religion from the state, not the other way around." He also called "a value-neutral education a contradiction in terms." In his view, to teach students without giving them their country's "ethics, morality, and values" meant "robbing them of their most precious inheritance—the wisdom of generations that is contained in our moral heritage." Jefferson and his contemporaries could hardly have imagined such false neutrality, he insisted: "Our forefathers found their inspiration, justification, and vision in the Judeo-Christian tradition that emphasizes the value of life and the worth of the individual. It most certainly was never their intention to bar God from our public life. And, as I have said before, the good Lord who has given our country so much should never have been expelled from our nation's classrooms." Reagan consistently described "faith in the dignity of the individual under God" as "the foundation for the whole American political experiment" and unhesitatingly declared that "the Western ideas of freedom and democracy spring directly from the Judeo-Christian religious experience."[25]

Culture Wars

But Reagan's rhetoric hardly gained universal assent. Liberals decried the religious right's attempts to restore traditional moral strictures under the banner of Judeo-Christianity. They portrayed the term "Judeo-Christian values" as a mark of bigotry, not a sign of inclusion. The journalist Richard Cohen, for example, found Falwell's adoption of Judeo-Christian rhetoric alarmingly outdated. The United States, Cohen pointed out, featured four million Buddhists and large groups of Hindus, Muslims, and nonbelievers as well. Falwell's language, he continued, portrayed the United States as "a vast private club" in which Falwell deigned to grant "full citizenship to Jews" but kept others out. In other words, Cohen charged, Falwell had retained the underlying idea of "America as a quasi-religious state" that "withholds 100 percent citizenship from those who are neither Christian nor Jewish, and suggests that their rights are dispensed by the majority." People for the American Way founder Norman Lear joined Cohen in dismissing Falwell's "recantation" as too little and too late. "A Judeo-Christian republic is as much of an assault on separation of church and state as a Christian republic," Lear insisted. "Pluralism is not the co-existence of two religious traditions in a Biblical state but freedom for all."[26]

The phrase "culture wars" soon emerged as a common way of capturing the new dynamics in American public life. The culture wars framework identified two clearly delineated sides in the struggles of the day: on the one hand, advocates of traditional, Judeo-Christian values, and on the other, secular, pluralistic liberals. One early proponent of this interpretation was the Lutheran-turned-Catholic Richard John Neuhaus, a former 1960s radical who moved sharply rightward after *Roe v. Wade* and helped to broker the Catholic-evangelical alliance that anchored the religious right. Neuhaus contended in 1983 that Americans had divided into two groups of "ethical strangers," with little in common besides formal citizenship. Neuhaus blamed liberal apostasy. Up until the 1960s, he asserted, Americans had shared "a basic set of social and moral values that are reflected in political democracy and the Judeo-Christian tradition." Since then, the country had gone off the rails, leaving a saving remnant of conservatives to defend genuine American values against a militantly secular mainstream.[27]

The culture wars interpretation gained plausibility from several writings and events in the early 1990s. An important academic landmark was the publication of the sociologist James Davison Hunter's *Culture Wars: The Struggle to Define America* in 1991. Hunter placed Judeo-Christian formulations front and center, seeing in recent American history the dissolution of a formerly robust "Judeo-Christian consensus." Shortly thereafter, Hunter's book received a tremendous boost when the Catholic conservative Pat Buchanan injected the culture wars framework into the popular conversation. In a fiery speech to the 1992 Republican National Convention, Buchanan identified the struggle over Judeo-Christian values as the successor to the recently ended Cold War. There was "a religious war" in modern America, said Buchanan: "a culture war, as critical to the kind of nation we shall be as was the Cold War itself." At stake was nothing less than "the soul of America." As William Safire noted, Buchanan, who wore his hostility to Jews and other minorities on his sleeve, nevertheless began "studding his statements with 'Judeo-Christian values'" after Buckley's *National Review* accused him of anti-Semitism. At the 1992 convention, Buchanan targeted secular humanism and relativism, locating the key to "national salvation" in "the words of the Old and New Testament" and "the old conscience-forming and character-forming institutions of society: family and church, home and school." Buchanan hoped, in Safire's words, that "our Judeo-Christian values are going to be preserved and our Western heritage is going to be handed down to future generations and not dumped into some landfill called multiculturalism."[28]

As the 1980s gave way to the 1990s, other conservatives joined Safire in identifying multiculturalism and "political correctness," alongside secular humanism, as mortal threats to Western civilization. Conservatives watched with horror as scholarly critics of the Western canon highlighted the contributions of figures other than "dead white men" and sometimes even traced foundational Western commitments to other cultural and geographical areas. One professor cited Saint Augustine's African roots, arguing that the Judeo-Christian tradition had "thrived in Africa and Asia before becoming a major force in the West." Conservatives connected the assault on the "Western Civ" framework of mid-twentieth-century academia with campaigns for feminism and gay rights; each upended traditional understandings, sowing relativism and anarchy. The campaign against multiculturalism and political correctness enabled various groups of conservatives and neoconservatives to identify a shared enemy: not just secular educators and Hollywood liberals but also mainstream scholars across the disciplines. This approach helped to solidify the fractured conservative coalition of the 1990s by conceptually fusing Western civilization with a set of traditional moral values and religious tenets.[29]

The 1992 election demonstrated how central "God talk" had become to American party politics. Though an unlikely culture warrior himself, the stiff, Yale-educated incumbent George H. W. Bush gamely parried Buchanan's attack from the right and the folksy, populist evangelicalism of Arkansas governor Bill Clinton by meeting them on the ground of faith. Belatedly following Reagan by adding Judeo-Christian rhetoric to his arsenal, Bush identified the United States as a divinely chosen nation and argued that the Constitution was written by men "steeped . . . in the faith and philosophy of the Judeo-Christian tradition." Reagan offered his imprimatur, painting Bush as a conservative stalwart who "stands for the bedrock Judeo-Christian moral principles that guide us and our children." No one was going to mistake Bush for Buchanan, but the campaign showed how important it had become for Republican candidates to plausibly align themselves with the values and the language of the religious right.[30]

Not surprisingly, the Republican Party platforms of both 1988 and 1992 featured prominent invocations of Judeo-Christianity. The earlier document fused social, economic, and political conservatism by pitting the Christian family against a grasping state:

Republicans believe, as did the framers of the Constitution, that the God-given rights of the family come before those of government. That separates us from liberal Democrats. We seek to strengthen the family. Democrats try to supplant it. In the 1960s and 1970s, the family bore the brunt of liberal attacks on everything the American people cherished. Our whole society paid dearly. . . . The family's most important function is to raise the next generation of Americans, handing on to them the Judeo-Christian values of Western civilization and our ideals of liberty. More than anything else, the ability of America's families to accomplish those goals will determine the course our country takes in the century ahead.

By contrast, the 1992 platform took a different tack. No doubt reflecting the burden of twelve years of incumbency, as well as Bush's calls for a new "compassionate conservatism," it stated, "Unlike our opponents, we are inspired by a commitment to profound change . . . a positive vision of a vigorous America: prosperous and tolerant, just and compassionate."[31]

Yet the platform again dwelled on "timeless beliefs," including "individual freedom, hard work, and personal responsibility," "the fundamental goodness of the American people," "traditional family values," and "the Judeo-Christian heritage that informs our culture." It also spelled out the party's position on church-state matters, particularly in public education. "America must remain neutral toward particular religions, but we must not remain neutral toward religion itself or the values religion supports," the platform declared. "Mindful of our country's Judeo-Christian heritage and rich religious pluralism, we support the right of students to engage in voluntary prayer in schools and the right of the community to do so at commencements or other occasions." Softening the rigorously antigovernment stance of earlier platforms, the 1992 document focused more squarely on school prayer and other religiously charged issues at the heart of the era's cultural conflicts.[32]

Meanwhile, President Bush began to follow other conservative leaders in adapting the phrases "religious pluralism" and "religious freedom" to their own purposes. He attached those terms to the accommodationist argument that strict church-state separation undermines the freedom of believers to collectively express their faith in public. After the Supreme Court declared in the June 1992 *Lee v. Weisman* decision that a public school could not feature a nondenominational prayer at its graduation, the president defended the "venerable and proper American tradition of nonsectarian prayer at public celebrations." The United States "is a land of religious pluralism, and this is one of our Nation's greatest strengths," his statement asserted. "While we must remain neutral toward particular religions and protect freedom of conscience, we should not remain neutral toward freedom itself." As would so many religious conservatives after him, Bush reframed the protection of religious minorities as the oppression of a religious majority and associated both religious pluralism and religious freedom with that majority's desire to express its faith in public settings.[33]

Multireligious America Ascendant

The growing tendency of conservatives to weld the concept of religious pluralism to accommodationism helped shift the linguistic landscape after Democrats regained the White House in the 1992 election. Although battles over religion, morality, and politics roared through the 1990s and into the twenty-first century, Judeo-Christian formulations largely disappeared from the rhetorical toolkits of American presidents. Ironically, this held true despite the fact that evangelicals occupied the presidency for sixteen years after George H. W. Bush left office. Although their social views differed substantially, the Southern Baptist Bill Clinton and the evangelical Methodist George W. Bush felt a common imperative to stress the country's religious diversity. Clinton, facing an increasingly conservative Republican opposition, eschewed the Judeo-Christian formulations embraced by so many presidents before him. So, more surprisingly, did George W. Bush. Despite his theological and political conservatism, Bush worked hard to tamp down anti-Muslim sentiment among his evangelical and neoconservative followers in the wake of the September 11, 2001, attacks. Strikingly, Republican Party platforms also omitted Judeo-Christian language after 1992; it would not reappear until John McCain, a staunch user of Judeo-Christian terminology, became the candidate in 2008. In the intervening years, Clinton, Bush, and many other national leaders explored new ways of characterizing the religious makeup of an increasingly diverse country.

Early in his presidency, Clinton experimented with various formulations of American religious identity. In November 1993, Clinton celebrated diversity on a global scale, offering a musical analogy akin to Horace Kallen's orchestra metaphor and referring to religiously grounded civilizations. "I hear the complex music of our many different languages," Clinton told a group of international business leaders, "and I know that in each of them, our words for work, for opportunity, for children, for hope carry the same meaning. I see the roots of our many ancient civilizations, whether Confucian, or Islamic or Judeo-Christian. I know there is much we can learn from each other's rich and proud cultures." A few years later, Clinton's lauded his own country's "great and noble struggle to make our national voice a chorus of unity—varied by differing intonations, but carried and lifted by a rich harmony."[34]

However, while Clinton's use of musical images persisted, he avoided the term "Judeo-Christian" after 1993. Instead, Clinton settled on "multireligious" as his descriptor of choice for American religious identity. In so doing, he echoed the Harvard University scholar Diana L. Eck, a specialist on Hinduism and religious pluralism who founded the Pluralism Project at Harvard in 1991. The term "multireligious" appeared throughout Eck's influential writings of the 1990s. For example, shortly after George H. W. Bush mobilized "religious pluralism" to defend the right of Christians to pray in public schools, Eck penned a widely reprinted editorial that characterized religious pluralism as a sustained, dialogical form of engagement across group boundaries. Warning that theorists of multiculturalism had ignored the religious dimensions of cultural differences, she emphasized that "America has not only a multicultural future but a multireligious one." Yet a religiously diverse country would founder, she continued, if its inhabitants lacked "knowledge of one another." Genuine pluralism "must be more than just plurality," Eck insisted. Turning the bare fact of religious diversity into intergroup amity would require of all citizens "active engagement and a level of public religious literacy and inter-religious dialogue that we have not yet begun to achieve." Eck's portrait of America as a multireligious nation gained additional visibility with the publication of her 1993 book *Encountering God: A Spiritual Journey from Bozeman to Banaras*. There, she invoked the term "multireligious" repeatedly, describing "the world of multireligious America in the late twentieth century" as "truly a new frontier." Subsequent statements included Eck's 1997 digital resource *On Common Ground: World Religions in America* and the widely read *A New Religious America: How a "Christian Country" Has Become the World's Most Religiously Diverse Nation*, published shortly before 9/11.[35]

Clinton may have encountered Eck directly in September 1993, at a breakfast meeting with religious leaders during the centennial celebration of the World's Parliament of Religions. Eck called that gathering "a wake-up call to Protestants, conservatives, evangelicals, and even the Jewish people," signaling the emergence of "a radically new multi-religious social reality." Whatever the precise nature of the influence, Clinton soon settled on the multireligious formulation, which he used as early as February 1993 and typically combined with one or more parallels, calling the United States "multiracial and multiethnic and multireligious." Clinton also stated on many occasions that his own religious journey had been "immeasurably enriched by the power of the Torah, the beauty of the Koran, the piercing insights of the religions of East and South Asia and of our own Native Americans, the joyful energy that I have felt in black and Pentecostal churches, and yes, even the probing questions of the skeptics."[36]

Clinton's vision of America as multireligious thus challenged the religious right with a message of unity amid open-ended diversity. Speaking to the American Council on Education in February 1997, Clinton praised Americans for rejecting "dangerous rhetoric" that "seeks to divide us against one another based on our racial or ethnic or religious or other differences," and instead embracing the view that "it is actually a great godsend for us to be the world's most multiethnic, multiracial, multireligious democracy." What, then, held the country together? The answer was simple, Clinton told a Georgetown University audience: "America is an idea. We're not one race. We're not one ethnic group. We're not one religious group. We do share a common piece of ground here. But you read the Declaration of Independence and the Constitution: This country is an idea." To Clinton, American unity was civic, not religious. Arguing that the country's wealth, both financial and spiritual, flowed from its unparalleled diversity, Clinton called on Americans to "move beyond division and resentment to common ground." He admonished them to create a "chorus of harmony" where "you know there are lots of differences, but you can hear all the voices." With the post-1965 immigrants and their descendants starting to gain political influence, Clinton's language reflected a simple demographic fact that Eck had exhaustively highlighted: the United States housed Buddhists, Hindus, Sikhs, Muslims, and many others alongside Protestants, Catholics, and Jews.[37]

For his part, George W. Bush assigned religion a more direct political role than did Clinton. Yet he joined his predecessor in downplaying Judeo-Christian terminology and in emphasizing religious diversity. After the 9/11 attacks Bush repeatedly insisted that Muslims were not the enemy in the new "war on terror," and Islam was not inimical to American principles. As "this great Nation of many religions understands," he told an audience in January 2002, "our war is not against Islam or against faith practiced by the Muslim people; our war is a war against evil." Bush aligned Islam and other faiths firmly with Christianity and Judaism in the battle of "good versus evil." In fact, Bush had begun reaching out to Muslim Americans even before al-Qaeda struck. He continued a tradition, begun by Ford and Carter and renewed by Clinton in 1994, of issuing statements on Muslim holidays. Bush commemorated the Eid al-Fitr in March 2001 and continued to mark Muslim holidays through his presidency.[38]

Up to 2001, the new immigrants that had arrived since 1965—including large groups of Muslims—had generally come to American shores, settled, and raised families without sparking the kinds of bitter public referenda on their political capacities that earlier generations of immigrants had faced. Racial tensions certainly arose, as during the years of Japanese ascendance in the automobile sector. Personal bigotry toward the new immigrant groups was widespread, as were structural disadvantages. And dislike of Muslims in particular remained strong. A Christian suspicion of Islam dating back to the Crusades, coupled with more recent associations of the Middle East with terrorist violence, still colors the thinking of many Americans about the relationship between Muslims and liberal democracy. For these reasons and many others, Islamophobia—including suspicion of the homegrown "Black Muslims" of the Nation of Islam as well as Muslims of foreign origin or parentage—has been a powerful force in American culture since the nineteenth century. Moreover, specific situations abroad, including the Iran hostage situation, a pair of wars with Iraq, and the ongoing Israel-Palestine conflict, have continued to stoke such fears. More generally, Samuel Huntington's 1996 book *The Clash of Civilizations and the Remaking of World Order* expressed a tendency among many American commentators to divide the world into religiously defined and mutually opposing spheres. Still, such tensions rarely produced concerted public challenges to the democratic bona fides of the growing American Muslim community. All of the new immigrant groups faced much more opposition on racial and cultural rather than political grounds; there was comparatively little public debate on whether their faiths comported with democracy, of the type that Catholics and Jews had faced.[39]

Little, that is, until 9/11. All of that changed with al-Qaeda's attacks on American soil on September 11, 2001. In many minds, a question raised by Huntington instantly came to the fore: Was Islam compatible with democracy? To Bush's right, many conservatives answered Huntington's question with a resounding no. Conservative evangelicals such as the Reverend Franklin Graham, Billy Graham's son, called Islam "a very evil and wicked religion" and argued that Muslims worshipped "a different God" than did Jews and Christians. But the president himself took a more conciliatory tack. Emphasizing that the vast majority of Muslims the world over were peace-loving people, he decried efforts to hold them collectively responsible for the extreme actions of a few of their coreligionists. Bush also reached out to Islamic leaders—for example, by visiting the Islamic Center in Washington a week after 9/11—and repeatedly stressed that "Islam is peace," a religion "based upon love, not hate." Bush's cabinet members followed his lead, though the new approach did not always come naturally—as in late 2003, when Secretary of State Colin Powell offhandedly referred to America as a "Judeo-Christian" nation, then quickly caught himself and called it "a country of many faiths." Journalists at Reuters and elsewhere criticized Powell's original statement, conjecturing that his remarks could "antagonize millions of American Muslims, most of whom want to be included in the mainstream."[40]

Reuters added, "Some American Muslims have coined the term Judeo-Christian-Islamic to reflect their ideal of what the United States should be." Indeed, there had been occasional calls since the 1970s to replace the concept of a Judeo-Christian tradition with a "Judeo-Christian-Islamic tradition" or an "Abrahamic tradition," thereby bringing Muslims under the umbrella of Americanism. Such assertions of theological and religio-political kinship multiplied in the wake of 9/11, with the simpler "Abrahamic" generally finding favor over its more precise, hyphenated counterpart. Like Judeo-Christian rhetoric before it, the Abrahamic discourse aimed to knit a distrusted group into the American social fabric by emphasizing points of theological, historical, and ethical commonality between monotheistic religions. In this case, the main point of continuity lay in the fact that Jews, Christians, and Muslims each trace their lineages directly to the covenant between God and Abraham described in Genesis. Jews and Christians trace the line of descent through Isaac, the son of Abraham and Sarah; Muslims through Ishmael, the son of Abraham and Hagar. The Abrahamic concept highlights the shared descent from Abraham and a set of basic theological commitments—starting with monotheism, the worship of a single, transcendent God—associated with the Abrahamic covenant between God and the Israelites.[41]

Since emerging in the 1970s, the Abrahamic framework had gradually made its way among some scholars of religion and interfaith advocates, and occasionally found expression in broader discourses as well. Jimmy Carter, for example, famously sought to mediate tensions in the Middle East by identifying a common Abrahamic heritage that he believed could foster improved political relations. Carter repeatedly referred to Muslims, Christians, and Jews as the "children of Abraham." Later, Bill Clinton became the first president to employ the specific term "Abrahamic." In December 2000, when Clinton commemorated the Eid al-Fitr alongside Hanukkah and Christmas, he employed Abrahamic language in all three documents and called that year's chronological overlap between the holidays "a powerful reminder of the fundamental values we share: a reverence for our Creator, a belief in human dignity, and a conviction that we must love our neighbors as ourselves." Even some conservative evangelicals began to extend tolerance to Muslims in the late 1990s.[42]

The 9/11 attacks gave a major boost to efforts at Abrahamic reconciliation among liberals, even as they ratcheted up suspicion of Islam among other commentators. "Abraham salons" and "Daughters of Abraham" book clubs flourished as citizens explored Islam's role in American culture. The prominent journalist Bruce Feiler wrote a study guide for the salons, which were accompanied by a series of "Abraham summits" of prominent religious commentators. *National Geographic* ran a cover story titled "Abraham: Father of Three Faiths," and *Time* used a cover portrait of Abraham to accompany a lengthy story inspired by Feiler's influential book *Abraham: A Journey to the Heart of Three Faiths*. Like many Catholics and Jews before them, Muslim leaders, who were becoming better established and better educated, made concerted efforts to promote new constructions of American identity after 9/11. In May 2003, the nation's top Muslim organizations—including the American Muslim Alliance, the Council on American-Islamic Relations, the Muslim American Society, and the American Muslim Council—implored "Americans to stop using the phrase 'Judeo-Christian' when describing the values and character that define the United States" and to say instead "Judeo-Christian-Islamic" or "Abrahamic." Muslim leaders such as Feisal Abdul Rauf, the imam of a mosque near the World Trade Center, emphasized—again, like some Catholics and Jews of an earlier era—that their faith comported uniquely well with American democracy.[43]

Yet resistance to the Abrahamic conception of American identity could be heard on many sides. Other religious minorities, who were likewise beginning to find their political voices, protested their linguistic exclusion from the high-profile expressions of civil religion that followed 9/11. If Abrahamic monotheism stood in a unique relationship to American democracy, as many proclamations seemed to suggest, what of Hinduism, Buddhism, and other faiths that were not monotheistic—let alone nontheists? Following a memorial at the National Cathedral, a Hindu scholar whose nephew had died in the World Trade Center attack wrote, "There is more to America than the 'Abrahamic' religions, and people do go to places other than a church, synagogue, or mosque to pray." The Hindu International Council against Defamation petitioned Bush to include Hindus in his invocations of American religiosity. Scholars chimed in as well, noting that "'Abrahamic,' a term invented to include Muslims along with Christians and Jews, excludes Buddhists and Sikhs."[44]

Meanwhile, many religious conservatives retained the Judeo-Christian framework. The National Association of Evangelicals and Richard John Neuhaus, among others, decried attempts by liberal groups such as the National Council of Churches to replace "Judeo-Christian" with "Judeo-Christian-Islamic" or "Abrahamic." Giving in to this multicultural impulse, Neuhaus warned, would only hasten the devolution of American religious identity into an absurdity—the United States as a "Judeo-Christian-Buddhist-Hindu-Islamic-Agnostic-Atheist society." The initial burst of popular interest in Islam after 9/11 also gave way to mounting suspicion, as the number of Americans viewing Islam unfavorably grew from roughly one-third of the population in

2002 to over half by 2010. Most Americans continued to think of their country as Christian, Judeo-Christian, or broadly pluralistic, not Abrahamic.[45]

Perhaps for these reasons, President Bush and his allies steered clear of Abrahamic terminology—in fact, all concrete descriptions of American religious identity—even as they reached out to the Muslim community. In his March 2000 Eid al-Adha message, Bush did raise the Abrahamic possibility. Muslims celebrating that year's Hajj, he stated, "honor the great sacrifice and devotion of Abraham as recognized by Judaism, Christianity, and Islam." By teaching other Americans about Islam, Bush added, "you enrich the lives of others in your local communities." But such rhetoric did not recur after 9/11, even as Bush stressed religious diversity and reached out to Muslims in particular. Unlike Clinton, Bush never adopted a single term such as "multireligious" for his vision of religious diversity. Instead, he used lists of faiths—often, but not always, singling out Christians, Jews, and Muslims—or cited a broadly shared "spiritual foundation," a bedrock set of moral principles that underpinned all faiths and the American way of life. Bush also referred regularly to America as a country made up of "many faiths" or "different faiths" and, like Clinton, made much of its devotion to "religious diversity" and "religious freedom." The phrase "religious tolerance" found a place in Bush's lexicon as well, a unique linguistic feature of the post-9/11 context in which he spoke.[46]

Overall, Bush's religious rhetoric asserted the value of all faiths even as he implicitly assimilated them to his own evangelical vision. "I believe the Lord can work through many faiths," Bush said in 2003, "whether it be the Christian faith, Jewish faith, Muslim faith, Hindu faith. When I speak of faith, I speak of all faiths, because there is a universal call, and that main universal call is to love your neighbor. It extends throughout all faith." Although theological liberals could have endorsed that sentiment, many of Bush's comments accompanied his controversial program of federal support for "faith-based initiatives," which operated on the principle that many "seemingly intractable" social problems "can be solved by helping a soul change their heart." Bush's overtures to Muslims, like his faith-based initiatives, rested on a universalistic but evangelically tinged conception of religion. Proclaiming a National Day of Prayer in April 2001, Bush averred that Americans of all faiths "worship the Almighty in different ways" and "ought to encourage faith-based programs to help solve problems," as part of a national "moral and spiritual renewal."[47]

*

Judeo-Christian rhetoric hardly vanished in the first years of the twenty-first century, but the term's use as a descriptor of America's past, and especially its present and future, was increasingly confined to the right wing of the Republican Party. There, social traditionalists decried the collapse of a moral consensus—and an accompanying framework of "family values"—that they believed had held sway in the United States until the 1960s. Yet the growing association of Judeo-Christian language with the religious right helped to further erode its popularity among other groups, to whom the term increasingly smacked of kitschy 1950s sitcoms and suburban conformity rather than deep spiritual convictions capable of grounding social action, and even social criticism.

Meanwhile, the underlying question of America's religious identity remained wide open as the new century progressed. Muslims, Hindus, Buddhists, and other groups began to find a place in the political and cultural firmament, while the mainline Protestant churches continued to shrink precipitously. A growing minority of religious "nones"—those unaffiliated with any religious body—began to make its voice heard as well. The campaign for gay rights took major steps forward, as large numbers of citizens came to accept gay marriage and to identify an open and affirming stance toward LGBTQ persons as a moral imperative. And in 2008, the American people elected a president who was not only black but also had family ties to Islam and shared his middle name—Hussein—with the Iraqi dictator against whom they had fought two wars. Judeo-Christian discourse faced potent new obstacles, at a time when changing patterns of religious diversity and rapidly increasing mobility strained even the expansive multireligious framework. Was Judeo-Christian America dead and gone, as many pluralists and nonbelievers already assumed, or was its day yet to come, as most traditionalists continued to hope?

Conclusion

The Future of Judeo-Christian Discourse

BEYOND MULTIRELIGIOUS AMERICA?

What lies ahead as the second decade of the twenty-first century draws to a close? Some believe that Judeo-Christian discourse has reached the end of its road in American public life. Barack Obama's presidency may have epitomized the multireligious vision, or it could mark the onset of a new way of thinking about religion and identity in more hybridized terms. Donald Trump's ascension may signal the start of a new phase in the history of Judeo-Christian (or Christian) nationalism, or it may hasten the decline of religious nationalism among conservatives. Have we been witnessing the globalization of the culture wars, perhaps fueled by the relentless march of capitalism? How will the growing power of millennial and "Generation Z" voters shape the religious right's future and the wider political landscape? Is the United States now "postsecular," or is it undergoing a new phase of secularization, albeit one obscured by perceptions of religion's omnipresence in American culture? Questions such as these offer rich fodder for journalists and academics alike. But as recent history has forcefully reminded us, the past, while suggestive, does not necessarily presage the future. On the other hand, stories about the past are crucial resources in dreaming the future and creating social change. America's fortunes in the 2020 elections will depend in large part on how each of the parties understand and mobilize the abolitionist Wendell Phillips's prophetic admonition, "The heritage of the past is the seed that brings forth the harvest of the future."

One thing is clear, however: Although cultural conflicts resembling those of the 1970s continue to rage on, we should be wary of simply projecting contemporary dynamics into the future. Indeed, there have been significant changes in American public life since the advent of the culture wars, and especially since 2008. Some of the shifts began earlier, as with the rise of religious "nones": those who mark "No Religion" when surveyors ask their religious affiliation. As cultural warfare crested in the 1990s, Americans increasingly disavowed religious belonging altogether. From 1990 to 2007, the number of nones rose from 8 percent of the population to 16 percent—in absolute terms, from fourteen million to thirty-four million—making them larger than all non-Christian religious groups combined and the fastest-growing belief community over that period. The pace of growth slowed dramatically after 2001, perhaps in response to 9/11, but then rose again after 2007; the nones now account for some 23 percent of the US population. Meanwhile, the percentage of nones correlates strongly with decreasing age, rising to nearly a third among millennials.[1]

Significantly, the growth of the nones came to national attention only in 2008, with the publication of a major study by the Pew Research Center. That timing roughly corresponds with the newfound acceptability of "atheist" as a personal identifier, especially among younger Americans. Religious skeptics no longer felt a need to label themselves "humanists" or to indicate in other ways that they, too, had a belief system and moral commitments. Indeed, the resurgence of the "atheist" label signaled the culmination of a long-standing shift toward equating the term "religion" itself with the views of those Christian conservatives—mainly evangelical Protestants, conservative Catholics, and Mormons—most strongly tied to the rise of the religious right. Though changing beliefs matter as well, it is revealing that a far higher percentage of nones—though still a small fraction—called themselves atheists in Pew's 2014 study than had done so in 2007. Here, too, strong generational shifts are evident: In a 2016 survey, 13 percent of thirteen- to eighteen-year-olds identified as atheists.[2]

Other changes concerning religious pluralism have been afoot as well. As early as 2007, 70 percent of respondents affiliated with religious institutions told pollsters that many religions could lead to eternal life. Even 57 percent of evangelicals allowed for that possibility. A follow-up study in 2008 showed that Christians have warmed toward not only other versions of Christianity but also non-Christian faiths, although Islam continues to inspire considerable hostility, especially among evangelical Protestants. Another 2008 survey found that nearly a quarter of Americans—24 percent—believe in reincarnation. And a 2017 poll showed that fully one-third of Americans profess belief in a higher power that is not the God of the Bible. Meanwhile, more than a quarter of US Christians—including 32 percent of Catholics—are unfamiliar with the term "Protestant." In a variety of ways, Americans have become less inclined to think of the various religions in exclusive terms and more inclined to see them as alternative, even equally valid, spiritual paths. Although

American religion remains robust in many ways, contemporary forms of faith are less closely tied to specific religious institutions, practices, and theological claims than their predecessors.[3]

Not surprisingly, studies of intermarriage across religious lines reveal analogous trends. A 2014 survey revealed that 19 percent of Americans married before 1960 were in interfaith marriages, whereas the equivalent number for those married since 2010 was 39 percent. Almost half of the growth in that number had come since 1990, and much of it reflected the rise of the nones as a distinct group, particularly among millennials. Meanwhile, the rate for unmarried couples living together was even higher: A full 48 percent had partners of another faith. Clearly the American religious landscape has changed a great deal since the 1930s, when Judeo-Christian discourse first emerged, and even the 1970s, when that language's center of gravity shifted rightward with the rise of the religious right.[4]

*

New possibilities can be discerned in American political rhetoric as well, especially since 2008. Barack Obama's public statements, coupled with his complex personal identity, broke significantly with precedent. At first glance, Obama would seem to have adopted the rhetorical norms of the multireligious paradigm. But in key respects, his style of religio-political communication departed markedly from patterns prevailing since the 1970s. One clue to the novelty of Obama's rhetoric was his repeated acknowledgment of the existence and rights of nonbelievers. During his first term, Obama always mentioned "nonbelievers" when delineating America's religious diversity. In his second term, he specified further, including both "atheists and agnostics." No other modern president's public speeches have ever extended such systematic recognition to this widely despised subset of Americans. This practice implicitly challenged the understandings of democracy that emerged in the Cold War, which cast serious doubts on nonbelievers' loyalty and capacity for democratic leadership.

Throughout the twentieth century, in fact, most presidents—including Eisenhower, the only president besides Obama to mention atheists and agnostics in the same breath—openly acknowledged nonbelievers solely to reject their views, or even to question their very existence. As was customary in tri-faith America, Eisenhower held that nonbelievers knew in their hearts that God existed and ruled over human affairs. He contended that democracy rested on this premise of God's existence and power, and of humanity's dependence on the divine. To publicly disagree with these assertions during the early Cold War years was to risk seeming antidemocratic, un-American, subversive, immoral, abnormal, irrational, or perhaps even insane—associations that still persist in many locales. During the tri-faith era, presidents from Eisenhower to Gerald Ford routinely proclaimed that there were "no atheists in the foxholes." Ford, after a rather tongue-in-cheek promise to be "the President of black, brown, red, and white Americans, of old and young, of women's liberationists and male chauvinists, and all the rest of us in-between, of the poor and the rich, of native sons and new refugees, of those who work at lathes or at desks or in mines or in the fields, of Christians, Jews, Moslems, Buddhists, and atheists," then added, "if there really are any atheists after what we have all been through." As the tri-faith understanding gave way to its multireligious successor during the 1970s, atheists continued to appear, in the minds of many Americans, as either victims of false consciousness or dangerous subversives.[5]

This pattern of treating atheism as retrograde or even beyond the pale largely continued through the shift toward a multireligious perspective. On one atypical occasion in 1990, George H. W. Bush asserted that Americans "cherish dissent," including "the fact that we have many, many faiths," and thus guarantee "even the right to disbelieve." But Americans, he explained, tolerated such aberrations precisely because the citizenry was "truly religious." Bush also linked his discussion of religious freedom to the waning Cold War, highlighting the persecution of Christian leaders under communism. Most of his speech emphasized the usual themes: that "Americans are religious people"; that the Founders wrote, "All men are endowed by their Creator with certain unalienable rights"; and that the nation stood on the verge of a renewal of faith in "the Word of God." The tendency to marginalize nonbelievers can also be seen in Bill Clinton's felt need to emphasize that he had "even" learned from skeptics on his faith journey.[6]

Obama, by contrast, identified atheists as simply one more community of belief, with their own language—and, crucially, with their own moral commitments. Meanwhile, he defined the United States itself in formally secular terms. Obama raised hackles a few months after his election when he told a Turkish audience that the United States, despite its "very large Christian population," was "a nation of citizens who are bound by ideals and a set of values," not "a Christian nation or a Jewish nation or a Muslim nation." These statements reflected Obama's commitment to a secular public sphere, a view he connects to his liberal Protestant religious identity. On the hotly contested question of religion's role in public life, Obama offered a deft compromise grounded in a subtle distinction: Following theorists such as John Rawls and Jürgen Habermas, Obama urged the faithful to embrace the inescapable imperative to translate their beliefs into public reasons capable of persuading citizens who hold different views. At the same time, he insisted that "secularists are wrong when they ask believers to leave their religion at the door before entering the public sphere." Rigidly separating personal faith from public debates was both "a practical absurdity" and a tremendous loss of moral resources, Obama argued. But in a "deliberative, pluralistic democracy," he emphasized, "the religiously motivated" still needed to "translate their concerns into universal, rather than religion-specific, values" in order to make any headway in convincing those unlike themselves. To this end, Obama called on all Americans to employ, in their public deliberations, "a language that allows for argument, allows for debate, and also allows that we may be wrong."[7]

The complexity of Obama's religio-racial identity likewise challenged both the tri-faith and multireligious models. In his openness about how he negotiated this complexity, and in the language he used to describe it, Obama's personal story mirrored what will likely become a defining mode of American experience as the twenty-first century unfolds. Having come to Christianity as an adult, Obama called himself "a Christian by choice" in a 2010 interview and forthrightly acknowledged his parents' nonparticipation in institutionalized religion. At the same time, Obama described his mother as "one of the most spiritual people I knew," even though "she didn't raise me in the church." Indeed, Obama's religious background is even more multifaceted than that; he spent two and a half years at an Indonesian-language Catholic school in Jakarta as a young boy, and during his childhood his estranged Kenyan father moved from Islam to Anglicanism to atheism before marrying a Jewish woman.[8]

While president, Obama repeatedly cited his own hybridized identity "as an American, as a Christian, a person partly of African descent, born in Hawaii," when reflecting on the character of his country. In the aforementioned 2010 interview, Obama pivoted from his personal faith to his vision of America: "I'm also somebody who deeply believes that the—part of the bedrock strength of this country is that it embraces people of many faiths and of no faith, that this is a country that is still predominantly Christian, but we have Jews, Muslims, Hindus, atheists, agnostics, Buddhists, and that their own path to grace is one that we have to revere and respect as much as our own." Even as he identified religious multiplicity as the source of America's strength, Obama's phrasing pointed to another dimension of his commitment to toleration—namely, humility about his view of American religious identity, which he presented as his own belief rather than as an objective fact. Obama's language in the 2010 interview implicitly acknowledged the deep opposition in some quarters to his understanding of religious difference and American belonging.[9]

Well before Obama entered the Oval Office, the new tone of relaxed openness he took toward religious difference was already evident in his 2006 book *The Audacity of Hope*. There, Obama described himself as both "a Christian and a skeptic" and warned of "the dangers of sectarianism": "Whatever we once were," he declared, "we are no longer just a Christian nation; we are also a Jewish nation, a Muslim nation, a Buddhist nation, a Hindu nation, and a nation of nonbelievers." Obama made his expansive understanding of religious diversity clear on the campaign trail as well, where he routinely offered similar statements. And it shone through in his 2009 inaugural, where Obama used the folksy phrase "patchwork heritage" when calling the country's long-standing diversity—again, as "a nation of Christians and Muslims, Jews and Hindus, and non-believers"—the source of its great strength.[10]

Not surprisingly, Obama's rhetoric drew much criticism from the right. Detractors cast doubt on his personal religious authenticity, in part because he consistently included both nonbelievers and Muslims in his accounts of America's religious heritage. Obama's sharpest critics charged that he was an atheist or a Muslim in liberal Protestant garb. Yet Obama did not defend himself by mobilizing Christian or Judeo-Christian renditions of American nationalism. Nor did he revert to Clinton's preferred term "multireligious." Instead, Obama took care to list America's major faith communities by name, always including nonbelievers, Muslims, and at least one Asian-origin faith community alongside Jews and Christians. (On the few occasions when he used a shorthand expression, he employed "many faiths" rather than "many religions" or "multireligious"; this usage enabled him to include nonbelievers and the religiously unaffiliated.) During the 2008 campaign and throughout his first term, Obama's characteristic phrasing encompassed "Christians and Muslims, Jews and Hindus, and nonbelievers." Not surprisingly, he added new groups over time. In 2010, Obama began to publicly commemorate the Diwali holiday and to mention Buddhists and Sikhs in his speeches as well. Importantly, Obama's delivery usually conveyed that these lists were not meant to be comprehensive but instead pointed toward an even more expansive, open-ended pluralism amenable to future growth and change.[11]

During the 2012 campaign, Obama offered fewer litanies of religious diversity, perhaps to quell attacks on his own religious identity and its authenticity in a democratic context. However, he soon resumed the earlier pattern.

On Religious Freedom Day in 2014, Obama issued arguably the quintessential expression of his vision:

> America embraces people of all faiths and of no faith. We are Christians and Jews, Muslims and Hindus, Buddhists and Sikhs, atheists and agnostics. Our religious diversity enriches our cultural fabric and reminds us that what binds us as one is not the tenets of our faiths, the colors of our skin, or the origins of our names. What makes us American is our adherence to shared ideals— freedom, equality, justice, and our right as a people to set our own course.

As usual, Obama coupled an expansive rendering of religious diversity with a purely civic understanding of what Americans held in common and how they ought to defend their views in public. Although he referred frequently to "my Christian faith," he never conflated that faith with American ideals.[12]

On the few occasions when Obama employed Judeo-Christian terminology, he did so in highly specific, carefully bounded ways. For instance, he asserted that much of American law derived historically from the Judeo-Christian tradition. Yet Obama relegated that inheritance to the distant past and drew a distinction between the country's historical provenance—the fact that American democracy had sprung from Judeo-Christian teachings—and the logically distinct claim that democracy requires Judeo-Christian tenets as its philosophical and cultural foundation. Instead, he argued that every generation of Americans, dating back to the "pilgrims who sought refuge from persecution," had "seen people of different faiths join together to advance peace, justice, and dignity for all." Obama portrayed the United States as a religiously pluralistic country knit together by civic ideals and interfaith tolerance and cooperation. In his view, the country featured a formally secular state and a deep tradition of religious freedom and voluntarism, alongside a wide range of faith communities offering invaluable moral resources in civil society.[13]

Anchoring Obama's vision was his genuine conviction that Judeo-Christian principles reflected broader, universal truths that he hoped would become more fully realized in the future. In 2015, Obama made such a reference to the Judeo-Christian ideal when he expressed his hope that Americans and Israelis would "embody the Judeo-Christian and, ultimately then, what I believe are human or universal values that have led to progress over a millennium." Obama elaborated on this idealistic, universalistic stance in 2013. Prodded to discuss "the common Judeo-Christian or, even further, Muslim background to the belief that we have a social responsibility" for the unfortunate, Obama responded by widening the lens still further: "There's no great religion that doesn't speak to this. At root, every great religion has some equivalent of the golden rule, some equivalent of the idea that I am my brother's keeper and my sister's keeper, some notion that, even as we each take individual responsibility for acting in a responsible and righteous way, part of our obligation is to the larger world and future generations." Elsewhere, Obama shorthanded the values he associated with the Judeo-Christian pluralistic ideal as a "shared spirit of humanity that inhabits us all, Jews and Christians, Muslims and Hindus, believers and nonbelievers alike," even as "we worship in different ways."[14]

Obama's strong penchant for universalism marked his holiday addresses as well. Jesus, he typically declared, had brought the world "a message that says we have to be our brother's keepers, our sister's keepers; that we have to reach out to each other, to forgive each other; to let the light of our good deeds shine for all; to care for the sick and the hungry and the downtrodden; and of course, to love one another, even our enemies, and treat one another the way we would want to be treated ourselves." However, Obama then tempered his universalism with a pluralistic note by emphasizing that Jesus's ethical message "grounds not just my family's Christian faith, but that of Jewish Americans, Muslim Americans, nonbelievers, Americans of all backgrounds." Obama also brought his inclusive account of America's religions to the National Prayer Breakfast, where earlier presidents had often issued ringing statements of Christian or Judeo-Christian exceptionalism. There, Obama rigorously separated religion from ethics, insisting that Christian values "can be found in many denominations and many faiths, among many believers and among many nonbelievers." Even as Obama's public statements affirmed the Christianity of his family and many other Americans, they also drew a wide "circle of we" based on shared ethical commitments, and thus capable of including members of all faiths, as well as religious skeptics. Whereas previous presidents could not have spoken convincingly for such a wide range of traditions, Obama managed to do so precisely because of the hybridized nature of his own identity.[15]

On the international stage, Obama's rhetorical approach enabled him to present the United States as both a microcosm and a champion of global religious and cultural diversity, simultaneously reflecting both a reality and an aspiration. "Our story is shaped by every language; it's enriched by every culture," he told listeners abroad. "We have people from every corner of the world." Speaking to the British Parliament in May 2011, Obama acknowledged that America's diversity created tensions around issues such as "immigration and assimilation." But both Britain and the United States, he continued, ultimately regarded their "patchwork heritage" as "an enormous source of strength." This embrace of diversity, he continued, showed an increasingly interconnected world that "it is possible for people to be united by their ideals, instead of divided by their differences." As he had elsewhere, Obama presented himself as an individual example of global interconnectedness and diversity—as living proof that "the grandson of a Kenyan who served as a cook in the British Army" could ascend to the presidency, just as "the sons and daughters of the former colonies" could be elected to Parliament.[16]

Obama's remarkably fluid ability to speak about religious difference in America illustrates a phenomenon that could become increasingly central to American religious life in the twenty-first century: Personal experience with religious multiplicity can facilitate a capacity to think and speak from diverse perspectives, without necessarily eliminating the ability to occupy a single faith tradition. There was surely some political opportunism in Obama's mentions of non-Judeo-Christian religious groups, which were growing in both numbers and influence during his two terms. Yet the president's own background also shaped his replacement of the generic "multireligious" with a more complex, open-ended language that invoked "faiths" rather than "religions" and centered more squarely on individuals than on groups. Obama told a Burmese audience he had learned "the power of diversity" from both "my own country and my own life." When he took up the presidential challenge of articulating a civic "we," Obama did so in unprecedented ways, referring constantly to both his personal faith and the diversity of the United States and the world. By referring openly to his own religious and racial hybridity, Obama grounded his claims about American identity in personal experience.[17]

Obama's thoroughgoing departure from past religious patterns helps explain why he elicited such vitriol from conservatives. It is important to recognize that Obama was not just the country's first African American (and biracial) president. He was also the first president to embody in his person a model of religious diversity stretching beyond Judeo-Christian boundaries. Obama exemplified new modes of self-understanding that had emerged in cosmopolitan cities and on college and university campuses, and to some extent in military communities as well, and were starting to make their way into everyday life across the country. His approach provoked outrage because it rejected not only the notion of a Judeo-Christian America but also the deeper Cold War logic that still persists in the early twenty-first century. These interrelated concepts defined the United States as a religious nation beset by the forces of secularism, both abroad and at home. By contrast, Obama defined the country in purely civic terms. If the multireligious model challenged the assertion that Judaism and Christianity possessed unique democratic resources, Obama's emphasis on civic ideals struck at the assumption that personal and communal religion underwrites democracy. From the vantage point of Judeo-Christian (and Christian) exceptionalists on the religious right, Obama offered nothing but an unvarnished—and implicitly totalitarian—secularism.

To be sure, much of Obama's success stemmed from his capacity to create a skillfully balanced amalgam of religious rhetorics both familiar and new. Thus, he appeared black and Christian to some supporters and biracial and religiously hybrid to others. But at a deeper level, Obama's new approach to religious rhetoric challenged the multireligious understanding of the United States as a collection of self-contained religious groups that simply needed to make peace. His approach portrayed religious difference not as a static condition to be managed but rather as a vital dynamic, spawned by religious mobility and border crossings, to be actively celebrated. This newly articulated hybrid sensibility highlighted the fact that religious diversity, long emphasized by the multireligious-America model, operates inside the lives of single individuals as well as between them. Obama's unprecedented example as a president who had navigated multiple faith traditions and racial identities, encountering such borders within himself, gave new momentum to the emerging fascination with both racial and religious hybridity.

*

Donald Trump's refusal to follow long-established rules of conservative public piety has also revealed the changed conditions of American public life. Most of Obama's conservative critics and challengers reasserted either the Christian or Judeo-Christian character of the United States. As elsewhere, however, Trump has broken the mold in the realm of presidential rhetoric, showing little facility with the term "Judeo-Christian." He has largely replaced that term with language that signals Christian nationalism but often ignores, or even violates, basic theological tenets. Instead, Trump appeals instrumentally to Christian conservatives as an interest group, promising to protect them from perceived threats to Judeo-Christian morality, especially on matters of sexuality and gender norms. We may never know whether Trump's clumsy professions of faith and the testimonials about his personal beliefs from friends and spiritual advisers actually convinced voters that genuine religious commitment lay behind his political pandering or whether they simply voted against his opponent, "crooked Hillary." But there is some reason to suspect the latter. After all, Trump stands well outside the broad cultural matrix of conservative Christian America, even if he shares many of its political agendas. An erstwhile secular urbanite with little knowledge of Christianity's content and even less respect for personal piety, Trump is, at bottom, a cutthroat realist with no obvious moral compass. He seems to view the world as a site of constant power struggles wherein strong, virtuous winners defeat weak, undeserving losers, a view likely buttressed in part by lessons learned in his youth from the positive-thinking guru Norman Vincent Peale. Trump, who identifies as a Presbyterian, may be *for* conservative Christians politically, but he is definitely not *of* them culturally. At one point, he even joked that advancing the religious right's political interests was "the only way I'm getting to heaven."[18]

Thus far exempted from the usual requirement to model personal piety, Trump also ignores long-standing linguistic conventions—including tipping his hat to even the narrowest uses of the term "Judeo-Christian"—in describing the country's religious character. To date, he has employed Judeo-Christian rhetoric only twice and has done so in a predictably hollow and supersessionist manner. At the October 2017 Values Voter Summit, for example, Trump characteristically congratulated himself for "stopping cold the attacks on Judeo-Christian values" in the United States: "We're saying 'Merry Christmas' again," he boasted. In a bid to activate the "family values" logic long associated with the term "Judeo-Christian," Trump intoned, "Bureaucrats think they can run your lives, overrule your values, meddle in your faith, and tell you how to live, what to say, and how to pray. But we know that parents, not bureaucrats, know best how to raise their children and create a thriving society." Assuring his audience that Americans "don't worship government, we worship God," Trump pledged his loyalty to "our cherished friend and partner, the state of Israel" and his antipathy toward "radical Islamic terrorism." Trump's rhetoric has laid bare the common tendency of many on the religious right to equate "Judeo-Christian" with a specifically Christian agenda. For the most part, Trump simply relies on amorphous phrases—"people of faith," "faith in God and his teachings"—or contends, as he did in his earlier remarks to the 2016 Values Voter Summit, that under his watchful eye the nation's "Christian heritage will be cherished, protected, defended, like you've never seen before."[19]

To some degree, Trump's rhetoric recaptures the stark binary of religion and secularism that has shaped American public discourse since the World War II era. A proclamation declaring Trump's inauguration day a "National Day of Patriotic Devotion" insisted that preserving American freedoms requires "faith in our sacred values and heritage." At a deeper level, however, Trump's political rhetoric illustrates new patterns. He certainly does not toe the multireligious line; few on the right cavil when he categorically attacks Muslims, just as George W. Bush warned Americans not to do in the wake of 9/11. Nor, however, does Trump's rhetoric fit into the tri-faith mold and the Cold War logic of the mid-twentieth century. Thus far, he has hardly ever relied on either Judeo-Christian formulations or the constitutive contrast between a pious America and a secular, totalitarian other. Perhaps eschewing words like "godless" or "secular" to avoid drawing attention to his own religious marginality, Trump prefers instead to follow business conservatives in calling liberals and progressives "socialists." Trump did attempt to stoke the cultural offensive against secularism when he lambasted "the war on Christmas," but for the most part he barely acknowledges religion when he looks at the United States or around the world, with the notable exception of US-Israel relations.[20]

Abroad, as at home, Trump sees the world in terms of winners and losers. Despite his affinity for "clash of civilizations" thinkers such as his former adviser Steve Bannon, an economic and political nationalist, Trump seems to view countries largely according to their desirability as resort locations and to trace their conditions to the personal qualities of either their citizens or their leaders. Meanwhile, he treats Islam as a violent, anarchic force, not as an implicitly totalitarian faith, and likewise views other immigrant groups through the lenses of criminality and economic productivity. In short, Trump fixates mainly on social differences, not religious ones.

Even more strikingly, Trump departs from the age-old tendency to define American democracy in terms of shared spiritual values, whether Christian, Judeo-Christian, or broadly civic. Indeed, he bothers little with ideals of any kind, barely even mentioning democracy itself. Rather, Trump portrays national institutions as tools for advancing the material interests of citizens. He largely ignores the theological content of the Christian tradition, leaving only the bald equation of religion with capitalism, plaudits for economic winners, and disdain for the unfortunate. To be sure, Trump has piggybacked on the nativist and anti-immigrant tendencies of the Tea Party movement, which took aim at the multireligious approach. Yet he displays no inclination to provide even his supporters with a clearly articulated vision of America's moral or religious identity or a set of guiding ideals, beyond the crass association of Christianity with success and power. Here, too, we see the weakened force of both the tri-faith and multireligious paradigms, and the emergence of a new religio-political climate wherein religious commitments are intimately related to other axes of identity such as class, race, gender, and sexuality.

In this respect, as in so many others, Trump stands at some remove from religious conservatives within the Republican Party. His predecessors repeatedly used Christian or Judeo-Christian rhetoric to shore up their support from these quarters. On the campaign trail before the 2008 election, John McCain, despite having bucked his Episcopalian upbringing to become a

Southern Baptist, still needed to mend fences with religious conservatives who had not forgotten his sharp attacks on Jerry Falwell and Pat Buchanan in the 2000 primaries. Thus, McCain said the most pressing question for voters in the 2008 election should be "Will this person carry on in the Judeo Christian principled tradition that has made this nation the greatest experiment in the history of mankind?" And in 2012, Mitt Romney invoked Judeo-Christian terminology in part to assuage the suspicions of evangelical Protestant and conservative Catholic voters regarding his Mormonism. Romney traveled to Liberty University, founded by Jerry Falwell, to reassure evangelicals that "our Judeo-Christian tradition" explained the country's greatness. The attraction of conservative evangelicals to Christian Zionism has further strengthened the association of Judeo-Christian language with the religious right in recent years. Particularly influential here has been the political activism of Christians United for Israel leaders John Hagee and David Brog.[21]

Perhaps reflecting McCain's influence, Judeo-Christian terminology returned to Republican Party platforms in 2008 after an absence since 1992. The 2008 platform blamed activist judges for seeking to "drive faith out of the public arena," arguing that "public display of the Ten Commandments does not violate the US Constitution and accurately reflects the Judeo-Christian heritage of our country." Similarly, the 2012 Republican platform devoted an entire section to the "war on religion," wherein "liberal elites try to drive religious beliefs—and religious believers—out of the public square." It accused the Obama administration of seeking "to compel faith-related institutions, as well as believing individuals, to contravene their deeply held religious, moral, or ethical beliefs regarding health services, traditional marriage, or abortion."[22]

Trump has benefited greatly from many evangelicals' belief that Democrats seek to stamp out religion. As internecine strife erupted in the Republican Party in 2016, its platform took a page from the Eisenhower-Reagan playbook and reasserted the foundational political status of America's "Judeo-Christian heritage." After rehearsing liberal offenses, the platform turned to the claim that democratic rights come from God:

> Our First Amendment rights are not given to us by the government but are rights we inherently possess. The government cannot use subsequent amendments to limit First Amendment rights. The Free Exercise Clause is both an individual and a collective liberty protecting a right to worship God according to the dictates of conscience. Therefore, we strongly support the freedom of Americans to act in accordance with their religious beliefs, not only in their houses of worship, but also in their everyday lives.

As before, Republicans identified student prayer and public displays of the Ten Commandments as constitutionally protected religious expressions. Yet Trump himself, unlike past candidates and presidents, barely bothered to cloak his Christian agenda in Judeo-Christian terminology. In other words, he has thus far largely dispensed with the religious convention that had shaped Republican presidential politics in the mold of Reagan's conservatism since the 1980s. In so doing, Trump abandoned not only lingering antipathies to Russia but also the basic premises of the Cold War redefinition of democracy. He thereby demonstrated that most religious conservatives would reflexively vote Republican, no matter what religio-political label the party's candidate attached to their policy preferences.[23]

✶

The place and meaning of Judeo-Christian language is far less clear in today's emerging political climate than in earlier ones. Nonetheless, the long history of Judeo-Christian discourse in the United States does offer several clues about where the country may be headed. First, a number of factors would seem to militate against the hope of some interfaith activists and scholars that the term "Abrahamic" will come to perform the same integrative function that "Judeo-Christian" did in postwar America. The long, fraught history of Western relations with the Islamic world, as well as more recent developments, has fostered anxieties about Islam that helped to catapult Donald Trump into office in 2016. Meanwhile, a term that singles out Muslims and ignores Hindus, Buddhists, and other minorities (including nonbelievers) likely will not appeal to those with a more expansive understanding of American identity, even if that language works to mitigate suspicion of Muslims in other quarters.[24]

There are also many other reasons why the tri-faith dynamics of the 1940s and 1950s are unlikely to simply repeat themselves with Muslims. The remarkable power of Judeo-Christian rhetoric in its heyday reflected not only its assertion of equality among Protestants, Catholics, and Jews but also its congruence with population patterns and its association with a series of widely endorsed cultural projects. Judeo-Christian formulations became enormously popular in the mid-twentieth century because they seemed to capture demographic and historical realities as well as normative ideals. Of course, such descriptions of American religious pluralism did not fully account for realities on the ground, as when a Sikh won election to Congress in 1956. But Judeo-Christian language did help Americans come to grips with the sweeping demographic changes that had taken place from the 1880s to the 1920s, when industrialization transformed an overwhelmingly Protestant country into one with substantial populations of Catholics and Jews. Even in 1956, it was true that the vast majority of Americans came from Protestant, Catholic, or Jewish backgrounds.[25]

Yet demographics alone do not transform discourses on national identity. There is typically a significant delay between the movement of populations and the moment of conceptual reckoning, when cultural and political shifts—in many cases, shifts unrelated to the original demographic phenomenon itself—make it both possible and necessary to acknowledge new patterns of diversity and assign meaning to them. In the case described here, the waves of immigration accompanying Gilded Age industrialization set the stage for America's Judeo-Christian discourse. But the decisive factor—that which determined *how* the nation accommodated its Catholic and Jewish minorities—was the ideological warfare of the mid-twentieth century. This fact helps to explain why democracy and national identity figured so prominently in Judeo-Christian discourse during those years. The imperative to defend democracy against totalitarian challengers led Americans to define the "we" of their democracy—to specify the common political ideas and commitments that a diverse conglomeration of Americans shared.

Many uses of Judeo-Christian rhetoric during the tri-faith era thus took their shape from the widespread perception that the fates of both Western civilization and democracy hung in the balance. It is no accident that America's emergence from World War II as the self-identified leader of the "free world" coincided with the rise of Judeo-Christian terminology. Many Americans believed that their country's new international role entailed spreading democracy and human rights, both of which were widely viewed as products of Judeo-Christianity. This political context virtually ensured that the immigrants of 1870–1924 and their descendants would be defined primarily as Catholics and Jews rather than Italians, Poles, and Russians. The power of Judeo-Christian discourse in mid-twentieth-century American culture stemmed from its dual capacity to acknowledge new demographic realities at home and to make sense of America's growing global power. For some Americans, intense fears of secularization reinforced the tendency to believe that practicing Protestants, Catholics, and Jews stood shoulder to shoulder with one another in the defense of democracy. Others worried about the abridgement of civil liberties, including freedom of religion, under fascism and communism. But in both cases, the correspondence between demographics and political sensibilities reinforced the view that the United States and Europe traced their roots to a coherent "Judeo-Christian tradition."

We can see now, from an increasingly distant remove, that the period from World War II to the early 1970s was a unique moment in both American and global history. It was a time when the West harbored illusions about its power and grandeur, based on fictions about human and natural resources that rested in turn on the intertwined histories of colonialism and industrialization. It was a moment when Americans self-consciously took over leadership of "Western civilization" from Europeans and easily traced that civilization back to Judeo-Christian roots. It was a period of tremendous affluence, which allowed American leaders to avoid hard choices between competing agendas. It was an era when national policy was defined by an overarching goal: defeating totalitarianism, once and for all. And it was a time when the main enemy against which Americans defined themselves—communism— was militantly secular.

The cultural imperative to define and defend democracy has taken new forms since the Cold War's end. Few of today's global threats present a secular, Marxist guise, even though conservatives still find plenty to fear in atheism and religious heterodoxy at home. With the exception of Islamic radicalism, policymakers say little about the ideological dimensions of global competitors. North Korea appears as a military threat, China as an economic power (despite some evangelicals' concern for Chinese Christians), and Russia as a political challenge, viewed largely in isolation from the Orthodox Church's influence there. Even Mexican immigrants, the bugaboo of many Trump supporters, figure primarily as an economic and racial phenomenon, not an ideological or religious one. A growing number of Americans, it seems, have begun to move beyond the Cold War redefinition of democracy, in which a tri-faith America stood over and against an antireligious, totalitarian enemy.

Changing personal experiences matter as well. Both the tri-faith and multireligious frameworks defined citizens as adherents to discrete, coherent faith traditions. Today, a growing number of Americans struggle to locate themselves within a single religious community—or, for that matter, under the aegis of institutional religion at all. They experience religion as a matter of individuals standing at the intersections of multiple systems of belief and practice. Like the absence of a secular, totalitarian challenger, the ongoing shift from group-based thinking toward a more individualized and hybridized conception of religious identity is fundamentally altering the conditions of American public life.

These far-reaching changes have begun to undermine many of the familiar rhetorical imperatives of American political discourse. Obama can assert the moral legitimacy of nonbelievers without committing political suicide. Meanwhile, Trump can invoke America's "Christian heritage" despite having a Jewish son-in-law, daughter, and grandchildren. He can also cozy up to Russia without causing his supporters—even his evangelical Christian advocates—to question his personal religious authenticity as they did Obama's. There are hardly any similarities in how Obama and Trump have approached religion; whereas Obama took religion to be a matter of individual commitment under the shared umbrella of a universalistic and pluralistic ethic, Trump seems to regard religious communities primarily as interest groups. Yet Obama and Trump share a common historical context, in a United States no longer governed by the religio-political logics that defined the realm of the politically possible from the World War II era into the first decade of the twenty-first century.

Still, the question of how Judeo-Christian terminology will fare in the future remains wide open at present. Some speculate that Trump's presidency will undermine the religious right itself, along with the Judeo-Christian rhetoric it has used so effectively since the 1970s. Yet it is suggestive that many of today's leading conservatives—including figures as diverse as Steve Bannon and his former Breitbart News colleague Ben Shapiro, whose commitments to free trade and the global promotion of human rights have made him a fierce critic of Bannon's nationalistic sensibility—identify their core principles as outgrowths of a Judeo-Christian tradition and posit a Manichean divide between the (implicitly white) "Judeo-Christian West" and the alliance of "socialistic" liberals and "Islamic fascism" that threatens it.[26]

Such examples attest to the remarkable staying power and elasticity of Judeo-Christian terminology, even as the landscape of personal faith and religious identity continues to shift dramatically in the United States. The recent attempts of the Trump administration to project American cultural conflicts onto the rest of the world reveal the multiple and often diametrically opposed meanings that the term "Judeo-Christian" has taken on. That discourse has always worked on many levels at once. Perhaps, in the future, it will work in ways as yet unimagined. Over the years and decades to come, all of us will be marked, in one way or another, by the broad trends that have made religious identities increasingly individualized, malleable, multifaceted, hybridized, and transnational in the United States. To survive, Judeo-Christian discourse will have to contend with these forces as well.

If past experience suggests anything, it is that the emergence of a new, more fluid understanding of religion and public life will spawn a sustained backlash, just as its tri-faith and multireligious counterparts did in the 1930s and the 1970s. As has always been the case in the history of American religious difference, there is a significant and politically consequential lag between the experiences of urban dwellers and those in less cosmopolitan settings. These divergences have always shaped the fortunes of collective descriptors such as "Judeo-Christian" (or even "tri-faith"). In more provincial areas—especially but not exclusively in the South—many have not yet wavered in their sense of America as a Christian nation. Today, liberals in overwhelmingly Protestant contexts might still use Judeo-Christian language to signal their solidarity with non-Protestants, even as many in urban areas scoff at its antiquated ring. And an overwhelmingly white, conservative hard core of Americans will continue to insist that America is a Christian or a Judeo-Christian nation, always and forever. Yet such usages, too, will inevitably reflect new possibilities in the cities, driven by generational changes as well as the inroads of cosmopolitanism, globalization, and hybridization. Millennials and Generation Z, facing the harsh realities of economic insecurity and climate change, will continue to question the values and choices of previous generations, slowly reshaping the contours of American identity even as they fall into more stable patterns as they age. Barring total environmental destruction, the twenty-first-century United States will likely give rise to new possibilities, while continuing to nurture old ones.

The coming decades will also speak to a final, persistent question at the heart of this book: Can people know who they are—as members of national communities, or even as human beings, for that matter—without delineating who they are not? Does identity formation always require a foreign outsider, an enemy within, a threatening Other? If we are currently witnessing a shift from a multireligious America to some new vision, what enemy or enemies haunt that emerging paradigm? If the specter of totalitarianism sustained the tri-faith paradigm, and the specter of terrorism has sustained the multireligious paradigm, what fears and hatreds may lurk in the shadows of the coming era, shaping both individual psyches and group identities while defining the realm of the politically possible?

The divergent examples of Obama and Trump, combined with ongoing shifts in the religious identities and self-understandings of ordinary Americans, suggest that we are entering another period of open-ended conflict over the country's religious identity. In many respects, the current situation mirrors that of the interwar years, when the paradigm of a Protestant America gave way to its Judeo-Christian successor. Of course, contemporary patterns also differ in important ways. But today, as in the 1920s and 1930s, a narrow but well-established conception of American identity—in that case, the equation of Americanism with Protestantism; in this case, the religious right's ideal of a Judeo-Christian America—is coming under fire from critics favoring a range of more inclusive visions, for reasons that reflect deep-seated cultural shifts as well as the political maturation of recently arrived religious minorities and long-standing controversies over sexual politics, immigration, and other issues. In the current climate, some describe the United States as

Abrahamic; others call it multireligious; still others label it secular—or some combination of these and other paradigms. And the words of Obama and Trump suggest that additional possibilities, as yet unrealized, may also be emerging. The future trajectories of Judeo-Christian rhetoric, and the wider cultural currents in which that discourse flows, will tell us a great deal about the twenty-first-century United States—and the dynamics of identity more broadly.

*

At bottom, this book has been an extended meditation on the political importance of language. In the middle decades of the twentieth century, the prevailing religio-political visions in the United States became tied up with Judeo-Christian terminology in ways that continue to resonate down to the present. The fraught history of Judeo-Christian discourse reminds us of the power of our words to fashion our world, even—or perhaps especially—in the age of the sound bite and the tweet. In ways we seldom stop to consider, choosing one word over another can be a profoundly political act, especially when we are describing collective identities and aspirations. In public debate, our word choices are deeply freighted because they convey powerful logics— underlying narrative structures that draw causal, if-then links between particular actions and their likely or threatened consequences. Increasingly, informed democratic participation in a highly diverse and media-driven democracy requires the capacity to read in and around the words of political leaders and commentators, assessing the persuasiveness of their respective visions and ferreting out who might benefit from their formulations. This process of closely reading political rhetoric is at once a practical necessity and an ethical practice. Indeed, the study of history (and the other liberal arts, for that matter) teaches us that all human language simultaneously describes and prescribes. Our word choices reflect real-world arrangements, and they have the power to enact real-world consequences. Words do not always serve single, clearly defined interest groups. Nor do they always work in straightforward and predictable ways. At bottom, however, they do operate as instruments of power that tend to produce winners and losers, if only by training a spotlight on certain actors while consigning others to the shadows.[27]

Above all, the story of America's Judeo-Christian discourse highlights the power of words to simultaneously include and exclude. This paradoxical tendency has characterized all Judeo-Christian formulations, regardless of their intent—just as it does all collective descriptions of human groups. The term "Judeo-Christian" has conveyed dreams of unity and universality that particular subgroups sought to enact but could never fully realize. The story of America's Judeo-Christian discourse, then, underscores both the efficacy and the limitations of our conceptual and linguistic imaginations. Indeed, it highlights the inevitable gap between our ideals and our capacity to realize them—between "the 'isness' of our being" and "the 'ought-ness' of our highest ideals," as Martin Luther King Jr., echoing Reinhold Niebuhr, put it.[28] Calling some users of Judeo-Christian discourse "pluralists" signals their stated ambition to widen the "circle of we" beyond Jewish and Christian confessional boundaries. It does not mean they actually attained the quixotic goal of total inclusion. They clearly could not have done so, since their definition of religious authenticity marginalized or excluded those who did not share their comparatively broad understanding of tolerance. Likewise, labeling others "Judeo-Christian exceptionalists" does not mean they rejected religious diversity per se. Rather, their insistence on the unique relationship between the Judeo-Christian faiths and democracy enforced a narrower definition of religious authenticity that marginalized or excluded wide swaths of the population, both outside and within the Judeo-Christian fold. In other words, these divergent frameworks within America's Judeo-Christian discourse authorized competing patterns of inclusion and exclusion—patterns with tremendous linguistic and political consequences in their day and our own.

Rather than attempt to debunk Judeo-Christian discourse by tracing its history, this book has sought instead to reinvigorate, through description and analysis, our perpetual search for words—whether crafted in past contexts or still waiting to be coined—to help us reimagine American democracy. Even if the vision of a Judeo-Christian America proves to have reached the end of its long career—a prospect I find highly unlikely—we still need to understand its full history in order to chart a linguistic and political path forward. The language of Judeo-Christianity once conveyed many of the hopes and dreams of liberal democracy, as its pivotal role in the civil rights movement attests. Might it, or the successor term "Abrahamic," assume a similarly foundational role in the future? Or could some other collective descriptor—such as "secular," "multireligious," or a term as yet unused—take the place of "Judeo-Christian" in an increasingly diverse and fractured America?[29]

The uncertain future of America's Judeo-Christian discourse also calls into question the "culture wars" framework that has structured so much media commentary on religion and politics in the United States since Ronald Reagan and the religious right rose in tandem. This book has proposed pushing back the origin point of today's conflicts over religio-political issues to the 1940s and 1950s, when Americans disagreed sharply over religion's role in their public institutions. From another angle, however, the preceding chapters also suggest the inadequacy of the culture wars framework itself, at least in its shorthand versions. As that narrative has developed and taken hold, its powerful oppositional logic has evacuated layer after layer of complexity from our public discourse. Its portrayal of American politics as a standoff between Christian conservatives and secular cosmopolitans—an analysis, we should note, that mirrors the Cold War binary of Judeo-Christian democracy and godless communism—enforces a model of religious authenticity based on the views of theologically and socially conservative Christians and hides all other groups from sight. Missing from the culture wars framework are the actual views of a majority of Americans, including progressive evangelicals, Catholics, and Mormons, liberal and mainline Protestants, Jews of every stripe, racial and ethnic minorities within every faith tradition, non-Judeo-Christian minorities (including Muslims, Hindus, Buddhists, and numerous others), those who consider themselves "spiritual but not religious," and the many agnostics and non-believers who do not harbor ill will toward their devout fellow citizens.

Thus, the culture wars narrative teaches media consumers (and scholars of religion, for that matter) a host of false lessons. Among the most damaging are its implications that all theologically conservative Christians are socially conservative, and that all cosmopolitan urbanites are militant secularizers—avowed atheists who have no religious identities, lack robust ethical commitments, and want to stamp out all forms of religion. As our media images and even our polling techniques reanimate and reinscribe the dubious assumptions about religion and ethics that anchor the culture wars paradigm, other religious positions come to seem inauthentic, incongruous, idiosyncratic, or even incoherent.[30] At a time when Americans face enormously consequential political choices, those whose identity commitments disrupt the foundational assumptions of the culture wars framework could play a particularly important role in shaping the country's future by challenging the caricatures produced by that framework and asserting the authenticity of their own positions.

Judeo-Christian discourse has fostered controversy since its inception in the 1930s because that language, like the culture wars idea, has called attention to deeply contested questions about the legitimacy of secularism and unbelief, the promises and perils of pluralism, and the proper place of religious belief in a spiritually and demographically heterogeneous democracy. Does a democracy require a virtuous citizenry? If so, which attributes constitute democratic virtue, and how can they be cultivated? Such thorny political questions have always given America's Judeo-Christian discourse much of its resonance.

And the questions remain, even as our answers and language shift. If we are indeed witnessing the birth of a new era, shorn of the Cold War logic that sustained the tri-faith and multireligious paradigms, this portends significant and wide-ranging consequences for the public culture of the United States, and for the country's role in the world. Whether or not Judeo-Christian visions vanish from the field, the story of America's Judeo-Christian discourse makes one thing abundantly clear: In the future, as in the past, our dreams of America will powerfully shape our language and our actions alike.

Bibliographic Essay

Mark Silk's groundbreaking 1984 article "Notes on the Judeo-Christian Tradition in America" and the corresponding chapter in his book *Spiritual Politics: Religion and America since World War II* (1988) inaugurated the serious historical study of Judeo-Christian formulations and laid out a chronological frame that has proven remarkably durable in the face of the information revolution that has taken place since the 1990s: Judeo-Christian formulations of American democracy and national identity emerged in the late 1930s and then spread widely during World War II, persisting throughout the 1950s and 1960s, before increasingly coming under fire in the 1970s. According to Silk, the "Judeo-Christian tradition," constructed during World War II, became enshrined in national lore during the early Cold War years and played a decisive role in the civil rights movement of the 1950s and 1960s as well. Silk also called attention to the diversity and ambiguity of the meanings assigned to the Judeo-Christian discourse and the lingering opposition to the very use of the concept in certain quarters.

Subsequent scholars, often drawing on Silk's work, have emphasized that liberal campaigns for tolerance, targeting both fascism abroad and anti-Semitism at home, drove Judeo-Christianity's rise to prominence as a descriptor of American democracy and national identity. A classic example is Martin E. Marty's 1986 *Christian Century* article, "A Judeo-Christian Looks at the Judeo-Christian Tradition." There, Marty wrote that the term's orientation had changed markedly in the 1970s and 1980s, when Judeo-Christian discourse became a tool for the promotion of the Christian right's conservative agenda. The earlier uses, he assumed, had been thoroughly liberal and inclusive by contrast.

Between 1998 and 2004, a number of studies fleshed out this account of tri-faith and Judeo-Christian constructions as outgrowths of a liberal antifascism that made Jews full participants in the American project. Deborah Dash Moore turned from public discourse to institutions—in this case, the military branches—in "Jewish GIs and the Creation of the Judeo-Christian Tradition" (1998) and *GI Jews: How World War II Changed a Generation* (2004). Indeed, Moore called the Judeo-Christian tradition "largely a creation of the American military in World War II." Meanwhile, William R. Hutchison, in *Religious Pluralism in America: The Contentious History of a Founding Ideal* (2003), argued that the term "Judeo-Christian" had been largely stripped of its supersessionist meanings and repurposed as a tool for liberal inclusion in the mid-twentieth century. For his part, Stephen Prothero argued in *American Jesus: How the Son of God Became a National Icon* (2003) that Silk had over-emphasized both the extent of Jewish skepticism about the Judeo-Christian discourse and the contributions of "neo-orthodox" Protestants. In fact, he claimed, Jewish thinkers such as the rabbi Stephen S. Wise and the "Jewish Jesus" proponents John Cournos and Sholem Asch had pioneered the term's modern use.

Since 2008, the number of analysts of Judeo-Christianity in the United States has grown considerably and the interpretive landscape has become more diversified. In *Inventing the "American Way": The Politics of Consensus from the New Deal to the Civil Rights Movement* (2008), Wendy L. Wall identified the Judeo-Christian tradition as one of many competing visions of consensus that emerged during the World War II era. J. Terry Todd's 2010 essay "The Temple of Religion and the Politics of Religious Pluralism: Judeo-Christian America at the 1939–1940 New York World's Fair" argued that the "new tri-faith model" of American identity projected by the New York Temple actually embodied a "politics of exclusion" that shut out other religious minorities. (Todd's argument encapsulates the argument of the volume in which it appears, *After Pluralism: Reimagining Religious Engagement* [2010], edited by Courtney Bender and Pamela Klassen.) Meanwhile, Kevin M. Schultz's *Tri-Faith America: How Catholics and Jews Held Postwar America to Its Protestant Promise* (2011) has reinforced the long-standing perception of Judeo-Christian discourse as a tool of liberal inclusion, emphasizing especially the role of the National Conference of Christians and Jews. Ronit Y. Stahl revisited the military side of the story in *Enlisting Faith: How the Military Chaplaincy Shaped Religion and State in Modern America* (2017). On tri-faith visions, see also David Mislin, *Saving Faith: Making Religious Pluralism an American Value at the Dawn of a Secular Age* (2015).

On broader questions about religion in American public life, this book builds on canonical works such as Robert T. Handy's *Undermined Establishment: Church-State Relations in America, 1880–1920* (1991) and especially Robert Wuthnow's *The Restructuring of American Religion: Society and Faith since World War II* (1988). Wuthnow argues that the postwar period witnessed an unprecedented "politicization of religion," a growing liberal-conservative divide within each of America's major religious groups that fostered cross-confessional, religio-political alliances. An even older work, Edward A. Purcell Jr.'s *The Crisis of Democratic Theory: Scientific Naturalism and the Problem of Value* (1973), set the stage for subsequent analyses of debates over the cultural foundations of democracy: see, for example, the writings of Philip Gleason, especially *Speaking of Diversity: Language and Ethnicity in Twentieth-Century America* (1992), and David A. Hollinger, whose *Science, Jews, and Secular Culture* (1996) brings naturalists into the history of religion. On the interwar and postwar transformation of mainline Protestantism in response to growing religious pluralism, as well as the emergence of an interfaith movement among Protestants, Catholics, and Jews in the 1920s, see also Hollinger's *After Cloven Tongues of Fire* (2013) and *Between the Times: The Travail of the Protestant Establishment in America, 1900–1960* (1989), edited by William R. Hutchison. For more on the demographic and cultural shifts brought about by the influx of Catholic and Jewish immigrants between 1880 and 1920, see R. Laurence Moore, *Religious Outsiders and the Making of Americans* (1986). Important recent works on American civil religion include Philip S. Gorski, *American Covenant: A History of Civil Religion from the Puritans to the Present* (2017); Matthew Bowman, *Christian: The Politics of a Word in America* (2018); and Daniel Rodgers, *As a City on a Hill: The Story of America's Most Famous Lay Sermon* (2018).

Religious liberty and church-state relations have generated an explosion of scholarly interest in recent years. Scholars of religion and the law have made decisive contributions in this area, including Winnifred Fallers Sullivan, *The Impossibility of Religious Freedom* (2005); Sarah Barringer Gordon, *The Spirit of the Law: Religious Voices and the Constitution in Modern America* (2010), Steven K. Green, *The Second Disestablishment: Church and State in Nineteenth-Century America* (2010); Linda Przybyszewski, *Religion, Morality, and the Constitution Order: New Essays on American Constitutional History* (2011); and Green, *The Third Disestablishment: Church, State, and American Culture, 1940-1975* (2019). David Sehat's widely heralded *The Myth of American Religious Freedom* (2011) traces the persistence of Protestant renderings of American national identity in the nineteenth and twentieth centuries. Kathleen Holscher addresses church-state questions from the standpoint of local schools in *Religious Lessons: Catholic Sisters and the Captive School Crisis in New Mexico* (2012). Tisa Wenger's *We Have a Religion: The 1920s Pueblo Indian Dance Controversy and American Religious Freedom* (2009) explores how discourses of religious freedom figured in Pueblo resistance to Anglo-Protestant cultural dominance, and Wenger's *Religious Freedom: The Contested History of an American Ideal* (2017) embeds that story in a broader analysis of religious liberty and structures of racial domination.

Chroniclers of American Catholicism have added many insights on the public roles of religion, even as they have insisted that Catholics had little incentive to participate in the Judeo-Christian discourse and plenty of reasons to abstain. Indeed, in *Catholicism and American Freedom* (2003), John T. McGreevy characterized Judeo-Christian formulations as implicitly anti-Catholic, due to their rejection of top-down authority and their emphasis on the prophetic and scriptural foundations of Judeo-Christian faith. On Catholicism and liberalism, see also Jay P. Corrin, *Catholic Intellectuals and the Challenge of Democracy* (2002). At the level of social history, Joshua M. Zeitz's *White Ethnic New York: Jews, Catholics, and the Shaping of Postwar Politics* (2007) offers a fascinating portrait of the ethno-religious dimensions of postwar politics.

In recent years, scholarship on Protestant evangelicals has defined the study of religion and politics and decisively impacted our understanding of American political culture more broadly. Key studies include Darren Dochuk, *From Bible Belt to Sunbelt: Plain-Folk Religion, Grassroots Politics, and the Rise of Evangelical Conservatism* (2012); Matthew Avery Sutton, *American Apocalypse: A History of Modern Evangelicalism* (2014); and Melani McAlister, *The Kingdom of God Has No Borders: A Global History of American Evangelicals* (2018). Conservative evangelicals also figure prominently in the burgeoning literature on the synergism of capitalism and religion: e.g., Bethany Moreton, *To Serve God and Wal-Mart: The Making of Christian Free Enterprise* (2010); Kevin Kruse, *One Nation under God: How Corporate America Invented Christian America* (2015); Kathryn Lofton, *Consuming Religion* (2017); and Darren Dochuk, *Anointed with Oil: How Christianity and Crude Made Modern America* (2019).

Also helpful are several recent books on the intersection between religion, culture, and politics during the interwar and postwar years; see especially Benjamin L. Alpers, *Dictators, Democracy, and American Public Culture: Envisioning the Totalitarian Enemy, 1920s–1950s* (2003); William Inboden, *Religion and American Foreign Policy, 1945–1960: The Soul of Containment* (2008); Diana Selig, *Americans All: The Cultural Gifts Movement* (2008); Andrew Finstuen,

Original Sin and Everyday Protestants: The Theology of Reinhold Niebuhr, Billy Graham, and Paul Tillich in an Age of Anxiety (2010); Mark Thomas Edwards, *The Right of the Protestant Left: God's Totalitarianism* (2012); and Matthew S. Hedstrom, *The Rise of Liberal Religion: Book Culture and American Spirituality in the Twentieth Century* (2013). On war and civil religion, see also Jonathan Ebel, *Faith in the Fight: Religion and the American Soldier in the Great War* (2010); Raymond Haberski Jr., *God and War: American Civil Religion since 1945* (2012); and *From Jeremiad to Jihad: Religion, Violence, and America* (2011), edited by John D. Carlson and Jonathan Ebel. On international relations, see Melani McAlister, *Epic Encounters: Culture, Media, and U.S. Interests in the Middle East since 1945* (rev. ed., 2011), and Andrew Preston, *Sword of the Spirit, Shield of Faith: Religion in American War and Diplomacy* (2012). On the culture wars, see Andrew Hartman, *A War for the Soul of America: A History of the Culture Wars* (2015); and Stephen Prothero, *Why Liberals Win the Culture Wars (Even When They Lose Elections)* (2016). Recent conflicts over sexuality are well covered in books such as Heather R. White, *Reforming Sodom: Protestants and the Rise of Gay Rights* (2015); Anthony M. Petro, *After the Wrath of God: AIDS, Sexuality, and American Religion* (2015); and R. Marie Griffith, *Moral Combat: How Sex Divided American Christians and Fractured American Politics* (2017).

In critical theory and religious studies, a host of recent books have explored how the category of "religion" has been constituted in particular contexts, especially in relation to "secularism" and "pluralism." Key works include Jonathan Z. Smith, "Religion, Religions, Religious," in his *Relating Religion: Essays in the Study of Religion* (2004); Talal Asad, *Genealogies of Religion: Discipline and Reasons of Power in Christianity and Islam* (1993); José Casanova, *Public Religions in the Modern World* (1994); Asad, *Formations of the Secular: Christianity, Islam, Modernity* (2003); David Chidester, *Authentic Fakes: Religion and American Popular Culture* (2005); Tomoko Masuzawa, *The Invention of World Religions: or, How European Universalism Was Preserved in the Language of Pluralism* (2005); Wendy Brown, *Regulating Aversion: Tolerance in the Age of Identity and Empire* (2006); Tracy Fessenden, *Culture and Redemption: Religion, the Secular, and American Literature* (2007); Elizabeth Shakman Hurd, *The Politics of Secularism in International Relations* (2008); Janet R. Jakobsen and Ann Pellegrini, eds., *Secularisms* (2008); Courtney Bender and Pamela E. Klassen, eds., *After Pluralism: Reimagining Religious Engagement* (2010); and Kathryn Lofton, *Oprah: The Gospel of an Icon* (2011). For more historical approaches, see Stephen Prothero, ed., *A Nation of Religions: The Politics of Pluralism in Multireligious America* (2006); Charles Mathewes and Christopher McKnight Nichols, eds., *Prophesies of Godlessness: Predictions of America's Imminent Secularization from the Puritans to the Present Day* (2008); and Charles L. Cohen and Ronald L. Numbers, eds., *Gods in America: Religious Pluralism in the United States* (2013). Helpful accounts of American skeptics include Susan Jacoby, *Freethinkers: A History of American Secularism* (2004); and Leigh Eric Schmidt, *Village Atheists: How America's Unbelievers Made Their Way in a Godly Nation* (2016). From a political-theoretical perspective, Emilio Gentile's *Politics as Religion* (2006) explores the dividing lines that separate religion from politics and the religious from the secular. Much of the recent interest in religion and secularism takes as its starting point the philosopher Charles Taylor's massive study *A Secular Age* (2007).

Notes

Introduction

1. Catherine Albanese has vividly recalled the moment, at a graduate student conference during her final year at the University of Chicago, when her adviser, Jonathan Z. Smith, first posed this question. I have borrowed it here because "How do you dream America?" strikes me as a much preferable alternative to the concept of "civil religion." Albanese, "Echoes of American Civil Religion," *Immanent Frame*, February 12, 2010, https://tif.ssrc.org/2010/02/12/american -civil-religion.

2. Important studies of this discourse and the associated "tri-faith" conception of American identity include Mark Silk, "Notes on the Judeo-Christian Tradition," *American Quarterly* 36, no. 1 (Spring 1984): 65–85; Silk, *Spiritual Politics: Religion and America since World War II* (New York: Simon and Schuster, 1988); Deborah Dash Moore, "Jewish GIs and the Creation of the Judeo-Christian Tradition," *Religion and American Culture* 8, no. 1 (Winter 1998): 31–53; Moore, *GI Jews: How World War II Changed a Generation* (Cambridge: Harvard University Press, 2004); and Kevin M. Schultz, *Tri-Faith America: How Catholics and Jews Held Postwar America to Its Protestant Promise* (New York: Oxford University Press, 2013).

3. An especially good example of the typical approach is William R. Hutchison's *Religious Pluralism in America* (2004). Hutchison, like many other authors, treats the postwar rise of Judeo-Christian formulations as evidence of a gradually widening sphere of inclusion. On the illusory notion of Cold War–era consensus, see Wendy L. Wall, *Inventing the "American Way": The Politics of Consensus from the New Deal to the Civil Rights Movement* (New York: Oxford University Press, 2008); and Alan Brinkley, "The Illusion of Unity in Cold War Culture," in *Rethinking Cold War Culture*, ed. Peter J. Kuznick and James Gilbert (Washington, DC: Smithsonian Institution Press, 2001): 61–73.

4. For instructive uses of "religio-racial," see Judith Weisenfeld, *New World A-Coming: Black Religion and Racial Identity during the Great Migration* (New York: New York University Press, 2016); and Josef Sorett, "Cultural Production and American Religion," in *Proceedings: Fifth Biennial Conference on Religion and American Culture* (Indianapolis, IN: Center for the Study of Religion and American Culture, 2017), 51–53.

5. Like "religio-racial," the term "religio-political" holds considerable explanatory power in

relation to Judeo-Christian discourse. Applying such terms, which are typically used to describe individual or collective identity, to a corporate religious concept such as "Judeo-Christian" opens up a host of compelling questions about American politics and culture in the round. As this book will show, Judeo-Christian discourse features a constant slippage between the ideal and the real that is obscured by debates over whether the discourse is essentially political or religious. Each of those labels captures important dimensions of the discourse, but neither is sufficient; it is both ideological and theological at once. Indeed, the choice of one interpretation over the other obscures key reasons why Judeo-Christian discourse has proven so compelling, for so long, in American public life.

6. My invocation of the phrase "the circle of 'we'" here borrows from David A. Hollinger's essay "How Wide the Circle of 'We'? American Intellectuals and the Problem of the Ethnos since World War II," *American Historical Review* 98, no. 2 (April 1993): 317–37. There, Hollinger admonishes would-be historicists "to acknowledge that the communities providing moral and cognitive standards come into being under a great variety of circumstances, are perpetuated for many distinctive ends, and are driven by very different distributions of power. He writes, "No sooner do we ask, 'How wide the circle of the we?' than we ought to ask, 'What identifies the we?' and 'How deep the structure of power within it?' and 'How is the authority to set its boundaries distributed?'" To this end, Hollinger invokes "Fernand Braudel's dictum that from 'the question of boundaries' all other questions flow: 'To draw a boundary around anything is to define, analyse, and reconstruct it'" (329). Hollinger's attention to boundary-drawing exercises here and elsewhere speaks to the constructed nature of religion as a category. For a widely cited meditation on the binary between "the religious" and "the secular," see Talal Asad, *Formations of the Secular: Christianity, Islam, Modernity* (Stanford: Stanford University Press, 2003). For more on good/bad religion, see Robert A. Orsi, *Between Heaven and Earth: The Religious Worlds People Make and the Scholars Who Study Them* (Princeton: Princeton University Press, 2004).

7. Emmet John Hughes, *The Ordeal of Power: A Political Memoir of the Eisenhower Years* (New York: Atheneum, 1963), 11.

8. Conservative Protestants are the key actors in Kevin M. Kruse, *One Nation under God: How Corporate America Invented Christian America* (New York: Basic Books, 2015).

9. For the latter argument, see Tracy Fessenden, *Culture and Redemption: Religion, the Secular, and American Literature* (Princeton: Princeton University Press, 2007).

10. Recent works that use the Judeo-Christian category in other ways include Andrew Preston, *Sword of the Spirit, Shield of Faith: Religion in American War and Diplomacy* (New York: Knopf, 2012); Cara Lea Burnidge, *A Peaceful Conquest: Woodrow Wilson, Religion, and the New World Order* (Chicago: University of Chicago Press, 2016); David Mislin, *Saving Faith: Making Religious Pluralism an American Value at the Dawn of a Secular Age* (Ithaca: Cornell University Press, 2015); and Ronit Y. Stahl, *Enlisting Faith: How the Military Chaplaincy Shaped Religion and State in Modern America* (Cambridge: Harvard University Press, 2017).

11. Recent histories of American religion have tended to include an even narrower cast of characters, focusing largely on the conservative evangelical Protestants whose views have increasingly become synonymous with the term "religion" in the contemporary United States. Yet this group did not act in isolation from the Catholic, liberal Protestant, Jewish, and secular Americans who were their contemporaries. Scholars should work to reintegrate the history of religious and political conservatism into a broader narrative, featuring a much wider cast of characters.

12. Will Herberg, *Protestant-Catholic-Jew: An Essay in American Religious Sociology* (Garden City, NY: Doubleday, 1955), 274.

13. For a summary of this argument, see K. Healan Gaston, "Demarcating Democracy: Liberal Catholics, Protestants, and the Discourse of Secularism," in *American Religious Liberalism*, ed. Leigh E. Schmidt and Sally M. Promey (Bloomington: Indiana University Press, 2012), 337–58.

14. As I have argued elsewhere, this view undergirded the cultural logic of the Cold War: K. Healan Gaston, "The Cold War Romance of Religious Authenticity: Will Herberg, William F. Buckley Jr., and the Rise of the New Right," *Journal of American History* 99, no. 4 (March 2013): 1109–32.

15. Wendy Brown, *Regulating Aversion: Tolerance in an Age of Identity and Empire* (Princeton: Princeton University Press, 2006); Courtney Bender and Pamela E. Klassen, eds., *After Pluralism: Reimaging Religious Engagement* (New York: Columbia University Press, 2010). "One man's 'cultural pluralism,'" observed Robert Bellah in 1975, can represent "another man's 'nativism,' with all the classic elements of violence and oppression that entails." Bellah, *The Broken Covenant: American Civil Religion in Time of Trial* (New York: Seabury Press, 1975), 110.

16. David Hollinger has noted the crucial role of competing definitions of religious authenticity. He suggests that we ought to think of religious groups—in his case, evangelical Protestantism and Judaism—as representing discrete "model[s] of religious authenticity." "Jewish Intellectuals and the De-Christianization of American Public Culture in the Twentieth Century," in Hollinger, *Science, Jews, and Secular Culture: Studies in Mid-Twentieth-Century American Intellectual History* (Princeton: Princeton University Press, 1996), 31. See also Hollinger's reflections on identity and authenticity in *Postethnic America: Beyond Multiculturalism* (New York: Basic Books, 1995), 119, 160.

17. Matthew Avery Sutton, "Was FDR the Antichrist? The Birth of Fundamentalist Antiliberalism in a Global Age," *Journal of American History* 98, no. 4 (March 2012): 1052–74; Sutton, *American Apocalypse: A History of Modern Evangelicalism* (Cambridge: Belknap Press of Harvard University Press, 2014).

18. On the rejection of Judeo-Christian language by conservative evangelicals, most Catholics, and Mormons, see esp. Neil J. Young, *We Gather Together: The Religious Right and the Problem of Interfaith Politics* (New York: Oxford University Press, 2016).

19. In adopting the heuristic terms "exceptionalist" and "pluralist" for the competing sensibilities that shaped Judeo-Christian discourse, I rejected many promising alternatives, including "exclusivist" and "inclusivist." Some readers will protest that both groups were pluralists of a kind, insofar as each asserted the compatibility of more than one religious confession with democracy. Conversely, it is also possible to regard both groups as species of exceptionalists, since many pluralists were as intolerant of Catholicism and supernaturalism as the more extreme Judeo-Christian exceptionalists were of secularism and naturalism. Other readers might prefer to see pluralists labeled "cosmopolitans" or "universalists." But in much of the literature on American religious diversity and pluralism, these terms tend to connote liberal naïveté of the kind that either expects everyone to magically converge on a single framework of thought or discerns such a framework already in existence beneath all actual differences of opinion. In light of such potential misunderstandings, I opted to highlight the open-ended character of the position by using the term "pluralist," which typically means an expansive orientation that contrasts with exceptionalism's narrower delineation of acceptable faiths. Meanwhile, "exceptionalist" offers the exact connotation needed to describe that position. Its advocates held that certain religious faiths were exceptional in their ability to provide the core tenets of democracy. All of the participants in Judeo-Christian discourse were conceptual innovators, pushing beyond

the narrowly confessional terms employed by their predecessors. But exceptionalists offered a far more specific demarcation of which confessions could support democracy than did their pluralist opponents. Exceptionalists charted a middle path between older, intensely parochial definitions of American national identity and the broad, open-ended tolerance espoused—if not always enacted—by pluralists.

20. Of course, "Judeo-Christian" continues to serve scholars as a professional term of art, although increasingly they either include Islam in the Judeo-Christian fold or use the more inclusive term "Abrahamic." The analysis in this book focuses on the synergism of the Judeo-Christian discourse with democracy, not its specialized scholarly uses.

21. Silk, "Notes on the Judeo-Christian Tradition."

Chapter 1

1. See esp. Tomoko Masuzawa, *The Invention of World Religions* (Chicago: University of Chicago Press, 2005). Cf. Hugh McLeod, *Secularisation in Western Europe, 1848–1914* (New York: St. Martin's, 2000); and J. W. Burrow, *The Crisis of Reason: European Thought, 1848–1914* (New Haven: Yale University Press, 2000).

2. Shalom Goldman, ed., *Hebrew and the Bible in America: The First Two Centuries* (Hanover, NH: University Press of New England, 1993); Goldman, *God's Sacred Tongue: Hebrew and the American Imagination* (Chapel Hill: University of North Carolina Press, 2004).

3. Benedict Anderson, *Imagined Communities: Reflections on the Origin and Spread of Nationalism*, rev. ed. (New York: Verso, 1991).

4. Peter C. Hodgson, *Hegel and Christian Theology: A Reading of the Lectures on the Philosophy of Religion* (New York: Oxford University Press, 2005), 228–37; Hegel quoted in Susannah Heschel, *Abraham Geiger and the Jewish Jesus* (Chicago: University of Chicago Press, 1998), 113; Joël Sebban, "The Genesis of 'Judeo-Christian Morality': On the Origin of an Expression Used in the French Intellectual World," *Revue de l'histoire des religions* 229, no. 1 (2012): 85–118. See also David Lincicum, "F. C. Baur's Place in the Study of Jewish Christianity," in *The Rediscovery of Jewish Christianity from Toland to Baur*, ed. F. Stanley Jones (Atlanta: Society of Biblical Literature, 2012): 137–66; and Emmanuel Nathan and Anna Topolski, eds., *Is There a Judeo-Christian Tradition? A European Perspective* (Boston: De Gruyter, 2016).

5. Masuzawa, *Invention of World Religions*, 147–49.

6. Mark Silk, "Notes on the Judeo-Christian Tradition in America," *American Quarterly* 36, no. 1 (Spring 1984): 71–72; Arnold quoted in John Storey, "Matthew Arnold: The Politics of an Organic Intellectual," *Literature and History* 11, no. 2 (Autumn 1985): 223–25. See also Peter Melville Logan, "Fetishism and Freedom in Matthew Arnold's Cultural Theory," *Victorian Literature and Culture* 31 (2003), esp. 557; and David J. DeLaura, *Hebrew and Hellene in Victorian England: Newman, Arnold, and Pater* (Austin: University of Texas Press, 1969).

7. Quoted in Flavia M. Alaya, "Arnold and Renan on the Popular Uses of History," *Journal of the History of Ideas* 28, no. 4 (October–December 1967): 561. See also Shirley Robin Letwin, "Matthew Arnold: Enemy of Tradition," *Political Theory* 10, no. 3 (August 1982): 339–47; Donald D. Stone, "Arnold, Nietzsche, and the 'Revaluation of Values,'" *Nineteenth-Century Literature* 43, no. 3 (December 1988): 307–9; and Terry G. Harris, "Matthew Arnold, Bishop Joseph Butler, and the Foundation of Religious Faith," *Victorian Studies* 31, no. 2 (Winter 1988): 189–208.

8. Stone, "Arnold, Nietzsche, and the 'Revaluation of Values,'" 307–9; Julian Young, *Nietzsche's Philosophy of Religion* (New York: Cambridge University Press, 2006).

9. In fact, an 1866 article on Renan offered one of the earliest American uses of "Judeo-Christian": "Ernest Renan's 'Les Apotres': Conclusion," *Albion* 44, no. 28 (July 14, 1866): 353.

10. Heschel, *Abraham Geiger and the Jewish Jesus*, 151, 15–16, 162–63; Masuzawa, *Invention of World Religions*, 173–74; David C. J. Lee, *Ernest Renan: In the Shadow of Faith* (London: Duckworth, 1996).

11. Quoted in Masuzawa, *Invention of World Religions*, 174, 177–78.

12. Philip C. Almond, *The British Discovery of Buddhism* (New York: Cambridge University Press, 1988), 126–28; Masuzawa, *Invention of World Religions*, 140–41; Daniel Dubuisson, *The Western Construction of Religion: Myths, Knowledge, and Ideology* (Baltimore: Johns Hopkins University Press, 2003).

13. Hodgson, *Hegel and Christian Theology*, 95–98; Masuzawa, *Invention of World Religions*.

14. "Jacob Frank: Founder of the Sect of Franks in Poland," *Weekly Messenger* 7, no. 2 (September 29, 1841): 1254.

15. W. Bacher, "Judaeo-Christian Polemics in the Zohar," *Jewish Quarterly Review* 3 (July 1891): 781–84; Theodore Dwight Woolsey, "Notice of a Life of Alexander the Great," *Journal of the American Oriental Society* 4 (1854): 410; "The Fifth Gospel," *Chicago Daily Tribune*, June 15, 1879, 9; John Tyndall, "The Sabbath: An Address," *Eclectic Magazine of Foreign Literature* 33, no. 1 (January 1881): F2; H. P. Smith, "Some Recent German Books," *Hebraica* 1, no. 4 (April 1885): 260.

16. Samuel Garner, "Reports," *American Journal of Philology* 3, no. 9 (January 1, 1882): 102. Cf. F. York Powell, "Recent Research on Teutonic Mythology," *Folk-lore* 1, no. 1 (March 1890): 126; and Alfred Nutt, "Celtic Myth and Saga," *Folk-lore* 1, no. 2 (June 1890): 260.

17. *El Paso Herald*, rpt. in "The State Press," *Dallas Morning News*, October 8, 1894, 4.

18. Maurice Bloomfield, "Contributions to the Interpretation of the Veda," *Journal of the American Oriental Society* 16 (1896): 22; cf. J. Estlin Carpenter, "The Place of Immortality in Religious Belief," *New World* 6, no. 24 (December 1897): 608; J. Rendel Harris, "The Grenfell-Hunt Papyri," *Independent* 49, no. 2451 (August 12, 1897): 7.

19. William James, review of *Personal Idealism: Philosophical Essays by Eight Members of the Oxford University*, *Mind*, n.s., 12, no. 45 (January 1903): 96. Cf. Max Radin, *The Jews among the Greeks and Romans* (Philadelphia: Jewish Publication Society of America, 1915).

20. Maurice Vernes, cited in "Notes and Abstracts," *American Journal of Sociology* 9, no. 2 (September 1903): 278.

21. On the humanities, see Bruce Kuklick, "The Emergence of the Humanities," *South Atlantic Quarterly* 81 (1990): 194–206. On Western civilization, see Gilbert Allardyce, "The Rise and Fall of the Western Civilization Course," *American Historical Review* 87, no. 3 (June 1982): 695–725; and James Turner, *The Liberal Education of Charles Eliot Norton* (Baltimore: Johns Hopkins University Press, 1999).

22. Caroline Winterer, *The Culture of Classicism: Ancient Greece and Rome in American Intellectual Life, 1780–1910* (Baltimore: Johns Hopkins University Press, 2002); George M. Fredrickson, *The Inner Civil War: Northern Intellectuals and the Crisis of the Union* (Urbana: University of Illinois Press, 1993).

23. Andrew Jewett, *Science, Democracy, and the American University: From the Civil War to the Cold War* (New York: Cambridge University Press, 2012); T. J. Jackson Lears, *No Place of Grace: Antimodernism and the Transformation of American Culture, 1880–1920* (New York: Pantheon, 1981), esp. 141–81; Nicholas Murray, *A Life of Matthew Arnold* (London: Hodder and Stoughton, 1996).

24. James Freeman Clarke, *Ten Great Religions: An Essay in Comparative Theology* (Boston:

Houghton Mifflin, 1871), vii–viii, ix–x, 29–31; Almond, *British Discovery of Buddhism*, 74. For Clarke's German influences, see John Wesley Thomas, *James Freeman Clarke: Apostle of German Culture to America* (Boston: Luce, 1949), 117–18; and Arthur S. Bolster Jr., *James Freeman Clarke: Disciple to Advancing Truth* (Boston: Beacon, 1954), 293.

25. Lears, *No Place of Grace*, 175–76; Shalom Goldman, introduction to Goldman, ed., *Hebrew and the Bible in America*, xv–xviii, xxvii–xxviii; Goldman, *God's Sacred Tongue*, 201, 235–52; Winterer, *Culture of Classicism*, esp. 10–43; Carl J. Richard, *The Founders and the Classics: Greece, Rome, and the American Enlightenment* (Cambridge: Harvard University Press, 1994).

26. Egal Feldman, *Dual Destinies: The Jewish Encounter with Protestant America* (Urbana: University of Illinois Press, 1990), 123, 139–43; Crawford Howell Toy, *Judaism and Christianity: A Sketch of the Progress of Thought from Old Testament to New Testament* (Boston: Little, Brown, 1890), 39, 45.

27. Turner, *Liberal Education of Charles Eliot Norton*, 384–88, 233–34.

28. William S. Knickerbocker, preface to Matthew Arnold, *Culture and Anarchy* (New York: Macmillan, 1925), xxii. Cf. Paul Elmer More, "Judaeo-Christianity," in More, *The Sceptical Approach to Religion* (Princeton: Princeton University Press, 1934).

29. A classic study of American liberal Protestantism is William R. Hutchison, *The Modernist Impulse in American Protestantism* (Cambridge: Harvard University Press, 1976).

30. W. H. C. Frend, "Church Historians of the Early Twentieth Century: Adolf von Harnack (1851–1930)," *Journal of Ecclesiastical History* 52, no. 1 (January 2001): 83–102; Adolf von Harnack, *What Is Christianity?*, trans. Thomas Bailey Saunders (New York: G. P. Putnam's Sons, 1901).

31. Christopher H. Evans, *The Kingdom Is Always but Coming: A Life of Walter Rauschenbusch* (Grand Rapids, MI: William B. Eerdmans, 2004); Walter Rauschenbusch, *A Theology for the Social Gospel* (New York: Macmillan, 1917), 25.

32. Arthur O. Lovejoy, "Religion and the Time-Process," *American Journal of Theology* 6, no. 3 (July 1902): 448; Daniel J. Wilson, *Arthur O. Lovejoy and the Quest for Intelligibility* (Chapel Hill: University of North Carolina Press, 1980), 22; Lovejoy, "The Origins of Ethical Inwardness in Jewish Thought," *American Journal of Theology* 11, no. 2 (April 1907): 228–49.

33. Lovejoy, "Religion and the Time-Process," 448; Lovejoy, "The Origins of Ethical Inwardness in Jewish Thought," 248–49. Buddhism, like Judaism, served as a major comparison point for Christianity in Lovejoy's early writings: e.g., "The Entangling Alliance of Religion and History," *Hibbert Journal* 5 (1907): 260, 276.

34. Morris Jastrow, *The Study of Religion* (New York: Charles Scribner's Sons, 1901), 78, 76, 220–21, 202, 115. On Jastrow, see Bruce Kuklick, *Puritans in Babylon: The Ancient Near East and American Intellectual Life, 1880–1930* (Princeton: Princeton University Press, 1996); Masuzawa, *Invention of World Religions*, 117–19; and Kathryn Lofton, "Liberal Sympathies: Morris Jastrow and the Science of Religion," in *American Religious Liberalism*, ed. Leigh E. Schmidt and Sally M. Promey (Bloomington: Indiana University Press, 2012): 251–69.

35. Horace M. Kallen, *Judaism at Bay: Essays toward the Adjustment of Judaism to Modernity* (New York: Bloch, 1932), 54–55, 48–49.

36. Ibid., 41, 48, 38–39, 13.

37. Ibid., 8–9, 41, 9–10, 15.

38. Lewis Fried, "Creating Hebraism, Confronting Hellenism: The *Menorah Journal* and Its Struggle for the Jewish Imagination," *American Jewish Archives Journal* 52 (2001): 147–74 (quote on 151); Daniel Greene, *The Jewish Origins of Cultural Pluralism: The Menorah Association and American Diversity* (Bloomington: Indiana University Press, 2011).

39. Oswald Spengler, *The Decline of the West*, trans. Charles Francis Atkinson (New York: A. A. Knopf, 1926).

40. Edwyn R. Bevan and Charles Singer, preface to *The Legacy of Israel*, ed. Bevan and Singer (Oxford: Clarendon Press, 1927), v, xxxv–xxxvi.

41. Diana Selig, *Americans All: The Cultural Gifts Movement* (Cambridge: Harvard University Press, 2008); Horace M. Kallen, "Democracy versus the Melting-Pot," *Nation* 100 (February 18–25, 1915): 190–94, 217–20.

42. Daniel A. Segal, "'Western Civ' and the Staging of History in American Higher Education," *American Historical Review* 105, no. 3 (June 2000): 782, 777–78, 781; Allardyce, "The Rise and Fall of the Western Civilization Course," 706; Peter Novick, *That Noble Dream: The "Objectivity Question" and the American Historical Profession* (New York: Cambridge University Press, 1988). Progressive politics reinforced the orientation toward Europe: Daniel T. Rodgers, *Atlantic Crossings: Social Politics in a Progressive Age* (Cambridge: Belknap Press of Harvard University Press, 1998).

43. Paul Scott Mowrer, "Pan-Latinism Rises as a World Force," *New York Times*, May 8, 1927, SM20. Cf. George Sarton, "The New Humanism," *Isis* 6, no. 1 (1924): 25; and Sarton, "Eighteenth Critical Bibliography of the History and Philosophy of Science and the History of Civilization," *Isis* 8, no. 3 (July 1926): 532.

44. Markku Ruotsila, *John Spargo and American Socialism* (New York: Palgrave Macmillan, 2006), 41–42, 65–67; "'Judeo-Christian' Socialism," *Nation* 102, no. 2644 (March 2, 1916): 257–58; John Spargo, *Marxian Socialism and Religion: A Study of the Relation of the Marxian Theories to the Fundamental Principles of Religion* (New York: B. W. Huebsch, 1915), 176

45. Quoted in Herbert Danby, *The Jew and Christianity: Some Phases, Ancient and Modern, of the Jewish Attitude towards Christianity* (New York: Macmillan, 1927), 110–13, 118. Klausner's book is *Jesus of Nazareth: His Life, Times, and Teaching*, trans. Danby (New York: Macmillan, 1925). For the time being, the older meanings of the compound term "Judeo-Christian" survived even among interfaith activists: e.g., Isidor Singer, *A Religion of Truth, Justice and Peace* (New York: Amos Society, 1924), 279–80; review of Singer, *Religion of Truth*, *Methodist Review* 40, no. 5 (September 1, 1924): 828; Stephen S. Wise quoted in "Praises 'Island Within,'" *New York Times*, April 16, 1928, 26.

46. John Haynes Holmes, "If I Were a Jew!" *The Community Pulpit*, series 1930–31, no. 5, 6; cf. George Foot Moore, rpt. in Singer, *Religion of Truth*, 300.

47. Reinhold Niebuhr, "Hebraism and Hellenism," *The Community Pulpit*, series 1928–29, no. 9, 9, 11, 14.

48. Horace M. Kallen, *Why Religion* (New York: Boni and Liveright, 1927), 40; Kallen, *Culture and Democracy in the United States* (New York: Boni and Liveright, 1924).

49. P. W. Wilson, "An Epic View of Christianity," *New York Times*, December 20, 1931, BR19.

Chapter 2

1. Franklin Hamlin Littell, *From State Church to Pluralism: A Protestant Interpretation of Religion in American History* (New York: Macmillan, 1962), 149; Robert Wuthnow, *The Restructuring of American Religion: Society and Faith since World War II* (Princeton: Princeton University Press, 1988), 18–20.

2. Egal Feldman, *Catholics and Jews in Twentieth-Century America* (Urbana: University of Illinois Press, 2001), 1.

3. John Higham, *Strangers in the Land: Patterns of American Nativism, 1880–1925*, 2nd ed. (New Brunswick: Rutgers University Press, 1988), 194–263; Lynn Dumenil, *The Modern Temper: American Culture and Society in the 1920s* (New York: Hill and Wang, 1995).

4. Benjamin Justice, *The War That Wasn't: Religious Conflict and Compromise in the Common Schools of New York State, 1865–1900* (Albany: State University of New York Press, 2005); Tracy Fessenden, *Culture and Redemption: Religion, the Secular, and American Literature* (Princeton: Princeton University Press, 2007); Steven K. Green, *The Bible, the School, and the Constitution: The Clash That Shaped Modern Church-State Doctrine* (New York: Oxford University Press, 2012); Paula S. Fass, *Outside In: Minorities and the Transformation of American Education* (New York: Oxford University Press, 1989).

5. Judah L. Magnes, "Attitude of the Jews toward Week-Day Religious Instruction," *Religious Education* 11, no. 3 (June 1916): 226–30; Abba Hillel Silver, "The Organized Conspiracy against the Public School" (1924), in Daniel Jeremy Silver, ed., *In the Time of Harvest: Essays in Honor of Abba Hillel Silver* (New York: Macmillan, 1963), 44; Philip R. McDevitt, "The Problem of Curriculum for Week-Day Religious Instruction," *Religious Education* 11, no. 3 (June 1916): 231–38; Floyd S. Gove, *Religious Education on Public School Time* (Cambridge: Harvard University Press, 1926), 119–20.

6. David A. Hollinger, "Jewish Intellectuals and the De-Christianization of American Public Culture in the Twentieth Century," in Hollinger, *Science, Jews, and Secular Culture: Studies in Mid-Twentieth-Century American Intellectual History* (Princeton: Princeton University Press, 1996), 17–41.

7. Shailer Mathews, "Present Co-Operative Action by the Churches," *Biblical World* 49, no. 2 (February 1917): 70.

8. John T. McGreevy, *Catholicism and American Freedom: A History* (New York: W. W. Norton, 2003),182; James Hennesey, SJ, *American Catholics: A History of the Roman Catholic Community in the United States* (New York: Oxford University Press, 1981), 248; David B. Tyack, "The Perils of Pluralism: The Background of the *Pierce* Case," *American Historical Review* 74 (October 1968): 82; Thomas J. Shelley, "The Oregon School Case and the National Catholic Welfare Conference," *Catholic Historical Review* 75, no. 3 (July 1989): 451.

9. Robert A. Slayton, *Empire Statesman: The Rise and Redemption of Al Smith* (New York: Free Press, 2001), 295, 268, 238; McGreevy, *Catholicism and American Freedom*, 148–49; Lawrence H. Fuchs, *The Political Behavior of American Jews* (Glencoe, IL: Free Press, 1965), 66–67; Ronald S. Steel, *Walter Lippmann and the American Century* (New Brunswick, NJ: Transaction, 1999), 247.

10. John Dewey, "Why I Am for Smith," *New Republic* 56 (November 7, 1928): 320–21.

11. Fulton J. Sheen, *God and Intelligence in Modern Philosophy* (New York: Longmans, Green, 1925), 8; William H. Halsey, *The Survival of American Innocence: Catholicism in an Era of Disillusionment, 1920–1940* (Notre Dame: University of Notre Dame Press, 1980), 156–59.

12. McGreevy, *Catholicism and American Freedom*.

13. "Serfs of the State," *America* 32, no. 24 (March 28, 1925): 566–67; Zachary R. Calo, "'The Indispensable Basis of Democracy': American Catholicism, the Church-State Debate, and the Soul of American Liberalism, 1920–1929," *Virginia Law Review* 91 (2005): 1063; "Why Catholics Are Loyal," *America* 31, no. 25 (October 4, 1924): 594.

14. "State Rights and Human Rights" and "Serfs of the State," *America* 32, no. 24 (March 28, 1925): 566–67.

15. Quoted in Calo, "'The Indispensable Basis of Democracy,'" 1046, 1053, 1050–51; John A. Ryan, "Church, State and Constitution," *Commonweal* 5, no. 25 (April 27, 1927): 680.

16. Quoted in Calo, "'The Indispensable Basis of Democracy,'" 1057–58; Carlton J. H. Hayes, "Obligations to America. I. Catholic America," *Commonweal* 1, no. 8 (December 31, 1924): 200–201.

17. "Half-Way Houses," *Commonweal* 5, no. 2 (November 17, 1926): 31–32; Carlton J. H. Hayes, "Obligations to America. III. A Turning Point in History," *Commonweal* 1, no. 10 (January 14, 1925): 255–56; Hayes, "Obligations to America. II. Civic Duties of Catholics," *Commonweal* 1, no. 9 (January 7, 1925): 227–28. Cf. T. Lawrason Riggs, "Religious Tolerance," *Commonweal* 1, no. 3 (November 26, 1924): 60–62; and John A. Ryan, "The Doctrine of Fascism," *Commonweal* 5, no. 2 (November 17, 1926): 42.

18. A. M. Riordan, "Is One Religion as Good as Another?" *America* 31, no. 4 (May 10, 1924): 81; "The Holy Name at Washington," *America* 31, no. 25 (October 4, 1924): 594. Riordan's article nicely summarizes the content of the Catholic secular.

19. Michael Williams, "At Dayton, Tennessee," *Commonweal* 11, no. 2 (July 22, 1925): 265; John McHugh Stuart, "Dark Waters Stirring," *Commonweal* 11, no. 14 (August 12, 1925): 326; T. Lawrason Riggs, "Fundamentalism and the Faith," *Commonweal* 2, no. 15 (August 19, 1925): 344–45; Frederick Joseph Kinsman, "The Writing on the Wall" pt. 2, *Commonweal* 2, no. 17 (September 2, 1925): 388–89.

20. Winfred Ernest Garrison, *Catholicism and the American Mind* (Chicago: Willett, Clark and Colby, 1928), 267.

21. Dumenil, *Modern Temper*, 226–35; Fuchs, *Political Behavior of American Jews*, 190; Hennesey, *American Catholics*, 231–32.

22. Paul S. Boyer, *Purity in Print: The Vice-Society Movement and Book Censorship in America* (New York: Charles Scribner's Sons, 1968); McGreevy, *Catholicism and American Freedom*, 155; Kathleen A. Tobin, *The American Religious Debate over Birth Control, 1907–1937* (Jefferson, NC: McFarland, 2001).

23. George N. Shuster, *The Catholic Spirit in America* (New York: Dial, 1927), 175.

24. Shailer Mathews, in "The Use of the Bible in Public Schools: A Symposium," *Biblical World* 27, no. 1 (January 1906): 61; "An Antidote to Secularism," *America* 31, no. 18 (August 16, 1924): 426–27.

25. "Concerning the Scopes Case," *Commonweal* 2, no. 4 (June 3, 1925): 85–86; Michael Williams, "Summing-Up at Dayton," *Commonweal* 2, no. 13 (August 5, 1925): 305; Williams, "At Dayton, Tennessee," 262–63, 265.

26. "Osborn on Religion," *Commonweal* 3, no. 13 (February 3, 1926): 343; "The Holy Name at Washington," 594; "Why Catholics Are Loyal," 594; Catherine Radziwill, "Bolshevism—A Universal Danger," *Commonweal* 1, no. 24 (April 22, 1925): 655.

27. John A. Ryan, "Legislation and Liberty," *Commonweal* 6, no. 20 (September 21, 1927): 463; "The Organized Minority," *America* 31, no. 21 (September 6, 1924): 499–500; Mark O. Shriver, "Our Changing Constitution," *Commonweal* 5, no. 18 (March 9, 1927): 487–88; NCWC quoted in Elizabeth McKeown, *War and Welfare: American Catholics and World War I* (New York: Garland, 1988), 189; "State Aid for the Catholic School" and "Freedom in Education," *America* 31, no. 26 (October 11, 1924): 619.

28. McGreevy, *Catholicism and American Freedom*, 170; Steel, *Walter Lippmann*, 236; Shuster, *Catholic Spirit*, 281; Morris S. Lazaron, *Common Ground: A Plea for Intelligent Americanism* (New York: Liveright, 1938), 273–74.

29. John A. Ryan, "Fascism in Practice," *Commonweal* 5, no. 3 (November 24, 1926): 74, 76; Harvey Wickham, "The Facts of Fascism," *Commonweal* 5, no. 8 (December 29, 1926): 205.

30. Lawrence G. Charap, "'Accept the Truth from Whomsoever [sic] Gives It': Jewish-Protestant Dialogue, Interfaith Alliances, and Pluralism, 1880–1910," *American Jewish History* 89, no. 3 (September 2001): 268–76; C. E. Silcox and Galen M. Fisher, *Catholics, Jews and Protestants: A Study of Relationships in the United States and Canada* (New York: Harper, 1934), 313–17; Robert T. Handy, *Undermined Establishment: Church-State Relations in America, 1880–1920* (Princeton: Princeton University Press, 1991), 188; Benny Kraut, "A Wary Collaboration: Jews, Catholics, and the Protestant Goodwill Movement," in *Between the Times: The Travail of the Protestant Establishment in America, 1900–1960*, ed. William R. Hutchison (New York: Cambridge University Press, 1989), esp. 196, 198; Higham, *Strangers in the Land*, 279.

31. Benny Kraut, "Towards the Establishment of the National Conference of Christians and Jews: The Tenuous Road to Religious Goodwill in the 1920s," *American Jewish History* 77, no. 3 (March 1988): esp. 392–93, 395, 401; Kraut, "A Wary Collaboration"; NCCJ quoted in C. E. Silcox, "Protestant-Catholic-Jewish Relations: A Seminar at Columbia University," *Religious Education* 24 (March 1929): 207.

32. Kraut, "Towards the Establishment of the National Conference of Christians and Jews"; Silcox and Fisher, *Catholics, Jews and Protestants*, 332–33; Kraut, "A Wary Collaboration," 213–14.

33. Silcox, "Protestant-Catholic-Jewish Relations," 207, 209–10 (quoted), 217; Silcox and Fisher, *Catholics, Jews and Protestants*, 305.

34. Quoted in Silcox, "Protestant-Catholic-Jewish Relations," 215–16.

35. Leo P. Ribuffo, *The Old Christian Right: The Protestant Far Right from the Great Depression to the Cold War* (Philadelphia: Temple University Press, 1983), xii, 4; Matthew Avery Sutton, "Was FDR the Antichrist? The Birth of Fundamentalist Anti-liberalism in a Global Age," *Journal of American History* 98, no. 4 (March 2012): 1052–74; Sutton, *American Apocalypse: A History of Modern Evangelicalism* (Cambridge: Belknap Press of Harvard University Press, 2014).

36. Quoted in Robert A. Slayton, "Al and Frank: The Great Smith-Roosevelt Feud," in *FDR, the Vatican, and the Roman Catholic Church in America, 1933–1945*, ed. David B. Woolner and Richard G. Kurial (New York: Palgrave Macmillan, 2003), 55–56. See also Thomas E. Lifka, *The Concept "Totalitarianism" and American Foreign Policy, 1933–1949* (New York: Garland, 1988), 37; and Hennesey, *American Catholics*, 254.

37. Philip Gleason, "American Catholics and Liberalism, 1789–1960," in *Catholicism and Liberalism: Contributions to American Public Philosophy*, ed. R. Bruce Douglass and David Hollenbach (New York: Cambridge University Press, 1994), 57; Steven M. Avella, "California Catholics and the Gubernatorial Election of 1934," in Woolner and Kurial, *FDR, the Vatican, and the Roman Catholic Church in America*, 68.

38. McGreevy, *Catholicism and American Freedom*, 150–51; Jay P. Corrin, *Catholic Intellectuals and the Challenge of Democracy* (Notre Dame: University of Notre Dame Press, 2002), 220–21; Aaron I. Abell, *American Catholic Thought on Social Questions* (Indianapolis: Bobbs-Merrill, 1968), xxxi-xxxii. For Dewey's views, see Robert B. Westbrook, *John Dewey and American Democracy* (Ithaca: Cornell University Press, 1991), 225–26, 244–49.

39. Anthony Burke Smith, "John A. Ryan, the New Deal, and Catholic Understandings of a Culture of Abundance," in Woolner and Kurial, *FDR, the Vatican, and the Roman Catholic Church in America*, 49, 51; Gerald P. Fogarty, "Roosevelt and the American Catholic Hierarchy," in ibid., 16, 18; Hennesey, *American Catholics*, 259, 269, 195–96, 200–201, 32, 201; Abell, *American Catholic Thought on Social Questions*, xxxi; George Q. Flynn, *American Catholics and the Roosevelt Presidency, 1932–1936* (Lexington: University of Kentucky Press, 1968), 26, 44–45, 49, 195; McGreevy, *Catholicism and American Freedom*, 152–53; Kevin E. Schmiesing, *Within the Market*

Strife: American Catholic Economic Thought from Rerum Novarum to Vatican II (Lanham, MD: Lexington Books, 2004), 102; Wuthnow, *The Restructuring of American Religion*, 6–7; Robert Wuthnow, *The Struggle for America's Soul: Evangelicals, Liberals, and Secularism* (Grand Rapids, MI: William B. Eerdmans, 1989), 108; Lizabeth Cohen, *Making a New Deal: Industrial Workers in Chicago, 1919–1939* (New York: Cambridge University Press, 1990), 221.

40. "The Atheistic College," *America* 56, no. 4 (October 31, 1936): 85; "Communism in the Schools," *America* 56, no. 9 (December 5, 1936): 206; "Dictatorship through the Schools," *America* 55, no. 22 (September 5, 1936): 516–17.

41. George M. Marsden, *Fundamentalism and American Culture: The Shaping of Twentieth-Century Evangelicalism, 1870–1925* (New York: Oxford University Press, 1980), esp. 206–8; Corrin, *Catholic Intellectuals and the Challenge of Democracy*, 272–91. For an early Protestant overture, see J. Gresham Machen, *Christianity and Liberalism* (New York: Macmillan, 1923), 23, 52.

42. Leonard Dinnerstein, "Jews and the New Deal," *American Jewish History* 72, no. 4 (1983): 461–62; Ribuffo, *Old Christian Right*, 17, 157; Ronald H. Carpenter, *Father Charles E. Coughlin: Surrogate Spokesman for the Disaffected* (Westport, CT: Greenwood, 1998), 135; Donald I. Warren, *Radio Priest: Charles Coughlin, the Father of Hate Radio* (New York: Free Press, 1996), 29–30, 26; Alan Brinkley, *Voices of Protest: Huey Long, Father Coughlin, and the Great Depression* (New York: Knopf, 1982), esp. 128–33.

43. Ribuffo, *Old Christian Right*, 116, 91 (quoted), 40, 52–53, 147; Donald S. Strong, *Organized Anti-Semitism in America: The Rise of Group Prejudice during the Decade 1930–40* (Washington: American Council on Public Affairs, 1941), 147.

44. Strong, *Organized Anti-Semitism in America*, 133; John LaFarge, SJ, "Christian Front to Combat Communism," *America* 55, no. 22 (September 5, 1936): 508–10.

45. John P. Diggins, "American Catholics and Italian Fascism," *Journal of Contemporary History* 2, no. 4 (October 1967): 51–68; Hennesey, *American Catholics*, 272; J. David Valaik, "In the Days Before Ecumenism: American Catholics, Anti-Semitism, and the Spanish Civil War," *Journal of Church and State* 13 (1971): 465–77, esp. 470–71; Fogarty, "Roosevelt and the American Catholic Hierarchy," 26, 23, 26, 30. On fascism as the lesser evil, see "Fascism and Communism in Spain," *America* 56, no. 19 (February 13, 1937): 433; Wilfrid Parsons, "Fascist-Communist Dilemma," *Commonweal* 25, no. 16 (February 12, 1937): 429–31; John LaFarge, SJ, "Fascism or Communism: Which the Greater Danger?" *America* 56, no. 1 (October 10, 1936): 4-5; and Wilson D. Miscamble, "The Limits of American Catholic Antifascism: The Case of John A. Ryan," *Church History* 59, no. 4 (December 1990): 533.

46. Stanley Coben, *Rebellion against Victorianism: The Impetus for Cultural Change in 1920s America* (New York: Oxford University Press, 1991).

47. "The Defense of Democracy," *Commonweal* 25, no. 14 (January 29, 1937): 370.

48. *Man and Modern Secularism: Essays on the Conflict of the Two Cultures* (New York: National Catholic Alumni Federation, 1940).

49. John F. O'Hara, *Religion in Education* (n.p., 1936), 4–7.

50. Charles Clayton Morrison, "A Free Church beside a Free State in a Free Society," in *A Forum of Freedom: Findings and Addresses of the National Conference on Religious Liberty*, ed. Rufus W. Weaver (Washington: Continuation Committee on Religious Liberty, 1940), 87; William Adams Brown, *A Creed for Free Men: A Study of Loyalties* (New York: Charles Scribner's Sons, 1941), 225.

51. *The Public Papers and Addresses of Franklin D. Roosevelt*, vol. 8 (New York: Macmillan, 1941), 1–2. A number of widely read online articles have argued that Roosevelt helped establish

the concept of a Judeo-Christian America by speaking broadly of "faith" or "religion" rather than Christianity in particular: e.g., Andrew Preston, "A Very Young Judeo-Christian Tradition," *Boston Globe* online, July 1, 2012, https://www.bostonglobe.com/ideas/2012/06/30/very-young -judeo-christian-tradition/smZoWrkrSLeMZpLou1ZGNL/story.html; Gene Zubovich, "The Strange, Short Career of Judeo-Christianity," *Aeon*, March 22, 2016, https://aeon.co/ideas/the -strange-short-career-of-judeo-christianity. However, Roosevelt's public utterances remained rooted in Christianity, and his desire to keep Catholics and Jews in his Democratic coalition clashed with his private sense that the country still understood itself as Protestant or Christian. To my knowledge, Roosevelt never used Judeo-Christian terminology, despite his occasional references to the tri-faith idea. For a judicious account of early tri-faith initiatives, see David Mislin, *Saving Faith: Making Religious Pluralism an American Value at the Dawn of a Secular Age* (Ithaca: Cornell University Press, 2015).

52. Jones quoted in Edwin E. Aubrey, *Secularism a Myth: Spiritual Values in Secular Culture* (New York: Harper and Brothers, 1954), 17; Grant Wacker, "A Plural World: The Protestant Awakening to World Religions," in Hutchison, *Between the Times*, 259–60; William R. Hutchison, *Errand to the World: American Protestant Thought and Foreign Missions* (Chicago: University of Chicago Press, 1987), 159; "Christian Engineering," *Time*, October 17, 1932. On Jones's role, see also Samuel McCrea Cavert, *The American Churches in the Ecumenical Movement, 1900–1968* (New York: Association Press, 1968), 134. On the Hocking report, see "William Ernest Hocking and the Liberal Protestant Origin of Human Rights," in *Christianity and Human Rights Reconsidered* (forthcoming).

53. Reinhold Niebuhr, *The Nature and Destiny of Man: A Christian Interpretation*, 2 vols. (New York: Charles Scribner's Sons, 1941/1943). "Theological renaissance" is from Douglas Sloan, *Faith and Knowledge: Mainline Protestantism and American Higher Education* (Louisville, KY: Westminster John Knox Press, 1994).

54. Louis Minsky, "The United Front," *Commonweal* 35, no. 17 (February 19, 1937): 457–58; Rabbi Louis L. Mann, "Religious Liberty—The Cornerstone of All Liberties," in Weaver, *Forum of Freedom*, 69.

55. Quoted in Weaver, *Forum of Freedom*, 44; Louis Minsky, "You're a Fascist! And You're a Communist!" *America* 56, no. 25 (March 27, 1937): 582. On the broader history of this charge against Jews, see Paul Hanebrink, *A Specter Haunting Europe: The Myth of Judeo-Bolshevism* (Cambridge, MA: Belknap Press of Harvard University Press, 2018).

56. O'Hara, *Religion in Education*, 9.

57. Edward A. Purcell Jr., *The Crisis of Democratic Theory: Scientific Naturalism and the Problem of Value* (Lexington: University Press of Kentucky, 1973); Lazaron, *Common Ground*, 283–84; Una M. Cadegan, "Guardians of Democracy or Cultural Storm Troopers? American Catholics and the Control of Popular Media, 1934–1966," *Catholic Historical Review* 87, no. 2 (2001): 252–82; Harold Brackman, "The Attack on 'Jewish Hollywood': A Chapter in the History of Modern American Anti-Semitism," *Modern Judaism* 20, no. 1 (February 2000): 1-19; Felicia Herman, "American Jews and the Effort to Reform Motion Pictures, 1933–1935," *American Jewish Archives Journal* 53 (2001): 11–44.

58. Samuel McCrea Cavert, "The Separation of Church and State," in Weaver, *Forum of Freedom*, 78, 80–81, 83.

59. Stephen A. Schmidt, *A History of the Religious Education Association* (Birmingham, AL: Religious Education Press, 1983); John L. Elias, "Catholics in the REA, 1903–1953," *Religious*

Education 99, no. 3 (2004): 225–46, quoted in John Wiltbye, "Public Schools Imperil Religion: Legally Wrong to Teach Children to Be Good," *America* 55, no. 25 (September 26, 1936): 584.

60. Silcox and Fisher, *Catholics, Jews and Protestants*, 331–33; Everett R. Clinchy, *All in the Name of God* (New York: John Day, 1934).

61. Clinchy, *All in the Name of God*, 177–78, 165. Diana Selig analyzes the "cultural gifts" model that Clinchy echoed: *Americans All: The Cultural Gifts Movement* (Cambridge: Harvard University Press, 2008). Benny Kraut notes Clinchy's foreshadowing of Herberg in "A Wary Collaboration," 200.

62. On Hayes, see esp. Patrick Allitt, *Catholic Converts: British and American Intellectuals Turn to Rome* (Ithaca: Cornell University Press, 1997). In a frequently updated volume, Ross lauded church-state separation: *Ethics from the Standpoint of Scholastic Philosophy* (New York: Devin-Adair, 1938), 323–24.

63. Patrick J. Hayes, "J. Elliot Ross and the National Conference of Christians and Jews: A Catholic Contribution to Tolerance in America," *Journal of Ecumenical Studies* 37, no. 3–4 (Summer–Fall 2000): 321–32; Carlton J. H. Hayes, "The Contribution of History to Group Relations," in *The American Way: A Study of Human Relations among Protestants, Catholics, and Jews*, ed. Newton Diehl Baker, Hayes, and Roger Williams Straus (New York: Willett, Clark, 1936), 115, 114; Hayes, "Comments," in ibid., 148, 152.

64. Baker, Hayes, and Straus, *American Way*, 102.

Chapter 3

1. P. W. Wilson, "An Epic View of Christianity," *New York Times*, December 20, 1931, BR19; Wilson, "Man's Hope of Immortal Life," *New York Times*, September 25, 1932, BR10.

2. Representative publications include *Liberty and Religion: A Reply to Certain Bishops* (London: James Clarke, 1906); *A Layman's Confession of Faith* (New York: Fleming H. Revell, 1924); *Is Christ Possible? An Inquiry into World Need* (New York: Fleming H. Revell, 1932); and *Newtopia, the World We Want* (New York: Charles Scribner's Sons, 1941).

3. *C. Silvester Horne, in Memoriam* (London: n.p., 1914).

4. P. W. Wilson, *After Two Years: A Study of American Prohibition* (London: United Kingdom Alliance, 1922): 7, 114.

5. See, for example, P. W. Wilson, *The Irish Case before the Court of Public Opinion* (New York: Fleming H. Revell, 1920). Wilson sharply distinguished Christian universalism from nationalism: "Asia Minor's Leaven of Nationalism," *New York Times*, July 31, 1932, BR9.

6. P. W. Wilson, "The World Stirred by Religious Strife," *New York Times*, September 24, 1933, SM9.

7. Wilson, "World Stirred by Religious Strife," SM18. For other uses of "Judaeo-Christian," see P. W. Wilson, "The Bible as Dr. Fosdick Interprets It," *New York Times*, December 4, 1938, BR9; and Wilson, "Story of the Most-Told of Stories," *New York Times*, December 22, 1935, SM5, SM17.

8. P. W. Wilson, "The Christian Faith through the Ages since Calvary," *New York Times*, June 28, 1931, BR14; Wilson, "Modern Puritans and Parting Ways," *New York Times*, July 2, 1922, 33; Benjamin Alexander Moses Schapiro, *Why I, a Jew, Am a Christian* (New York: Hebrew-Christian Publication Society, 1923). Wilson also supplied the foreword for Schapiro's *Love Begets Love: A Meditation on the Book of Ruth* (New York: Hebrew-Christian Publication Society, n.d.).

On the wider movement, see Michael R. Darby, *The Emergence of the Hebrew Christian Movement in Nineteenth-Century Britain* (Boston: Brill, 2010).

9. "Good-Will Barred to Nazis by Rabbis," *New York Times*, June 16, 1934, 16. The Jewish writer Ludwig Lewisohn, another early user of Judeo-Christian language, may have influenced Wise; see Lewisohn, "The New Kultur," *Nation* 136, no. 3546 (June 21, 1933): 695–96, 695, and Wise's remarks quoted in "Praises 'Island Within,'" *New York Times*, April 16, 1928, 26.

10. "Hope of Protest on Terrorism Seen," *New York Times*, October 23, 1938, 21; "Decalogue Held Antidote to War," *New York Times*, January 28, 1940, 12; "Pitiless Nazism Scored by Rabbis," *New York Times*, May 5, 1940, 27; "Jewish Sermons Plead for Peace," *New York Times*, December 26, 1937, 32; "Democracy's Crisis Is Theme of Rabbis," *New York Times*, April 9, 1939, G6.

11. Roger Williams Straus, *Religious Liberty and Democracy: Writings and Addresses* (New York: Willett, Clark, 1939), ix, 44; Isaac E. Marcuson, ed., *Proceedings of the Fiftieth Annual Convention of the Central Conference of American Rabbis* 49 (Washington: Central Conference of American Rabbis, 1939), 205–6; "Rabbis Invoke Aid of God for Britain," *New York Times*, September 29, 1940, 6.

12. "Rabbis Bid World to Repent Its Sins," *New York Times*, October 12, 1940, 17; "'Jesus vs. Hitler,' Topic of Sermon by Rabbi Wise," *Boston Globe*, January 13, 1941, 5.

13. Maurice Samuel, *The Great Hatred* (New York: A. A. Knopf, 1940); Philip S. Bernstein, "The Roots of Anti-Semitism," *Nation* 151, no. 23 (December 7, 1940): 578; Koppel S. Pinson, review of Samuel, *The Great Hatred*, *American Historical Review* 46, no. 4 (July 1941): 964.

14. Eugene S. Tanner, review of Sholem Asch, *The Nazarene*, *Journal of Bible and Religion* 8, no. 2 (May 1940): 100; "Religious Books Recently Published," *New York Times*, May 17, 1941, 13.

15. Stephen Prothero, *American Jesus: How the Son of God Became a National Icon* (Farrar, Straus and Giroux, 2003), 258–61, 231, 253; John Cournos, "An Epistle to the Jews," *Atlantic Monthly*, December 1937, 723–38; "Totalitarianism Is Scored: Dr. Wise Declares Jews Cannot Believe in 'Christ of Dogma,'" *New York Times*, April 18, 1938, 15.

16. Victor J. Bondi, "The Origins of the Theory of Totalitarianism" (PhD diss., Boston University, 1993), 2; Thomas E. Lifka, *The Concept "Totalitarianism" and American Foreign Policy, 1933–1949* (New York: Garland, 1988), 8–10, 15; Walter Lippmann, "Autocracy versus Catholicism," *Commonweal* 5, no. 23 (April 13, 1927): 627; Giovanni Gentile, "The Philosophic Basis of Fascism," *Foreign Affairs* 6, no. 2 (January 1928): 290–304. For more on early uses of the term, see also Benjamin L. Alpers, *Dictators, Democracy, and American Public Culture: Envisioning the Totalitarian Enemy, 1920s–1950s* (Chapel Hill: University of North Carolina Press, 2003).

17. Lippmann, "Autocracy versus Catholicism," 627.

18. Lifka, *The Concept "Totalitarianism" and American Foreign Policy, 1933–1949*, 13, 15–16, 22, 46–47, 38.

19. E.g., George F. Thomas, "Myth and Symbol in Religion," *Journal of Bible and Religion* 7, no. 4 (November 1939): 167.

20. Paul Tillich, "The Totalitarian State and the Claims of the Church," *Social Research* 1, no. 4 (November 1934): 405–33; Reinhold Niebuhr, "Religion and the New Germany," *Christian Century* 50, no. 26 (June 28, 1933): 843–45.

21. Richard Wightman Fox, *Reinhold Niebuhr: A Biography* (Ithaca: Cornell University Press, 1985), 147–50; Reinhold Niebuhr, *Reflections on the End of an Era* (New York: Charles Scribner's Sons, 1934), 201; Niebuhr, "Optimism, Pessimism and Religious Faith" (1934), reprinted in *Christianity and Power Politics* (New York: Charles Scribner's Sons, 1940), 180.

22. Reinhold Niebuhr, "Why German Socialism Crashed," *Christian Century* 50, no. 14

(April 5, 1933): 451–53; Niebuhr, "Notes from a London Diary," *Christian Century* 50, no. 28 (July 12, 1933): 903–4; Niebuhr, "A Christian Philosophy of Compromise," *Christian Century* 50, no. 23 (June 7, 1933): 746–48.

23. John Alexander Mackay, "The Titanic Twofold Challenge," *New York Times*, May 7, 1939, SM1.

24. Ibid.

25. Dorothy Thompson, "On the Record: Goering and the Prodigal Son," *Boston Globe*, October 27, 1937, 16; Thompson, "On the Record: To a Jewish Friend," *Washington Post*, November 14, 1938, X9; Thompson, "On the Record: V—There Is a Tide," *Washington Post*, December 27, 1939, 7; Thompson, "Which New Order? Our Opportunity and Our Aim," *Washington Post*, December 23, 1940, 13.

26. Clinchy quoted in Dr. Herman L. Turner, "Happenings in Church World," *Atlanta Constitution*, January 15, 1939, 3K; F. Ernest Johnson, "Religion and the Philosophy of Education," *Vital Speeches of the Day* 7, no. 2 (November 1, 1940): 39 (cf. William Scott, "The Teaching of Religion and the Democratic Ideal," *Journal of Bible and Religion* 8, no. 1 [February 1940]: 4); Henry A. Wallace, "Judaism and Americanism," *Menorah Journal* 28, no. 2 (July–September 1940): 127, 137.

27. John T. McGreevy, *Catholicism and American Freedom: A History* (New York: W. W. Norton, 2003), 176.

28. Jacques Maritain, *Some Reflections on Culture and Liberty* (Chicago: University of Chicago Press, 1933), 25; Maritain and Mary Morris, "Sign and Symbol," *Journal of the Warburg Institute* 1, no. 1 (July 1937): 9; Maritain, *True Humanism* (New York: Charles Scribner's Sons, 1938), 39; Maritain, "The Immortality of Man," *Review of Politics* 3, no. 4 (October 1941): 422.

29. Carlton J. H. Hayes, *Essays on Nationalism* (New York: Macmillan, 1926), 1, 12, 26, 104–5, 109–10.

30. Ibid., 115, 29, 117, 104, 124–25, 114.

31. Ibid., 114, 113, 258–59, 209, 121, 118–19; Hayes, "The Contribution of History to Group Relations," in *The American Way: A Study of Human Relations among Protestants, Catholics, and Jews*, ed. Newton Diehl Baker, Hayes, and Roger Williams Straus (New York: Willett, Clark, 1936), 114–15.

32. Hayes, *Essays on Nationalism*, 213–15, 204–6, 200–202.

33. Ibid., 97, 99–100, 93, 258. On Hayes, see Edward Mead Earle, introduction to *Nationalism and Internationalism: Essays Inscribed to Carlton J. H. Hayes*, ed. Earle (New York: Columbia University Press, 1950), xiv; and Patrick Allitt, "Carlton Hayes and His Critics," *U.S. Catholic Historian* 15, no. 3 (Summer 1997): 23–37.

34. Carlton J. H. Hayes, "From One Age to Another," *Commonweal* 21, no. 2 (November 2, 1934): 12–13; Hayes, "The Challenge of Totalitarianism," *Public Opinion Quarterly* 2, no. 1 (January 1938): 22–23

35. Hayes, "The Challenge of Totalitarianism," 22–23.

36. Carlton J. H. Hayes, "The Novelty of Totalitarianism in the History of Western Civilization," *Proceedings of the American Philosophical Society* 82, no. 1 (February 1940): 96–97, 93–94.

37. Ibid., 95–96, 101–2.

38. Ibid., 97–98.

39. The English-language literature on personalism, particularly in its Catholic form, is spotty. The best overviews are Kevin Schmiesing, "A History of Personalism," available at https://papers.ssrn.com/sol3/papers.cfm?abstract_id=1851661; and Thomas D. Williams and Jan

Olof Bengtsson, "Personalism," in *Stanford Encyclopedia of Philosophy* (Winter 2018 ed.), ed. Edward N. Zalta, https://plato.stanford.edu/archives/win2018/entries/personalism. On Catholic formulations, see also John Hellman, *Emmanuel Mounier and the New Catholic Left, 1930–1950* (Buffalo, NY: University of Toronto Press, 1981); and Mark Zwick and Louise Zwick, *The Catholic Worker Movement: Intellectual and Spiritual Origins* (Mahwah, NJ: Paulist Press, 2005).

40. John Macmurray, *Creative Society: A Study of the Relation of Christianity to Communism* (New York: Association Press, 1936), 55–56, 59, 115. See also Macmurray, *The Clue to History* (New York: Harper, 1939); and Mark Bevir and David O'Brien, "From Idealism to Communitarianism: The Inheritance and Legacy of John Macmurray," *History of Political Thought* 24, no. 2 (Summer 2003): 305–29.

41. Herbert Agar et al., *The City of Man: A Declaration on World Democracy* (New York: Viking Press, 1940), 27–28, 32.

42. Ibid., 34–35, 41, 43.

43. Robert O. Ballou, ed., *The Bible of the World* (New York: Viking, 1939).

44. "Houck Names Stars to Guide Our Destiny," *New York Times*, December 1, 1941, 14.

45. "Peace Aims Hailed as War Weapon," *New York Times*, August 17, 1941, 29; Albert J. Gordon, "Unity of Faiths Is Urged in Crisis," *New York Times*, August 31, 1941, 20; advertisement, *New York Times*, September 21, 1941, BR33; "Bible's Influence in War Stressed," *New York Times*, December 7, 1941, 58.

46. "Strengthened Bond between World Religions Seen as Result of Chaos of 20th Century," *Los Angeles Times*, March 30, 1941, 10; Beatrice Jenney, ed., *Protestants Answer Anti-Semitism* (New York: Protestant Digest, 1941), quoted in Mark Silk, *Spiritual Politics: Religion and America since World War II* (New York: Simon and Schuster, 1988), 41.

47. Urey quoted in "Berle Sees Nazis Losing Strength," *New York Times*, September 9, 1941, 26; Muzumdar quoted in Matthew Benjamin Shindell, "The New Prophet: Harold C. Urey, Scientist, Atheist, and Defender of Religion" (PhD diss., University of California, San Diego, 2011), 257–58; "Text of Sermon Outline Suggested by Mayor La Guardia to Pastors," *New York Times*, November 9, 1941, 32.

48. Thomas F. Woodlock, "Thinking It Over," *Wall Street Journal*, December 9, 1940, 4; Francis E. McMahon, review of *The City of Man*, *Review of Politics* 4, no. 3 (July 1942): 363–64.

49. John F. Cronin, "Catholicism and Democracy: Is the Church of Rome on the Side of Democracy or Totalitarianism?" *Common Sense* 9 (October 1940): 3-6; Gordon, "Unity of Faiths Is Urged in Crisis," 20; Carlton J. H. Hayes, *A Generation of Materialism, 1871–1900* (New York: Harper, 1941), 135; Walter W. Ruch, "Calls Nazi Way Alien to Church," *New York Times*, November 19, 1941, 11.

50. Louis Finkelstein, J. Elliot Ross, and William Adams Brown, *The Religions of Democracy: Judaism, Catholicism, and Protestantism in Creed and Life* (New York: Devin-Adair, 1941), iv. William R. Hutchison interprets this book as a paradigmatic statement of pluralistic liberalism: *Religious Pluralism in America: The Contentious History of a Founding Ideal* (New Haven: Yale University Press, 2003).

51. Robert A. Ashworth, preface to Finkelstein, Ross, and Brown, *Religions of Democracy*, iv–viii.

52. J. Elliot Ross, "The Roman Catholic Religion in Creed and Life," in ibid., 161–62, 165, 167, 154. On Ross, see Patrick J. Hayes, "J. Elliot Ross and the National Conference of Christians and Jews: A Catholic Contribution to Tolerance in America," *Journal of Ecumenical Studies* 37, no. 3-4 (Summer–Fall 2000): 321–32.

53. Louis Finkelstein, "The Beliefs and Practices of Judaism," in Finkelstein, Ross, and Brown, *Religions of Democracy*, 6-7; Finkelstein, "Faith for Today: A Jewish Viewpoint," in Stanley High et al., *Faith for Today: Five Faiths Look at the World* (Garden City, NY: Town Hall, 1941), 160–62, 181–82, 173.

54. Gerald Groveland Walsh, "Faith for Today: A Catholic Statement," in High et al., *Faith for Today*, 150, 123–24, 99–100, 130, 150.

55. Stanley High, "Religion," in ibid., 16–18, 7-9, 19–20, 24–25.

56. George V. Denny Jr., introduction to ibid., xi, viii. Even Denny, however, argued that secular education inculcated "a philosophy of expediency rather than justice." "Postscript," in ibid., 259–60.

57. Frank Kingdon, "Faith as Experience," in ibid., 41–42, 47, 62–63, 77, 74; Swami Nikhilananda, "Faith for Today: The Hindu Viewpoint," in ibid., 233–34, 228, 244, 188, 192, 216, 219.

Chapter 4

1. Hyman J. Schachtel quoted in "Triumph of Godly over Nazis Seen," *New York Times*, December 27, 1942, 9; "Essayists Appeal for World Unity," *New York Times*, April 8, 1943, 19.

2. F. Ernest Johnson, introduction to *Religion and the World Order: A Series of Addresses and Discussions*, ed. Johnson (New York: Institute for Religious Studies, 1944); Edward A. Purcell Jr., *The Crisis of Democratic Theory: Scientific Naturalism and the Problem of Value* (Lexington: University Press of Kentucky, 1973). For Johnson's exceptionalist answer, see his "Religious Liberty," *Christendom* 9, no. 2 (Spring 1944): 181–94.

3. Walter M. Horton, "Chasms and Bridges between Christianity and Judaism," in *Approaches to Group Understanding*, ed. Lyman Bryson, Louis Finkelstein, and Robert M. MacIver (New York: Harper and Brothers, 1947), 745.

4. Deborah Dash Moore, "Jewish GIs and the Creation of the Judeo-Christian Tradition," *Religion and American Culture* 8, no. 1 (Winter 1998): 31–53. On the *Dorchester* incident, see also William R. Hutchison, *Religious Pluralism in America: The Contentious History of a Founding Ideal* (New Haven: Yale University Press, 2003).

5. Stephen S. Wise, ed., *Never Again! Ten Years of Hitler: A Symposium* (New York: Jewish Opinion Publishing Corporation, 1943). The volume also included Israel Goldstein, a frequent user of Judeo-Christian formulations before American intervention.

6. "Church Report Protests Jews' Persecution," *Washington Post*, May 8, 1943, 12; Kevin M. Schultz, *Tri-Faith America: How Catholics and Jews Held Postwar America to Its Protestant Promise* (New York: Oxford University Press, 2011), 16, 58, 61. The NCCJ itself occasionally used Judeo-Christian rhetoric in association with its annual Brotherhood Week, but it did not always do so. See, for example, "25th Annual Brotherhood Week Observation Starts Sunday," *Baltimore Afro-American*, February 21, 1953, 8; "Significance of National Brotherhood Week Explained," *Norfolk Journal and Guide*, February 21, 1953, 22; and "Today to Mark Opening of Brotherhood Week," *Los Angeles Times*, February 20, 1955, A10.

7. William Scott, "The Teaching of Religion and the Democratic Ideal," *Journal of Bible and Religion* 8, no. 1 (February 1940): 4; Eugene S. Tanner, review of Sholem Asch, *The Nazarene*, *Journal of Bible and Religion* 8, no. 2 (May 1940): 100.

8. Nikolai Berdyaev, *Slavery and Freedom* (New York: Charles Scribner's Sons, 1944), 14.

9. Charles Clayton Morrison, *Can Protestantism Win America?* (New York: Harper, 1948); Morrison, "A Free Church beside a Free State in a Free Society," in *A Forum of Freedom: Findings*

and Addresses of the National Conference on Religious Liberty, ed. Rufus W. Weaver (Washington: Continuation Committee on Religious Liberty, 1940), 87, 96.

10. For more on these dynamics, see esp. Mark Edwards, *The Right of the Protestant Left: God's Totalitarianism* (New York: Palgrave Macmillan, 2012).

11. Douglas Sloan, *Faith and Knowledge: Mainline Protestantism and American Higher Education* (Louisville, KY: Westminster John Knox Press, 1994); Clarence Prouty Shedd, "Religion in the Colleges," *Journal of Bible and Religion* 8, no. 4 (November 1940): 179, 182; "Conversations on Higher Education and Religion," *Hazen Pamphlets* 3 (New York: Edward H. Hazen Foundation, 1942), 18, 20; H. Shelton Smith, review of Hugh Stevenson Tigner, *No Sign Shall Be Given*, *Journal of Religion* 23, no. 2 (April 1943): 151. Cf. Arnold S. Nash, *The University and the Modern World: An Essay in the Philosophy of University Education* (New York: Macmillan, 1943), 93, 253.

12. Luther A. Weigle, "Public Education and Religion," *Religious Education* 35, no. 2 (April–June 1940): 70–74; *Christian Education Today: A Statement of Basic Philosophy* (Chicago: International Council of Religious Education, 1940), 3, 10, 146–47.

13. Quoted in Paul M. Limbert, "F. Ernest Johnson: Prophetic Interpreter of Christian Ethics (1885–1969)," *Religious Education* 64, no. 6 (November–December 1969): 500; F. Ernest Johnson, "Democracy and Discipline," *Christianity and Crisis* 3, no. 21 (December 13, 1943): 1–2; Johnson, "Contemporary Secularism as an Impediment to Religious Effort," in Johnson, *Religion and the World Order*, 11. For Johnson's critique of the Reformation, see "Religion and the Philosophy of Education: Interpretive Forces in Human Life," *Vital Speeches of the Day* 7, no. 2 (November 1940): 35–39.

14. F. Ernest Johnson, "Religious Liberty," *Christendom* 9, no. 2 (Spring 1944): 183, 185 (quoting Frankfurter), 187–88, 186. By contrast, the *Christian Century* endorsed the decision: "Religious Liberty and Fraud," *Christian Century* 61, no. 19 (May 10, 1944): 585.

15. Johnson, "Religious Liberty," 188–92, 194. Cf. Gregory Vlastos, "The Religious Foundations of Democracy, Fraternity and Liberty," *Journal of Religion* 22, no. 1 (January 1942): 1–19.

16. John H. Hallowell, *The Decline of Liberalism as an Ideology, with Particular Reference to German Politico-Legal Thought* (Berkeley and Los Angeles: University of California Press, 1943), 17–20, 71–72, 108–11, 118–19.

17. Reinhold Niebuhr, "A Faith for History's Greatest Crisis," *Fortune* 26 (1942) 99–100, 122, 125, 126, 128, 131, at 99–100; Niebuhr, *The Children of Light and the Children of Darkness: A Vindication of Democracy and a Critique of Its Traditional Defense* (New York: Charles Scribner's Sons, 1944), xv, 135; K. Healan Gaston, "'A Bad Kind of Magic': The Niebuhr Brothers on 'Utilitarian Christianity' and the Defense of Democracy," *Harvard Theological Review* 107, no. 1 (January 2014): 1–30.

18. John A. Mackay, *Heritage and Destiny* (New York: Macmillan, 1943), 15, 22, 82–83, 85–88; Mackay, "Emergent Clericalism," *Christianity and Crisis* 5, no. 2 (February 19, 1945): 1. See also James Leo Garrett, "John A. Mackay on the Roman Catholic Church," *Journal of Presbyterian History* 50, no. 2 (Summer 1972): 111–28.

19. M. Searle Bates, *Religious Liberty: An Inquiry* (New York: International Missionary Council, 1945), 310, 312–14, 324–25, 339.

20. "Religious Training in Schools Urged," *New York Times*, June 5, 1940, 21.

21. E.g., "Laski Is Assailed on Vatican Attack: Commander of Catholic War Veterans Charges Insult to Millions of Americans," *New York Times*, October 9, 1945, 2.

22. J. Elliot Ross, "Catholics and Anti-Semitism," *Ecclesiastical Review* 10, no. 5 (May 1939): 416, 418; Ross, *Jews Should Be More Jewish* (New York: n.p., 1942), n.p.; Ross, "The Roman

Catholic Religion in Creed and Life," in Louis Finkelstein, Ross, and William Adams Brown, *The Religions of Democracy: Judaism, Catholicism, Protestantism in Creed and Life* (New York: Devin-Adair, 1941), 160.

23. Connell cited in John Courtney Murray, "Current Theology: Christian Co-operation," *Theological Studies* 3 (September 1942): 414–15; Vincent A. Brown, "Cooperating with Non-Catholics," *Ecclesiastical Review* 108, no. 5 (May 1943): 386.

24. Quoted in John LaFarge, SJ, "Some Questions as to Interdenominational Cooperation," *Theological Studies* 3, no. 3 (September 1942): 325–26; Carlton J. H. Hayes, "In Summary," in *The American Way: A Study of Human Relations among Protestants, Catholics, and Jews*, ed. Newton Diehl Baker, Hayes, and Roger Williams Straus (New York: Willett, Clark, 1936), 152.

25. Quoted in LaFarge, "Some Questions as to Interdenominational Cooperation," 325–26.

26. Hayes quoted in ibid., 325–26; Francis J. Connell, "To the Editor," *Theological Studies* 3, no. 4 (December 1942): 622, 621; Connell quoted in Murray, "Current Theology: Christian Co-operation," 414, 416. Cf. Paul Hanly Furfey, "To the Editor," *Theological Studies* 4 (September 1943): 468; Furfey, "Intercredal Co-operation: Its Limitations," *American Ecclesiastical Review* 111, no. 3 (September 1944): 161–75; and Elmer A. McNamara, "Brotherhood, Unity, and Christ," *Ecclesiastical Review* 105, no. 3 (September 1941): 211–18.

27. Carlton J. H. Hayes, "To the Editor," *Theological Studies* 4, no. 2 (June 1943): 315–16.

28. Jacques Maritain, *Some Reflections on Culture and Liberty* (Chicago: University of Chicago Press, 1933), 4, 2; Maritain, *A Christian Looks at the Jewish Question* (New York: Longmans, Green, 1939); Maritain, *The Rights of Man and Natural Law* (New York: Charles Scribner's Sons, 1943), 23–25, 30, 33.

29. John Courtney Murray, *Matthias Scheeben on Faith* (1937), Toronto Studies in Theology, vol. 29 (1987); Murray, "Current Theology: Intercredal Co-operation: Its Theory and Its Organization," *Theological Studies* 4 (June 1943): 257–86; Murray, "Necessary Adjustments to Overcoming Practical Difficulties," in *Man and Modern Secularism: Essays on the Conflict of the Two Cultures* (New York: National Catholic Alumni Federation, 1940), 155; Murray, "To the Editor," *Theological Studies* 4 (September 1943): 472; Murray, "Current Theology: Christian Co-operation," 421.

30. See esp. John Courtney Murray and the Ethics Committee, *The Pattern for Peace and the Papal Peace Program* (Washington: Catholic Association for International Peace, 1944) and Murray, "Freedom of Religion, I. The Ethical Problem," *Theological Studies* 6 (June 1945): 229–86.

31. John Courtney Murray, "Towards a Theology for the Layman: The Pedagogical Problem," *Theological Studies* 5 (September 1944): 350–51; Murray, "On the Problem of Co-operation: Some Clarifications," *American Ecclesiastical Review* 112 (March 1945): 214; Murray, "To the Editor," 472–74; Murray, "Current Theology: Christian Co-operation," 413, 425, 428, 430; Murray, "Current Theology: Intercredal Co-operation," 260, 262, 274, 276–77; Murray, "Current Theology: Co-operation: Some Further Views," *Theological Studies* 4 (March 1943): 105–11.

32. Murray and the Ethics Committee, *The Pattern for Peace and the Papal Peace Program*, 2, 31–32 (quoted), 3, 16, 25, 11–12. For signatories, see "Religious Leaders Issue Peace Plan," *New York Times*, October 7, 1943, 15.

33. "Catholics Will Collaborate!" *Christian Century* 56, no. 1 (January 5, 1944): 6–7.

34. "No Truce between Russia and the Vatican," *Christian Century* 61, no. 7 (February 16, 1944): 196; "Collaboration without Compromise," *Christian Century* 61, no. 35 (August 30, 1944): 990–92.

35. Murray, "Current Theology: Freedom of Religion," *Theological Studies* 6 (March 1945):

106–7, 109–11, 102, 94–95; Murray, "Freedom of Religion, I. The Ethical Problem," 244–46, 249, 263, 255–56.

36. Murray, "Freedom of Religion, I. The Ethical Problem," 242–43, 263.

37. Murray, "Current Theology: Freedom of Religion," 109, 102–3, 107; Murray, "Freedom of Religion, I. The Ethical Problem," 262–63, 255–56, 258, 269–70.

38. Murray, "Freedom of Religion, I. The Ethical Problem," 269–70, 252–53, 266; Murray, "Current Theology: Freedom of Religion," 97, 104.

39. Murray, "Freedom of Religion, I. The Ethical Problem," 279–81, 284–86.

40. John Gilland Brunini, review of Finkelstein, Ross, and Brown, *The Religions of Democracy*, *Commonweal* 34, no. 23 (March 28, 1941): 577.

41. Jerome Nathanson, preface to *The Authoritarian Attempt to Capture Education: Papers from the Second Conference on the Scientific Spirit and Democratic Faith* (New York: King's Crown Press, 1945), v; Sidney Hook, "Sidney Hook Holds Conference a Direct Threat to the Liberal Tradition," *Humanist* 3, no. 1 (Spring 1943): 38; Max Savelle, "The Flight from Reason," *Journal of Modern History* 17, no. 1 (March 1945): 160.

42. Mackay, *Heritage and Destiny*, 27, 33; Mackay quoted in Samuel McCrea Cavert to H. Richard Niebuhr, January 14, 1939, folder 9, box 1, H. Richard Niebuhr Papers, Andover-Harvard Theological Library, Harvard Divinity School.

43. Marc Dollinger, *Quest for Inclusion: Jews and Liberalism in Modern America* (Princeton: Princeton University Press, 2000), 61, 73, 78; Paul Winkler, "Program of Death," *Washington Post*, December 16, 1943, 14.

44. Theodor H. Gaster, "A Judeo-Christian Civilization?" *Commentary* 1, no. 5 (March 1946): 91; Joshua Bloch, "Rab Saadia Gaon," *Jewish Quarterly Review*, n.s. 36, no. 1 (July 1945): 83; Frederick Burkhardt, "Democracy and Our Religious Heritage," *Humanist* 3, no. 1 (Spring 1943): 21, 23; Daniel D. Williams, review of George F. Thomas, ed., *The Vitality of the Christian Tradition*, *Journal of Religion* 25, no. 3 (July 1945): 218–19.

45. Horace M. Kallen, "Jewish Right, Christian Power," *Contemporary Jewish Record* 6, no. 6 (December 1943): 563, 577; Kallen, "Of Humanistic Sources of Democracy," *Journal of Legal and Political Sociology* 4, nos. 1-2 (Winter 1945–1946): 53–75.

46. John Dewey, "President Hutchins' Proposals to Remake Higher Education," in *The Later Works, 1925–1953*, vol. 11, ed. Jo Ann Boydston (Carbondale: Southern Illinois University Press, 1981), 400.

47. Horace M. Kallen, "Of the American Spirit: An Open Letter to Teachers of English," *English Journal* 35, no. 6 (June 1946): 290–91; J. Hutton Hynd, "The Greatest Hoax in History—The Claim to Infallibility," *Humanist* 5, no. 2 (Summer 1945): 56, 59; Edwin H. Wilson, "Clerical Fascism and Totalitarianism," *Humanist* 5, no. 1 (Spring 1945): 52, 49, 52.

48. Louis Finkelstein, "Faith for Today: A Jewish Viewpoint," in Stanley High et al., *Faith for Today: Five Faiths Look at the World* (Garden City, NY: Town Hall, 1941), 181; quoted in James Gilbert, *Redeeming Culture: American Religion in an Age of Science* (Chicago: University of Chicago Press, 1997), 72.

49. Gilbert, *Redeeming Culture*, 75, 59; quoted in Fred Beuttler, "Organizing an American Conscience: The Conference on Science, Philosophy, and Religion, 1940–1968" (PhD diss., University of Chicago, 1995), 122–23, 3; Albert Einstein, "Science and Religion," *Union Review* 2, no. 1 (November 1940): 5–7, 28; "Union of Science and Democracy for Human Betterment Is Urged," *New York Times*, September 12, 1940, 26.

50. J. Douglas Brown et al., "The Spiritual Basis of Democracy," in *Science, Philosophy, and*

Religion: Second Symposium, ed. Lyman Bryson and Louis Finkelstein (New York: Conference on Science, Philosophy, and Religion, 1942), 255; Beuttler, "Organizing an American Conscience," 203, 199, 207, 218.

51. Sidney Hook, "Theological Tom-Tom and Metaphysical Bagpipe," *Humanist* 2, no. 3 (Autumn 1942): 96, 100–102; Hook, "Sidney Hook Holds Conference a Direct Threat to the Liberal Tradition," 38; Horace M. Kallen, "Kallen Says Hook Upholds New Vision of Freedom," *Humanist* 3, no. 1 (Spring 1943): 30–31; John Dewey to Max C. Otto, July 31, 1940 (typos corrected), and Otto to Dewey, July 29, 1940, in *The Correspondence of John Dewey, 1940–1952*, vol. 3; Otto, "Take It Away!" *Humanist* 2, no. 1 (Spring 1942): 13–15; Otto, "Otto Finds Steady Anti-Democratic Drive in Conference," *Humanist* 3, no. 1 (Spring 1943): 29–30; Arthur E. Murphy, "Sectarian Absolutes and Faith in Democracy," *Humanist* 1, no. 3 (Autumn 1941): 106–8; Edwin H. Wilson, "Militant Orthodoxy Must Be Answered!" *Humanist* 2, no. 2 (Summer 1942): 72–73; Wilson, "Confusion—The Inevitable Result," *Humanist* 2, no. 3 (Autumn 1942): 113.

52. Harry A. Overstreet to John Dewey, November 17, 1942, in *The Correspondence of John Dewey, 1940–1952*, vol. 3. See also H[arry] A. Overstreet, "Overstreet Feels the Conference Indispensable," *Humanist* 3, no. 1 (Spring 1943): 28. Cf. Edwin E. Aubrey, "The Conference Should Take Up Concrete Tasks," *Humanist* 3, no. 1 (Spring 1943): 24–25; W. F. Albright, "Albright Claims Hook Prejudiced," *Humanist* 3, no. 1 (Spring 1943): 25–26; and R[obert] L. Calhoun, "Calhoun Says Hook Historically Inaccurate," *Humanist* 3, no. 1 (Spring 1943): 27–28.

53. Bloch, "Rab Saadia Gaon," 83.

54. Waldo Frank, "The Jew in Our Day: Preface to a Program," *Contemporary Jewish Record* 7, no. 1 (February 1944): 45, 40; Frank, "The Jew in Our Day: The American Jew," *Contemporary Jewish Record* 6, no. 5 (October 1943): 454–55; Frank, "The Jew in Our Day: Democracy and the American Jew," *Contemporary Jewish Record* 6, no. 6 (December 1943): 583–86; Frank, "The Jews *Are* Different," *Saturday Evening Post* 214, no. 38 (March 21, 1942): 57; Mark Silk, "Notes on the Judeo-Christian Tradition," *American Quarterly* 36, no. 1 (Spring 1984): 73.

55. Harry J. Ausmus, *Will Herberg: From Right to Right* (Chapel Hill: University of North Carolina Press, 1987), 65–66, 59 (quoted); K. Healan Gaston, "The Cold War Romance of Religious Authenticity: Will Herberg, William F. Buckley Jr., and the Rise of the New Right," *Journal of American History* 99, no. 4 (March 2013): 1133–58.

56. Ausmus, *Will Herberg*, 66–68; Will Herberg, "The Christian Mythology of Socialism," *Antioch Review* 3, no. 1 (Spring 1943): 131–32; Herberg, "The Crisis of Socialism," *Jewish Frontier* 11, no. 9 (September 1944): 30; Herberg, "The Ethics of Power," *Jewish Frontier* 12, no. 3 (March 1945): 21–23.

57. Herberg, "The Crisis of Socialism," 30, 26, 24; Herberg, "Semantic Corruption," *New Europe* 5 (July–August 1945): 10–11, 8; Herberg, "Personalism against Totalitarianism," *politics* 2, no. 12 (December 1945): 370, 372–74.

58. Herberg, "Personalism against Totalitarianism," 369, 373–74.

Chapter 5

1. Elizabeth Gray Vining, "The Educated Heart," *Vital Speeches of the Day* 20, no. 19 (July 15, 1954): 601; "Democracy's Roots Traced to Religion," *New York Times*, July 4, 1955, 6.

2. For a sharply critical account, see Philip Hamburger, *Separation of Church and State* (Cambridge: Harvard University Press, 2002).

3. A few studies have pointed toward antisecularism's importance: John C. Jeffries Jr. and James E. Ryan, "A Political History of the Establishment Clause," *Michigan Law Review* 100, no. 2 (November 2001): 279–370; Sarah Barringer Gordon, "'Free' Religion and 'Captive' Schools: Protestants, Catholics, and Education, 1945–1965," *DePaul Law Review* 56 (2007): 1177–1220; and James E. Zucker, "Better a Catholic than a Communist: Reexamining *McCollum v. Board of Education* and *Zorach v. Clauson*," *Virginia Law Review* 93, no. 8 (December 2007): 2069–2118.

4. John T. McGreevy, *Catholicism and American Freedom: A History* (New York: W. W. Norton, 2003), 176; Mark Silk, "Notes on the Judeo-Christian Tradition in America," *American Quarterly* 36, no. 1 (Spring 1984): 66, 76–77.

5. E.g., John LaFarge, "The Development of Cooperative Acceptance of Racial Integration," *Journal of Negro Education* 21, no. 3 (Summer 1952): 431.

6. James J. Hennesey, *American Catholics: A History of the Roman Catholic Community in the United States* (New York: Oxford University Press, 1981), 272. On the impact of fascism's disappearance, see also Joshua Zeitz, "Communist! Fascist! New York Jews and Catholics Fight the Cold War," *Studies in Contemporary Jewry* 22 (2005): 88–110; and Zeitz, *White Ethnic New York: Jews, Catholics, and the Shaping of Postwar Politics* (Chapel Hill: University of North Carolina Press, 2007).

7. McCaffrey quoted in "Laski Is Assailed on Vatican Attack," *New York Times*, October 9, 1945, 2; Anne O'Hare McCormick, "The War on the Side of the Angels," *New York Times*, April 5, 1947, C18. Cf. McCormick, "Abroad: Reflections on the Day after Christmas," *New York Times*, December 26, 1953, 12.

8. Clare Boothe Luce, "The Communist Challenge to a Christian World," *New York Herald Tribune*, November 24, 1946, 7; Luce, "The Real Reason," *McCall's* 74 (February, March, April, 1947): 16, 117–35; 16, 156–76; 26, 76–90.

9. William L. Rossner, SJ, "Today's Need: American Scholarship," *Vital Speeches of the Day* 21, no. 22 (September 1, 1955): 1451; Luigi Sturzo, "The Philosophic Background of Christian Democracy," *Review of Politics* 9, no. 1 (January 1947): 6; Carlton J. H. Hayes, "The American Frontier—Frontier of What?" *American Historical Review* 51, no. 2 (January 1946): 208–9.

10. Fulton J. Sheen, "Politics and Religion," *Vital Speeches of the Day* 12, no. 14 (May 1, 1946): 440; "Secularism Called Aid to Communists," *New York Times*, May 29, 1948, 16; "Easier Divorce Opposed," *New York Times*, January 19, 1950, 26.

11. Harry J. Ausmus, *Will Herberg: From Right to Right* (Chapel Hill: University of North Carolina Press, 1987), 1; Will Herberg, "Crucial Question—Collectivism: Totalitarian or Democratic?" *Commonweal* 43, no. 19 (February 22, 1946), 475–76; Herberg, "Bureaucracy and Democracy in Labor Unions," *Antioch Review* 3 (September 1943): 417; Herberg, "Semantic Corruption," *New Europe* 5 (July–August 1945), 10; K. Healan Gaston, "The Cold War Romance of Religious Authenticity: Will Herberg, William F. Buckley Jr., and the Rise of the New Right," *Journal of American History* 99, no. 4 (March 2013): 1133–58.

12. Will Herberg, "Democracy and the Nature of Man," *Christianity and Society* 11, no. 4 (Fall 1946), 12 (emphasis removed), 19, 18; Herberg, "Prophetic Faith in an Age of Crisis," *Judaism* 1, no. 3 (July 1952), 199; Herberg, "Personalism versus Totalitarianism," *politics* 2 (December 1945), 373, 370.

13. Will Herberg, "Faith and Politics: Some Reflections on Whittaker Chambers' *Witness*," *Christianity and Crisis* 12, no. 16 (September 29, 1952), 123; Herberg, "The Church and American Politics," *Commentary* 8, no. 2 (August 1949), 200; Herberg, "Democracy and the Nature of Man," 16; Herberg, "Personalism versus Totalitarianism," 373.

14. Will Herberg, "Religious Communities in Present-Day America," *Review of Politics* 16 (April 1954), 173; Herberg, "Secularism in Church and Synagogue," *Christianity and Crisis* 10, no. 8 (May 15, 1950): 58–59 (emphasis in original); Herberg, "Prophetic Faith in an Age of Crisis," 199.

15. Herberg, "Secularism in Church and Synagogue," 59–60; Herberg, "The Sectarian Conflict over Church and State," *Commentary* 14, no. 5 (November 1952), 457; Herberg, "Assimilation in Militant Dress: Should the Jews Be 'Like unto the Nations'?" *Commentary* 4, no. 1 (July 1947), 21–22; Herberg, "Jewish Existence and Survival: A Theological View," *Judaism* 1 (January 1952), 22, 24.

16. Herberg, "Assimilation in Militant Dress," 21; Herberg, "Secularism in Church and Synagogue," 59–60.

17. On Jewish secularism, see Laura Levitt, "Impossible Assimilations, American Liberalism, and Jewish Difference: Revisiting Jewish Secularism," *American Quarterly* 59, no. 3 (September 2007): 807–32.

18. Cyrus Eaton, "Atheists against Communism," *New York Herald Tribune*, November 28, 1946, 36; Edwin H. Wilson, "The Sectarian Battlefront," *Humanist* 6, no. 4 (April 1947): 199.

19. Gunnar Myrdal, *An American Dilemma: The Negro Problem and Modern Democracy* (New York: Harper and Brothers, 1944); "Randolph Warns of Dangers in 'Flirting with Communism,'" *Baltimore Afro-American* (December 14, 1946), 6; "Sees Religion Victor over Race Prejudice," *Philadelphia Tribune*, July 16, 1949, 16. Cf. "Next Sun. Is Annual NAACP Day," *Philadelphia Tribune*, February 22, 1949, 9. See, more generally, Wendy L. Wall, *Inventing the "American Way": The Politics of Consensus from the New Deal to the Civil Rights Movement* (New York: Oxford University Press, 2008).

20. Arthur E. Murphy, "Ideals and Ideologies: 1917–1947," *Philosophical Review* 56, no. 4 (July 1947): 386–88.

21. Horace M. Kallen, "Of the American Spirit: An Open Letter to Teachers of English," *English Journal* 35, no. 6 (June 3, 1946): 290; Kallen, "Human Rights and the Religion of John Dewey," *Ethics* 60, no. 3 (April 1950): 169–72.

22. Earl J. McGrath, "Fundamental Education," *Vital Speeches of the Day* 17, no. 5 (December 15, 1950): 152.

23. John Courtney Murray, "A Common Enemy, a Common Cause" (1948), published in *First Things* 26, no. 1 (October 1992): 34, 32, 37.

24. John Courtney Murray, review of M. Searle Bates, *Religious Liberty: An Inquiry*, *Theological Studies* 7, no. 1 (March 1946): 154; Murray, "How Liberal Is Liberalism?" *America* 751, no. 1 (April 6, 1946): 6-7.

25. Murray, review of Bates, 154. On the Christmas message, see Paul E. Sigmund, "Catholicism and Liberal Democracy," in *Catholicism and Liberalism*, ed. R. Bruce Douglass and David Hollenbach (New York: Cambridge University Press, 1994), 226, 229.

26. John Courtney Murray, "Separation of Church and State," *America* 76 (December 7, 1946): 261–63.

27. John Courtney Murray, "Separation of Church and State: True and False Concepts," *America* 76 (February 15, 1947): 541–45.

28. John Courtney Murray, "The Court Upholds Religious Freedom," *America* 76 (March 8, 1947): 628–30.

29. James M. O'Neill, "Church, Schools, and the Constitution," *Commentary* 3, no. 6 (June 1947): 562, 567, 566. Cf. O'Neill, *Religion and Education under the Constitution* (New York:

Harper, 1949); Wilfrid J. Parsons, *The First Freedom: Considerations on Church and State in the United States* (New York: D. X. McMullen, 1948).

30. John Courtney Murray, "Religious Liberty: The Concern of All," *America* 48, no. 19 (February 7, 1948): 513–16; Murray, "The Roman Catholic Church," *Annals of the American Academy of Political and Social Science* 256 (March 1948): 36–42. On POAU's membership, see esp. Gordon, "'Free' Religion and 'Captive' Schools," and Kathleen Holscher, *Religious Lessons: Catholic Sisters and the Captive School Crisis in New Mexico* (New York: Oxford University Press, 2012).

31. Murray, "A Common Enemy, a Common Cause," 34–35, 37.

32. George A. Kizer, "Federal Aid to Education: 1945–1963," *History of Education Quarterly* 10, no. 1 (Spring 1970): 84–102; Elizabeth A. Edmondson, "Without Comment or Controversy: The G.I. Bill and Catholic Colleges," *Church History* 71, no. 4 (December 2002): 820–47.

33. John Courtney Murray, "Reversing the Secularist Drift," *Thought* 24, no. 1 (March 1949): 36–46; Murray, "Current Theology: On Religious Freedom," *Theological Studies* 10, no. 3 (September 1949): 409–32; Murray, "Law or Prepossessions?" *Law and Contemporary Problems* 14, no. 1 (Winter 1949): 23–43.

34. John Courtney Murray, "The One Work of the One Church," *Catholic Mind* 48 (June 1950): 358–64.

35. Joseph A. Komonchak, "'The Crisis in Church-State Relationships in the U.S.A.': A Recently Discovered Text by John Courtney Murray," *Review of Politics* 61, no. 4 (Fall 1999): 675–714.

36. Ibid.

37. Reinhold Niebuhr, *The Children of Light and the Children of Darkness: A Vindication of Democracy and a Critique of Its Traditional Defence* (New York: Charles Scribner's Sons, 1944), xv, 41, 135.

38. Reinhold Niebuhr, "The Religious Level of the World Crisis," *Christianity and Crisis* 5, no. 24 (January 21, 1946): 4; Niebuhr, "Democracy as a Religion," *Christianity and Crisis* 7, no. 14 (August 4, 1947): 1–2.

39. "Faith for a Lenten Age," *Time*, March 8, 1948, 70–79; Reinhold Niebuhr, "The Pope on Property," *Christianity and Society* 9, no. 4 (Fall 1944): 6–8; Niebuhr, "A Catholic View," *Nation* 161, no. 25 (December 22): 695–96.

40. Reinhold Niebuhr, "Editorial Notes," *Christianity and Crisis* 6, no. 4 (March 18, 1946): 2; Niebuhr, "Editorial Notes," *Christianity and Crisis* 6, no. 6 (April 15, 1946): 2.

41. Reinhold Niebuhr, "Editorial Notes," *Christianity and Crisis* 7, no. 13 (July 21, 1947): 2.

42. Reinhold Niebuhr, "The Unity and Depth of Our Culture," *Sewanee Review* 52, no. 2 (April–June 1944): 193–98; Niebuhr, "The Religious Level of the World Crisis," 6.

43. Niebuhr, *Children of Light*, 3, 128, 124.

44. Reinhold Niebuhr, "Separation of Church and State," *Messenger* 12, no. 16 (August 5, 1947): 21.

45. Reinhold Niebuhr, "Our Relations to Catholicism," *Christianity and Crisis* 7, no. 15 (September 15, 1947): 5–7; Niebuhr quoted in Daniel F. Rice, *Reinhold Niebuhr and His Circle of Influence* (New York: Cambridge University Press, 2013), 213.

46. For more on this episode, see K. Healan Gaston, "Demarcating Democracy: Liberal Catholics, Protestants, and the Discourse of Secularism," in *American Religious Liberalism*, ed. Leigh E. Schmidt and Sally M. Promey (Bloomington: Indiana University Press, 2012), 337–58.

47. "Report of a Conference on Church and State, April 26, 1948," folder 13, box 3, National

Conference of Christians and Jews Records, Social Welfare History Archives, University of Minnesota; Murray, "A Common Enemy, a Common Cause," 36.

48. Reinhold Niebuhr, "Protestants, Catholics and Secularists," *Christianity and Society* 13, no. 2 (Spring 1948): 4–5; Niebuhr, "Editorial Notes," *Christianity and Crisis* 8, no. 5 (March 29, 1948): 34.

49. Niebuhr, "Protestants, Catholics and Secularists," 4–5; Niebuhr, "Religion and Tolerance," *Messenger* 13, no. 3 (June 22, 1948), 6.

50. William E. McManus memorandum, folder 23, box 9, series 7, Social Action Department Records, National Catholic Welfare Conference–U.S. Catholic Conference Papers, Catholic University of America, Washington, DC (henceforth "SAD-NCWC").

51. Ibid.

52. John C. Bennett, "Implications of the New Conception of 'Separation,'" *Christianity and Crisis* 8, no. 12 (July 5, 1948): 89–90. Interestingly, only three of the thirteen Protestants at the New York meeting—Bennett, Niebuhr, and Justin Wroe Nixon—signed the *Christianity and Crisis* statement. Much remains to be understood about that statement's provenance and the representativeness of its signers.

53. "Protestants Take the Catholic Line," *Christian Century* 65, no. 26 (June 30, 1948): 643.

54. John T. McGreevy, *Catholicism and American Freedom: A History* (New York: W. W. Norton, 2003), 166–67. Blanshard's book is *American Freedom and Catholic Power* (Boston: Beacon, 1949).

55. Mark Massa, "Catholic-Protestant Tensions in Post-War America: Paul Blanshard, John Courtney Murray, and the 'Religious Imagination,'" *Harvard Theological Review* 95, no. 3 (July 2002): 320. Philip A. Grant Jr., "Catholic Congressmen, Cardinal Spellman, Eleanor Roosevelt, and the 1949–1950 Federal Aid to Education Controversy," *Records of the American Catholic Historical Society of Philadelphia* 90, no. 1 (March–December 1979): 3-13.

56. James M. O'Neill, *Catholicism and American Freedom* (New York: Harper and Brothers, 1952); John Courtney Murray, "Review of *American Freedom and Catholic Power*," *Catholic World* 169 (June 1949), 233–34. See also Dale Francis, *American Freedom and Paul Blanshard* (Notre Dame, IN: Ave Maria Press, 1950).

57. W. Russell Bowie, "The Catholic Position: Protestant Concern over Catholicism," *American Mercury* 69 (September 1949): 261–73; John Courtney Murray, "The Catholic Position: A Reply," *American Mercury* 69 (September 1949): 274–83.

58. "Pooh! Pooh!" *Christian Century* 66, no. 38 (September 21, 1949): 1094–95; Reinhold Niebuhr, "The Pope's Domesticated God," *Christian Century* 67, no. 3 (January 18, 1950): 74–75; Niebuhr, "The Rising Catholic-Protestant Tension," *Christianity and Crisis* 9, no. 14 (August 8, 1949): 106–8.

59. Niebuhr, "The Rising Catholic-Protestant Tension."

60. "Dr. Niebuhr Speaks Out," *Ave Maria* 7 (May 1951).

Chapter 6

1. Quoted in Will Herberg, *Protestant-Catholic-Jew: An Essay in American Religious Sociology* (Garden City, NY: Doubleday, 1955), 258.

2. "Democracy's Roots Traced to Religion," *New York Times*, July 4, 1955, 6; R. H. Eckelberry, "Editorial Comments," *Journal of Higher Education* 24, no. 6 (June 1953): 328; "Europe's Christian

Democrats," *Time*, May 25, 1953, 34–35; Eugene Youngert, "Live Free or Die," *Vital Speeches of the Day* 21, no. 10 (March 1, 1955): 1082.

3. Harold C. Case, "The Mind's Adventure," *Vital Speeches of the Day* 18, no. 19 (July 15, 1952): 598; Samuel I. Clark, "Religion in Public Education," *Bulletin of the American Association of University Professors* 40, no. 4 (Winter 1954–55): 647–48.

4. Arthur Hays Sulzberger, "The Third Fear Is Ourselves," *New York Times*, December 31, 1951, SM5; Harry Emerson Fosdick, "Have We Lost Our Moral Heritage?" *Vital Speeches of the Day* 18, no. 20 (August 1, 1952): 630–31; David Sarnoff, "The Moral Crisis of Our Age," *Vital Speeches of the Day* 22, no. 4 (December 1, 1955): 120; Anne O'Hare McCormick, "Once More the Night before Christmas," *New York Times*, December 24, 1952, 16.

5. Virgil M. Hancher, "The Third Choice," *Vital Speeches of the Day* 16, no. 23 (September 15, 1950): 723; Waldo Frank, "'Anti-Communist Peril': Rediscovering Our Roots," *Nation* 178, no. 25 (June 19, 1954): 516–17.

6. C. A. Chick Sr., "Signs of Hope," *Vital Speeches of the Day* 20, no. 23 (September 15, 1954): 725; Ahmed Hussein, "The New Egypt," *Vital Speeches of the Day* 21, no. 11 (March 15, 1955): 1104; Edward J. Jurji, "Great Religions and International Affairs," *Theology Today* 12, no. 2 (July 1955): 172.

7. "Peril of Secularism Worse than A-Bomb, R.I. Cleric Declares," *Boston Globe*, February 5, 1953, D24; John O. Gross, "Religion and Education," *Peabody Journal of Education* 30, no. 6 (May 1953): 370; "Theobald Warns of Pagan Ideas," *New York Times*, January 24, 1953, 18; Ernest B. Koenker, "The Relationship of the Church to the National Culture," *Concordia Theological Monthly* 25, no. 11 (November 1954): 815–16.

8. "Patriotism and Religion," *Pittsburgh Courier*, July 8, 1950, 18; James A. Hagerty, "Fitzpatrick Lists More ALP 'Choices,'" *New York Times*, September 22, 1949, 36.

9. A. Powell Davies, "Congress Moves In on the Churches," *New Republic* 129, no. 1 (August 3, 1953): 8.

10. John Ellis Large, "What Is Man?" *Vital Speeches of the Day* 15, no. 24 (October 1, 1949): 756–57.

11. George M. Docherty, "Under God," sermon at New York Avenue Presbyterian Church, February 7, 1954, http://www.nyapc.org/wp-content/uploads/2014/01/Under_God_Sermon.pdf.

12. Henry Geiger, "The New 'Enemy': Secularism," *Manas* 5, no. 28 (July 9, 1952): 1–5.

13. A. J. Muste, "Possibility of Nonviolence," *New York Times*, October 8, 1954, 22.

14. Edwin E. Aubrey, *Secularism a Myth: An Examination of the Current Attack on Secularism* (New York: Harper, 1954), 11, 25, 12, 26. Other works on secularism were much more critical: e.g., J. Richard Spann, *The Christian Faith and Secularism* (New York: Abingdon-Cokesbury, 1948), Albert T. Mollegen, *Christianity and the Crisis of Secularism* (Washington: Henderson Services, 1951), and Georgia E. Harkness, *The Modern Rival of the Christian Faith: An Analysis of Secularism* (New York: Abingdon-Cokesbury, 1952).

15. Aubrey, *Secularism a Myth*, 182, 27, 30, 105, 136, 12–13.

16. Ibid., 121; Horace M. Kallen, *Secularism Is the Will of God* (New York: Twayne, 1954).

17. Kallen, *Secularism Is the Will of God*, 144, 219.

18. Ibid., 17, 217, 20, 22, 157.

19. Ibid., 160, 165, 11, 182, 184, 179–80, 182–83.

20. Ibid., 79–81, 143.

21. Paxton Blair, "Lawyers and Education," *Vital Speeches of the Day* 17, no. 24 (October 1, 1951): 761; Luther A. Weigle, "The Crisis of Religion in Education," *Vital Speeches of the Day* 20,

no. 5 (December 15, 1953): 148; John C. Bennett, review of James Hastings Nichols, *Democracy and the Churches*, *Journal of Religion* 31, no. 4 (October 1951): 282–83, 282.

22. Douglas Sloan, *Faith and Knowledge: Mainline Protestantism and American Higher Education* (Louisville, KY: Westminster John Knox Press, 1994); Russell J. Compton, "The Christian Heritage in Humanities Courses," *Journal of Bible and Religion* 20, no. 1 (January 1952): 20–21.

23. *Zorach v. Clauson* (1952), 343 U.S. 306, 315–16.

24. Anson Phelps Stokes, "God's Place in the School," *New York Times*, January 18, 1953, BR7.

25. John A. Mackay, "Religion and Government, Their Separate Spheres and Reciprocal Responsibilities," *Theology Today* 9, no. 2 (July 1952): 205, 211–13.

26. John Tracy Ellis, "Church and State in the United States: A Critical Appraisal," *Catholic Historical Review* 38, no. 3 (October 1952): 303–4; Clark, "Religion in Public Education," 647–48.

27. V. T. Thayer, "Our Secular Schools and Religion," *Phi Delta Kappan* 34, no. 9 (June 1953): 398.

28. "Secular Schools Defended by Conant in Baccalaureate," *Boston Globe*, June 19, 1950, 1, 11; "Dual School Rise Is Attacked Anew," *New York Times*, April 9, 1952, 25. Controversy also erupted at April's National Conference on Higher Education meeting: "Secularism Issue Splits Educators," *New York Times*, April 19, 1952, 17.

29. "Ethics as Essence of Religion Denied," *New York Times*, August 8, 1949, 13; "Archbishop Calls Conant Speech 'Exasperating,'" *Boston Globe*, April 14, 1952, 1; "Cushing Defends Parochial Schools," *New York Times*, April 14, 1952, 21; "Foes of Religion in Schools Scored," *New York Times*, April 21, 1952, 18.

30. "Agnes Meyer Calls Schools U.S. Bulwark," *Washington Post*, July 4, 1952, 9; Fulton J. Sheen, "Education in America," *Vital Speeches of the Day* 20, no. 16 (June 1, 1954): 504; "Protestant Group Warns of Inroads of Secular Trend," *New York Times*, December 13, 1952, 1, 17.

31. "Text of Statement by Catholic Bishops on Secularism and Schools," *New York Times*, November 16, 1952, 80; "Protestant Group Warns of Inroads of Secular Trend," 1, 17. One editorial noted both statements' similarity to Will Herberg's 1952 *Commentary* article, discussed later in this chapter: "Religion and the Schools," *Washington Post*, December 15, 1952, 10.

32. Charles Stinson, "Letter to the Editor: Catholics and Liberals," *New Republic* 126, no. 10 (March 10, 1952): 4.

33. John Cogley, *A Canterbury Tale: Experiences and Reflections, 1916–1976* (New York: Seabury, 1976); K. Healan Gaston, "Demarcating Democracy: Liberal Catholics, Protestants, and the Discourse of Secularism," in *American Religious Liberalism*, ed. Leigh E. Schmidt and Sally M. Promey (Bloomington: Indiana University Press, 2012): 337–58.

34. "Clearing the Air," *Commonweal* 52, no. 10 (June 16, 1950): 238; John Cogley, "The Unspoken Ism," *Commonweal* 54, no. 6 (May 18, 1951): 144–46.

35. John Cogley, "The Failure of Anti-Communism," *Commonweal* 52, no. 15 (July 21, 1950): 357; Cogley, "The Best Defense," *Commonweal* 51, no. 2 (October 21, 1949): 28.

36. John Cogley, "Question of Method," *Commonweal* 59, no. 23 (March 12, 1954): 570; "Democracy as Procedure and Substance," *America* 90, no. 25 (March 20, 1954): 646.

37. John Courtney Murray, "The School and Christian Freedom," *National Catholic Educational Association Proceedings* 48 (August 1951): 63–68; Murray, "The Natural Law," in *Great Expressions of Human Rights*, ed. Robert M. MacIver (New York: Harper, 1950), 12; Murray, "The Problem of Pluralism in America," *Thought* 24 (Summer 1954): 204.

38. J. Leon Hooper, *John Courtney Murray and the Growth of Tradition* (Kansas City, MO:

Sheed and Ward, 1996), 30; e.g., George W. Shea, "Catholic Doctrine and 'the Religion of the State,'" *American Ecclesiastical Review* 123 (1950): 161–74.

39. Murray, "The Natural Law," 12; Murray, "The Problem of Pluralism in America," 167–68; Murray, "The Church and Totalitarian Democracy," *Theological Studies* 14 (December 1952): 545.

40. Murray, "The Problem of Pluralism in America," 196, 201–4.

41. Ibid., 183, 208.

42. John Courtney Murray, "Leo XIII and Pius XII: Government and the Order of Religion," in *Religious Liberty: Catholic Struggles with Pluralism*, ed. J. Leon Hooper (Louisville, KY: Westminster John Knox Press, 1993), 54; Murray, "On the Structure of the Church-State Problem," in *The Catholic Church in World Affairs*, ed. Waldemar Gurian and M. A. Fitzsimons (Notre Dame: University of Notre Dame Press, 1954), 25.

43. Reinhold Niebuhr, "A Protestant Looks at Catholics," *Commonweal* 58, no. 5 (May 8, 1953): 118; Will Herberg, "A Jew Looks at Catholics," *Commonweal* 58, no. 7 (May 22, 1953): 174–76.

44. Niebuhr, "A Protestant Looks at Catholics," 118. See also Niebuhr, "Catholics and Politics: Some Misconceptions," *Reporter* 6 (January 22, 1952): 9-11.

45. Reinhold Niebuhr, "Love and Law in Protestantism and Catholicism," *Journal of Religious Thought* 9 (May 1952): 95–111.

46. Reinhold Niebuhr, *The Irony of American History* (New York: Charles Scribner's Sons, 1952); Richard Wightman Fox, *Reinhold Niebuhr: A Biography* (New York: Pantheon, 1985), 244–47; Niebuhr, "The Cultural Crisis of Our Age," *Harvard Business Review* 32, no. 1 (January–February 1954), 35.

47. Reinhold Niebuhr, "Utilitarian Christianity and the World Crisis," *Christianity and Crisis* 10, no. 9 (May 29, 1950): 66; Niebuhr, *Irony of American History.*

48. Will Herberg, *Judaism and Modern Man: An Interpretation of Jewish Religion* (New York: Farrar, Straus and Young, 1951); Herberg, *Protestant-Catholic-Jew.*

49. Will Herberg, "Secularism in Church and Synagogue," *Christianity and Crisis* 10, no. 8 (May 15, 1950): 60 (emphasis removed); Herberg, "Jewish Existence and Survival: A Theological View," *Judaism* 1, no. 1 (January 1952): 26; Herberg, "The Postwar Revival of the Synagogue," *Commentary* 9, no. 4 (April 1950): 324, 317; Herberg, "Religious Trends in American Jewry," *Judaism* 3, no. 3 (Summer 1954): 233.

50. Will Herberg, "The Sectarian Conflict over Church and State," *Commentary* 14, no. 5 (November 1952): 459; Herberg, "A Jewish Point of View," *Religious Education* 48 (May–June 1953): 139.

51. Herberg, "The Sectarian Conflict over Church and State," 455–56, 451, 454, 453; John C. Bennett, letter to the editor, *Commentary* 15, no. 1 (January 1953): 101; Herberg, "A Jewish Point of View," 136.

52. Will Herberg, "Anti-Semitism Today," *Commonweal* 60, no. 15 (July 16, 1954): 359, 361; Herberg, "The Sectarian Conflict over Church and State," 459.

53. Robert Gordis, letter to the editor, *Commentary* 3, no. 5 (May 1947): 490–91. On *Judaism*'s founding, see Laura Levitt, "Impossible Assimilations, American Liberalism, and Jewish Difference: Revisiting Jewish Secularism," *American Quarterly* 59 (September 2007): 820.

54. Paul Tillich, "Is There a Judeo-Christian Tradition?" *Judaism* 1, no. 2 (April 1952): 106, 109.

55. Bernard Heller, "About the Judeo-Christian Tradition: Some Comments on Paul Tillich's Article," *Judaism* 1, no. 3 (July 1952): 259–61.

56. Margaret L. Wiley, "Native Growth or Import?" *Journal of Higher Education* 23, no. 7

(October 1952): 350–58; Will Herberg, "Some Comments on Miss Wiley's Paper," *Journal of Higher Education* 23, no. 7 (October 1952): 367; Herberg, "Judaism and Christianity: Their Unity and Difference. The Double Covenant in the Divine Economy of Salvation," *Journal of Bible and Religion* 21, no. 2 (April 1953): 67.

57. Herberg, "Judaism and Christianity," 69, 72, 74–76.

58. Ibid., 76–77.

59. Robert Gordis, "The Nature of Man in the Judeo-Christian Tradition," *Judaism* 2, no. 2 (April 1953): 101–3, 104–6, 108. Ironically, another key difference lay in Christianity's emphasis on "the Prophets, while practically discarding the Law"; Judaism subordinated prophetic teachings to the Torah (101).

60. Bernard Heller, "The Judeo-Christian Tradition Concept: Aid or Deterrent to Goodwill?" *Judaism* 2, no. 2 (April 1953): 135–37, 139.

61. Leon Fram, "The Judaeo-Christian Tradition," *Judaism* 3, no. 1 (Winter 1954): 77–79.

62. "Old Faith to Meet Soviet Gain Urged," *New York Times*, May 12, 1948, 2.

63. John Foster Dulles to Everett R. Clinchy, April 9, 1948, folder "Correspondence 1941–1949," box 30, Everett R. Clinchy Papers, Social Welfare History Archives, University of Minnesota.

64. A recent account is Kevin M. Kruse, *One Nation under God: How Corporate America Invented Christian America* (New York: Basic Books, 2015), x–xiii. President Truman had repeatedly employed religious themes as well, and had invoked "our mutual Judaic Christian culture" in a 1946 letter to a Jewish leader: "American Jewish Cavalcade to Intensify Religious Activities Launched by U.A.H.C.," *JTA Daily News Bulletin*, November 4, 1946, 5.

65. Quoted in Martin E. Marty, *Modern American Religion, vol. 3, Under God, Indivisible, 1941–1960* (Chicago: University of Chicago Press, 1996), 306–7; William Lee Miller, *Piety along the Potomac: Notes on Politics and Morals in the Fifties* (Boston: Houghton Mifflin, 1964), 126–27. For a view of Eisenhower's rhetorical choices as more consciously chosen and strategic than usually assumed, see Paul Kengor, "Comparing Presidents Reagan and Eisenhower," *Presidential Studies Quarterly* 28, no. 2 (April 1998): 366–93.

66. "Spanish Consul Honored at Farewell Banquet," *Los Angeles Times*, April 12, 1953, A8; "Ike's Text at Jewish Tercentenary," *Boston Globe*, October 21, 1954, 7.

67. Dwight D. Eisenhower, "The Free World Challenged by Communism: We Must Have Unity and Faith," in *Selected Speeches of Dwight David Eisenhower* (Washington: GPO, 1970), 54. For more on this quote, see Patrick Henry, "'And I Don't Care What It Is': The Tradition-History of a Civil Religion Proof-Text," *Journal of the American Academy of Religion* 49, no. 1 (March 1981): 35–49.

68. "President-Elect Says Soviets Demoted Zhukov because of Their Friendship," *New York Times*, December 23, 1952, 1.

69. Dwight D. Eisenhower to Milton Stover Eisenhower, 1957, in Alfred D. Chandler Jr., ed., *The Papers of Dwight David Eisenhower*, vol. 18 (Baltimore: Johns Hopkins University Press, 1970), 88–89. In a characteristic speech at Goucher College in June 1961, Milton Eisenhower declared, "Communism strikes directly at the Judaic-Christian heritage—the abiding keystone of Western civilization." "Goucher Hears Dr. Eisenhower: Hopkins Head Sees Liberal Arts Unknown in Soviet," *Baltimore Sun*, June 12, 1961, 30.

70. Michelle Mart, *Eye on Israel: How America Came to View Israel as an Ally* (Albany: State University of New York Press, 2006); William R. Inboden, *Religion and American Foreign Policy, 1945–1960: The Soul of Containment* (New York: Cambridge University Press, 2008).

71. "Eisenhower Men Have Stag Lunch, Argue about UMT, Social Security," *Boston Globe*, January 20, 1953, 1.

72. *Dwight D. Eisenhower: Containing the Public Messages, Speeches, and Statements of the President, 1953–61* (Washington: GPO, 1960), 624.

73. On the differences between the two, see Daniel K. Williams, *God's Own Party: The Making of the Christian Right* (New York: Oxford University Press, 2010), 27–28.

74. Quoted in William Inboden, *Religion and American Foreign Policy, 1945–1960: The Soul of Containment* (New York: Cambridge University Press, 2008), 301; Dwight D. Eisenhower, "Statement by the President Upon Signing Bill to Include the Words 'Under God' in the Pledge to the Flag" (June 14, 1954), https://www.presidency.ucsb.edu/node/232153. Cf. Eisenhower, "Remarks at the Dedicatory Prayer Breakfast of the International Christian Leadership" (February 5, 1953), https://www.presidency.ucsb.edu/node/231800; and Eisenhower, "Address at the Second Assembly of the World Council of Churches, Evanston, Illinois" (August 19, 1954), https://www.presidency.ucsb.edu/node/232572. On foreign policy, see also Andrew Preston, *Sword of the Spirit, Shield of Faith: Religion in American War and Diplomacy* (New York: Knopf, 2012) and Seth Jacobs, *America's Miracle Man in Vietnam: Ngo Dinh Diem, Religion, Race, and U.S. Intervention in Southeast Asia, 1950–1957* (Durham: Duke University Press, 2004).

75. Paul Hutchinson, "The President's Religious Faith," *Life* 36, no. 12 (March 22, 1954): 160; Dwight D. Eisenhower, "Address at the Freedoms Foundation, Waldorf-Astoria, New York City, New York" (December 22, 1952), http://eisenhower.archives.gov/all_about_ike/quotes.html; "Texts of General Eisenhower's Addresses at Waldorf-Astoria Dinner and in Paterson Armory," *New York Times*, October 17, 1952, 18; Eisenhower, "Remarks Recorded for the 'Back-to-God' Program of the American Legion" (February 20, 1955), https://www.presidency.ucsb.edu/node /233928; "Ike's Text at Jewish Tercentenary," *Boston Globe*, October 21, 1954, 7; Eisenhower, "Remarks to the First National Conference on the Spiritual Foundations of American Democracy" (November 9, 1954), https://www.presidency.ucsb.edu/node/233269.

76. "4-Point Peace Plan Outlined by Eisenhower: President of Penn State Gives Address at Johns Hopkins Ceremony," *Baltimore Sun*, February 23, 1952, 20; Timothy Foote, "Luce et Veritas," *Time*, October 9, 1972, 96-97.

77. Dwight D. Eisenhower to Henry Luce, September 22, 1953, in Chandler, *The Papers of Dwight David Eisenhower* 14:534. For more on the NCCJ-McCarthy episode and Hughes's role in it, see Fred I. Greenstein, *The Hidden-Hand Presidency: Eisenhower as Leader* (New York: Basic Books, 1982).

78. Will Herberg to Hershel Matt and Gustine Matt, August 25, 1954, folder 27A, Will Herberg Collection, Drew University Archives, Madison, NJ; Herberg to June Bingham, April 13, 1955, Will Herberg file, box 26, June Bingham Correspondence, Reinhold Niebuhr Papers, Manuscript Division, Library of Congress, Washington, DC; "National Conference on the Spiritual Foundations of American Democracy, November 8–10, 1954," conference program, folder 35, box 10, series 7, SAD-NCWC; "Highlights, First National Conference on the Spiritual Foundations of Western Democracy," folder 80, box 1, John Courtney Murray Papers, Georgetown University, Washington, DC; Charles W. Lowry, foreword to *Conflicting Faiths: Christianity versus Communism*, ed. Lowry (Washington: Public Affairs Press, 1953), 3; Lowry, "Catholic-Protestant Relations: A Churchman Looks at Both," *Vital Speeches of the Day* 27, no. 5 (December 15, 1960): 130. For more on FRASCO, see Inboden, *Religion and American Foreign Policy*; and K. Healan Gaston, "The Cold War Romance of Religious Authenticity: Will Herberg,

William F. Buckley Jr., and the Rise of the New Right," *Journal of American History* 99 (2013): 1133–58.

79. "Highlights, First National Conference on the Spiritual Foundations of Western Democracy"; Will Herberg, "The Biblical Basis of American Democracy," *Thought* 30 (Spring 1955): 37–50; "Report on the National Foundation for Religious Action in the Social and Civil Order," folder 13, box 10, series 7, SAD-NCWC; "Memorandum on Foundation for Religious Action in the Social and Civil Order," October 25, 1954, folder 11, ibid.; John F. Cronin, "Report on the Foundation for Religious Action in the Social and Civil Order," folder 16, ibid.; Cronin to Archbishop Patrick A. O'Boyle, February 18, 1955, folder 14, ibid. On Cronin's role in FRASCO, see John T. Donovan, *Crusader in the Cold War: A Biography of Fr. John F. Cronin, S.S. (1908–1994)* (New York, 2005), 81–86.

80. Charles W. Lowry, *Communism and Christ* (New York: Morehouse-Gorham, 1953), 91; Cronin, "Report on the National Foundation for Religious Action in the Social and Civil Order."

81. "Memorandum on Foundation for Religious Action in the Social and Civil Order." Cf. Charles W. Lowry to *Christian Century*, December 24, 1955, folder 8, box 10, series 7, SAD-NCWC.

82. "Report on Conversations, Woodstock, November 27, 1954," folder 11, box 10, series 7, SAD-NCWC; Eugene J. Lipman, "Memorandum," November 10, 1954, folder 6, box 10, Abraham J. Feldman Papers, Jacob Rader Marcus Center of the American Jewish Archives, Cincinnati, Ohio. On ties between FRASCO and the Central Intelligence Agency, see Inboden, *Religion and American Foreign Policy*, 280–81.

83. Lipman, "Memorandum"; Judah Raby [Eugene J. Lipman], "Interfaith—On What Terms?" *Congress Weekly*, December 13, 1954, 6–7.

84. Lowry to Reinhold Niebuhr, April 17, 1956, folder "F: miscellaneous," box 6, General Correspondence, Niebuhr Papers.

85. Reinhold Niebuhr, "Democracy, Secularism, and Christianity," *Christianity and Crisis* 13, no. 3 (March 2, 1953): 19.

Chapter 7

1. James Reston, "Extremists Dominate Issue over Religion," *New York Times*, September 11, 1960, B3; "Christianity Losing Africa, Baptist Says," *Chicago Tribune*, March 20, 1960, B16; "Rabbi Scorns Temple Shelters as Yielding to Moscow Threat," *New York Times*, October 22, 1961, 82.

2. Kalman Siegel, "Israel to Step Up Aid to Neighbors," *Los Angeles Times*, November 20, 1960, 27; "Oxnam Sees Red Threat," *Washington Post and Times Herald*, November 27, 1958, B15; Benjamin Selekman, "Why Marx Had No Luck in America: There Is No Class Distinction Here, Thanks to Our Belief in Community of All," *Boston Globe*, January 5, 1958, A2; Arthur Krock, "Humanitarian Ethics of U.S. Protecting Cuba," *Los Angeles Times*, June 7, 1960, 2; "Bishop Pike Assails Marxism as Heresy," *New York Times*, February 24, 1961, 16; Richard Frohnen, "Youth Told to Cherish Our National Heritage," *Los Angeles Times*, February 11, 1960, C13; Kenneth Dole, "Christian Heritage Held Democracy's Only Hope," *Washington Post*, November 1, 1960, A10. Cf. Arnold Toynbee, "Spiritual Freedom Is the Great Difference," *New York Times*, January 5, 1961, SM8.

3. Richard Nixon, "Says U.S. Needs Talents of All," *Chicago Defender*, February 17, 1958, A9; "Brotherhood Week Begins Sunday," *New York Amsterdam News*, February 21, 1959, 23; "Bob

Hope to Head Brotherhood Week," *Chicago Defender*, December 17, 1960, 21; "Christians and Jews to Probe Religious Problems," *New Journal and Guide* (Norfolk, VA), July 15, 1961, 12.

4. "South Threatens American Survival," *Baltimore Afro-American*, April 21, 1956, 11; "Richmond Pastors Speak Out on Race," *Washington Post and Times Herald*, February 3, 1957, E3; "Along the N.A.A.C.P. Battlefront," *Crisis* 62, no. 10 (December 1955): 621–22.

5. Martin Luther King Jr., *Stride toward Freedom: The Montgomery Story* (New York: Harper, 1958), 205; King quoted in Richard Wightman Fox, *Reinhold Niebuhr: A Biography* (New York: Pantheon, 1985), 283; King, "The Negro and the American Dream," in *The Papers of Martin Luther King, Jr.*, vol. 5, ed. Clayborne Carson et al. (Berkeley: University of California Press, 1992), 508.

6. Cal Adams, "Lunch Counter Bias Deplored," *Pittsburgh Courier*, March 19, 1960, 3; "An Unknown Tune," *Carolina New Journal and Guide*, December 10, 1960; "New Negro Is Theme of Catholic Meeting," *Chicago Defender*, June 8, 1961: 19; "Jesuit Priest Condemns Advocates of Gradualism," ibid., October 30, 1961. See also "National YWCA Endorses Student Sit-Down Movement," *New Journal and Guide* (Norfolk, VA), April 23, 1960: A10.

7. "Text of Speech by Dulles before the B'nai B'rith on North Atlantic Council Session," *New York Times*, May 9, 1956, 4; Kenneth Dole, "Dulles Sees 'Dark Age' If Reds Win," *Washington Post and Times Herald*, January 23, 1958: A1; "Lodge Tells Russian What Makes U.S. Tick," Chicago Tribune, September 18, 1959: 5.

8. Dwight D. Eisenhower, "Address at U.S. Naval Academy Commencement" (June 4, 1958), https://www.presidency.ucsb.edu/node/233512; Eisenhower, "Annual Message to the Congress on the State of the Union" (January 10, 1957), https://www.presidency.ucsb.edu/node/233260; Eisenhower, "Remarks at the Cornerstone-Laying Ceremony for the Interchurch Center, New York City" (October 12, 1958), https://www.presidency.ucsb.edu/node/234073.

9. Emmet J. Hughes, *The Ordeal of Power: A Political Memoir of the Eisenhower Years* (New York: Atheneum, 1963).

10. "Is Our Religious Revival Real?" *McCall's* 82 (June 1955): 25; "The Unreal Revival," *Time*, November 26, 1956, 57; Sockman quoted in George Dugan, "Methodists Map World Message," *New York Times*, September 12, 1956, 14; Fromm quoted in Kenneth Dole, "News of the Churches: Psychoanalyst Hits at Religious Revival," *Washington Post*, January 29, 1955, 11; Judah Pilch, "Changing Patterns in Jewish Education," *Jewish Social Studies* 21, no. 2 (April 1959): 97–98; A. Roy Eckardt, *The Surge of Piety in America: An Appraisal* (New York: Association Press, 1958); Stanley J. Rowland, *Land in Search of God* (New York: Random House, 1958); Martin E. Marty, *The New Shape of American Religion* (New York: Harper, 1959); Gibson Winter, *The Suburban Captivity of the Churches: An Analysis of Protestant Responsibility in the Expanding Metropolis* (New York: Doubleday, 1961); Peter L. Berger, *The Noise of Solemn Assemblies: Christian Commitment and the Religious Establishment in America* (Garden City, NY: Doubleday, 1961).

11. Edward L. R. Elson, "Evaluating Our Religious Revival," *Journal of Religious Thought* 14, no. 1 (Autumn–Winter 1956–57): 55–57, 61; Talcott Parsons, "The Pattern of Religious Organization in the United States," *Daedalus* 87, no. 3 (Summer 1958): 80; Robert J. McCracken, "Religion: A House of Many Mansions," *New York Times*, April 29, 1956, 287.

12. Reinhold Niebuhr, "Is There a Revival of Religion?" *New York Times*, November 19, 1950, SM7; Niebuhr, "Prayer and Politics," *Christianity and Crisis* 12, no. 18 (October 27, 1952): 138–39; Niebuhr, "Religiosity and the Christian Faith," *Christianity and Crisis* 14, no. 24 (January 24, 1955): 186; Niebuhr, "Religiosity versus the Christian Gospel," *Episcopal Churchnews* 120, no. 2 (January 23, 1955): 12; K. Healan Gaston, "'A Bad Kind of Magic': The Niebuhr Brothers on 'Utili-

tarian Christianity' and the Defense of Democracy," *Harvard Theological Review* 107, no. 1 (January 2014): 1–30.

13. Niebuhr, "Religiosity versus the Christian Gospel," 12; Niebuhr, "Religiosity and the Christian Faith," 185; Niebuhr, "Billy Graham's Christianity and the World Crisis," *Christianity and Society* 20, no. 2 (Spring 1955): 3–4; Niebuhr, "Varieties of Religious Revival," *New Republic* (June 6, 1955): 15–16. See also Niebuhr, "Christian Faith—A 'Live Option,'" *Episcopal Churchnews* 120, no. 10 (May 15, 1955): 11; and Niebuhr, "Religious Faith and Conformity," *Episcopal Churchnews* 120, no. 12 (July 24, 1955): 10.

14. John M. Krumm, review of Will Herberg, *Protestant-Catholic-Jew*, *Union Seminary Quarterly Review* 11 (May 1956): 64; Will Herberg, *Protestant-Catholic-Jew: An Essay in American Religious Sociology* (Garden City, NY: Doubleday, 1955), 101–2.

15. Herberg, *Protestant-Catholic-Jew*, 23, 7, 85, 257; Will Herberg, "Religious Trends in American Jewry," *Judaism* 3 (Summer 1954): 232.

16. Herberg, *Protestant-Catholic-Jew*, 3; Nathan Glazer, "Religion without Faith," *New Republic* 133, no. 20 (November 14, 1955): 18–20; Rudolf Flesch, "Conversation Piece: America and the Great Faiths," *Los Angeles Times*, February 17, 1960, B5; Chad Walsh, "America May Go Shinto," *Living Church* 131, no. 22 (November 27, 1955): 5.

17. John Courtney Murray, "The School Question in the Mid-Twentieth Century," in *The Role of the Independent School in American Democracy*, ed. William H. Conley (Milwaukee: Marquette University Press, 1956), 4–5, 9. For John Cogley's appreciation of an earlier Herberg article on Paul Blanshard, see "Question of Method," *Commonweal* 59, no. 23 (March 12, 1954): 570.

18. Will Herberg, "Communism, Democracy, and the Churches: Problems of 'Mobilizing the Religious Front,'" *Commentary* 19, no. 4 (April 1955): 386–93.

19. K. Healan Gaston, "The Cold War Romance of Religious Authenticity: Will Herberg, William F. Buckley Jr., and the Rise of the New Right," *Journal of American History* 99 (2013): 1133–58. Much more remains to be said about the tri-faith character of Buckley's new conservatism.

20. "A New Experiment in Co-operation," *Priest* 12, no. 1 (January 1956): 21–25; Charles Lowry, "Catholic Protestant Relations," speech to First National Conference on the Spiritual Foundations of Western Democracy, folder 35, box 10, series 7, SAD-NCWC.

21. Eisenhower, "Remarks to the First National Conference on the Spiritual Foundations of American Democracy" (November 9, 1954), https://www.presidency.ucsb.edu/node/233269; Lowry quoted in "Highlights, First National Conference on the Spiritual Foundations of Western Democracy," folder 80, box 1, John Courtney Murray Papers, Georgetown University, Washington, DC.

22. Egal Feldman, *Catholics and Jews in Twentieth-Century America* (Urbana: University of Illinois Press, 2002), 74–78.

23. "Church Cites Pope on Birth Control," *New York Times*, July 24, 1958, 27; "U-I Film 'Condemned,'" *New York Times*, March 6, 1960, 26; John L. Thomas quoted in Richard Philbrick, "Medic Urges Firm Stand by Parents," *Chicago Tribune*, February 3, 1958, B16.

24. John Courtney Murray, *We Hold These Truths: Catholic Reflections on the American Proposition* (New York: Sheed and Ward, 1960), 16, 99.

25. Edmund Fuller, ed., *The Christian Idea of Education: Papers and Discussions* (New Haven: Yale University Press, 1957), 33.

26. Ibid.

27. John Courtney Murray, "Freedom, Responsibility, and the Law," *Catholic Mind* 56 (September–October 1958): 436–37, 440.

28. Kallen's continued explorations included "Secularism as the Common Religion of a Free Society," *Journal for the Scientific Study of Religion* 4, no. 2 (Spring 1965): 145–51.

29. Reinhold Niebuhr, "Reply to Interpretation and Criticism," in *Reinhold Niebuhr: His Religious, Social, and Political Thought*, ed. Charles W. Kegley and Robert W. Bretall (New York: Macmillan, 1956), 434.

30. Reinhold Niebuhr, "Christian Faith and Political Controversy," *Christianity and Crisis* 12, no. 13 (July 21, 1952): 97–98; Niebuhr, "The Relation of Religious to Political Convictions," *Messenger* 17 (1952): 7; Niebuhr, "About Christian Apologetics," *Episcopal Churchnews* 120, no. 8 (April 17, 1955): 13.

31. Niebuhr, "About Christian Apologetics," 13.

32. Reinhold Niebuhr, "Abundance of Things a Man Possesses," *Episcopal Churchnews* 120, no. 17 (August 21, 1955): 18. Sources that cited or were influenced by Herberg include "Christian Faith—A 'Live Option'" and "Varieties of Religious Revival." Niebuhr's reviews are "America's Three Melting Pots," *New York Times*, September 25, 1955, BR6, and "The Role of Religion," *Messenger* 20, no. 16 (September 6, 1955): 7.

33. Reinhold Niebuhr, *Pious and Secular America* (New York: Charles Scribner's Sons, 1958), 2–3, 51, 5–6.

34. Dan McKanan, ed., *A Documentary History of Unitarian Universalism, Volume 2: From 1900 to the Present* (Boston: Skinner House Books, 2017); Duncan Howlett, *The Fourth American Faith* (New York: Harper and Row, 1964), 55, 215.

35. John Cogley, *A Canterbury Tale: Experiences and Reflections, 1916–1976* (New York: Seabury, 1976); "Speech of Senator John F. Kennedy, Greater Houston Ministerial Association" (September 12, 1960), https://www.presidency.ucsb.edu/node/274502.

36. John F. Kennedy, "Inaugural Address" (January 20, 1961), https://www.presidency.ucsb .edu/node/234470.

37. Gustave Weigel, *The Modern God: Faith in a Secular Culture* (New York: Macmillan, 1963), 127.

38. John Cogley, "What Is a 'Liberal Catholic'?" *New Republic* 138, no. 7 (February 17, 1958): 18.

39. On Murray's role, see esp. Barry Hudock, *Struggle, Condemnation, Vindication: John Courtney Murray's Journey toward Vatican II* (Collegeville, MN: Liturgical Press, 2015).

40. Susannah Heschel, "Two Friends, Two Prophets: Abraham Joshua Heschel and Martin Luther King Jr.," *Plough Quarterly* 16 (Spring 2018); King quoted in Lewis V. Baldwin, *The Voice of Conscience: The Church in the Mind of Martin Luther King, Jr.* (New York: Oxford University Press, 2010), 145, 90. For a particularly reductive rendering of the Judeo-Christian tradition by another advocate of nonviolence, see Leilah Danielson, *American Gandhi: A. J. Muste and the History of Radicalism in the Twentieth Century* (Philadelphia: University of Pennsylvania Press, 2014), 210, 347.

41. "Birmingham Manifesto" (April 2, 1963), http://www.thekingcenter.org/archive /document/birmingham-manifesto; King quoted in Baldwin, *Voice of Conscience*, 125; Martin Luther King Jr., "From the Birmingham Jail," *Christian Century* 80, no. 24 (June 12, 1963): 767–73.

42. J. Alfred Dinsmore, letter to the editor, *Boston Globe*, September 14, 1963, 4; Gladwin Hill, "Suit Asks Change in Pledge to Flag," *New York Times*, June 20, 1963, 20; Robert W. Haney, letter to the editor, *New York Times*, July 28, 1963: 137; "Religious Leaders in L.A. Differ Widely on School Prayer Ruling," *Los Angeles Times*, June 18, 1963, 1.

43. Billy Graham, "My Answer," *Detroit Free Press*, January 23, 1962, 30.

Chapter 8

1. "Prolific Prophet," *Time*, June 14, 1963, 50; Martin E. Marty, "The Status of Societal Religion in the United States," *Concordia Theological Monthly* 36, no. 10 (November 1965): 688; Marty, "The Triumph of Religion-in-General," *Christian Century* 75, no. 37 (September 10, 1958): 1016–17; Marty, *The New Shape of American Religion* (New York: Harper, 1959); Marty, *Second Chance for American Protestants* (New York: Harper and Row, 1963). Meanwhile, the book that emerged from Marty's dissertation can be seen as an extended exploration of Herberg's "vanishing atheist" theme, with extensive quotes from Herberg in the final chapter: *The Infidel* (New York: Meridian, 1961).

2. Robert N. Bellah, "Civil Religion in America," *Daedalus* 96, no. 1 (Winter 1967): 1–21; Harvey Cox, *The Secular City: Secularization and Urbanization in Theological Perspective* (New York: Macmillan, 1965), 118; Edward B. Fiske, "There's Piety in Our Politics," *New York Times*, January 16, 1967, E9.

3. Cox, *Secular City*, 118–19; Peter L. Berger, *The Sacred Canopy: Elements of a Sociological Theory of Religion* (Garden City, NY: Doubleday, 1967).

4. Cox, *Secular City*, 118–19.

5. Berger, *Sacred Canopy*, 165, 108; Berger, *The Noise of Solemn Assemblies: Christian Commitment and the Religious Establishment in America* (Garden City, NY: Doubleday, 1961); Berger, "Between Tyranny and Chaos," *Christian Century* 85, no. 44 (October 30, 1968): 1370.

6. Will Herberg, *Judaism and Modern Man: An Interpretation of Jewish Religion* (New York, 1951), 7, 163; Herberg, "Jewish Existence and Survival: A Theological View," *Judaism* 1 (January 1952): 26.

7. Andrew M. Greeley, "After Secularity: The Neo-Gemeinschaft Society: A Post-Christian Postscript," *Sociological Analysis* 27, no. 3 (Autumn 1966): 119–20, 125–26; Will Herberg, "Secularism in Church and Synagogue," *Christianity and Crisis* 10, no. 8 (May 15, 1950): 60–61. Greeley's first study, like those of Marty and Berger, took direct inspiration from Herberg's *Protestant-Catholic-Jew* and quoted extensively from it: *The Church and the Suburbs* (New York: Sheed and Ward, 1959), xi, 41–49.

8. Eugene B. Borowitz, "Jewish Theology Faces the 1970's," *Annals of the American Academy of Political and Social Science* 387 (January 1970): 27, 22. Cf. Borowitz, "The Postsecular Situation of Jewish Theology," *Theological Studies* 31, no. 3 (September 1, 1970): 460.

9. Robert Gordis, *Judaism in a Christian World* (New York: McGraw-Hill, 1966), 155, 96–97; Gordis, *The Root and the Branch: Judaism and the Free Society* (Chicago: University of Chicago Press, 1962). For a fascinating account of the Jewish embrace of "religious liberty" rather than "religion" as the essence of democracy, see Mia Sara Bruch, "The Fatherhood of God and the Brotherhood of Man: American Jews and American Religious Pluralism, 1939–1960" (PhD diss., Stanford University, 2006).

10. Arthur A. Cohen, *The Myth of the Judeo-Christian Tradition* (New York: Harper and Row, 1970), 126, 82; Cohen, *The Natural and the Supernatural Jew: An Historical and Theological Introduction* (New York: Pantheon, 1962).

11. Cohen, *Myth of the Judeo-Christian Tradition*, 219, 221, 223.

12. Murdock M. MacLennan, letter to the editor, *Wall Street Journal*, December 28, 1970, 8; Linda Mathews, "Teacher Admits Atheism, Pacifism: Court Hears Battle for Citizenship," *Los Angeles Times*, December 13, 1967, B1.

13. "Viewpoint of the Times: 'Big Brother' May be a Computer," *Los Angeles Times*, Octo-

ber 8, 1967, M7; Harry Nelson, "Religion vs. Science Struggle Predicted," *Los Angeles Times*, January 21, 1968, 1; Frank L. Ayd, Jr., "Drugs and Men: The Effort to Control Behavior," *Los Angeles Times*, March 22, 1970, F1.

14. "Doctrines of the Dropouts," *Time*, January 5, 1968, 72; June Bingham, "The Intelligent Square's Guide to Hippieland," *New York Times*, September 24, 1967, 255; Russell Chandler, "Sun Shines Bright on Brotherhood," *Los Angeles Times*, February 3, 1974, B1; "Astrology Has No Future in Torrance," *Los Angeles Times*, February 6, 1972, CS2; Kitte Turmell, "Questioning Religion," *Boston Globe*, March 26, 1967, A34.

15. "Chaplain Believes the World Is Safe," *Los Angeles Times*, April 17, 1970, D8; Steven Kelman, "A Harvard Student Looks at Northwestern," *Chicago Tribune*, June 1, 1970, 1; George Collins, "Idealists' Limits Cited," *Boston Globe*, October 10, 1966, 22.

16. Martin Luther King Jr., "My Dream: Peace in Vietnam God's, Man's Business," *Baltimore Afro-American*, December 18, 1965, 20; King, "Beyond Vietnam—A Time to Break Silence" (April 4, 1967), http://www.americanrhetoric.com/speeches/mlkatimetobreaksilence.htm.

17. Weusi Weusi, letter to the editor, *Baltimore Afro-American*, July 6, 1968, A3; Sterling Plumpp, "Educating the Un-Educated," *Black Books Bulletin* 1, no. 1 (Fall 1971): 20; "Church Seen as Next Target of the Black Militants," *Chicago Defender*, November 30, 1968, 8; Stephen Clarke, "The Moral Muddle and the Schools," *Boston Globe*, October 26, 1969, B20; Ossie Davis, "When Is a Camera a Weapon?" *New York Times*, September 20, 1970, 123. For samples of Judeo-Christian rhetoric by King's followers, see Charles W. Bowser, "The Way I See It: Decade of the Sixties Belonged to Dr. King," *Philadelphia Tribune*, January 20, 1970, 9; Ben A. Franklin, "Protesters Call for Sharing of Nation's Affluence by All," *Washington Post*, June 20, 1968, 1; Joseph Howard, "Law Day: 'Justice, Equality Depend on Law—and You,'" *Baltimore Afro-American*, May 3, 1969, 1; and "Nonparty Voting Urged for Blacks," *New York Times*, September 6, 1970, 40.

18. Melani McAlister, *Epic Encounters: Culture, Media, and U.S. Interests in the Middle East since 1945* (Berkeley: University of California Press, 2005), 92 (quoted), 94; Malcolm X, "God's Judgement of White America," in *The End of White World Supremacy: Four Speeches*, ed. Imam Benjamin Karim (New York: Arcade Publishing, 2011); Malcolm X with Alex Haley, *The Autobiography of Malcolm X* (New York: Grove Press, 1965).

19. Carlton B. Goodlett, "The Difficult Road from Racism to Justice," *Sun Reporter* (San Francisco), November 27, 1971, 24; "The Slaying of Joetha," *Chicago Defender*, June 12, 1971, 8; Preston N. Williams, "The Black Experience and Black Religion," *Theology Today* 26, no. 3 (October 1969): 256; "Dr. Jackson Hits Civil Disobedience: Baptist Leader Says 'Follow Law,'" *Chicago Defender*, July 5, 1966, 4. Cf. "An Education in Universal Blackness," *Bay State Banner* (Boston), March 19, 1970, 12.

20. "Bishop Pike Calls War Opposition 'Moral' Act," *Los Angeles Times*, March 9, 1968, B6; Robert Levey, "Growth in Minority Sects: There Is a Religious Revival Abroad As Some Seek New Answers, Meaning," *Boston Globe*, September 27, 1970, A19; Prentiss Pemberton and Homer Page, "Translating Antiwar Protest into Political Power," *Christian Century* 85, no. 1 (January 3, 1968): 14.

21. Jean Murphy, "Antiwar Activity Shifts to Church and Synagogue," *Los Angeles Times*, April 11, 1972, G1; Robert F. Goheen, "Vietnam's Sad Lesson for the U.S.," *Los Angeles Times*, June 7, 1972, E7.

22. "West Fails to Make Use of Its Philosophical Edge," *Chicago Defender*, December 24, 1966, 10; Richard Halloran, "Church Thrives in Hilly Korean Area," *Washington Post*, October 21, 1967, B4; Robert S. Elegant, "Singapore and Malaysia Are Struggling to Solve Their Tense Racial

Problems," *Los Angeles Times*, June 22, 1971, A6; Robert G. Kaiser, "Corruption Is Vietnam's Way," *Washington Post and Times-Herald*, July 7, 1969, A12; Dan L. Thrapp, "Lawyer Takes Christ's Case to Japanese," *Los Angeles Times*, November 1, 1970, E6.

23. Aldo Leopold, "The Arboretum and the University" (1934), in Leopold, *"The River of the Mother of God" and Other Essays* (Madison: University of Wisconsin Press, 1991), 209; Lynn White Jr., "The Historical Roots of Our Ecologic Crisis," *Science* 155 (1967): 1203–7; Shepard Krech III, *The Ecological Indian: Myth and History* (New York: W. W. Norton, 1999), 20; Walter Sullivan, "A New Effort to Save Our Environment," *New York Times*, June 8, 1969, E6; Craig Hodgetts, "Concentrating on Ecology," *Los Angeles Times*, April 19, 1970, R11; "The Link between Faith and Ecology," *New York Times*, January 4, 1970, 145; William R. MacKaye, "Psalms Appropriate for Lunar Trip," *Washington Post*, July 19, 1969, D10. Cf. Leo Marx, "American Institutions and Ecological Ideals," *Science* 170, no. 3961 (November 27, 1970): 945–52; Theodore Roszak, *Where the Wasteland Ends: Politics and Transcendence in Postindustrial Society* (Garden City, NY: Doubleday, 1972).

24. Vine Deloria Jr., *Custer Died for Your Sins: An Indian Manifesto* (New York: Macmillan, 1969), 124; Deloria, "An Indian's Plea to the Churches," *Los Angeles Times*, February 6, 1972, G1; L. Dana Gatlin, "Wounded Knee: Religious Parlay," *Washington Post and Times Herald*, December 28, 1973, C8; Deloria, *God Is Red* (New York: Grosset and Dunlap, 1973).

25. Mary Barber, "Woman, Who Told You to Be Sweet?" *Los Angeles Times*, March 27, 1969, SG4; Elizabeth Shelton, "Women Not Just a Chip off Adam's Rib," *Boston Globe*, June 1, 1969, A1; "Father God, Mother Eve," *Time*, March 20, 1972.

26. Mary Daly, *Beyond God the Father: Toward a Philosophy of Women's Liberation* (Boston: Beacon, 1972), 3, 47, 149.

27. Sheila D. Collins, *A Different Heaven and Earth* (Valley Forge, PA: Judson, 1974); Jean MacRae, "Feminism and Patriarchal Christianity," *Christian Century* 92, no. 28 (September 3–10, 1975): 769–71; Collins, "Women and the Church: Poor Psychology, Worse Theology," *Christian Century* 87, no. 52 (December 30, 1970): 1558–59.

28. "Area Mayors Proclaim Law, Morality Week," *Los Angeles Times*, August 17, 1967, WS2; "Church Leaders Disagree on Cambodia Issue," *Los Angeles Times*, May 12, 1970, A1; Herbert Brucker, "Where Are All the Rules to Live By?" *Boston Globe*, July 29, 1974, 14.

29. "Ecumenical Heads Speak Out against Murderous Trend," *New Pittsburgh Courier*, June 3, 1972, 26; "We Are All Guilty," *Wall Street Journal*, May 17, 1972, 24; James Strong, "Daley Backed by Wilson: Orders to Shoot Also Draw Individual, Group Protests," *Chicago Tribune*, April 17, 1968, 1; Robert Sheehan, "Britian [*sic*] Gives U.S. Lesson on Riot Control," *Boston Globe*, September 8, 1968, 4A; Charles G. Hurst, Jr., "Needed: Community Control of Prisons," *Chicago Defender*, June 7, 1972, 8.

30. Richard Buffum, "Time and a Place," *Los Angeles Times*, April 22, 1971, B1. On sexual issues more generally, see esp. R. Marie Griffith, *Moral Combat: How Sex Divided American Christians and Fractured American Politics* (New York: Basic Books, 2017).

31. Abigail Van Buren, "Sexual Fantasies Normal as Long as They Stay Thoughts," *Los Angeles Times*, September 2, 1969, E11; Jim Carter, "Why All the Fuss about Pornography?" *Philadelphia Tribune*, April 29, 1972, 2; Pat Bryant, "Decision on Lewd Act Law Will Be Appealed," *Los Angeles Times*, November 24, 1972, SF3; Martin Duberman, "Homosexual Literature," *New York Times*, December 10, 1972, BR6; Alvin Ward, "Opening of Girlie Movie House Fought by 30th Ward Councilman," *Call and Post* (Cleveland), October 21, 1967, 3A.

32. Robert Turner, "'A Judeo-Christian Neighborhood': Residents Close Allston Book Store,"

Boston Globe, April 20, 1973, 3; David Rosenzweig, "Community College Board May Appeal Metzger Decision," *Los Angeles Times*, October 31, 1972, 3; Richard Bergholz, "Conservative GOP Group Asked to Be 'Patient' with Nixon," *Los Angeles Times*, March 23, 1969, B2; Hal Leiren, "Sex Education Gaining in Fight for Acceptance," *Los Angeles Times*, July 13, 1969, A1; Mable A. Mize, letter to the editor, *Chicago Tribune*, February 9, 1974, N10.

33. "Nixon Abortion Statement," *New York Times*, April 4, 1971, 28.

34. "The Right to Life," *Boston Globe*, May 28, 1974, 16; Harry Nelson, "Medical Assn. Abortion Position under Attack," *Los Angeles Times*, March 14, 1971, B8; Frank Viz, letter to the editor, *Chicago Tribune*, April 10, 1970, 14; Carol Liston, "Abortion Issue vs. the Church," *Boston Globe*, March 25, 1971, 39; "Text of Archbishop's Pastoral Letter on Abortion," *Boston Globe*, March 28, 1971, A7; Nick Thimmesch, "Beware of Killers Advocating a 'New Biological Ethic,'" *Los Angeles Times*, October 21, 1971, D7; David Nyhan, "Right-to-Life Movement a Growing Force in Nation," *Boston Globe*, May 6, 1974, 1.

35. "Workers Don't Fret about What to Do on Long Vacation," *Los Angeles Times*, October 23, 1966, B1; "The Work Ethic," *Chicago Tribune*, March 4, 1968, 20; untitled quotation from Francis R. Schanck, *Chicago Tribune*, December 25, 1967: H7.

36. Steven Robert Ott, "What Obligation to Help World's Poor?" *Los Angeles Times*, October 16, 1973, A6; James Crowley, "Thinking about the New Pension Law," *Boston Globe*, October 13, 1974, B36; Elliot Richardson, "Keep It Local," *New York Times*, January 31, 1973, 41; "Notable & Quotable," *Wall Street Journal*, September 13, 1972, 18.

37. Robert L. Krause, letter to the editor, *Wall Street Journal*, July 2, 1969, 14; caption to untitled photograph, *Call and Post* (Cleveland), March 10, 1973, 1A; Alfred Baker Lewis, letter to the editor, *Chicago Tribune*, June 7, 1975, 10.

38. Dana McLean Greeley, letter to the editor, *Boston Globe*, November 4, 1968, 10; Isabella Halsted, letter to the editor, *Boston Globe*, September 19, 1970, 6; Robert J. Donovan, "The U.S. and Israel: A 'Special Commitment,'" *Los Angeles Times*, July 20, 1975, D5. Cf. James P. Shannon, "California Vote for Death Penalty Bucks Trend of More Humanitarian Legislation," *Los Angeles Times*, November 25, 1972, 24.

39. Mary McGrory, "Language Lovers Wince at Rocky," *Boston Globe*, May 5, 1968, A5.

40. "Transcript of Governor Rockefeller's News Conference on Entering G.O.P. Race," *New York Times*, May 1, 1968, 30; Thomas P. Ronan, "Rockefeller Sees a Limit to Taxing," *New York Times*, December 30, 1967, 1; "Excerpts from the Message by Governor Rockefeller on the State of the State," *New York Times*, January 4, 1973, 28; "A Strange Conversion," *Chicago Defender*, September 20, 1975, 6; Vernon Jarrett, "Rocky Executes a Reverse Twist," *Chicago Tribune*, September 21, 1975, A6.

41. George Dugan, "Jersey Church Built in Form of Dove," *New York Times*, May 11, 1969, 69; "DePaul Black Students Elated over School's Approval of Demands," *Chicago Defender*, May 23, 1968, 12; Mike McManus, "Is He One of the Few Relevant White Men in This City?" *Washington Post*, June 1, 1969, 14; "Request for Reparations Received by S.F. Bishop," *Oakland Post*, May 15, 1969, 7; "Heads of 3 Major Religious Organizations Urge Congress to Pass Welfare Reform Bill," *New York Times*, April 6, 1970, 21; "Homosexuals and the City," *New York Times*, May 5, 1974, E6; Christopher Lydons, "Shriver's Catholicism Pictured as Something Close to Politics," *New York Times*, September 16, 1972, 12; Robert F. Drinan, "A Violation of Church-State Separation," *Los Angeles Times*, October 28, 1973, G1.

42. "Christ Lobby Brings Moral Eye to Politics," *Los Angeles Times*, August 13, 1972; Malcolm Boyd, "The Cult of the Potomac," *New York Times*, February 17, 1972, 37.

43. "Churchman of the Year," *Newsweek*, May 25, 1970, 96; "Episcopalian Is Named Clergyman of the Year," *New York Times*, June 11, 1971, 17; Charles P. Henderson Jr., "Richard Nixon: Theologian," *Nation*, September 21, 1970, 234.

44. Edward B. Fiske, "Praying with the President in the White House," *New York Times*, August 8, 1971, SM14; George Collins, "Rev. Boyd Scores Nixon-Graham Ties," *Boston Globe*, October 25, 1971, 24; "Billy Graham Apologizes to Jews for His Remarks on Nixon Tapes," *New York Times*, March 3, 2002, 28; Billy Graham, "Watergate and Its Lessons of Morality," *New York Times*, May 6, 1973, 251.

45. "Religious Americans 'Not Mad' at Nixon, 'Just Hurt,'" *Washington Post*, May 28, 1974, A12; Earl Belle Smith, "A Concept for Watergate," *New Pittsburgh Courier*, January 19, 1974, 7.

46. Evelyn G. Johnson, letter to the editor, *Boston Globe*, August 26, 1975, 18.

47. Clare Boothe Luce, "The Significance of Squeaky Fromme," *Wall Street Journal*, September 24, 1975, 24; Harold Blake Walker, "Living Faith," *Chicago Tribune*, November 17, 1971, E5; Walker, "No Philosophy—No Rules," *Chicago Tribune*, December 7, 1975, 91.

48. "The Judeo-Christian Tradition: The Joy of Sects," *National Lampoon*, December 1974.

Chapter 9

1. Ben Pleasants, "A Poetic Sampling of California Gumbo," *Los Angeles Times*, September 30, 1979, L18.

2. The term comes from Diana Eck, of Harvard University's Pluralism Project: *A New Religious America: How a "Christian Country" Has Become the World's Most Religiously Diverse Nation* (New York: HarperOne, 2001).

3. For examples, see John Dart, "Moslems in US Seek Recognition by Nixon," *Los Angeles Times*, December 5, 1970, A29; Aly Wassil, *Dear Mr. President: An Open Letter to Richard Milhous Nixon* (Los Angeles: Omniworld, 1972); and Dart, "Buddhist Selected as Chaplain of Senate," *Los Angeles Times*, December 7, 1974, 33.

4. On the importance of sexual issues in particular, see R. Marie Griffith, *Moral Combat: How Sex Divided American Christians and Fractured American Politics* (New York: Basic Books, 2017).

5. "Republican Party Platform of 1980," https://www.presidency.ucsb.edu/node/273420.

6. See, for example, Jerry Falwell, *Listen, America!* (Garden City, NY: Doubleday, 1980).

7. Jimmy Carter, *Keeping Faith: Memoirs of a President* (New York: Bantam, 1982), 281.

8. Richard Nixon, "Statement about Desegregation of Elementary and Secondary Schools" (March 24, 1970), https://www.presidency.ucsb.edu/node/241065; Nixon, "Statement about the Dedication of the American Museum of Immigration" (September 26, 1972), https://www.presidency.ucsb.edu/node/255077; Nixon, "Radio Address on Crime and Drug Abuse" (October 15, 1972), https://www.presidency.ucsb.edu/node/255210. Elsewhere, Nixon inflected the term "pluralism" with a small-state, probusiness ethos: e.g., "Special Message to the Congress Urging Expansion of the Minority Business Enterprise Program" (October 13, 1971), https://www.presidency.ucsb.edu/node/241056.

9. John F. Kennedy, "Address in Berkeley at the University of California" (March 23, 1962), https://www.presidency.ucsb.edu/node/236213.

10. Jimmy Carter, "'Our Nation's Past and Future': Address Accepting the Presidential Nomination at the Democratic National Convention in New York City" (July 15, 1976), https://www.presidency.ucsb.edu/node/244286; Carter, "Jewish High Holy Days Statement by the President" (September 22, 1978), https://www.presidency.ucsb.edu/node/243282.

11. Jimmy Carter, "Inaugural Address" (January 20, 1977), https://www.presidency.ucsb.edu/node/241475.

12. Jimmy Carter, "World Jewish Congress Remarks at the Meeting of the General Council" (November 2, 1977), https://www.presidency.ucsb.edu/node/242474.

13. Jimmy Carter, "Atlanta, Georgia, Remarks at Emory University" (August 30, 1979), https://www.presidency.ucsb.edu/node/249384.

14. Jimmy Carter, "Department of Health, Education, and Welfare Remarks and a Question-and-Answer Session with Department Employees" (February 16, 1977), https://www.presidency.ucsb.edu/node/243981; "1980 Democratic Party Platform" (August 11, 1980), https://www.presidency.ucsb.edu/node/273253.

15. Jimmy Carter, "Baltimore, Maryland Remarks at the Opening Session of the White House Conference on Families" (June 5, 1980), https://www.presidency.ucsb.edu/node/252059; "Alabama Will Bypass the Conference on Families," New York Times, February 12, 1980, B6.

16. Jimmy Carter, "National Bible Week Remarks at a White House Reception for Ministers and Religious Leaders" (November 25, 1980), https://www.presidency.ucsb.edu/node/251092.

17. David Farber, Taken Hostage: The Iran Hostage Crisis and America's First Encounter with Political Islam (Princeton: Princeton University Press, 2004), 16.

18. Jimmy Carter, "Relations with Islamic Nations: Statement by the President" (February 7, 1980), https://www.presidency.ucsb.edu/node/249921; Jimmy Carter, "Philadelphia, Pennsylvania Address before the World Affairs Council of Philadelphia" (May 9, 1980), https://www.presidency.ucsb.edu/node/250175; "1980 Democratic Party Platform."

19. Ronald Reagan, "Remarks at the Ethics and Public Policy Center Anniversary Dinner" (November 18, 1986), https://www.presidency.ucsb.edu/node/258186. Elsewhere, Reagan cited Justice Potter Stewart's warning that a ban on voluntary prayer in schools amounted to an "establishment of a religion of secularism": "Radio Address to the Nation on Prayer in Schools" (February 25, 1984), https://www.presidency.ucsb.edu/node/260442.

20. Morton Kondracke, "GOP Fumbles Its Play for the Jewish Vote," Los Angeles Times, September 17, 1984, C5; Kathy Sawyer, "Falwell Attempts to Mend Interfaith Fences," Washington Post, April 4, 1985, A4; David Brog, Standing with Israel: Why Christians Support Israel (Lake Mary, FL: Charisma House, 2006). An earlier text from the religious right that used "Judeo-Christian" frequently was Franky Schaeffer, A Time for Anger: The Myth of Neutrality (Wheaton, IL: Crossway, 1982). On Christian Zionism, see esp. Caitlin Carenen, The Fervent Embrace: Liberal Protestants, Evangelicals, and Israel (New York: New York University Press, 2012) and Samuel Goldman, God's Country: Christian Zionism in America (Philadelphia: University of Pennsylvania Press, 2018).

21. "Sampler of Haig's Views: Soviet Arms Buildup," New York Times, December 18, 1980, B16; Steven R. Weisman, "Black and a Woman Are Among 5 Named to Reagan Cabinet," New York Times, December 23, 1980, A1, A12; Norman Podhoretz, "Haig, and Reagan's Mandate," New York Times, December 23, 1980, A15; Donna Scheibe, "Sen. Schmitz' Wife out to Defeat ERA: Crusading Wife of Senator Campaigns to Defeat ERA," Los Angeles Times, February 1, 1976, 1; Mel and Norma Gabler cited in William C. Martin, With God on Our Side: The Rise of the Religious Right in America (New York: Broadway Books, 1996), 122; Ruth Washington, "Common Sense: We Need Prayer in Our Schools," Los Angeles Sentinel, July 7, 1983, A6; William Safire, "On Language: Haigravations Spinach," New York Times, February 22, 1981, SM3.

22. Ronald Reagan, "Remarks on Private Sector Initiatives at a White House Luncheon for National Religious Leaders" (April 13, 1982), https://www.presidency.ucsb.edu/node/244933;

Reagan, "Proclamation 4936—Jewish Heritage Week" (April 27, 1982), https://www.presidency.ucsb.edu/node/245395; Reagan, "Remarks to Members of the Congregation of Temple Hillel and Jewish Community Leaders in Valley Stream, New York" (October 26, 1984), https://www.presidency.ucsb.edu/node/260424.

23. Ronald Reagan, "Address Accepting the Presidential Nomination at the Republican National Convention in Detroit" (July 17, 1980), https://www.presidency.ucsb.edu/node/251302; Reagan quoted in in A. James Reichley, "The Conservative Roots of the Nixon, Ford, and Reagan Administrations," *Political Science Quarterly* 96, no. 4 (Winter 1981–1982): 543.

24. "Bennett Equates Religious and American Values, Supports Parochial School Aid," *Baltimore Sun*, August 8, 1985, A3.

25. Ronald Reagan, "Remarks and a Question-And-Answer Session with Women Leaders of Christian Religious Organizations" (October 13, 1983), https://www.presidency.ucsb.edu/node/261741; Reagan, "Written Responses to Questions Submitted by France Soir Magazine" (November 3, 1984), https://www.presidency.ucsb.edu/node/260658; Reagan, "Radio Address to the Nation on Education" (August 24, 1985), https://www.presidency.ucsb.edu/node/260498; Reagan, "Remarks at the Centennial Meeting of the Supreme Council of the Knights of Columbus in Hartford, Connecticut" (August 3, 1982), https://www.presidency.ucsb.edu/node/246276.

26. Richard Cohen, "Jerry Falwell and Buddha," *Washington Post*, April 6, 1985, A19; Norman Lear, "Whose Vision for America?" *Jewish Press*, July 12, 1985, 1.

27. Andrew Walsh, "Theologian Says U.S. Needs Shared Moral, Social Values," *Hartford Courant*, October 15, 1983, B5.

28. James Davison Hunter, *Culture Wars: The Struggle to Define America* (New York: Basic, 1991), 77; Pat Buchanan, "Address to the Republican National Convention" (August 17, 1992), http://voicesofdemocracy.umd.edu/buchanan-culture-war-speech-speech-text; William Safire, "Buchanan's Campaign," *New York Times*, December 16, 1991, A19; James Perry, "Buchanan Launches Presidential Bid, Says Bush Has Abandoned GOP Tenets," *Wall Street Journal*, December 11, 1991, A18; William Safire, "Pat Buchanan's Small World," *New York Times*, January 13, 1992, A14; Pat Buchanan, "Why I Am Running for President," *Human Events* 51, no. 52 (December 28, 1991), 11. Richard John Neuhaus had used the term "culture wars" earlier in 1991: Steven P. Miller, *The Age of Evangelicalism: America's Born-Again Years* (New York: Oxford University Press, 2014), 91.

29. Larry Scanlon, "Roots of Western Tradition Lie in the East," *New York Times*, October 12, 1988, A30; Andrew Hartman, *A War for the Soul of America: A History of the Culture Wars* (Chicago: University of Chicago Press, 2015).

30. Brian T. Kaylor, *Presidential Campaign Rhetoric in an Age of Confessional Politics* (Lanham, MD: Lexington Books, 2010), 74; Ronald Reagan, "Remarks at a Republican Campaign Rally in Palos Hills, Illinois" (November 4, 1988), https://www.presidency.ucsb.edu/node/252673. In his culture war speech, Buchanan similarly labeled Bush "a champion of the Judeo-Christian values and beliefs upon which America was founded": "Address to the Republican National Convention."

31. "Republican Party Platform of 1988," https://www.presidency.ucsb.edu/node/273433; "Republican Party Platform of 1992," https://www.presidency.ucsb.edu/node/273439.

32. "Republican Party Platform of 1992."

33. George Bush, "Statement on the Supreme Court Decision on the Lee v. Weisman Case" (June 24, 1992), https://www.presidency.ucsb.edu/node/267124.

34. William J. Clinton, "Remarks at a Dinner for the APEC Forum and Business Leaders in

Seattle" (November 19, 1993), https://www.presidency.ucsb.edu/node/218036; Clinton, "Procla-mation 6908—A National Month of Unity, 1996" (July 1, 1996), https://www.presidency.ucsb.edu/node/222644.

35. Diana L. Eck, "True Liberty Cherishes Difference: Our Ethnic Diversity Includes Forms of Worship Brought by Immigrants and Adapted to American Life," *Los Angeles Times*, July 5, 1992, M5; Eck, *Encountering God: A Spiritual Journey from Bozeman to Banaras* (Boston: Beacon, 1993), xv, 37; Eck, *On Common Ground: World Religions in America* (New York: Columbia University Press, 1997); Eck, *A New Religious America: How a "Christian Country" Has Become the World's Most Religiously Diverse Nation* (San Francisco: HarperSanFrancisco, 2001).

36. Quoted in Kathryn Rogers, "World's Religions Give 'Wake-up Call,'" *St. Louis Post-Dispatch*, September 5, 1993, 20; William J. Clinton, "Remarks on the Economic Program in Santa Monica, California" (February 21, 1993), https://www.presidency.ucsb.edu/node/217827; Clinton, "Remarks Announcing Guidelines on Religious Exercise and Religious Expression in the Federal Workplace" (August 14, 1997), https://www.presidency.ucsb.edu/node/224263.

37. William J. Clinton, "Remarks to the American Council on Education" (February 24, 1997), https://www.presidency.ucsb.edu/node/223708; Clinton, "Remarks at Georgetown University" (July 6, 1995), https://www.presidency.ucsb.edu/node/221675. Clinton also eschewed the phrase "religious pluralism" throughout his presidency, speaking instead of "religious diversity."

38. George W. Bush, "Remarks at a Townhall Meeting in Ontario, California" (January 5, 2002), https://www.presidency.ucsb.edu/node/211771; Bush, "Message on the Observance of Eid al-Adha" (March 6, 2001), https://www.presidency.ucsb.edu/node/214457.

39. Samuel P. Huntington, *The Clash of Civilizations and the Remaking of World Order* (New York: Simon and Schuster, 1996). On Islamophobia, see Melani McAlister, *Epic Encounters: Culture, Media, and U.S. Interests in the Middle East since 1945* (Berkeley: University of California Press, 2005); Timothy Marr, *The Cultural Roots of American Islamicism* (New York: Cambridge University Press, 2006); and Rosemary R. Corbett, *Making Moderate Islam: Sufism, Service, and the "Ground Zero Mosque" Controversy* (Stanford: Stanford University Press, 2017).

40. Graham quoted in Stephen Prothero, "Love Bombs at Home: A New Holy Trinity Tradi-tion: Judeo-Christian-Islamic," *Wall Street Journal*, December 14, 2001, W21; Bush quoted in Prothero, "How 9/11 Changed Religion in America," *USA Today*, September 10, 2011; "Powell Calls U.S. 'Judeo-Christian,' Then Amends," *Reuters News*, September 23, 2003.

41. "Powell Calls U.S. 'Judeo-Christian,' Then Amends." Early uses of "Judeo-Christian-Islamic" include Aly Wassil, *The Wisdom of Christ* (New York: Harper and Row, 1965), and "Area Islamic Leader Denounces Violence," *Los Angeles Times*, September 7, 1972, A24. On the trajec-tory of the Abrahamic discourse, see Mark Silk, "The Abrahamic Religions as a Modern Con-cept," in *The Oxford Handbook of the Abrahamic Religions*, ed. Adam J. Silverstein and Guy G. Stroumsa (New York: Oxford University Press, 2015), 71–87; and K. Healan Gaston, "The Judeo-Christian and Abrahamic Traditions in American Public Life," in *The Oxford Encyclopedia of Religion in America* (New York: Oxford University Press, 2018).

42. William J. Clinton, "Message on the Observance of Hanukkah, 2000" (December 21, 2000), https://www.presidency.ucsb.edu/node/228382; Steven Waldman, "Doubts among the Faithful," *New York Times*, March 7, 2001, A19. See also Clinton's analogous Christmas statement of 2000 (https://www.presidency.ucsb.edu/node/228414) and the rather differently phrased Eid al-Fitr statement (https://www.presidency.ucsb.edu/node/228318). A fuller statement of Carter's views appears in his *The Blood of Abraham* (Boston: Houghton Mifflin, 1985).

43. Jane Lampman, "Exploring the Power of Abraham's Legacy," *Christian Science Moni-*

tor, October 17, 2002, 15; "Daughters of Abraham Women's Interfaith Book Group," Pluralism Project profile, http://pluralism.org/profile/daughters-of-abraham-womens-interfaith-book -group; Amy Frykholm, "Grassroots Interfaith Efforts . . . Seattle's Interfaith Amigos: Three Faiths, Three Friends," *Christian Century* 125, no. 17 (August 26, 2008): 22-25; "Abraham: Journey of Faith," *National Geographic* 200, no. 6 (December 2001): 90-129; David Van Biema, "The Legacy of Abraham," *Time*, September 30, 2002, 64; "'Judeo-Christian' Label Assailed," *Washington Post*, May 17, 2003, B9; Jane Lampman, "A Bridge Builder between America and Islam," *Christian Science Monitor*, July 6, 2004, 15. Feiler's book is *Abraham: A Journey into the Heart of Three Faiths* (New York: William Morrow, 2002).

44. Lampman, "A Bridge Builder between America and Islam"; Prema A. Kurien, "Multiculturalism and 'American' Religion: The Case of Hindu Indian Americans," *Social Forces* 85, no. 2 (2006): 723-41; Alan Wolfe, "The God of a Diverse People," *New York Times*, October 14, 2001, WK13.

45. Richard John Neuhaus, "While We're at It," *First Things* 135 (August–September 2003): 71-72; Prothero, "How 9/11 Changed Religion in America." See also Yvonne Yazbeck Haddad, Jane I. Smith, and John L. Esposito, eds., *Religion and Immigration: Christian, Jewish, and Muslim Experiences in the United States* (New York: AltaMira, 2003), 2-3.

46. George W. Bush, "Message on the Observance of Eid al-Adha" (March 6, 2001), https:// www.presidency.ucsb.edu/node/214457; Bush, "Message on the Observance of Eid al-Adha, 2002" (February 21, 2002), https://www.presidency.ucsb.edu/node/214590.

47. George W. Bush, "Remarks at the Power Center in Houston, Texas" (September 12, 2003), https://www.presidency.ucsb.edu/node/212154; Bush, "Proclamation 7430—National Day of Prayer, 2001" (April 27, 2001), https://www.presidency.ucsb.edu/node/217090.

Conclusion

1. Pew Forum on Religion and Public Life, "U.S. Religious Landscape Study: Religious Affiliation" (February 1, 2008), http://www.pewforum.org/2008/02/01/u-s-religious-landscape -survey-religious-affiliation; Pew Forum on Religion and Public Life, "America's Changing Religious Landscape" (May 12, 2015), http://www.pewforum.org/2015/05/12/americas-changing -religious-landscape; Matthew S. Hedstrom, "Rise of the Nones," in *Faith in the New Millennium: The Future of Religion and American Politics*, ed. Matthew Avery Sutton and Darren Dochuk (New York: Oxford University Press, 2016), 250-68.

2. Pew Forum on Religion and Public Life, "America's Changing Religious Landscape"; Barna Group, "Atheism Doubles among Generation Z" (January 24, 2018), https://www.barna .com/research/atheism-doubles-among-generation-z.

3. Pew Forum on Religion and Public Life, "New Report from the Pew Forum on Religion and Public Life Finds Religion in U.S. Is Non-Dogmatic, Diverse, and Politically Relevant" (June 23, 2008); http://www.pewforum.org/2008/06/23/new-report-from-the-pew-forum -on-religion-amp-public-life-finds-religion-in-us-is-non-dogmatic-diverse-and-politically -relevant; Pew Forum on Religion and Public Life, "Many Americans Say Other Faiths Can Lead to Eternal Life" (December 18, 2008), http://www.pewforum.org/2008/12/18/many-americans -say-other-faiths-can-lead-to-eternal-life; Pew Forum on Religion and Public Life, "Many Americans Mix Multiple Faiths" (December 9, 2009), http://www.pewforum.org/2009/12/09 /many-americans-mix-multiple-faiths; Pew Forum on Religion and Public Life, "When Americans Say They Believe in God, What Do They Mean?" (April 25, 2018), http://www.pewforum

.org/2018/04/25/when-americans-say-they-believe-in-god-what-do-they-mean; Pew Forum on Religion and Public Life, "U.S. Protestants Are Not Defined by Reformation-Era Controversies 500 Years Later" (August 31, 2017), http://www.pewforum.org/2017/08/31/u-s-protestants-are -not-defined-by-reformation-era-controversies-500-years-later.

4. Pew Forum on Religion and Public Life, "Interfaith Marriage is Common in U.S., Particularly Among the Newly Wed" (June 2, 2015), http://www.pewresearch.org/fact-tank/2015/06/02 /interfaith-marriage.

5. Eisenhower, "Remarks at Annual Breakfast of the International Council for Christian Leadership" (February 2, 1956), https://www.presidency.ucsb.edu/node/233762; Gerald Ford, "Commencement Address at Warner Pacific College in Portland" (May 23, 1976), https://www .presidency.ucsb.edu/node/258542; Ford, "Address to a Joint Session of the Congress" (August 12, 1974), https://www.presidency.ucsb.edu/node/256489.

6. George Bush, "Remarks at the Annual National Prayer Breakfast" (February 1, 1990), https://www.presidency.ucsb.edu/node/263826; William J. Clinton, "Remarks Announcing Guidelines on Religious Exercise and Religious Expression in the Federal Workplace" (August 14, 1997), https://www.presidency.ucsb.edu/node/224263.

7. Barack Obama, "The President's News Conference with President Abdullah Gul of Turkey in Ankara, Turkey" (April 6, 2009), https://www.presidency.ucsb.edu/node/286349; Obama, *The Audacity of Hope: Thoughts on Reclaiming the American Dream* (New York: Crown, 2006), 218–19; Obama, "Remarks at the Compassion Forum" (April 13, 2008), https://www.presidency.ucsb .edu/node/277451.

8. Barack Obama, "Remarks and a Question-and-Answer Session in Albuquerque, New Mexico" (September 28, 2010), https://www.presidency.ucsb.edu/node/288727.

9. Barack Obama, "Remarks at a Memorial Service for Former President Shimon Peres of Israel in Jerusalem" (September 30, 2016), https://www.presidency.ucsb.edu/node/319102; Obama, "Remarks and a Question-and-Answer Session in Albuquerque, New Mexico."

10. Obama, *Audacity of Hope*, 9, 218; Obama, "Remarks at the Compassion Forum"; Obama, "Remarks on Faith-Based Organizations in Zanesville, Ohio" (July 1, 2008), https://www .presidency.ucsb.edu/node/278624; Obama, "Inaugural Address" (January 20, 2009), https:// www.presidency.ucsb.edu/node/217053.

11. Barack Obama, "Remarks during a Meeting with Business Leaders in Mumbai" (November 6, 2010), https://www.presidency.ucsb.edu/node/288364; Obama, "Remarks at the Iftar Dinner" (August 13, 2010), https://www.presidency.ucsb.edu/node/288935; Obama, "Statement on the Observance of Diwali" (November 4, 2010), https://www.presidency.ucsb.edu/node/288306.

12. Barack Obama, "Proclamation 9076—Religious Freedom Day, 2014" (January 15, 2014), https://www.presidency.ucsb.edu/node/305210; Obama quoted in Martin Saunders, "The Faith of President Obama—In Six Quotes and One Hymn," *Christian Today*, August 1, 2015, https:// www.christiantoday.com/article/the-faith-of-president-obama-in-six-quotes-and-one-hymn /60652.htm.

13. Barack Obama, "Proclamation 8926—Religious Freedom Day, 2013" (January 16, 2013), https://www.presidency.ucsb.edu/node/303746. For the most part, Obama's scattered uses of "Judeo-Christian" involved US-Israel relations: e.g., "Remarks at a Memorial Service for Former President Shimon Peres of Israel in Jerusalem."

14. Barack Obama, "Interview with Jeffrey Goldberg of 'The Atlantic'" (May 19, 2015), https://www.presidency.ucsb.edu/node/323779; Obama, "Interview with Chris Matthews on MSNBC's 'Hardball' at American University" (December 5, 2013), https://www.presidency.ucsb

.edu/node/327088; Obama, "The President's Weekly Address" (April 3, 2010), https://www.presidency.ucsb.edu/node/288042.

15. Barack Obama, "Remarks on Lighting the National Christmas Tree" (December 1, 2016), https://www.presidency.ucsb.edu/node/320048; Obama, "Remarks at the National Prayer Breakfast" (February 2, 2012), https://www.presidency.ucsb.edu/node/299411.

16. Barack Obama, "Remarks at the University of Yangon in Rangoon, Burma" (November 19, 2012), https://www.presidency.ucsb.edu/node/302656; Obama, "Remarks to the Parliament in London" (May 25, 2011), https://www.presidency.ucsb.edu/node/290331.

17. Obama, "Remarks at the University of Yangon in Rangoon."

18. J. Randy Forbes, "Obama Is Wrong When He Says We Are Not a Judeo-Christian Nation," *U.S. News & World Report*, May 7, 2009; Daniel Burke, "Romney Appeals to Evangelicals through Shared 'Judeo-Christian' Values," *Religion News Service*, September 28, 2011, https://religionnews.com/2012/09/28/romney-appeals-to-evangelicals-through-judeo-christian-values/; Donald J. Trump, "Remarks to the 11th Annual Values Voter Summit in Washington, DC" (September 9, 2016), https://www.presidency.ucsb.edu/node/319637.

19. Donald J. Trump, "Remarks at the Family Research Council's Values Voter Summit" (October 13, 2017), https://www.presidency.ucsb.edu/node/331276; Trump, "Remarks to the 11th Annual Values Voter Summit in Washington, DC." Trump also used "Judeo-Christian" in "Remarks at a 'Make America Great Again' Rally in Pensacola, Florida" (December 8, 2017), https://www.presidency.ucsb.edu/node/331865.

20. Donald J. Trump, "Proclamation 9570—National Day of Patriotic Devotion" (January 20, 2017), https://www.presidency.ucsb.edu/node/322256.

21. "John McCain: Constitution Established a 'Christian Nation,'" *Beliefnet*, September 29, 2007, http://www.beliefnet.com/news/politics/2007/06/john-mccain-constitution-established-a-christian-nation.aspx; Burke, "Romney Appeals to Evangelicals through Shared 'Judeo-Christian' Values"; Brad Knickerbocker, "Mitt Romney Courts Evangelicals at Liberty University," *Christian Science Monitor*, May 12, 2012; Caitlin Carenen, *The Fervent Embrace: Liberal Protestants, Evangelicals, and Israel* (New York: NYU Press, 2012); David Brog, *In Defense of Faith: The Judeo-Christian Idea and the Struggle for Humanity* (New York: Encounter, 2010). See also Kathryn Lofton, "John McCain: No God but Country," *Religion Dispatches*, June 14, 2009, http://religiondispatches.org/john-mccain-no-god-but-country.

22. "2008 Republican Party Platform" (September 1, 2008), https://www.presidency.ucsb.edu/node/278999; "2012 Republican Party Platform" (August 27, 2012), https://www.presidency.ucsb.edu/node/302338.

23. "2016 Republican Party Platform" (July 18, 2016), https://www.presidency.ucsb.edu/node/318311.

24. K. Healan Gaston, "The Judeo-Christian and Abrahamic Traditions in American Public Life," in *The Oxford Encyclopedia of Religion in America* (New York: Oxford University Press, 2018).

25. Gurinder Singh Mann, "Making Home Abroad: Sikhs in the United States," in *A Nation of Religions: The Politics of Pluralism in Multireligious America*, ed. Stephen Prothero (Chapel Hill: University of North Carolina Press, 2006), 166.

26. Gwynn Guilford and Nikhil Sonnad, "What Steve Bannon Really Wants," *Quartz*, February 3, 2017, https://qz.com/898134; Christopher Caldwell, "What Does Steve Bannon Want?" *New York Times*, February 26, 2017, SR1; "Shapiro Champions Judeo-Christian Values before 11,000 at Liberty University," *Daily Wire*, April 25, 2018, https://www.dailywire.com/news/29901

/watch-shapiro-champions-judeo-christian-values-daily-wire. Other Trump administration officials likewise portray Judeo-Christian values as under assault by a liberal elite: e.g., Betsy DeVos, quoted in Sam Tanenhaus, "'I'm Tired of America Wasting Our Blood and Treasure': The Strange Ascent of Betsy DeVos and Erik Prince," *Vanity Fair*, October 2018. On the contemporary use of Judeo-Christian rhetoric as a code word for whiteness, see, for example, Aamna Mohdin, "Jewish Americans Are Shunning the Term 'Judeo-Christian' Thanks to Donald Trump," *Quartz*, October 17, 2017, https://qz.com/1104073/jewish-americans-want-nothing-to-do-with-the-term -judeo-christian-thanks-to-donald-trump; "Judeo-Christian Foreign Policy," Centre for Feminist Foreign Policy, April 8, 2018, https://centreforfeministforeignpolicy.org/journal/2018/3/30 /the-anti-semitic-and-islamophobic-nature-of-judeo-christian-foreign-policy-part-i; and Hila Hershkoviz, "Ben Shapiro's 'Judeo-Christian' Complex," *Vision*, July 30, 2018, https://visionmag .org/2018/07/30/ben-shapiros-judeo-christian-complex.

27. Likewise, our descriptions of the past imply particular understandings of the present that help to shape the future. Even professional historians, known for their empiricist approach and reluctance to tell readers what to think or do, speak constantly—if usually indirectly—to such normative questions through their choices of wording, content, and structure. No matter how hard historians work to treat competing viewpoints fairly, they cannot help but take sides through their choices of language, as well as narrative form and content. This book is certainly no exception.

28. Martin Luther King Jr., "The Human Tension" (sermon, between 1948 and 1954), Martin Luther King, Jr. Papers Project, https://kinginstitute.stanford.edu/king-papers/documents /human-tension.

29. Of course, secularisms differ across time and space and are shaped by dominant religious traditions themselves. Scholars have variously identified evangelical, Protestant, Christian, and Judeo-Christian secularisms in the United States: John Lardas Modern, *Secularism in Antebellum America* (Chicago: University of Chicago Press, 2011); Tracy Fessenden, *Culture and Redemption: Religion, the Secular, and American Literature* (Princeton: Princeton University Press, 2007); Linell E. Cady and Tracy Fessenden, eds., *Religion, the Secular, and the Politics of Sexual Difference* (New York: Columbia University Press, 2013); and Elizabeth Shakman Hurd, *The Politics of Secularism in International Relations* (Princeton: Princeton University Press, 2009). For the broader point, see also Janet R. Jakobsen and Ann Pellegrini, eds., *Secularisms* (Durham, NC: Duke University Press, 2008); and Linell E. Cady and Elizabeth Shakman Hurd, eds., *Comparative Secularisms in a Global Age* (New York: Palgrave Macmillan, 2010).

30. For a cogent analysis of how polling techniques and reporting patterns replicate prevailing narratives about faith and politics, see Robert Wuthnow, *Inventing American Religion: Polls, Surveys, and the Tenuous Quest for a Nation's Faith* (New York: Oxford University Press, 2015).

Index

Made in United States
Troutdale, OR
07/20/2023

11438180R00206